$ 12.95

order from.

Speak Out

P.O. BOX 9895

Reno, NV 89507

SEX
AND
THE
PULPIT

SEX
AND
THE
PULPIT

Rabbi Abraham L. Feinberg

1981

∩ Methuen

Toronto   New York   London   Sydney   Auckland

Canadian Cataloguing in Publication Data

Feinberg, Abraham L., 1899–
  Sex and the pulpit

Bibliography: p.
ISBN 0-458-94550-1

1. Sex and religion. 2. Sex and Judaism.
3. Sex (Theology). I. Title.

BL65.S4F44   291.1′78357   C81-095001-4

Printed and bound in Canada

1 2 3 4 5 81 86 85 84 83 82

To Patricia, whose love and devotion,
answering to mine, brought me home again
and renewed my zest for life and my zeal for
writing what I think and feel about life.

Contents

Acknowledgments

This book has been known to me by a name reflecting our personal private relationship: "Moby Dick." Like Captain Ahab in Herman Melville's novel, I vowed to subdue the Great White Whale, to "finish it before it finishes me." The obsessed sailor hunter had only one leg; I have only one operative eye—and even it is impaired. And now, eighty-two years of age by count, I had to dig a book out of my own mind, memories and research—alone, not at all a spokesman for any thoughts or opinions save mine as an individual. For me there is no other way. So I lashed myself to the mast, my desk, for three years. Bouts of illness, physical and mental exhaustion, uncertain stamina, all these and more plagued my efforts. Now the task is done, whatever the result, good or bad—and Pat and I can relax.

This could not have happened without the stimulus and morale-sustaining spiritual presence of Holy Blossom Temple in Toronto, for which I have profound affection, and beloved friends such as Jack Clarke, Alan Walker, Franc Joubin, Margaret David-son, Cecil Williams, Donovan Roberts, and many others. Whether in New York, Jerusalem, Toronto, San Francisco or Reno, their vibes touched me to faith in myself. I'm not sure they will all like *Sex and the Pulpit*. I hope and think they have learned to take me as I am.

In the actual creation of this book I would like to thank three people, all truly great human beings. One is Lesley Wyle, trade editor of Methuen Publications, whose guidance and confidence from the first have been of enormous and indispensable value to me. Another is Wayne Herrington, editorial co-ordinator with the same company, who copy-edited the book with unflagging care and interest. The third is Yvonne L. Kirk; without her limitless patience, concern and skill in typing my handwritten pages, incredibly and unreadably confused by poor eyesight and a Virgo's compulsive perfectionism, "Moby Dick" still would be at sea instead of being imprisoned within the covers of a book.

For my long deceased immigrant parents and the generations before them who remained in the doomed ghettos of Eastern

Europe, I express deep thanks to God. From them I learned to love the "little people" of our world—and to seek knowledge.

Finally, I salute an endangered species—the men and women who in the name of individual freedom release themselves from the bonds of respectability, reverence and obedience that they might help release our society from religious dictatorship, social injustice, self-non-acceptance and sexual oppression.

ABRAHAM L. FEINBERG
Reno, Nevada

Preface

"Jews love three things: sex, Torah and revolution." Thus spoke Dr. Morris Feitelzohn, mentor of the compulsive satyr Aaron in Nobel Laureate Isaac Bashevis Singer's novel *Shosha*. Like most grandiloquent generalizations, its categorical judgment envelops only a deceptively inflated smidgen of truth. No less and no more than Gentiles, all adult and able-bodied Jews I know love sex, most honor the Torah (often in breach rather than observance), and regrettably only a few radicals are glassy-eyed for revolution. And if "Torah" is anglicized to "Divine teaching," "love" reduced to "being personally enmeshed" and "revolution" pinpointed as "sexual," the exact replica of Dr. Feitelzohn's epigram might be applied to *all clergymen*. What is the theme of *Sex and the Pulpit* if not the close involvement of clergymen with sex in relation to Divine teaching during a time of sexual revolution? It is not a "how to" book. The know-how of making love matches in complexity the vaunted American know-how of making spaceships. Indeed, the common use of the participle "making" signifies artificial manufacture. In an age pathetically aware of its erotic apparatus, a slight shift of pelvic nerve-end or muscle can stack the cards for ecstasy or tears. Sexologists, on the trail of a saleable slogan, have found "performance." In my youth the noun alluded to the stage or the athletic field; now it is more apt to mean coupling in bed.

I once overheard a group of divorcées exchange evaluations of bed partners they all had tested; the criteria were no less specific than the number of feet racked up in a pole vault. Coeds have been known to devise a rating system; fraternity Don Juans loftily doom awkward females with an epithet denoting "a poor fuck." Sundry Ladies' Auxiliary church members, one of them informed me, "even mark for sex arousal the clergyman's pulpit voice and his masculinity."

The devotion to arithmetic has begotten another institution of our computer-enslaved time: the scientific survey. Bedroom olympics spawn statistics no less profusely than corporate boardroom xeroxes on the state of the treasury. To paraphrase Ecclesiastes, "Of the making of surveys there is no end." Their

xii / Sex and the Pulpit

pronouncements sound a warning signal in the wilderness through which we clerics must pick a lonely and semi-monastic way. But we are not an island; in matters of sex, our distinction is not *being* "above" sex; it is being *expected* to be, by congregants eager for faith, by the media eager for scandal and by lecherous "he-men" who insist on pulpit purity as their surrogate offerings to God. Unlike feminists Friedan and Steinem, most clergymen are officially resigned to their "double standard" as a universally endorsed condition; some pastors even rejoice in a holier-than-thou mandate that enhalos a calling acclaimed as "sacrificial."

Whatever the corrosive impact of new-fangled fashions on Dr. Kinsey's Bloomington shrine may be, the founder of sexology has awakened countless North Americans to the fact that people lead sexual lives very different from their own and yet remain well within the bounds of "normalcy." Private clerical conduct ranges on a gamut wide enough for any non-criminal layman. Save for lower echelons of the Catholic priesthood, the hallmark of ministers is individualism; rabbis are proverbially self-directed. Let me add that the reminiscences and opinions submitted in this book are mine alone, though I believe they mirror, *au fond*, the hardcore, all too human fragility of the soul the cloth dare not plumb.

The average person knows little more than the tangible externals of his/her own sexuality, much less that of others. In my boyhood days, before the celebrated sexual revolution, proper women of Middle America were too embarrassed even to peer into the forbidden cavity between their legs or to admit to themselves their joy in having it filled. Male solid citizens confined their recognition of the penile presence to poolroom and tavern jokes that concealed their dread of bowing audibly to King Phallus. Perhaps the taboo harks back to Ham, the biblical son of Noah who was punished through his progeny, generation after generation, because he looked upon his father's nakedness. Despite millenial change, more than a mite of that ancient recoil from verbalized, seriously discussed sexuality is still a habitué of the North American mind. The domain of Eros is *terra incognita*.

The sexual propensities of the average human being are a locked treasure chest. Nothing is incredible. Who among the civilized urbane is immune to macabre fantasies? Only a fraction, luckily, are mad enough to try to *live* them. Potentialities in human deportment are limited only by the self-malleability of God in whose image man was created.

What realm of discourse is hospitable to more evasiveness and dissembling than intimate revelations about one's sexuality? Do interviews rate high as channels to the underground? In contrast to the cliché-lisping elite who frequent seminars and the minority who can afford the psychiatrist's couch, the eager middle-class North Americans whom surveys attract, I suspect, are likely to underscore their normalcy when not exaggerating their devilry out of manly (or womanly) pride. Can any naiveté be more astonishing than that of "experts" who almost reverently enshroud for computation the anatomical reactions of subjects trussed up with wires and electrodes for "scientific" inquiry into a process so unpredictably affected by winds of change as coitus? Margaret Mead once warned against supposing that these descriptions of what people are doing should be taken as the basis for what is *right*. Shall we accept them holus-bolus as the basis for what is *true*?

Bertrand Russell towers high among the greats of this century. Deeply distressed by the painful effects of religion-sponsored sexual morality, he warmly welcomed a swing of the pendulum. Is that swing threatening to shatter the grandfather's clock? Joseph Epstein, editor of *American Scholar*, says yes. "Where Bertrand Russell once stood, a tall symbol of enlightened values, now stands Masters and Johnson," he wrote. They glue eyes to their camera lenses and plug in electronic equipment to count clitoric or prostatic actions, labeling them with words such as "glands, protuberances, engorgements, contraction, and high-frequency impulses." Epstein charges that Freud's campaign against undue abstinence has been translated into the notion that sexual activity in itself is a form of health. . . . So much for what sex-liberated circles label a negligible minority report.

Is Epstein's polemic cool, cautious and correct? A native endowment of skepticism toward Delphic oracles in general persuades me also to question the obeisance given to Masters and Johnson. The value of their methodology seems unassailable only for that segment of the North American populace which doesn't mind being manipulated in a laboratory equipped with monitoring devices similar in purpose to an Auschwitz gas-chamber peep-hole. Will they finally perfect a wiring system whose beeps can launch lovers into simultaneous orgasm-Nirvana?

The findings of many surveys, not excluding Masters and Johnson's, will be quoted in this book on the principle that, when experts disagree, laymen are well advised and free to consult their own intelligence, common sense and experience.

All religions have some truth; none have *the* truth! So it is with sex codes. Whether proclaimed from the papal throne or in the manifestos of COYOTE, created by Margo St. James to secure the elementary rights of prostitutes as human beings, whether sounded in the call to arms of Pro-Lifers or in the piety-drenched power ploys of the theocratic-autocratic rabbinical faction in Israel—I am not disposed to confound pastoral postures. All pontifical noises are not hollow! Once unleashed from the idolatry of computer printouts and the ferocity of evangelical research zealots, they often help conquer the obscurantism that hounds rational sex study.

"Don't do as I do; do as I say!" That hoary phrase tagged to clergy by their detractors is irrelevant! The most powerful sermons of a dynamic preacher are those in which he delivers a moral challenge to *himself*; all too visible to him is the distance between his "say" and "do." The chief target of homiletical admonition may be the conscience of the admonisher! My "personal" approach to sex and the clerical mind needs no apology.

1

The Way It Was

"Do you plan to start a religion?" Voltaire reputedly advised an eager-beaver acolyte: "Then get yourself crucified!" It seems, however, that religion was born millenia before Jesus died and emerged where all animal life comes forth—from the loins.

The marriage of sex and religion was solemnized when a pre-historic hominid linked edible vegetation blossoming in the earth and the fruitfulness of animal bodies, including his own, with circumambient, possibly dream-bred demons to whom he must offer tribute for survival. A watershed was reached when shamans and medicine-man priests convinced him that they alone had access to these omnipotent gods who dispensed blessing and curse. The practice and paraphernalia of worship burgeoned into escalating mystification with the brain-boggling discovery, after aeons of "miraculous," chronological, nine-months' happenstance, that a partnership in creation had been granted to mortal flesh through the interplay of penis and pudenda. Perhaps that was the launching point of man's intellectual evolution, a breakthrough much more portentous than the use of fire and wheel. Never throughout the intervening expanse of time, I believe, have religious activity and meditation been severed from their roots in the genitals.

That the rite of gods-worship was in effect a by-product of the rite of coitus does not lower the dignity of "organized" religion (henceforth to be designated simply as the church—synagogue included). For many North Americans, sex *is* religion. Obsessive craving for euphoria (turn-on), proliferating diversity of ritual (fellatio-cunnilingus), glorification of communion with wine and water (physical coitus), eucharistic dramatization (fantasies of carnal semi-divine ecstasy), Gospel-celebrating festivals (group orgies), Reformation (sexual revolution), sacred Scripture (Kinsey reports), charismatic priesthood (Masters and Johnson), symbols of Divine omnipotence (all-ruling phallus), mystic transcendance (orgasm)—what *other* appurtenances of religion are required?

Consciously or unconsciously, acknowledged or muted, openly or secretly, a spokesman for structured religion becomes in his person and his pulpit the subject and object of sexuality. I am in my eighty-third year. The angel-adversary sex has entombed in my memory both grievous wounds and wondrous delights. History, theology and those unlocked reprises of time past—and what I observe today—are like the lamps I saw fastened on coal miners' caps as they descended into the pits, long ago when I was very young. They, I trust, will guide me through the underground labyrinth of clerical sexuality. The "coal" I bring to the surface will not coruscate with a golden hue—but it will be my own.

Our post-Judeo-Christian age has further ensnarled the underbrush that always has cluttered the sexual development of the clergy. Every aware churchman becomes a battleground in spirit between his humanity and his vocation. Before defining the "way it is" today, one needs to describe the "way it was." The convolutions of the pastor's internal and external sex pattern have a backdrop. From what conditioning did my generation of clergymen emerge—what were the sociosexual assumptions, let us say, in the early decades of the twentieth century? To this day, those assumptions shape the eroticism, by negation, of a lad whose possibly congenital dissidence, allied with an active libido, set him unalterably against the petrified sex morality of the "church."

I was born just prior to the dawn of the twentieth century in a grimy semi-rural mining and mill town, "across the tracks," on the banks of the Ohio River. The way it was began, for me, on a humid summer day about 1911 in the steamy kitchen of a wooden frame house that clung to a hillside high above the river. My Gentile pal, Jim, had hollered to me "Milk and cookies, Abe!" in our creek swimming hole at the sycamore tree. The tangy babble of unkosher salt pork frying on the coal stove stirred in me a guilty ache of proscribed hunger when I saw cloudlets of smoke puffing out through the cracks in its iron belly. Jim yelled, "I'm going to the store for mom," but I had become numb to the sense of hearing. Sensuality alone gripped me at the sight of his mother's ample bosom quivering under a thin, sweat-dampened house dress that stroked her limbs and buttocks like a second skin, at the acrid smell of warmth that exuded from her body, at the shimmer of a rumpled pink satin nightgown through the open door of a rear room—and the drumbeat sound of my heart as I sat like a stone watching her loose-jointed hips rise and fall with undulatory twitches at every pad of her slippered feet.

That single-raimented vision and Jim's dad, a gaunt glass blower, were Mr. & Mrs.! What did they do together? That night I lay rigid beside an elder brother as a troop of vivid answers heated my veins. Dirty, wrong! Delight tingled like a song in the secret places of my flesh—harbinger of unspoken raptures to come. Yet I curled up in terror.

The ignorance of "our gang," a multi-racial bunch from across the tracks, was total, undiluted by even a shred of fact. Well-nigh nothing we believed was true, and of the truth we knew nothing. The mere thought of questioning my immigrant parents twisted my viscera into knots. The sole bond between us was love too deep for demonstration. The Feinberg family did not "let go." The more heavily feeling pressed down on our relations with one another, the more rare was its expression. The cramped quarters in which we lived—parents, kids, anywhere from seven to ten at home, and often a nephew or a niece my father had brought over from the Lithuanian *shtetl* (little village) of his birth to share our poverty—seemed to constrain our spirits as well as our bodies. We siblings found it easier to mock and argue than to show our common frustrations and our love. It was tragic! How often I ached to tell my mother, a truly beautiful, selfless votary of family, people and God, how much I adored her. For weeks on end I invented intimate chats with my father. Between the dappled gray matter in my cranium and his immersion in rabbinic learning, there stretched a distance from earth to Betelgeuse. The peddler's pittance he earned had to be supplemented with the pennies wrung from picking up bottles, carrying luggage, running errands, hawking newspapers—every available odd job in town. Pop's dependence on our meager contributions didn't raise his self-esteem.

Yet I wanted to know—above all—everything about sex. The gang made fun of my addled haste to know. I gasped in astonishment when I found out at last, in my junior year at high school, just where babies came from.

Classroom talks on physiology didn't help. Like the hospital nurses' baths we students got sick for in college, they reached down as far as possible, up as far as possible, but never arrived *at* the possible. Special doctor lectures in elementary grade school depicted on slides the harm done by too little ventilation, too much whisky, too tight corsets—and cigarettes. The last-named rated high in my estimation for the crotch-tickling arousal I got from the picture cards of slinky actresses we salvaged from spent packets of cigarettes in Duffy's poolroom. Street dogs stuck together at the genitals were more informative than the teachers Misses Smythe and Hawkins. We proudly recited the Latin-derived names of brain sections and botanical cotyledons, while alley conferences on sex organs were held in one-syllable Anglo-Saxon.

On a safari to a lush hilltop glade for pawpaws, our gang would clasp hands in a circle and dare each other to "say it." A half-century later the Berkeley free speech movement would scrawl on placards a call to F-U-C-K the Establishment. Within that cool glade, redolent of buttercups and nearby haystacks, the four-letter scare word was no less taboo than the invocation of Yahweh in the Jerusalem temple of the ancient Israelites. Fingers interlocked in a collective paroxysm of dread, none of us could wrap teeth and lips around that syllable. Did we expect to be struck by lightning? Instead of challenging God to punish us—like Sinclair Lewis's gaudy gesture when he proclaimed his atheism—we clamped our mouths.

Everything You Wanted to Know about Sex and Were Afraid to Ask had not yet been printed. *Trees of Knowledge* provided only tantalizing fruit. Jubilant barnyard visits to fetch Passover kosher milk in leaven-free pails ended my puzzlement over what I assumed were cows frantically trying to mount other cows as they were being driven along the road to the abattoir, as well as the sight of the stiff cock of a rapt, love-sick horse stretching downward with a slight curve from its underbelly. Then there were anatomical studies advancing from the tattered pages of a medical book pinched from a physician's waiting room, and knot-holes enlarged with a pen-knife in the planks of a wooden bridge lured us to crouch under them and wait for the flounce of lace petticoats worn by devout ladies on their daily rounds to attend Mass in the nearby Catholic Church. The ladies would have been shocked to learn that they were stimulating our youthful libidos!

Jim's cousin had told him that "jacking off" and wet dreams could use up so many sperms that you might never have children when you got married. "We have only a certain amount!" he'd said. In panic, some of us squeezed the private member a split second before ejaculation to abort the emission. . . . Naked, we romped "up on the hill" and enacted an improvised "corn-hole" ballet in a hesitant escalation of fondle, stroke and climactic.

Intrinsically, the interlocking of bodies contorted by hot desire, and without the redemptive intercession of passionate love cosmetics like darkness, "atmosphere" and boudoir space-decor—that is, the unadorned *act* of intercourse—lags far behind the *idea* of intercourse. I dare to submit that coitus in itself is not at all beautiful. The always-available Man from Mars would be stupefied by the tangled angles of limbs. He would guffaw if he were to read the sublime *Letters of Heloîse and Abélard*, listen to *Tosca*, or gaze at Rodin's "The Kiss." Gymnastics, stertorous breathing, incontrolled exertion—is that ballet? Nonsense!

The Right Reverend Wesley Frensdorff, Episcopal Bishop of Nevada, once asked, "What kind of a God could invent this incredible foolishness to be the physical means of sharing the greatest of life's intimacies and participating in the creative process?" A God who dwells, I suspect, in the cosmic vastness above all human folly—except his weakness for irony. He may have turned the whole comic bit over to Mother Nature, who was deputized to guarantee the survival of the Father's creation. Placing sex in her hand, like a sword of knighthood, He bade her use it so that life might be multiplied. With all the astuteness of motherhood, she made sex resplendently beauteous to attract and channel the life-continuing energy of mankind. (Darwin noted that even the color of flowers is designed to attract certain pollen bearing insects.)

In our jejeune eagerness to attain sex erudition we pursued diverse academic researches into the subject of fallen women. A laborious pursuit of the word "prostitute" in the library yielded only frustration; "whore" was easier to say. The cheapest one in town, we whispered, was "Trolley Car"—anyone could get on for a nickel. For a week we followed her inebriated peregrinations like hounds smelling out spoors—but we never found her engaged. The word "bastard" was not quite as elusive. The fluids that flowed with heightening velocity below the navel hinted at the cause of the disgrace that befell laughing black "Topsy" down in Ramcat Alley and honey-haired Maribelle from "uptown" who had to quit school and move away. . . .

Dead-Eye Dick, Fred Fearnot, Frank Merriwell—frayed dime novels that I hid from my mother's reach—gave us preliminary boot-camp training in machismo. Horatio Alger's gallery of stalwart heroes, Jim the Newsboy, Tom the Boot-Black, Bob the Farm Lad—pure-minded paragons of athleticism, capitalist thrift and sexless probity—tipped us off that fiscal success through marriage to a tycoon's daughter, and not the prodigal joys of fast living, was the gleaming goal of a true American boy. *Shepherd of the Hills, Girl of the Limberlost, Graustark*—these treacly romances left lying around by my grownup sister were devoured and soon cast aside as non-inflammatory. Harold Bell Wright contributed nothing to my education in the fact of sex. He did shift the burden of my sexual brooding from the epidermal itch that stings and inflames all people to the light that never was on sea or land: the romantic ideal of Woman. That wistful image of feminine perfection has never been entirely absent from any subsequent encounter I had with Woman, in whatever corporeal guise she may have appeared to me.

One thing I *knew*: girls were pure and unblemished; they were immaculate as the driven snow near the bobsled run. Stationed in front of the Presbyterian Church to sell Sunday-morning newspapers to the emerging parishioners, I heard girls daintily chirping in the Philathea Bible class. At school they huffed away from crayon sketches hurled at them by "the bad boys"; they glided through the air like an angelic choir. Gentile girls, I thought, were all alabaster and ethereality, encased in delicate skin unbeaded with sweat and unheated by the imperatives of sex. Not until my first day at college, in the Varsity lunchroom, did I confront the fact of female carnality—hundreds of them biting, chewing, presumably digesting their food. They did have alimentary canals and colons! The pedestal shook but has endured to this day.

In my early teens I often stole away after supper, unless Sabbath prayers detained me, to the "girl of my dreams"; she sold tickets at the nickelodeon. Like a starry-eyed sentinel, I kept silent watch at the curb, feasting on her peaches-and-cream complexion and what I fancied was a Grecian profile. Nickels were scarce. When Fatty Arbuckle, the Keystone Kops and "Two-Gun" William S. Hart surrendered my private pantheon to Theda Bara, the aboriginal sex goddess of the silver screen, I leaped to the bait of the repulsively fat movie-palace owner who "let me in free" and then, in the last row, directed my hand through his fly to a limp penis. My senses, thanks to Theda, were totally enthralled not by repulsive touch but by the sight of her hypnotic lashes and heaving breasts.

After my vigil at the curb one sultry evening, when again I

failed to pull a glance from the pale-blue eyes of my dream girl, sub-umbilical stirrings despatched an urgent message to my brain: "Stalk up to the ticket cage, tell her everything—everything—and run!" A second message canceled the coup. Anton Krulenko had been caught humming at some girls in the playground, "I've gotta cunt, I've gotta cunt, I've gotta county wagon"; he was led off to reform school.

"Post-office"—a special-delivery letter meant a kiss. "Spin-the-bottle"—where it stopped spinning, a hug might start. Whispered tales of mild lubricity at gaslight-dimmed parties were tantalizing. My lips fairly slavered at stories of nearby farm kids who snuggled in the hay at milking time. When would I tear away the veil and penetrate the strata of mystery, layer upon layer? I would need to get married, and that was farther away than the moon. And I still didn't know *exactly* how babies were made. Nor did any of my friends.

At seminary (Hebrew Union College; entrance—1916) there were interludes of campus high-jinks: affectionate mimicry of professorial eggheads who had blotted out their youth in the oceanic vastness of European Jewish scholarship, Purim-spiels, basketball games and minstrel shows that juxtaposed clever satiric song parodies of *The Vamp* and *Dardanella* with raunchy, grass-skirted bookworms imitating hula dancers on the Elysian beaches of Hawaii. At the Cincinnati Conservatory of Music I snatched morsels of expansive joy from vocal lessons that I attended on a scholarship and from doing exalting solos in the seminary choir under an organist who gave me free coaching— and lasting disdain of racial and nationalistic barriers, he being German and a "dead ringer" for Kaiser Wilhelm, the villain whom four of my older brothers serving in France with the American Expeditionary Force had vowed to "hang."

I became a junior member of a lofty-nosed seminary clique that wolfed down accounts of erotic acrobatics in secretly circulated books written by Krafft-Ebing, Havelock Ellis and eventually a Viennese Jew named Sigmund Freud. Freud enabled us to defuse the guilt of our clamorous passions by consigning them to the subconscious. We intoned Omar Khayyam's "A loaf of bread, a jug of wine, and thou" with more enthusiasm than the verb conjugations in our Hebrew lessons. Frazer's *Golden Bough* convinced us that morality was relative to time and place. We pounced on the debunking dynamite of George Bernard Shaw, reveled in H. L. Mencken, and vicariously flaunted the tantalizing sensuality of Baudelaire and Byron. We feasted on James Branch Cabell's proscribed *Jurgen* that resonated the dictum of Epicurus not to avoid pleasures but to select them. We whispered Nietzsche's "Goest thou to woman, forget not thy whip!" to the bathroom wall and went to bed with the female conquests of Don Juan and Boccaccio. It did not help. The entire spectrum of masturbatory verbalization merely aggravated what I once called the "non-scratchable rash at the bifurcation point of the forked radish." While pedagogues droned, our hormones danced.

At last, after endless nocturnal mutterings into my pillow, I got up enough courage to make a date with a damsel who resided in the impeccably respectable Jewish suburb of Avondale. It was like going over the top on a dawn patrol from the trenches in France. "Operation Shirley," "Mission Reconnaissance." Objective: a davenport in the family livingroom. My objective was achieved—but I was still in No Man's Land. I was so nervous I couldn't stop talking. My monologue began with some prickly epigrams lifted from Oscar Wilde's *The Importance of Being Earnest*; I sneaked into Beethoven's *Fifth Symphony*, sidled into President Woodrow Wilson's "Fourteen Points," and then solved the problem of cost-of-living-consumer-goods-distribution. I sailed non-stop through the hemlock speech of Socrates, Beatrice Webb's Fabian socialism, Ludwig Lewisohn's *Upstream* and George Jean Nathan's theatrical reviews in *The Nation*. Then I spoke about my summer job at the steel mill during the war, telling her what I hoped to accomplish as a rabbi and why I believed in God. . . . Silence, accompanied by a further tightening of my visceral muscles, was followed by a paroxysm of indecision. Should I reach out and touch her hand? She let me land a goodbye peck on the cheek.

Frustrated and disgusted, I told my roommate Rube all about it. His smoothness at stringing along girls often had left me spellbound with admiration. Rube assured me that I had made a good start: "Give yourself time!" he said.

"'To know,' it says in the Bible, is to have intercourse, Rube," I replied. "I am beginning to understand the connection. A woman's vagina is the gateway to the meaning of everything—life. I've got to know a woman!"

The seminary's response was silence. Despite the staff's rampant individualism that often reached bravura proportions, and despite their untrammeled classroom audacity in personal behavior and opinion that evoked my adulation, they were like undifferentiated peas in a pod about sex, as though they and their children had been produced by the gods on Olympus. I felt cheated. I had hoped that ancient rabbinic wisdom would lead me by the hand through the mazes of Venus.

Recall of my student days is almost total. Yet I remember only four pedagogical allusions to sexual behavior during the entire seminary period: a professor of Jewish philosophy had related uniquely human face-to-face intercourse to an encounter with God; another, during a Talmud class, suddenly sputtered, "Feinberg, you got sex troubles?" (he had caught me gazing through the window dreaming of a willowy girl who had sent me running like a deer after she had stretched out on the grass before me on my twilight trek home); a third professor sprayed spittle over me while elaborating on the infidelities of Hosea's wife; finally, in medieval history, the Jewish family's strength was explained to me by turning to details about the correct amenities and modes of conjugal union recorded in the talmudic tractate *Nashim* (Women).

The Talmud (from the Hebrew root word "to learn") is a vast compilation in Hebrew and Aramaic dialect on practically every subject under the sun concerned with the elucidation of biblical law and its 613 commandments. The product of more than seven centuries of intellectual speculation and cultural activity in Palestine and Babylonia between about 200 B.C.E. (Before the Christian Era) and 500 C.E. (the Christian Era), it contains two million words. For centuries the debates and decisions of the rabbis were not written down lest they compete with the sacredness of the Bible itself, but were handed down by word of mouth. Traditional Judaism regards the written Talmud as the complement and fulfillment of Scripture, since all human conduct had been ordained by God in microcosm on Mount Sinai. About two-thirds is ritual, civil and criminal law, or *Halachah* (The Way), parts of it now irrelevant and obsolete for the mundane life of today. The remainder, *Agada*, is constant and current; it embodies the free play of the mind and imagination of a multitude of teachers and sages through the centuries. It is a rich tapestry of parables, folk tales, proverbs and the family, woven by the minds and spirits of inordinately wise and mature men for human guidance, as though all deliberations of the United States Supreme Court based on the Constitution (in Judaism, the first

five books of the Bible) had been gathered together for authoritative reference to the life of every American citizen. Although
talmudic mandates are no longer binding on modern Jews, all
rabbis, however liberal, still turn to them with reverence as an
expression of the God-search and godly conduct orientation of
Judaism.

In the chaos of my reveries on the subject of Woman, the "Sea
of the Talmud" was no more a purgative for sex hangups than the
kabbalistic computations in medieval mysticism, the *hapax
legomina* in the Book of Job, or the cold-shower remedy lam-
pooned in our bumming-room bull sessions.

It was a quote from the Talmud, however, and a telephone
number that led me out of impasse. The former permitted an
unwed male of marriageable age (eighteen) to go to a town where
he was not known, if his bachelordom was a result of, let us say,
economic circumstances. Rabbinical students were not excepted.
The same day that brought me that delightful euphemism also
brought me the post-graduate student who let me jot down her
telephone number. Singly, these two events were fortuitous and
trivial; paired, they bore an occult message and a promise.

Her name was Irene; her rooms in a small brick house facing
a quiet courtyard in a sedate residential section of the city were
antiseptically neat; her age—about thirty; her appearance—trim,
with russet hair, a fresh complexion and a figure that was firm
and rounded. She was gentle, soft-spoken, tender and responsive.
Her profession: prostitute. But the Irene totality was far more
than a depersonalized vessel for my pent-up eroticism. From the
start I always slipped the currency note with a minimal gesture
noiselessly under a jewel box on her dresser; a faint smile and swift
eye-spark always signaled that she had understood.

Was Irene a relationship? Did she signify emotional involvement? The German philosopher Immanuel Kant, who bestrides
abstruse academic speculation like a colossus, once said something about two people who enter into a pact to use each other's
genitals. The fiscal contract Irene and I had made was canceled
the moment we touched, and it never again resumed a place in our
minds. Our sporadic (affordable) linkage times had the non-arti-
ficial, non-mechanical, non-dehumanized quality of Martin
Buber's "I-Thou," a truly human osmosis of two personalities.
That may not add up to a "relationship" as defined by modern
standards of cohabitation, but it had mutuality and a beauty of its

own. In retrospect, abjuring both sentimentality and hard-nosed calculation, I still ask myself whether Irene saved me from what we then referred to as a "nervous breakdown." Two of my classmates had caved in because of "over-work." They had to leave school, but their erratic sex-drenched talk and solitary, secretive bathroom seances seemed to have been the unquestionable symptoms of repression "gone haywire." I cannot diagnose the degree of my vulnerability to such an aberration, but it is certain that my neurotic tensions folded their tents like Bedouins and crept away. Irene uncorked me. Her bed was balm. Once, at a convention a year or two later, a colleague told me Irene had asked about that "brown-eyed, skinny kid!" He was sure she had meant me. . . .

By gradually easing back my mind inside that "brown-eyed skinny, kid," I delved, one leisured summer, to the hub of the question why I had chosen the rabbinate as my life-work. First, as a Jew, I had been molded by almost four thousand years of dramatic, dynamic and enigmatic history—from Abraham to Moses, from Isaiah and Maimonides to Herzl and Einstein—of a people whose continued existence struck me with awe. I felt that I was born not only in Bellaire, Ohio, by physical happenstance, but also in Grinkishok, Lithuania, that poverty-blighted, pogrom-haunted *shtetl* of my parents, as well as in Jerusalem, where the inextinguishable light of the Jewish spirit had been ignited by a passion to know God's will and enter into covenant with Him.

The Ohio River, the hills above it and our polyglot proletarian gang from across the tracks had given me a Huckleberry Finn boyhood. Nostalgia floods from my memory-bank: riding the waves of a calliope-whistling steamboat in a skiff; noodling for tadpoles, roasting mickeys by a fire, diving off a stone bridge, driving the feed store man's horse-and-buggy, picking pawpaws and dewberries, hopping freight trains, snaring catfish which I couldn't bring home because they were not kosher, raiding apple orchards, bob-sledding and ice-skating on the frozen creek—these were frolicsome, sun-lit days.

Hebrew school (*Heder*) dug far deeper. There a starveling, itinerant teacher eked out a meager fare on the monthly pittance paid by immigrant peddlers to whom the knowledge of the "holy tongue" in Bible and prayerbook meant Bar Mitzvah for their boys (not girls), the God-commanded study of the Torah and the preservation of the Jewish people. The synagogue that housed the school was a weather-worn wooden shack; Jewish kids were hunched over the ancient texts after public school, while the Gentiles played baseball or mumbledy-peg; the paper-thin teacher relieved his melancholia by shouting and ear-twisting. But all that vanished in the fascinating lore of biblical heroes. I clad myself in the breastplate of the High Priest, while the classroom's tattered wallpaper burst into the golden pillars of Solomon's Temple. At home, when my mother blessed the candles on the Sabbath Eve, the universe seemed sunk in silent awe. When my father led his seven sons in the account of Israel's flight from Egypt to freedom on the Passover Eve, I dreamed that I was Elijah; I would announce deliverance for all the oppressed everywhere.

Second, as a Jew, I was "different." I didn't go to church, didn't attend Sunday School or celebrate Christmas. A sweet old lady who had hired me to deliver her Yuletide gifts once said to me, "You Feinberg boys are so nice. Too bad our Lord won't save you." I was often doused in the water fountain, and the coal miners' kids called me "sheeny." "Abie, the Jew baby" echoed in the school corridor. But Abraham was the father of my people—and the first name of Lincoln whom I loved—and mine! During a Yiddish lesson, which my mother taught me to make me part of the Jewish folk, she would describe life in Grinkishok so vividly that I still try to reconstruct mentally that lost world of Eastern European Jewry reduced by Hitler to bones and ashes. She told me how her family had bolted the door and stayed inside on Easter Sunday in fear of attack by the peasants who had been incited by the priests to avenge the Crucifixion.

Although I was the first Jewish president of a high school graduating class in 1916, no one ever invited me to a party. When Leo Frank was lynched in Georgia, I shivered in my bed all night. The Statue of Liberty softened my sense of alienation. I memorized Emma Lazarus's poem. Had not my parents been among the "huddled masses yearning to be free"? The torch in New York Harbor had led them out of bondage. At high school commencement, my valedictory was entitled "America First," yet every night I included in my prayer, "Oh God, bring the Jews back to Palestine," although I had never heard then of Zionism.

In body I was born on the Day of Atonement (Yom Kippur), the most sacred day in the Hebrew calendar. When word reached my father in synagogue that his seventh child had arrived, his prayers "stormed heaven," it was said, sped by the fact of having another mouth to feed. Pop could never master the American knack for business; he had devoted himself to rabbinical lore and works of piety. At my Bar Mitzvah ceremony during Yom Kippur worship, I was given special permission to make a speech, in both English and Yiddish; I vowed to serve the Jewish people, religion—and God.

Third, because I was "different," I became a dissident. The biblical prophets had directed me to social justice, and poverty had identified me with the "little people." Passion for the underdog still stirs me to indignation. I saw coal miners beaten on the streets by imported goons because they demanded a union; I saw a black playmate drown in the sycamore-tree swimminghole, stunned by rock-throwing rednecks yelling "nigger." Through tears, I promised God to defend the poor and the persecuted.

William Jennings Bryan electrified me with his oratory following a Roman-candle parade to elect him president. Everybody had said I was a fine speaker and writer. I too would be a tribune of the common people! Whenever I ascended a platform, self-doubt fell to the floor as the subject, the audience and I fused together. What couldn't I do as a preacher brandishing a sword for justice?

Fourth, as a dissident I also was a seeker for the truth. The two mysteries that belabored and beckoned me were God—and sex. At sixteen I was like the harp of King David on which the wayward winds of the desert played their mournful or mirthful tunes, except that the principal melody strummed on my spirit was a riddle as old as the human brain: the problem of evil. Every step I took crashed against it. Disease, sorrow, injustice, death, the floods that overflowed the Ohio River banks every spring and drove the stoic innocents in the "depressed" town section from their shabby homes and left the rich on Gravel Hill untouched. I brooded over the callousness of nature, from the iceberg that sank the *Titanic* in 1912, to the hot lava that caused volcanic eruptions in Asia. Could nature, the instrument of God, be so cruel? Thousands of Armenians were massacred by the Turks; coal miners' children begged for food at our kitchen door in hard times. There was so much undeserved suffering and unredeemed injustice. If God can abolish evil, and will not, He is wicked; if He would and cannot, He is weak.

What I would call *Weltschmerz* at seminary a year later bore down heavily upon my mind. However, I was sure that a rabbi could not only clarify the Great Unknowns but could put the chalice of healing wisdom to the parched lips of all mankind.

Sex! What was this unremitting vision that stalked my waking moments and shattered my sleep? What was this necromancer that alternately froze and embroiled my body? What was this yearning that began with gentle curiosity about girls' breasts I had never touched and ended with torment demanding that I touch the tingling protuberance whose arrogance did not recede until it was sated? How could I deal with it? What could I do? Where would I learn its secret? Surely the sages and scholars of my religion would guide me down the labyrinthine paths of a need and desire implanted by God himself. Rabbinic studies held the light. A Catholic priest confided to me years later that men sometimes enter the ministry of the church to throttle their sex problem because the decision to be celibate is mandatory and obviates the need to make an independent choice. I had no intention to invite control. I had to find my own way—*that* was it!

It was Abba Hillel Silver, the most renowned rabbi of modern times, who gathered into focus all the dreams and resolutions sprouting in my mind. I rode the trolley to his temple in Wheeling, West Virginia, one Sabbath Eve to hear him preach. All my misgivings and uncertainties fled before his magnetism, superb eloquence and luminous "being at one" with God and Israel. Debating teams, school plays and oratorical programs had given me some experience as a speaker. I knew I could be a good preacher—not an equal of Rabbi Silver certainly, but perhaps one able to inspire. Instead of declaiming on "Women's Suffrage" or "The Relative Harm of Corsets or Cigarettes," I would defend the Jewish people and do homage to God. I only needed to receive Rabbi Silver's blessing to enter Hebrew Union College, the famous Reform Jewish seminary in Cincinnati.

Ordination in 1924 and a two-year rehearsal gestation period in small congregations were followed by a weekend visit and sermon try-out at Temple Israel of the City of New York, then Manhattan's second largest Jewish Reform congregation after awesome Temple Emanuel, the cathedral synagogue of the Western Establishment. Instant election to the co-rabbinate with the ailing, distinguished septuagenarian Maurice Harris who was soon to retire—and what naive self-inflation called "my destiny"—cleared the path for me. At twenty-seven I was inducted into the rarefied atmosphere of a nationally prestigious New York pulpit by

Stephen S. Wise of Free Synagogue and Nathan Krass of Temple Emanuel, who together with Rabbi Silver formed the triumvirate that towered over world Jewry.

But from sunset to dawn one night, three years later, I transposed into words a non-stop total regurgitation of spiritual turmoil I could no longer curb or endure. It might have been laboriously indited by a medieval monk in his barren cubicle, but my cell was a plush Fifth Avenue hotel apartment. I had slain the big-city dragon, wooed and won Park Avenue—the Big Apple was in my pocket. Blessed (or cursed) with pulpiteering "flair," I preached to a sea of silver-topped noggins nodding to one another, a sea flecked by a few-score middle-aged housewives, some of them en route to a post-service luncheon at Schrafft's and a theater matinee. The temple executive director said I had the "biggest damn Saturday morning crowd in town." A newspaper columnist dubbed me a "radical young Lochinvar come to uphold the banner of social justice and champion the poor and down-trodden."

After years of trauma and stumbling to and fro in a morass where every healthy expression of gnawing sexuality was forbidden and nothing could be said, vociferous social radicalism gradually merged with repressed sexual radicalism. I was led into stabler waters by a black, slightly moth-eaten bathing suit on the most exquisite female form I had ever beheld. At seminary, the circle of self-conscious and intellectually snobbish elitists to which I clung had nourished "culture" pretensions. We had vowed to travel lightly; family cares would sabotage our fight for a new world order—we were not the marrying kind. But Ruth's rare and beautiful spirit toppled my vow of bachelorhood when I bared my soul to her on the rocky shore of Cape Cod. Her name was already legendary in the top echelons of Manhattan's glamorous realm of women's fashions, yet she had continued to make her home with parents and siblings; she laughed off my grandiloquence about her own apartment, along with my less circumlocutory modes of seduction. What but the disciplines of a mathematics major at Smith College could yoke such authentic innocence of spirit to a razor-sharp sophistication of mind?

On Election Day in November 1930 we began forty years of marriage that ended with our fore-doomed, desperately fought battle against her devastating cancer—and death-in-life for me. Grief for her suffering and my loss of the only non-blood-related person who had made the word "love" admissible to my tongue was intensified by a feeling of bafflement. Although Ruth shared and encouraged the social radicalism that embroiled me in many of my "lost-cause" conflicts with the military-industrial complex, she could not share my perpetual but also lost, private civil war with anarchic sexuality. Tragically, she knew nothing of it. There was a complete breakdown of communication, and I was the prime culprit! Since then, when I counsel couples I beseech them to level the barriers of reticence, disguised as delicacy.

A pair of lovers might with assurance of enormous survival-value inch back into the Garden of Eden before the alleged "Fall," when primal man and woman gazed upon each other's nakedness through the eyes of a new-born child. Does familiarity breed contempt? I submit that absence of total, unimpeded communication, for example, about each other's specific sexual needs, and one's most inward feelings, physical and emotional, can almost certainly breed frustration and cumulative, even unjustified resentment. Let not a woman believe that undressing in the closet is a badge of honor. It is a gesture of immaturity, of enslavement to primitive taboos. Even a rollicking smidgen of deliberate obscenity can break the ice. Although the first experimental utterance may evoke a flush in the cheeks and tension in the limbs, the second will produce a belly laugh and a stirring in the region below it.

On February 28, 1930 I resigned from Temple Israel. Was it moral "maladjustment" alone that made me decide to doff my rabbinical robe? There were other ingredients in the heady brew. On a New York Upper Broadway sidewalk I had caught the blood-reddened eyes of a khaki-clad torso strapped to roller skates—a basket-case shipped home from the Argonne shambles of World War I. I sped up Tenth Avenue beside the railroad tracks, hoping that the chug of shuttling freight trains would dull my senses. But I could not flee the thud of rubber handpads whereby the torso had propelled itself forward. Rather than wear an ROTC uniform, I had cut a whole semester at university. Now I would defy militarism from one of the most important pulpits in America. The next Sabbath I stood like a pillar of stone before the Ark of the Covenant. Approaching the sermon's end, I lifted my hand. "Religion dare not endorse war. I will never acclaim armed conflict for territory, trade, glamorous terminology or extravagant deification of national honor. Our true loyalty is man; our enemy—war!"

After the benediction, I strode down the aisle to wish the congregants *Gut Shabbas*, hands clenched in the pockets of my robe. I would not retreat! I would not truckle to a religion that pounced on pornography and prayed for "our God's side" in war, that parlayed shopworn platitudes into sonorous edicts from heaven and misshaped its clergy into fashionable friars pandering to the powerful. Mourners who had come to say *Kaddish*, the prayer for the dead, filed past me. Vacantly, I muttered words of solace. One woman sidled up to me, breathing, "As usual, Doctor, grand!" Another reminded me of my forthcoming book review of the novel *If Winter Comes* for a women's club tea; a third complained about my delay in visiting her hospitalized husband. A volunteer choir soprano playfully waggled her forefinger under my nose, cooing, "Remember, we have a dinner date tomorrow evening," and the chairman of the property committee, who inspected the premises after every service, gaily gripped my hand. "Brilliant, boy—but you can't get me upset! The stock market reached the highest point in history today!"

So much for the supposed attention-grabbing power of sermons. On the evidence, the revelation of homiletical anemia should not astonish anyone. Humanity has been bombarded with pulpit finger-pointing for well-nigh twenty-five centuries, since the time sermons began to develop out of the Jewish custom to expound the Torah reading at synagogue service. But I was not a long-term historian at the time of that sermonic flop; the immediate moment had significance enough. The preaching mission envisaged to crown my ministry no longer could be disguised; it was a romanticized chimera.

Another incident in the temple boardroom had made me wonder whether I wanted to be partner in a commercial enterprise, Religion Inc. During a routine monthly directors' meeting, which I attended regularly at their invitation, the discussion ranged around the sale of tickets for seats during the High Holyday Services. This year that source of funds was threatened by the calendar; New Year (Rosh Hashanah) would precede Memorial Day. "People will be stayin' in the country and attendin' services there! We won't be able to sell seats even in Gimbel's basement!" said one of them. "The Conservative *shul* around the corner raises its money from cemetery plots; they are letting tickets go at cut rates!" interjected another.

Remedies for the problem burst "hot and heavy." "Sell the

property we own next door to the old temple uptown. The real estate market is ripe for a killing!" "Put on a big dinner honoring some politician . . ." I listened no more. The debate stormed on with nary a word about religion. A poke in the ribs from the secretary returned me to earth from a tranquilizing snooze. The treasurer was standing, with his hands aloft. "Gentlemen, gentlemen!" he cried. "Don't forget our greatest asset, our handsome young rabbi! A star attraction! He'll bring 'em in! That's his business!"

Walking home across town through Central Park, I talked to myself and the dark solitude. Will I manipulate people according to their usefulness, camouflage self-promotion schemes as public services, scrutinize every word for its value to my popularity chart, keep my eyes peeled on becoming the biggest drawing-card in New York—a Super-Salesman Rabbi? No, by God! I'll be damned if I will!

Another incident occurred on a Sunday afternoon, in early September 1929 in a drab room off the main lobby of the Hebrew Settlement near Manhattan's eastside Jewish ghetto. An American flag stood in one corner, a tycoon philanthropist's portrait hung on the wall. On folding chairs arranged in neat rows sat several score of weary, worry-scarred Jewish men and women. They looked exhausted from the continuous grind of sweatshop pressing and sewing which they had done since the day they landed on Ellis Island as immigrants from Eastern Europe. The Settlement program director had invited me to entertain them with songs. Nodding to the Temple Sunday School music teacher at the piano, I began my program. These folk with gnarled hands and care-filled hearts must have joy tonight! "O Sole Mio," "Matinata," "Otchi Tchorniya," "I've Told Every Little Star," "The Student Prince Serenade." Wrinkles began to fade, heavy-lidded eyes brightened and tensed chins rose in laughter. "Mutter Herz" (Mother Heart), "Eili, Eili" (My God, My God, Why Hast Thou Forsaken Me) and other Yiddish songs followed. Tears began to glisten on their cheeks and then mine followed. This was a tribute to the choked-off warmth and joy of humble people who knew so little pleasure that the notes of a fumbling amateur tenor stretched their taut face muscles with spontaneous cries of rapture. For one golden evening we were all wrapped into one capsule of release from troubles. Never since ordination had my spirits soared so exultantly toward the light.

From the Settlement I went to a late evening party of the Temple Junior Society. Soon "Juniors" converged on me and "O Sole Mio" fled, to be replaced by a gaggle of staccato exclamations. "Kenneth's dad just bought him a Packard"; "Marilyn spent the summer taking ballet lessons in Paris"; "Susan has signed up for a Mediterranean cruise"; "Michael has been accepted by Andover Academy." I heard them all too clearly. With each announcement, my heart sank a degree lower. Then brash Lester, flushed with cocktails, thrust forward and fairly shouted in my ear, "How can you believe all that stuff, Rabbi? Money talks, that's all. . . ."

I walked home up Fifth Avenue. On Monday morning I made a phone call to Estelle Liebling, who had coached America's leading singers. "My friend," I said, "I'm giving up the rabbinate. I want to sing." "You're crazy," she gasped, "to give up serving in one of our most prominent and plush temples for a roller-coaster life; you'll starve!" I gulped but held fast. "The animals in the zoo are well-fed, too, Estelle, but caged. I want to be free."

Embedded in my farewell address on that Sabbath Eve in February 1930 was a clarion manifesto to Temple Israel's congregation: "Like the tomb of Tutankhamen, church and synagogue are full of splendor, but bereft of life. Organized religion is a deserted lighthouse; the tides of human energy beat on other shores."

I took off my black robe, laid it on the reading desk, and walked off the pulpit. Ruth had saved a seat beside her in the front row. Pausing for a few seconds, I looked out at the huge gathering. "Now I belong among you," I murmured, then sat down and took her hand.

My farewell sermon turned into a nation-wide brouhaha in ecclesiastical councils and in the press. The debate was heated up by the *New York Times*, which published a two-column report on my sermon in its Sunday edition, printing verbatim the negative anti-Establishment section but omitting the positive half, which had emphatically reiterated my undimmed faith in God and my personal regard for Temple Israel. Moscow's *Pravda* reprinted the *Times* report, crowing that it heralded American youth's espousal of atheism.

My formal letter of resignation spelled out a desire to study singing and music. One deep-rooted though undefined cause of my headlong flight was, as I see it now, a more profound desire for individual freedom, social and sexual. The incompatibility of that freedom with the moral commitment of a rabbi was complicated, I felt, by fear of detection, the personality split of a double life, and the scarcely audible whisper of faint, fading guilt. The litany of sins for which I beseeched the Lord's forgiveness on every Day of Atonement in unison with the throng of worshipers had lost its visceral impact.

More than by obligation to abstract morality, I was motivated by concern for the Jewish community. The Big Apple provided almost absolute "lost-in-the-crowd" protection against prying eyes and inquisitive noses, but my own senses did not shield me from a "still, small voice." Ego-stroking publicity heavily weighted the dangers to which I was subjecting the people of the beloved parents who had nurtured me. All the arguments wrestling for control of my mind, however, I could dismiss and shake off their threat to equanimity; but there remained one, unconquerable: *I have to be free*!

Stephen S. Wise blasted my goodbye address, declaring categorically that I "never had given support to Zionism." He must know, I stated in riposte, that I had made a pilgrimage to Palestine the preceding summer and had attended countless dinners to arouse monetary and moral enthusiasm for Zionist pioneers. His sacrifice of veracity to verbiage was my first embroilment in clerical politics.

A scholarship was awarded me to study grand opera under Salignac, the tenor star of *l'Opéra Comique*, at the Conservatoire Americaine in Fontainebleau, near Paris, the City of Light, known to me from previous visits as a bastion of personal liberty. That summer of 1930 I rode the screaming train almost daily. More than viewing the Louvre, I was amazed to encounter a review of myself. Sipping brandy at the Café de la Rotonde, buzzing center of stylized lubricity, sexual fantasies no longer alerted their penile servitor to arise. When accosted on the Boulevard des Italiens by the routine "voulez-vous coucher avec moi?" I would thumb with frowning concentration a match-book-size French-English dictionary and spread my hands in mockery of incomprehension. (My descent to callous comedy toward women compelled, for the most part, to "scour" the streets for an uncertain livelihood and suffer harassment was an exhibition of retarded adolescence; I regret it keenly.)

Was it the mythical beauty of Paris, the exhilaration of singing tenor arias from *Faust, Manon, Romeo and Juliet* on stage? It was, I believe, the bracing air of freedom and permissiveness that had altered the fulcrum of my consciousness. Release from the monolith of moral dictatorship had liberated me from the imperialism of sexuality. Whereas the pulpit had magnified the place of sexual indulgence in my value system, Paris had reduced it.

My verdict was fully validated when I returned to New York and a series of lucky events that peaked in an astonishing radio career. It all began with a fifteen-minute "sustaining" (unpaid) stint Saturday afternoons on a local radio station and progressed through successive implausible stages, as though propelled by a hidden hand, in a razmataz world for which I had had no training. A phone call came from the most talked about star-maker on Broadway, a try-out, a contract, a session with the photographer and, presto, I had my own unprecedented five nights a week program on the NBC-WJ2 network, broadcast from coast to coast. "You can't make cross-country love to every woman in America with a moniker like Abraham Feinberg!" manager Ed Wolfe said. I thus became "Anthony Frome, Poet-Prince of the Air Waves," named after Ethan Frome, hero of a beloved novel. Since then "Tony" and "Abe" have dwelt, not always amicably, inside my skin. Unlike Gilbert and Sullivan's "Wandering Minstrel," "a thing of shreds and patches," Anthony Frome received a glamorous blast-off to radio celebrity.

The early 1930s were eventful years for the American people, and for me. A cover-page photo and feature story in *Radio Guide*; songs in every genre, from Tin Pan Alley to the Metropolitan, in almost every tongue save Chinese, broadcast from Radio City, preceded on Friday by Roosevelt's "Fireside Chats"; movie shorts for Paramount; personal appearances in Atlantic seaboard theaters, including the New York Paramount at $1,500 per week—that was in 1933, the bottom year of the Great Depression.

Before every broadcast I read from the Hebrew Bible the Song of Songs, an interchange of carnal, even explicit love poems studded with erotic imagery. Talmudic savants long ago denatured the lovers, transforming their conjugal union into a "Covenant" between God and Israel, as the Christian Fathers did into Christ and the church at a later time, to shield the ever-susceptible populace and themselves from lust-kindling Scripture. In my mind the Song of Songs was a transfusion of vital juices, a dosage of life-affirmation more congenial to Judaism than the manufactured prudishness of theologians who dared to judge in God's name while defaming His creation. Reciting it generated the mood for "Anthony Frome" on the air.

I physically caressed the microphone with fingers and larynx, and through it, as surrogate, the libidos of frustrated housewives, nubile flappers and lonely men, by summoning all the craft I knew of nuance and *schmaltz*. At the same time, I think I assuaged the pain of the jobless, the hopeless, the bankrupt merchants and brokers who were selling apples on street corners. They were all victims of a Depression that had left thousands with no balm except to be able to forget. Yet, despite the pragmatic "sexiness" of my repertoire, the temptations of a Broadway "name" and of fluttering autograph-seekers, my radio years were the most nearly chaste period in my adult life.

The promoters of Anthony Frome had stifled the news as best they could that I was a married man. My career was powered by a tenacious manager who browbeat the National Broadcasting Company brass into giving me a "helluva" build-up—all puffed into print by a mendacious press agent. He fabricated into "exclusive" stories sundry "inside" tidbits about me and whispered them to the columnists. For example, they wrote that I did the show in socks because my shoes squeaked when I sidled back from the mike for a sexy fade-out. Italian fans of Metropolitan star Nino Martini mobbed me for autographs because I looked like him; my Neapolitan coach comforted himself for my failure to be born in Sorrento, where I would have "sucked opera with mother's milk," giving me an ear for *bel canto*.

"Tony, some of your hot fan letters should have been written on asbestos!" a Broadway wag bellowed by way of a compliment. It did not rejoice me. I could feel only compassion for "lonely hearts" whose lives were so empty they found a thrill in vicariously sharing mine. These were love-starved, simple people who got a fleeting fulfillment of their sex fantasies from the masturbatory letters they wrote to a warbler who drenched songs with that "bed time" feeling. The stage-door Jennies and Johnnies who stuck a stubbed pencil and a piece of paper into my hand for a name-scribble stirred in me a rash impulse to cry out, "For God's sake, seek love in a lover's body!" *The Court of the Poet-Prince* was a monthly paper mimeographed and circulated by my fan club, The Anthony Frome Fellowship. Aware of my previous life as a rabbi, the editors spelled out in every issue that the *Court*'s main purpose was to nurture racial and religious brotherhood. I was immeasurably proud of that and of Adele St. John's article entitled "From Pauper to Poet-Prince."

What a jolt I received from the new theatrical environment! Microphone and stage seemed almost antiseptic in comparison with the furtive, sniggering leers of the macho "boys" and "girls" in "church." The veterans with whom I, a top-billed interloper, was booked into movie-theater slots were an endangered species; their livelihood, precarious at best, was reduced to a doughnuts-and-coffee fare and a squalid room in a cheap hotel. They had come from the vaudeville circuit that now was banished by the movies. It was the publicity puffed stars who supplied Walter Winchell with scandal, while affluent bourgeois burghers aped the scabrous doings and sayings of the spoiled darlings of screen and radio. My dressing room was often visited by the other "acts"; they had gleaned from a *Radio Guide* story that I had been a rabbi. Their almost pathetic eagerness to talk about religion and God and their personal problems while still bedizened in makeup and costume warmed my heart, mitigated my stage fright and confirmed to me that the stage outdoes the pulpit as a pedagogue of simple decency.

That former rabbinical colleagues fumed at the admittedly garish setting of my personal appearances in movie theaters did not discomfit me. Embarrassment arose from the excessive monetary reward I received while scores of Americans obtained their sole nutrition from bread lines and soup kitchens. And my wide-ranging repertoire included only one song related to the punishing economic state of the day: "Brother, Can You Spare A Dime?"

Did I ever accuse myself of bartering dignity for the motley cap and bells of an entertainer? Not at all. Affection from the unseen congregation of the air was no less sincere than that of the good burghers who had faced me in the pews. On the pulpit I had talked *about* God; in song, I tried to talk *to* Him by thrusting voice and heart out to my invisible friends. The message I transmitted was to *love happily*. Instead of a professional word, a tool perfunctorily used in synagogue, "God" became the key to a personal encounter with Him.

My reveries began to toy with random thoughts on a bid to Hollywood—the movies—when three monstrous apparitions began to stalk from the shadowed wings to the center of my dream-lit stage. Benito Mussolini was the first of these apparitions. At seminary we had mimicked the iron-man's chin, sneering at the imperious Il Duce's will that had managed to persuade Italian trains to run on time. Now his black-shirted ruffians threatened to stomp freedom into the dust. Among his blustering heroics was the bombing of Ethiopian villages. Then press reports began to appear about a Colonel Francisco Franco who was spawning counter-revolutionary rumblings in Spain. Stories were circulating about his cloak-and-dagger recruitment of African Moors to help obliterate the republican regime in the name of the Roman Catholic religion and anti-Communist liberation. From a lofty studio perch in Radio City I could not yet decry the Italo-German planes freed to pulverize Loyalists who had been disarmed by the farce of American non-intervention, nor the carnage of Guernica. But I could sense that Spain was a "dry run" for the Axis' onslaught against individual liberty.

On January 30, 1933 I was seducing the wires, volts and fuses of radio into worship of Eros, chortling "Love in Bloom" with a fake plastic guitar to a bevy of long-limbed blondes lolling on the New York Paramount stage in a set suggesting Teutonic Valhalla. At the same time, Adolf Hitler was using radio to seduce Germans into worshiping *him* and sharing *his* Teutonic (Aryan) Valhalla. In the Fifty-Seventh Street apartment I happily shared with Ruth, an easy-chair had been used as background for a signed photo of romantic Anthony Frome, hair-grease and all, wearing a lounge-robe and smoking a borrowed pipe. The picture was to be mailed in "personal" response to fan letters. Sitting there, I could not yet physically see the Nazi juggernaut moving inexorably toward control of Europe, enslavement of mankind and the extinction of Jewry. But there was premonition in my bones. The next morning I remarked to Ruth, "A Jew *cannot* live, and a decent human being *will* not live, in a Fascist world." Soon I switched from reading *Variety* to articles written by Dorothy Thompson, Vincent Sheean, Stanley High, William Shirer, as well as reports of Hitler's speeches in the *New York Times*. Herr Goebbels surely must have smacked his lips over this unwitting propaganda channel bestowed on him by the Jewish-owned purveyor of "all the news that's fit to print." Books by Nora Waln and Gregor Ziemer littered my makeup table in various theater dressing rooms. I had a radio installed to be able to listen to Ed Murrow, Kaltenborn and Trout. Suddenly, fan letters and lavish gifts began to bore me; having my eyebrows plucked to prevent eye blackouts for movie shorts seemed ridiculous to me. Fingers that once had sinuously cupped the microphone now held it in a nervous clutch; I no longer held in my hands the cheeks of Roxy's Rockettes who had come to see my show, and I often forgot to remind Ruth to pin a cornflower on my lapel as she had done before each broadcast. Only when I stood under stage lights or in the Radio City studio to "do my number" could I forget and drown out Hitler's venomous tirades.

The day before the scheduled renewal of my sponsorship contract, I was rehearsing "Kol Nidre," the most moving of all synagogue melodies, chanted on the eve of Yom Kippur. For the first and only time, my manager and I had decided to include a cantorial number in my program. Before I reached the final swelling phrase of the chant, my eyes filled with tears. After the rehearsal, I telephoned Ruth and asked her to meet me for lunch. "I need to talk with the woman I love," I said. "What happened?" she asked as we sat down to eat. "Fascism is the ultimate enemy of all I stand for, darling." I hunched toward her across the table. "It's not just genocide of Jews; Fascism glorifies war, nullifies the mind, dehumanizes people and makes absolute obedience the leader of supreme law; it replaces individual worth with a brutalized herd and demands that all the world uproot every impulse to mercy." I bit my lips and went on, "I've saved up enough to cushion my exit from radio. I can subsidize myself as a rabbi for a few years. I've got to fight Fascism."

Ruth placed her hands over mine: "Tony, I have felt all along you would do this—and I'm glad!"

In May 1935 the press blared that Tony Frome was to be installed as Rabbi Abraham Feinberg at Mount Neboh Temple in Manhattan. The annual salary? What I had garnered in one month as "Poet-Prince." The Anthony Frome Fellowship magazine commented with more than mildly poignant sadness: "Oh minstrel, yet a prophet, seer/ Whose message reaches out afar/ You glorified the songs we hear/ And shed radiance like a star/. . . . The sincerity of our affection for him will continue to bind us together. . . . We shall miss the God-given voice more than he will ever know." A few months later, I was summoned to Arlington, Virginia, to officiate at the funeral of Leona Palmer, the paper's editor.

Another door opened. I joined the American League Against War and Fascism; I refused to speak on behalf of General Franco, thus turning aside a request from Cardinal Hays transmitted in a phone call by a Jewish Tammany Hall judge; I blasted the choice of Berlin for the 1936 Olympic Games; I bitterly criticized a plan to give the Duke of Windsor, who openly admired Hitler, a red-carpet welcome in New York. My ongoing feud with Fascism is on record, in press and magazine reports, in my books, in threats on my life—a half-century of combat on many fronts.

It also had become clear to me that Fascism was not limited to a specific nation or group. Soviet Communism cloaks itself in anti-Fascist phraseology—honing a state mechanism for Fascist crimes, even anti-Semitism. "Church" reveals a bent for Fascism by clamping a sexuality-morality code to the mind and body of the individual demanding obedience on penalty of punishment at the hands of God. Thus it erases the crucial margin of independent choice and the dignity guaranteed to every human being fashioned in the Divine image. Conformity to orders from above is the seminal matrix of Fascism. It is no fortuitous accident or historic whimsy that socioeconomic diehards who plump for rigid adherence to things as they were and despise innovation also pray for our national return to the tried and true morals of the horse-and-buggy era. Interplay between good piety and good politics is as American as apple-pie.

The following years moved me from a second Manhattan pulpit to a "prominent" position in Denver, Colorado, and finally to Toronto, Canada, and an eighteen-year span as a "controversial" rabbi. During that time my energy and time were often preempted by a string of involvements other than my pulpit—the Canadian Campaign for Nuclear Disarmament, including anti-nuclear demonstrations with Linus Pauling at home and Bertrand Russell and Canon Collins in England. After my "technical" retirement as rabbi of Holy Blossom Temple in Toronto, my unflagging opposition to the Vietnam adventure culminated in a 1967 civil disobedience journey to Hanoi and a half-day meeting with Ho Chi Minh, which in turn was climaxed by an ignored peace overture from Ho that I personally relayed to President Lyndon Johnson. My book *Hanoi Diary* is a blow-by-blow account of that mission. This was followed by a cross-continent speech junket for United States' withdrawal from Vietnam. Then came foreign travel on behalf of the State of Israel and survivors of the Holocaust.

On February 14, 1971 Ruth died. We had struggled together for almost three years to salvage a thread of hope. She was the twelfth in our immediate families to be destroyed by cancer. (In the following summer, I survived surgery against it.) My spirit shattered by grief and weariness, I fled from twenty-eight years of Canadian hospitality and beloved Toronto's friendships and the memories of lost happiness. My social justice battles largely lost, I began a "new life" as I had entered the old—alone, in Berkeley, California, and then moved to Reno, Nevada. "In my wildest nightmares, I never dreamed I would be living here," I used to say, with a laugh. But Reno has brought me companionship, a home and renewed zest for living.

2

In the Beginning was the Rod, and the Rod was God

The sexual act is a most divine and sacred sacrament. Men and women who are not sexually active . . . are spiritually barren. A man who does not unite with a woman in this life must return in another life and carry on this sacred duty to his Creator.
—Megene Gonzalez, *A Kabbalah for the Modern World*

For the early Fathers of Christianity, and the intransigent addicts to fear of the flesh today in and out of the church, the urgency of sex presented itself as the Devil's device for man's damnation. For normative Judaism it was the device for procreation, with pleasure, designed by God. For the mystic, somewhat marginal, Jewish Kabbalist sect of the fourteenth century and its present-day legatees, however few in number, the act of sex, beyond being a rule *by* God, is the road *to* him. Swift on the heels of that dazzling revelation comes an equally dazzling deduction: the phallus, the indispensable energizing vehicle of coitus, is *itself* of the nature of God.

That the genitals participate in the supreme power of the Almighty is a statement that is at the very heart of the centuries-hallowed fundamental Christian moral system, although it is theologically inadmissible to orthodox Christendom. How else may one interpret the centrality of "sinful" sex in the eternal destiny of those who practice it? When non-marital perforation of the hymen or the penetrating thrust of penis can sway Divine judgment, bringing doom and everlasting damnation in hell, do not hymen and penis reflect and represent Divine power and become His agent? Are not the alternatives of damnation *versus* salvation for all eternity the most awesome and fearsome of God's choices?

The genitals thus become a surrogate for God, the arbiter of human destiny. Essentially, is this functional deification of the phallus, as ordered by pristine fundamentalist Christianity, different from those primitive religious rites which demanded the performance of the sexual act to win from fertility gods the fruit of the womb and the earth for survival?

The fusion of sex and religion is so complete that we cannot discern where the one begins and the other ends; it is the appropriate extension of the biblical male-female formula: "They shall become one flesh."

The biography of the sex-religion axis began to be engraved on the deepest palimpsest of our racial memories long before human annals began to be inscribed on reed, papyrus and stone. The crude, to us exotic and over-explicit, language of the longest if not the sweetest story ever told may not soothe a queasy stomach or excite erogenous zones, but it needs to be recited. The tight embrace of the sexual and the religious is one of the crucial themes of this book. In our search for security with God and ecstasy in sex, only a resoldering of both in joy can redeem religion from hypocrisy and irrelevance—and sex from vulgarity and ugliness.

Since ancient times unhappy self-castrated courtiers of God the King have condemned sexual love with a frenzy that betrays their own abnormal preoccupation with its delights. By doing so they have stripped from their own votaries the privilege of adding erotic rapture not only to perfunctory religious observance but also religious spirituality to the carnal crudities of sex.

For generations Jews have celebrated the Friday-night arrival of the Sabbath as a wedding-feast. After welcoming the "Sabbath bride" with the traditional lyrical splendor of thanksgiving, the words of a song tell us how the husband embraces his bride and "does what is pleasing to her." Rabbinic literature designates marital relations on the eve of the Sabbath to be specially favored in God's sight as a warrant of human partnership. By our conjugal union with the Divine Creation, from which He rested on the Sabbath, the Holy Presence (*schechinah*) is evoked and puts forth His hand in blessing over the nuptial bed.

The yoke that binds religion and sex in symbiotic coexistence leaps back over the Hebrew calendar and the arithmetic of Bishop Ussher to a timespan germane to Darwinian evolution, beyond known history. Anthropology suggests that the body of prehistoric man dwelled in caves, but his mind cowered in a realm peopled by malevolent demons who could swallow the sun, crush him in a storm or earthquake and rend him with fang, tooth and claw. So he invested trees, beetles, stars or whatever else he could find with spirits that he could harness for his protection. Other than such dubious aids, one of the certain sources of incomparable pleasure and peace, however temporary, resided in his genitals. When an available female presented herself to him their sexual climax, in all likelihood, brought them both the only respite from danger, since consumption of food could be disrupted by envious predators.

I doubt that the hairy ape's club was ever a weapon used to persuade the lady; she had desire, but not for resistance. And when a random pair found that their genital contact was pleasurable beyond all others, I do not doubt that this encounter, now condescendingly termed "animalic," generated a semblance of "love." Sex, therefore, led to love—not the reverse, as moralists and poets tend to insist.

Did our remote ancestors know that sex leads to babies? Again, in my unresearched opinion, a regrettably impossible live interview with a resurrected fossil would confound the conventional. I am certain that the pleasure principle preceded the awareness of procreation. However, through aeons of time, his and her dim wits evidently must have toted up coitus, her abdominal swelling and a routine (nine-month) gestation period to hurtle them headlong into the amazing discovery that the mysterious, self-directed, alternately elongated and shrunken appendage below the navel of the male provided not only moments of insensate rapture but the miracle of new life. The squirming, crying, guzzling little creature so like himself or his female no longer was considered an accident or a benefice from the strange and terrible deities of sky and forest. It was the creation of the god-like instrument in his own loins which could spurt a magic fluid into a female's aperture just as it could squirt urine onto the ground.

The famed anthropologist-explorer Dr. Louis S. B. Leakey believed that the upward climb of our species started with the emergence of the tool-user man, *Homo habilis*. The club, the wheel, the axe, the stone knife and the plow supplied him with the rungs to power and the conquest *of* nature. But the tribe that solved the mystery of birth by tracing it to the penis-pudenda connection raised man to collaboration *with* nature and with benevolent gods as the source of life. It was the male's phallus that embodied their omnipotent and omnipresent power. The belief that the female sex apparatus had no active part in the reproductive process was maintained by no less a pundit than Aristotle, who perceived the vaginal region merely as the passive, non-contributing receptacle for male emissions. For centuries that fondly cuddled myth nurtured the masculine complacency of male chauvinists.

"Be fruitful and multiply," the first commandment in the Hebrew Bible, certifies the first consideration of pre-Margaret Sanger humanity. The sovereign influence of sex is illustrated in a talmudic legend according to which the Almighty One was once persuaded to cancel out sexual passion, *yetzer horah*, from all loving creatures. Thereupon families ceased to flourish, no more homes were constructed, men no longer built cities and industry, and even hens stopped laying. Life came to a standstill.

Did not the cosmic Creator place the sex organs at the center of the body where limbs and nerves converge? How much more vital was sex reproduction to the denizens of a world that subsisted solely by the labors of human hands and the clumsy tools they carved! One penis *plus* one vagina meant one or more helpers to hunt, fish, plant and fight. Once animals were domesticated, herds and flocks were also drawn into the cycle of multiplication. (I understand a low-cost chemical called gonadin trophin can now accelerate the mating schedule of dairy cows.)

In the scheme of things sexual congress moved from pleasure to procreation to elementary survival. Infants *must* emerge from the womb—alive! The phallus derives potency from and shared divinity with the ultimate phallus power of gods on whose favor alone it can rely. A life-line to these all-controlling, all-encompassing directors of human fate can be securely and effectively stretched from the place where the unbroken continuity of life is launched: in the pullulating orifice of the female's sexuality. It is sacred and revered because of its essential service to the phallus (rod)-god.

God did not create man. On the contrary, man fashioned an infinite enlargement of his own primary but finite self-image. As ancient man became aware of and exalted by his hitherto-puzzling penis as the creator of life that guaranteed survival and sexuality, it became the dominant strand in his nascent egoism, his sense of self. (It still is!)

The next step was inevitable. The developing human creature had to project that supremely important role onto a deity who had to be placated, persuaded and prompted, by whatever means, so that the generative seed of his penile divine emissary might bring forth abundant offspring.

Among nature's numerous deities which previously had been associated with fear and magic, the ruler of birth became king, and the sex drive concretized in the phallus was sufficiently powerful to possess his whole being. He whom we now hide and call many "bad" names thus became the most important of all gods: Phallus Rex.

Perhaps this awakening after long gestation gave birth to religion. The midwife was the rite of fertility. It reached a peak in song and dance that surrendered the entire human apparatus to ecstasy for fecundity, also releasing the worshiper from the strain of a constant struggle for survival. Under the guidance of various exotic-erotic "priests," religious rituals have enlivened the story of mankind to this moment, producing an efflorescence that left no region of our world unvisited.

Since man invented gods in his own image, he invested them with attributes that gave him the highest degree of delight. Therefore, the first act of coitus for a woman was often with the deity, through the priest. Herodotus, who can be considered a reliable Greek historian, made reference to cohabitation in the holy precincts of worship by most people for the sex god's vicarious pleasure. A virgin dwelling within the gates could fulfill her ordained function by bestowing a gift of her unsullied vagina on any stranger who enacted the initiatory rite on the altar of the sex god (or, quite often, goddess).

Virginity was considered sacred and became the exclusive playground of the gods; the priest whose virility was never questioned acted as their agent or incarnation. Often the sex god was the subject of legend in the guise of a bull, such as the virgin-consuming Minotaur of Crete, the taurobolium ritual that drenched a bull's servitors in its blood as a kind of mass aphrodisiac, the penis-proud bull-stud Apis of ancient Egypt which, in my guess, was worshiped in homage to divine sexuality by the back-sliding Children of Israel soon after their departure from Egypt (the biblical writers emasculated the story by substituting a golden calf).

Brides of Ancient Rome's aristocracy were selected to sacrifice their virginity to the statue of the god Priapus who was always shown in erection. Augustine informs us that Roman matrons regarded this custom as honest and religious, obliging the young maidens to come and sit upon the masculine monstrosity. Each bride was then led into a sacred chamber by a priest who verified the hymenal loss, while her parents and the groom waited in an anteroom of the Priapic shrine. In sculptured nakedness Babylon's goddess Mylitta and Greece's Aphrodite were said to have witnessed similar inanimate deflowerings in their temples.

Even today among some primitive tribes the priest as the surrogate of deity can deflower virgins. Indeed, they cannot marry until he has removed their maidenhood in the name of their god. He may even receive a remuneration for his services. Young girls belonging to the Aikuyu tribe of East Africa are "married" to the snake god first, and then his earthly vicars, the medicine men, consummate the union in huts specially constructed for that purpose. The offspring become the children of the snake god and henceforth can partake in his divine status. In other cultures, maidens writhe on the priest's couch in symbolic prayer for their people's participation in the gargantuan sexuality of the god, on whose behalf the priest gladly receives their votive offering.

Lest we smugly confine these sexual "superstitions" to barbaric tribes and times our "civilization" has, thank God, out-lived, we might reflect for a moment on an even more horrendous debacle of reason, namely, the Jonestown, Guyana, mass-suicide of nine hundred Americans—an inexpressibly macabre act which occurred at the command of the Reverend Jim Jones. He resembled the Aikuyu snake god not only in his omnipotent rule over human lives, but also in his claims that he possessed control over sexuality. Through the testimony of survivors it was ascertained that Jones demanded sex rights over every woman—and man—in Jonestown and forbade sexual intercourse without his consent, boasting that his penis was gigantic both in size and orgasmic capacity.

In remote regions of India it is not uncommon for a husband to accompany his wife to the priest and stand by as reverential spectator of an act expressing sexual union; definite days may be selected for visits of childless women to the temple where they receive the "blessing of creation" beyond the potency limits of their husbands. The adoring touch of a yogi's *lingam* (male genital; the female counterpart is *yoni*) by a barren wife is credited in some quarters with the power to impregnate.

It is plausible that persons of strict rectitude in everyday sex, such as the Kanchaluyas of India, were always more likely to break out in unrestrained sex at worship. Females would remove their outer garments before entering the temple, and the priest, after giving each one a number, would deposit their garments in a box. During an interval of prayer and dance, he would assign each woman to the man holding the corresponding number. No matter who the woman may have been—a stranger or a mother—her sacred duty was to fulfill with her partner the ritual of sex. In a maelstrom of shrieks and orgiastic exercises by all those present, an innocent ritual of piety was performed that would appear to us as a mass promiscuity operation.

In ancient times, communities were minuscule in membership and mystery clung to anyone hitherto unknown and unseen. It therefore may be pertinent to recall that the strangers who visited Abraham purported to be angels. By advising him that Sarah, though grown old beyond impregnation, would bear him a son, they sustained the miracle of fertility. And were not the Children of Israel bidden to bring the first fruits of the harvest and of the sexuality of their beasts to Yahweh's altar as a thanksgiving for His largesse? ("All that openeth the womb is Mine.") To this day observant Jews are expected to redeem their first-born sons, who would be "drafted" for temple service, by making a symbolic payment to a descendant of the priestly Levites. The breaking of a glass by the groom at a Jewish marriage ceremony *may* have started centuries before my Israelite ancestors swept into Canaan as a symbolic concession to the sex gods for the secular, unmediated rupture of the hymen. Let it be confessed that they borrowed and revised many pagan notions in the Promised Land.

Penile sanctity is encountered as a widespread fetish in the pages of history. Once the genitals were recognized as the essential means for executing the procreative powers of the gods, they became holy in themselves. Remote districts in India have records of priests wandering about naked in the streets ringing bells to summon women to perform their religious duties by piously embracing the sacred organs; in other lands males and females genuflect to the generative power of King Phallus with a kiss. In biblical times the penis was a sacred object on which to swear oaths. (The Bible is used for this purpose today.) When Abraham had Eliezer vow to find a proper wife for Isaac, he asked the servant to place his hand under his, Abraham's, "thigh" (a generic euphemism for the privates) stating, "Thus I will make thee swear by the Lord." The word "testament" is derived from *testes* (testicles); in imperial Rome "testimony" was submitted on the authority of "two little witnesses" (Latin: *testiculi*).

In Russia and other East European countries spite or defiance was expressed by extending the tip of the thumb between index and middle finger. This gesture was called "figa" or "fig," a male-genital symbol reminiscent of the Adam and Eve story, for which the fig-leaf was borrowed from Near Eastern mythology.

In certain other European regions persons of exceptional piety regarded the foreskin of Jesus, the Holy Prepuce, with earnest reverence. Until very recently as many as twelve such sacred relics of his circumcision have drawn attention from worshipful visitors. Many of these foreskins were the subjects of legends. The one relic deposited in the Abbey Church of Colomb in the French diocese of Chartres was believed to render barren women fruitful and lessen the pain of childbirth.

East Indian culture, one of the oldest, has retained other sociosexual artifacts. One of them, a smooth round stone protruding from an elongated saucer, depicts the union of yoni and lingam in honor of the mighty god Seva. In Celebes the image of yoni and lingam in fusion adorns temple posts to commemorate fallen warriors; the Greeks baked cakes that were eaten at religious ceremonies in the form of the two joined genitals; Congo tribes modeled the penis in clay, adorned it with feathers and carried it on high in ritual dances to celebrate the gods who blessed the womb; penis-pudenda in conjugation are represented at some European shrines that often are out of bounds to tourists. As late as the sixteenth century, in a chapel dedicated to St. Fontinat, wax figures with the same theme were suspended from the ceiling in such proximity that the noise they made when they struck against one another disturbed the devotions of the faithful. Throughout Egypt lingams hewn in stone celebrate the valor of Isis, the Mother Goddess and Queen of Heaven. According to the annals of Egypt's ancient dynasties, when Isis gathered up the remains of murdered Osiris, she noted the absence of his divine lingam and therefore had one copied in stone.

It is not beyond imagination that circumcision, initiated as a sign of the Abrahamitic covenant with Yahweh in the biblical account, is really a rationalized vestige of a pre-biblical rite which sacrificed the foreskin to fertility. Is it not possible that the bond of covenant-relation between God and Israel was assumed to confer special super-human distinctions on the anatomical spot where it is signed and sealed? To certain African tribes, foreskin removal signified initiation into manhood, as described in the television-movie *Roots*. Among some Arab tribes, male surgery is coupled with incision of a young maiden's clitoris or the infibulation of the *labia minora*. This practice has been condemned by enlightened women, including, I believe, the spouse of one Egyptian head of government, as a cruel device to lessen sexual stimulation and temptation. . . . All these "operations" may have originated in deference to the fertility gods who had to be appeased. Sacrificing the prepuce or the hymen was not really a hardship as neither was considered necessary for sexual intercourse and could even hinder it.

Before the human species began to gather historical data (a few seconds before midnight on a one-year scale of human evolution), sexual activity scarcely entered into man's consciousness beyond the play of muscle, membrane and nerve-ends. Alternating phallic penetration and withdrawal might have approximated to a degree the involuntary systole-diastole of the heart or the swing of a pendulum. One might assume that not until morality fettered the sex drive, shaping man's spirit around its control and imprisonment, did the genitalia enter the realm of decision and deliberation. The range of the forbidden grew with the size and complexity of social groups. Recovering from repeated bouts of exhaustion, man's concern for survival finally made him realize that his instinct had to be bridled by limiting promiscuity and outlawing incest. No more public demonstrations of madness or coitus at will!

Religion, in its earliest Corybantian aspects, moved in the *opposite* direction, through a wild pace of fertility rites. Far from being comparable to the involuntary or automatic movements of the body, it exercised every sinew, nerve and brain cell. Nowhere was this more evident than in erotic dances choreographed to flatter the sex gods by group imitation of their coital act. A grisly, near suicidal feature of these excesses was self-castration. Crotch mutilation attracted some early Christians during the infant stages of their new sect's denial of the flesh. Whereas St. Jerome and other early devout followers of Christ conceived deracination of the despised sex organ as the loftiest rung on their ascetic ladder to perfection and purity, the pagans, having denuded their bodies of something holy, presented their most sublime possessions to a god or gods in whose sight it was the epitome of creation.

Most pagan religious events escalated in a gradual crescendo of orgiastic excitement. The aboriginal cast in the drama, as I visualize it, must have been a slap-happy meeting of near-nude congregants under a leafy tree, with an enthusiastically undulating priest modeling and supervising the actions. The nuclear theme must have been recapitulation, by random pairs, of male-sky plummeting down to fertilize recumbent female-earth, with every woman squatting or swaying in eager response to the beckoning finger or budding rod of the man. The climax of the drama as performed by the priests of Cybels must have been the severance of genitals. After a bacchanale of mad dancing, drunken singing and flogging of torsos, the once-galvanic instruments of joy were placed upon the altar in affirmation of avowal to serve the sex goddess in female dress.

In the Phrygian "Great Mother" cult, candidates for the priesthood castrated themselves during orgy initiations. By contrast the Hebrew Bible specifically excluded priests with physical defects from participating in service at the altar; it even forbade the sacrificial offering of a defective animal, and castration of one's beasts by Jew or Gentile substitute was not tolerated. Although the eunuch was a common figure in the Near East, a Jewess was not permitted to marry one. According to Mosaic Law the hand of a woman could be cut off if she touched the genitals of a man other than her husband. In many parts of the world, to expose oneself was tantamount to a curse, and to uncover the nakedness of another constituted a sinful desecration.

Since the gift of sex outbids all others, the divine donor can be flattered and repaid by celebrating its voluptuous pleasures in his imagined presence. As marriage among the gods became a common factor in myth, it fostered elaborate idolatry of the Mother Goddess: Aphrodite, Demeter, Diana of Ephesus (spanned by seventy breasts), Astarte-Ishtar, Isis. Baal (Hebrew for "Master") under many aliases preempted the male slot; he was the chief target of the Hebrew prophets' denunciation of licentiousness. The virulence of their warnings that Yahweh would wreak dire punishment on the Hebrews for sexual abominations reveals how extensively these Canaanite revels had infiltrated the bastions of Hebraic sexual austerity, an abstemiousness which had its roots in the seminal Jewish concept of God, the stern, authoritarian

Father and Law-giver who demands self-discipline.

The Father-God of Israel had no consort, no identification with natural force or principle; he is Lord of *all*. The reproductive process is His forthright gift, neither intrinsically divine nor to be obtained by any imitative or reciprocal ceremony. Yahweh's purpose is fulfilled when man uses that process responsibly and not in mindless surrender to sensuality. One does not spurn sex; one controls it.

With the masculine entry into the pantheon of sex deities and to assure fertility, many people proceeded all the more intensively to bring the maternal and paternal principles into copulation. How? By doing it. Tribes in Central Africa would segregate men and women four days before seeding their fields and assemble there the night before planting to engage with pent-up fury in indiscriminate intercourse. Other less volatile groups molded a grotesquely gigantic penis and a yawning vagina out of red clay, then squeezed them together as soon as the blossoms appeared on the rice paddies. They would then coalesce their sweating limbs with grunts and shouts, making the rhythmic motions of pelvis and buttocks a microcosm of the alternating seasons of sowing and harvest. Zulu medicine men would fry the genitals of men who had died in full vigor, grind them and strew the powder, moistened with the milk of nursing mothers, over their fields. Similarly, inhibiting boundaries and slithering bodies melted into an indistinguishable mass during the Bacchic festivals of Greece or the saturnalia of Rome. European peasants in some stagnant rural enclaves still couple in the fields to win a bountiful crop.

Captain Cook described a Pacific Island practice in which a tall youth and a slight girl of twelve consummated conjugal union on a crude wooden altar while elderly women onlookers clucked and assisted them. According to historians many shrines permitted any male to emulate the priest and adopt the role of divine vicar, thus placing at his disposal the females, virgin or mated. The ensuing monetary transactions served to augment the coffers of temple functionaries. Some female frequenters of the shrine became permanent adjuncts, engaged in the performance of sex acts as tribute to and object lessons for the resident god; they were equal in dignity and sanctity to the priest. Their recompense was dual: an exalted sense of duty-fulfillment and abundant opportunity for sex-fulfillment. Male prostitutes subsequently lengthened temple rosters. (They were held up to unparalleled castigation by the Hebrew prophets, and the Torah banned such donations to Yahweh.)

These purveyors of sacred sex sold their expertise, but their occupation hardly ranked them as practitioners of prostitution for profit. The material gain was garnered by the religious institution, under the male priest's management. Organized prostitution's potential value to bolster celestial finances has never been shunned or scorned by the respectable. In the Middle Ages sundry church dignitaries deigned to wax opulent on the proceeds of personal indulgences to lucrative lubricity. And it was widely believed in supposedly knowledgeable New York circles that at one time the treasury of Manhattan's oldest and most revered Episcopal house of prayer was bulging with revenue from "Red Light" property.

For centuries remnants and reminders of orgiastic pagan excesses have challenged the sobriety and faith in virtue's triumph laboriously nourished by the church. These stubborn undergrowths on mankind's zigzag shuffle to perfection need not surprise us. We are still savage, if not beast, however much we tend to snub and upstage our ancestors.

The orgasmic sound of an appetitive male infant sucking, heaving and smacking his lips at the maternal nipple may persuade us that food for the emptiness in the alimentary canal packs greater power than filling the vaginal void, yet a female baby may seem the soul of innocence until its fingers find the vaginal cavity or the penile overhang. Breast-sucking evokes the mother's secret titillation and the infant's wide-eyed rapture. Lips have remarkably sensitive nerve-ends, which as every talented necker knows play a vital subsidiary role as a potential prelude to or substitute retardant of coitus. If the infant could talk, would it vote sex or victuals into priority? I wonder about that. One fact emerges out of such speculation: unsatisfied food-hunger debilitates and drains the will; frustrated sex-hunger rises in flood until the dam bursts. Revolutions are made by people hungry enough to be angry but not too hungry for energetic rebellion. . . . The open or masked fertility practices and paraphernalia scattered over the religious landscape since the heydays of paganism are the residue of bursting dams; self-denying codes were no less futile against them than the sacks ordained by New England Puritans to cover the lower parts of male-female bodies "bundled" in wall-beds to warm their courting and "innocent endearments." (More than half the births in Concord, Massachusetts, under Puritanism backed the legitimacy conferred by parental marriage.)

The carvings of exaggerated female genitals that crowned supporting columns of almost every temple in antiquity were found over the doorways of Christian cathedrals in Ireland, supposedly for protection against malevolent spirits. Sex goddesses like Artemis taunt the onlooker in nooks reserved for statues of Christian saints, and prized Madonna paintings have proliferated from pagan representations of a sex goddess and child. The odor of sanctity merges with the myrrh and frankincense of biblical assignations, as does the sultry fragrance of the Garden of Eden when its two inhabitants first "knew" their bodies; floral offerings on every altar murmur the immemorial syndrome, their bright colors designed by nature to attract insects bearing pollen for fertilization.

The maypole dance cannot entirely expunge traces of fertility-rite symbolism, since the pole itself externalizes the deified phallus, encircled by exuberant maidens usually clad in virginal white. The ceremonial was assigned by prelates to Whitsunday, when able-bodied Christians of medieval times ran into the woods to spend the night in revelry. According to a 1558 chronicler, morning witnessed their return with a decorated maypole and a manageable herd of oxen, their horns tipped with nosegays.

Was dancing condemned by some established church authoritarians because of its early association with fertility orgies? Emotional spontaneity, alleged to be a possible prelude to collective lewdness, has never enjoyed high ratings in circles geared to regimentation. Intermittent dance manias have gripped Christendom in the Middle Ages, and shaking and dancing rituals have persisted in enclaves of Christendom down to the nineteenth and twentieth centuries. What is the New Orleans Mardi Gras if not a hilarious, let-joy-be-unconfined genuflection to the "flesh" before the advent of discipline ordained by Lent?

When Christian missionaries converted the heathen Celts, surviving remnants of fertility ceremonial provided an opportunity for outbursts of frenetic eroticism connected with the growing of crops. Christmas mumming, a vestige of primitive man's anxiety over the darkness-versus-light combat during the winter solstice, may have been derived from the hysterical saturnalias of Rome.

Phallic worship was not readily abandoned by the founding followers of the risen Christ; penitential books and church edicts often refer to its persistence. Diggers into that dim time theorize that attempts were made to combine Christian philosophy with the Risen Phallus—furtively in the beginning, more frankly later on. An eighth-century ordinance set a forty-day penance of bread and water as penalty for continued phallic worship; a thirteenth-century cleric was chastised by his bishop for leading his flock around a phallic figure in the churchyard at Eastertime. In 1585 people prayed to a replica of the penis of St. Fontin, and women wanting to conceive made use of it in the same way that Roman wives inserted a wooden phallus before they entered the marriage bed. In a letter written as late as 1786 the British envoy to Naples described to the president of the Royal Academy how, in a little-known section of Issernia, the peasants worshiped the phallus of St. Cosimo. The women would kiss a hand-made waxen counterpart of the holy man's penis, present it to the priest and pray, *"Santo Cosimo benedetto, cosi io voglio,"* ("Blessed Saint Cosimo, this is how I want it").

Some years ago nation-wide shock and swift suppression followed the discovery of a phallus-worshiping sect in Kentucky. During the zenith period of the British Empire, six out of seven subjects worshiped fertility gods, which may explain why Pakistan rejected the Queen's entitlement as Defender of the Faith. Havelock Ellis, my favorite sex expounder, tells us that a W. J. Chidley advocated acceptance of the sex act as noble and even holy, worthy of performance in public on certain occasions without shame; Australians locked him up as insane.

A few decades ago "rip-roarin'" camp-meetings, the Bible Belt's peripatetic pressure-cooker, mirrored essential elements of a fertility rite. A circuit-riding preacher would gather great crowds on some grassy knoll under a tent and harangue hell-fire and brimstone until they shrieked, writhed and jerked on the ground, while hirsute men cooly bided their time until the panting, born-again women pulled up their dresses, initially for body ventilation under the hot sun. "T'was easy-pickins, like strippin' the husk off an ear o' corn," a local farmhand once explained to me between lip-smacking spits of scrap tobacco-juice. Some females landed in confinement nine months later, and at times "camp-meetin' children" were born to women whose husbands had been delivered from impotence by a "miracle" mediated through the preacher. To discuss the babes' striking resemblances to the reverend or his male assistants was by common consent forbidden, nor did anyone dare to reckon that the preacher had "made" more souls than he had "saved." The holy rollers of my Ohio boyhood, whose semi-nude floor-crawling, hysterical shouting and baptismal dunks in the Ohio River I used to watch in goggle-eyed amazement, were a close kin of the camp meetin' folk—both were spiritual descendants of the "little" people who had gyrated in the temples of Mylitta and Diana of Ephesus.

A zany return to fertility-centered origins was headlined in December 1979 by the self-styled "Children of God," who proposed, and I am told, still practice the use of sex ("flirty fishing") to lure recruits. In a tract showing couples in close embrace, their leader proclaimed, "People today are terrifically in need of sex. If you don't satisfy their sexual appetite, they have a hard time believing you really love them. . . . If you can't find it at home or in church, try us. . . . There is no such thing anymore as adultery. . . . For us, the Ten Commandments are out." A B'nai B'rith report catalogues the cult's sales pitch as a "farrago of Biblical misquotations, . . . predictions of earthly doom and . . . crude anti-Semitism," the denunciation of conventional churches. Given the current boom in irrationality, the cult's bombast is not significant; what is intriguing is the statistic that among "religions" that have sprouted in the North American subsoil since 1970, the "Children of God" or the "Love Family" now has eight thousand members, chiefly young people. It seems that evangelism's sex technique still wears the magic robe of success.

Only by stretching similarities can this atavistic phenomenon be called a fertility rite. It will not retreat that far into the past until rapt devotees grind their hips in half-naked, wanton abandon around an elevated likeness of Lord Phallus. Would the psychosociologist list the cult as a straw in the wind among weighty portents of the future? Who knows? We are privileged or condemned to occupy this planet at a time of prodigious opulence in the vagaries of human nature, when what seemed unthinkable yesterday already has happened, and the impossible, to use Abraham Maslow's word, is "actualized."

Can there be a revival of paganism? To the extent that it is divested of fairy-tale sex gods and goddesses as a cosmeticized offspring of prehistoric demonology, I think I might welcome what in the context of this book is its seminal insight, namely, the

Joy of Sex, that deftly laconic title of Alex Comfort's bestseller.

On second thought, I find unacceptable the abstract philosophy that underlay the ancient pagan's thought-style. He lived, moved and had his being under one conceptual umbrella: man can do nothing, even the gods can do nothing, to bring about what has never existed. Before the beginning of time the gods provided a mode for all human events, and we humans now merely reenact what they did before us. All our experiences are unalterable carbon copies of the gods' experiences, and that is how it will always be. Just like fertility rites, the rituals we perform to the gods today are ways of identifying ourselves with them, but these rituals are automatic. . . . Such a fatalistic view would erase man from history and history itself; for me, as a Jew and a stout believer in the human being's power to choose and act in a world partly of his making, it is anathema.

Joy in sex—to savor and to see—can be, on the highest possible plane, an enactment of the Divine Spirit that energizes every human being who can ignite it by his or her will. God gave life through the medium of sex; we worship the source of life by the exercise of sex: the thirst for sex is the thirst for God. Genuine reverence for the Divine expresses itself in reverence for life, life abundant, life in song and step and glance and touch.

Turning to the Bible and to talmudic tradition, I am puzzled and ask myself an irreverent, if not downright blasphemous question: Granted that the Kabbalah is in error, and God does not have genitalia, then why does He busy himself with such a plethora of sexual regulations, prohibitions and admonitions in the Torah that He revealed to us through Moses? Are His creatures consumed by such evil that He must transform their thoughts into moral commands? Were I a rabbinic sage living in the first century instead of a brash rabbi hoping to enter the twenty-first, I might address this query to the Almighty himself. But that must be postponed until Judgment Day.

Scripture and the sayings of venerable scholars abound in sex. If these saintly men are not ashamed, I need not be. Kabbalah says all souls in Heaven make love. In fact the Angels, and the Lord no less, engage in a higher kind of love. Though their ways are beyond our comprehension, I imagine they find it quite enjoyable.

The Talmud is so detailed and explicit on sex, it even concedes that the greater the man the greater is his passion, warning that God will call us to account for the permissible pleasures we have rejected. In the Hebrew Bible the words "sex" and "religion" were omitted by the deeply intuitive men who compiled it, perhaps out of the same delicacy that refined "defecate" into "covering the feet" (letting down one's robe) and black-listing specific reference to the penis. The same poetic sensibility is evident in the Song of Songs wherein the maiden summons her lover to the "fountain" and the "vineyard" in her pudenda.

Isaac Bashevis Singer, the first Yiddish Nobel prize winner, unequivocally certifies the implications of paganism emptied of superstition and wonder. The *leitmotif* of Judaism does not gainsay him. Singer has been lambasted for his alleged immersion in the erotic. True, he takes no pains to conceal a penchant for sex-induced aberrations; in *Shosha* the protagonist is involved with at least four women in the same mating season. He also turned the ultra-sensitive tentacles of his intellect from sex to religion by debating a crucial issue of theology: Why does God blind and blunt His all-seeing awareness of evil that permeates the universe? One of the characters in *Shosha* is convinced that the Almighty One has lost His way in Divine amnesia, "bewildered" by His own creation. It is a reflection of the shallowness of our society that a writer or preacher who tries to unravel the riddles of sexuality must necessarily be incompetent or indifferent in other spheres of vital import.

D. H. Lawrence launched the first major attack against the miasma of asexual self-righteousness; Lady Chatterley is the prototype of the more articulate liberated woman of today. For me, association with either of these writers would be a badge of honor.

Mildly pagan tunes can be heard from the staid voices in all three organized religions:

1. *A quotation from ancient rabbis*: "Know that sexual union properly achieved is a matter pure and sacred; let none think there is something ignoble and ugly in it. Intercourse with a virgin is preceded by a prayer of thanks to God for planting a nut-tree, a lily of the valley in the Garden of Eden, that no stranger may rule in the enclosed wall."

2. *Quotations from Hebrew mystics*: "A man is permitted to kiss his wife on any place but one." "During intercourse kissing should come as another expression of union that finds its expression in heaven."

3. *Father Russell Obata, C.S.S.R., Redemptorist priest*:

"Sex, with its unfailing appeal and intricate design, is a direct route to God. Preachers who frighten people into virtuous ways seem to indicate that sex is a super-highway to hell. And yet, sex is a constant reminder of God, a masterpiece of design. . . . The position of the sex faculties offers a maximum of protection. The external location of the male's manufacturing unit of sperm which prevents it from overheating, the proper heat of the female's body which encourages the sperm to journey forth and meet the egg as it descends, the 100-million or more sperm of a single act of sex that enter the race to capture the emerging egg— these are work of an infinite designer."

4. *Dr. Harvey Cox, Baptist minister, Associate Professor in Harvard Divinity School, author of "The Secular City"*: "Religious language, including the word God, will make sense again only when the lost experience to which such words point become a felt part of the human reality. If God returns we may have to find Him in the dance, not doctrine."

5. *Dr. Martin E. Marty, Lutheran minister, Associate Professor of Church History, University of Chicago, author of many books*: "Sexual intercourse is the deepest, highest, most profound, most engaging and involving human relationship, through which two people share a secret of personality and become 'one flesh.' We should not set aside copulation in an absolute way and say, 'Here is the line. On one side, with technical virginity, you are a saint; if you cross it, you go to hell.'"

Long ago, during my student days at rabbinical college, I brushed gently and lovingly with Hasidism, which brushed in the same manner with paganism; Hasidic champions and practitioners may be horrified at the merest whisper of such contaminating encounter. I even frightened my beloved wife by revealing to her, only half in jest, a persistent fantasy: to introduce at Holy Blossom Temple in Toronto that joyous acceptance of God-intoxicated naturalism into the majestic liturgy of God transcendant. A Hasid is not commanded to renounce, but to hallow. One can be a good Jew and yet taste good food, dance the roundelay, walk singing through the shaded woods, excrete, tie shoe laces, enfold a bedded woman in one's arms—all in holiness! What a contrast to the flagellating friars, the scripture-mouthing exemplars of rabbinic arrogance, and to the succubi-plagued hallucinations of confession-bleating saints! My father was a scholar trained for microscopic disputation in a citadel of unbending rabbinism, a "Litvak" (Lithuanian Jew), traditionally hostile to the Hasid's enthusiasm for life. But his genes were attuned to lyric song and the celebration of life. Like him, my soul belongs to the affirmation of the life-force.

More lucidly than any stroll back into ancestry for its birthplace my hankering for the pagan got its definitive expression in a poem I pasted on the wall over my attic study table at seminary more than sixty years ago. It was written by the famed Hebrew writer Saul Tchernikovsky:

> *Before the Statue of Apollo*
> I am the Jew; dost thou remember me?
> I kneel to life, to beauty and to strength,
> I kneel to all the passionate desires
> Which they, the dead in life, the bloodless ones
> The sick, have stifled in the living God,
> The God of wonders of the wilderness,
> The God of gods, Who took Canaan with storm
> Before they bound Him in phylacteries.

Sex and religion reign over the human condition as superpowers; they impart meaning to it, ruling in mutual dependence. The sex drive itself gave organized religion an opportunity to amass what was indisputably the greatest power ever lodged in human hands. The church established in the theologically untutored minds of men its claim, through unique access to God's will, that it had been granted a monopoly of Divine pardon and therefore the certainty of everlasting salvation or damnation. In return it demanded and received unquestioning obedience and support. In the very act of denouncing sex as sinful, requiring forgiveness, the church drew from it control of human lives. Religion owes to sex its existence as an instrument of authority over human behavior.

I believe the time has come to propose a policy of constructive coexistence. Religion will terminate its increasingly futile vendetta and recognize sex as the lawful and incomparable design of God for human happiness. Sex will elevate its goal beyond the currently popular and exaggerated hunt for orgasm to the quest, through phallic (rod) power, for a sense of the presence of God. The future of religion will be ever more precarious until it ceases to negate the joy of sex and begins to say "yes." When, how and why did the church ever say "no"?

3

Man of God
Wrestles
with Eros

Long ago I tabulated nine occupational hazards of the clergy: 1. pomposity; 2. sentimentality; 3. saccharinity; 4. insularity; 5. sycophancy; 6. egocentricity; 7. timidity; 8. triviality; 9. ambidexterity. I now would like to add sexuality, placing this tenth hazard at the top. All these hazards are symptomatic of a cleric's humanness, and each is magnified by the social conditioning and the personality structure of the average clergyman.

The New Testament's verdict on the roving eye testifies to the strength and authenticity of optic lust. I have been its indentured servant to this day. Sir Charles (Charlie) Chaplin, in his autobiography, confessed that he could never meet an attractive woman without measuring her potential for reproduction. If those were his genuinely felt sentiments, as I think they must have been, then the adorable tramp expressed in an astonishingly ponderous euphemism the simple fact that his probing eyes stripped women of their clothes and took them to bed. Did not Jimmy Carter as presidential-candidate admit to similar instant reflex actions in his *Playboy* interview?

Charlie and Jimmy, and Tom, Dick and Harry all share direct descent from prehistoric man who, feeling the immediate urgency of desire when seeing the female of the species, would lope forward on all fours—prior to his evolution into a biped— and mount her for the anal thrust enjoyed then by all non-humans. The female was ever-ready. There was no postponement awaiting the "in-heat" signal that can madden a male dog while he waits for a bitch, no limited rutting season that can deter two male moose from interlocking antlers in deadly combat for an expectant female.

Homo sapiens-Homo sexualis is the most continuously

47

lecherous of all major animals. Food-hunger diminishes in the later stages of deprivation because of physical debility, but sex-hunger may even be sharpened. Tumescence of the normal human penis, I am told, is not reduced by nor does it atrophy from disuse.

Is the clergyman a mutation, exempted by his genes from sexuality? Honest inquiry must begin with the seminal fact that the occupant of the pulpit dwells in the animal kingdom and is therefore subject to the wrench of its drives and dangers. The clergyman may reach his hands upward to a luminous heaven, but his feet remain deeply embedded in the mire of the same moral conflict as other humans. In the Hebrew Bible Abraham's descendants were linked in God's promise both to the lofty stars in the firmament and the lowly sands of the sea. The distance between these two metaphors marks the battleground where the pulpit stands.

Those who regularly attend church or synagogue, however, tend to extend their faith in God to their faith in His spokesmen, often merging the two. They may *beseech* the former to justify their faith, but from the latter they *demand* it, apparently out of a need to know that someone—if not they themselves—is immaculate. The cleric is seen as the embodiment of impeccable virtue, not only in the sight of his Maker, whose punishment may be postponed to a far-off time in the "other" world, but also in the sight of the persons dubiously termed his "flock." Christian clergymen ideally accept as their model Jesus Christ, the personification on earth of the Father's perfection. In turn, many laymen humbly transfer their adulation to His deputy. Similarly, the rabbi at best embodies in his person the sanctity of the *Torah*, the Teaching, and through it the holiness of the God who sent it as a revelation of His love for the Chosen People.

Practically all Western religions except Satanism—from Unitarian rationalism to Holy Roller hysteria—place their priesthood above the "common herd." Some individuals are well suited for the role, truly believing that they are "holier than thou." They ascend the pulpit in an unflappable inner state of self-assurance, even taking pride in humility. Like the saints of Catholicism and the memorial prayer *kaddish*-reciters of ultra-Orthodox Jewish piety, they consider themselves empowered to seek God's mercy for the departed, acting as lawyers for the defense in the Celestial Court.

I am particularly uneasy about deification by children. I recall a story about a rabbi who placed his hand on a little boy's head in blessing. The little boy looked up at him and said, "Thank you God," and the rabbi murmured in reply, "You're welcome, my son." Most clergymen are embarrassed by such readiness of parishioners to convert the pulpit into a pedestal. Whenever I was called upon to consecrate a group of "beginners" in religious school, raising my hands in the ancient priestly blessing with fingers forming the Hebrew letter "shin" for *Shaddai* the Almighty One, as I looked down at their fresh awestruck faces a stab of self-mockery would assail me. And afterwards when a parent would come up to tell me that I was "Susie's idea of God," my discomfort was not assuaged by Susie's anthropomorphism.

"And to think that they think you're the Messiah," I often would whisper as I looked into the shaving mirror. This self-directed irony and humor can shield a cleric from pretentiousness. Fortunately, mine surfaced in my formative years no further than private soliloquy. When on duty in the pulpit I could recite the liturgy and preach in God's presence without a shred of self-derogation. Congregants are inclined to accept their minister at his own estimate of himself. After all, Jesus' authentic sign of warm humanity was his reluctance to proclaim himself the Messiah. Public puncture of a clergyman's aspirations to *super* humanity can be a fatal stab of honesty for him as well as for a politician. Adlai Stevenson's Achilles heel in his bid for the presidency was his innate inability to think of himself alone as the bringer of salvation to America. He had the genuine intellectual's sense of the "littleness" of Man.

Whether it is a protective posture or a stifling encumbrance, the priestly breastplate worn willy-nilly by the clergyman is in fact a straight-jacket of impossible expectations. The feet of clay condoned in "ordinary mortals" are forbidden him on pain of disgrace and dismissal.

The debacle of my Canadian friend Reverend Russell Horsburgh is a microcosm of the pastor's built-in exposure to the judgmental fixation and endemic sex paranoia of Bible-directed pietists. He was arrested on June 29, 1964 at his office in Park Street United Church in Chatham, a small community of thirty thousand in western Ontario. Charged with eight counts of contributing to juvenile delinquency, his case went before the court on September 21 of that same year. His "offense," apart from running concerts, weekly dances and athletic programs for young people at the church, had been to arrange courses in sex education and a series of Sunday-night lectures on such topics as "The Modern Crisis in Sexual Morality." One pre-Easter Sunday I preached at his request on "A Jewish View of the Crucifixion"— in itself a provocative innovation. On that occasion I warned him that his lecture projects would "roil a nest of vipers" in that tight-laced rural community. But Reverend Horsburgh seemed bent on martyrdom.

At his trial sixty witnesses were heard, many of them teenagers he had tried to help. Fourteen testified against him. He took the stand in his own defense, denying that he had been aware of allegations that his church had been used to indulge in immoral acts and that he had encouraged teenagers to commit them.

After fourteen days, Russell Horsburgh was found guilty on five counts of contributing to juvenile delinquency. His sentence? One year of imprisonment. The day after his conviction he resigned, and it did not take long for the elders of Park Street United Church to vote against paying their former pastor's legal expenses.

Nor did it take long for two of the teenagers who had testified against him to come forward and recant their earlier accusations in sworn affidavits, one of them admitting that he had "conspired" with an adult against Horsburgh, and the other that he had been "influenced" by an adult. Based on these denials and twenty contradictions contained in testimony, an appeal was launched. It failed to reverse the conviction by a 3–1 vote. On June 26, 1967 the Supreme Court of Canada voted 4–3 to allow Reverend Horsburgh a new trial. Only three of the fourteen witnesses who earlier had testified against him appeared in the Chatham courtroom. Acquittal came on the day his second trial began, and he was released from prison after 107 days. The notorious teenage libertines had testified against him because they could not forgive his being "of the cloth," despite the "good fellow" image he had so assiduously cultivated. They had vented their spleen against adult critics through him, seeking to dilute their shameless sex delinquency by pilloring him as "contributor." He had become their sacrificial offering. But it was blindness and bigotry under religious auspices that really paved his road to jail. Hounded by a conspiratorial clique of church members and a macho police force battening on their gallant efforts to rescue the town's morals, and victimized by his own naiveté and honesty, Chatham's "man of God" became a caged pariah in penance for the sins of his parish.

During the trial I contributed letters to bolster his crumbling self-esteem, as well as money for his defense. But other ecclesiastical colleagues joined in the hosannas to flouted virtue, shaking their heads over Horsburgh's "injection" of sex into the antiseptic pulpit; he had dared to defy the ban on a rational probe of sexuality in the church. Even after his acquittal the United Church clerical body did not cancel its punitive edict of expulsion.

The more I pondered about the case, the more I realized that I was not alone sloshing through the sexual quagmire. I had stated in the introduction to Reverend Horsburgh's book *From Pulpit to Prison*, in which he gave a personal account of churchly persecution, "We clergymen are sacrificial holocausts to the privately owned deity who, pietists claim, chose them to cleanse their sin-soaked neighbors."

To the individual who regularly, rigidly and reverently sits in church or synagogue, any picayune change in custom often becomes a bogey-man. Teheran Moslems burned down a movie theater, killing four hundred people, in protest against the blasphemies of modernism some years before the Khomeini fundamentalist revolution. Just as radical students disturbed the peace by demonstrating against the Vietnam "holy war" against Communism, a clergyman can disturb the placidity of those sitting in the pew by daring to lift a pulpit voice against the "holy war" against sexual candor. How can man's capacity for independent thought be expected to survive as a petrified artifact overgrown by centuries of undeviating moralization? Even those religions that begin with a bang against stiffening of the intellectual joints often degenerate to uttering a prolonged burp at tentative signs of sexual eccentricity.

How often has the founder of a radical religious movement become its last defender? I suspect that the anti-Horsburgh party in Chatham, Ontario, took no pains to remember that Martin Luther led his reform of Roman Catholic sexual corruption into espousal of rank social injustice. Alleged sinning by lay dignitaries of the "church" usually meant a bit of a hug in a shadowy nave, a furtive pinch of a choirgirl's bottom, or a behind-the-hand whisper to the church secretary. This sort of thing could be waved aside as an all-too-human frailty; after all, the same Lord who forgave Jimmy Carter's lust by sight also would forgive them.

However, Reverend Horsburgh's misdeeds went beyond nervous fumbling under a chorister's robe or a compassionate pastoral-call kiss of an affection-starved parishioner. He wanted to open windows to let fresh air into the dark chambers where the church strangles the truth about sex and religion.

"High Church clerics chase boys, Low Churchmen chase girls." That irresponsible canard makes the rounds, illustrating the general readiness of the public to believe the worst about the pulpit. Yet sex problems in marriage must be swept away like gnats in a windstorm, and the immutable dogmas about sex behavior must remain the over-the-counter (pulpit) prescriptions to tranquilize the front-pew congregants. Secret misdemeanors argue respect for the rules, thereby acknowledging by default the authority of moral precepts; they offer God-fearing upholders of virtue a chance to imitate the Lord's grace. Does not the Creator himself cause the blood to converge from all parts into the "strategic" place? Did not precocious St. Augustine arise from the couch of multiple mistresses to lucubrate the lofty fortress of sex negation?

The run-of-the-mill man of God in our time has no license for *hidden* peccadillos, no coffee-breaks from wearing the black robe. Every step, big or little, that he takes is monitored. Where a few generous lay spirits may avert their eyes from a stumble, others will smack their lips drooling with gossip; most will weigh the matter heavily. And the penalty is a measure of inflated expectations if the stumbling is the result of an itch in the genitals. Such unseemly behavior constitutes a form of theft; the cleric has robbed his worshipers of their illusions. Whatsoever his self-identity, the people sitting in the pews are determined to believe that he is a man of God, a professional "holy man," and like the lotus-positioned yogi of India he must act the part. To exacerbate his tensions, the realization that tenure, repute and livelihood rest upon his ability to say "no" to female allure roils his mind with fear and fantasies, rendering him even more vulnerable to a self-fulfilling prophecy.

Russell Horsburgh may have had recourse to a mild dosage of voyeurism, and he could not pry away the sex taboo that may have obsessed his perhaps neurotically guilt-prone mind. But he was not charged with illicit intercourse. His wife, a rather pathetic figure as I remember her, offered no satisfying escape hatch. Had his super-refined Christian conscience permitted it, non-marital coitus might have stabilized the balance between spirit and body by proving to him that they are one.

The historic process whereby perforation of the hymen or frenetic friction of the penile epidermis became the gate to hell is probably the most intriguing stage in the evolution of human self-discipline. It bred such an imbalance of values that a human creature may be a monster in all human relations and at the same time a candidate for celestial bliss—if he or she never bedded with anyone except his or her lawful wedded spouse. This pivotal bond to an elementary anatomical fact can preempt a clergyman's total relationship to God, other persons and himself. Once Horsburgh began to be "talked about," the door to his vocation began to close. I believe that a double life, had he been able to rationalize it, would have kept him "alive," although when he eventually died in 1971 the cause of death was cancer.

At times the sacrificial lamb of Chatham unveiled his innermost thoughts to me. These disclosures led me to conclude that, for him, physical love, Eros, had been replaced by Agape, the self-denying intoxication of spiritual love. As a devout and romantic acolyte he would almost certainly have been sucked into that fascinating, unrealistic cult. The agape syndrome is alluded to again and again in the New Testament as the implicit ideal set forth by Christ for his followers. Its dominance of the biblical guidelines for Protestant clergy has been more than a moderately activating agent of sexual problems.

Women-power! That was the central reality with which my friend Russell Horsburgh had *not* "lost" touch—simply because he never had it. He rarely smiled, he did not know how to quip, socially he was a zero, he had no skills in the adroit verbalization of flattery. Nathan Krass, the superstar rabbi of New York's awesome Temple Emanuel, once confided to me the bedrock of his battle-plan: "Be intellectual with pretty women, frivolous with intellectual ones, saucy with old ladies—and mildly, though gallantly, flirtatious with all women."

The first lesson I learned in the practical rabbinate was never to slight the female psyche. The studiously circumspect but "knowing" manipulation of a woman's special sensibilities will go far to secure internal control and political tenure, as any alert parish cleric will tell you. Religion-shirking husbands absorbed in the marketplace usually will cede to their "better halves," as they shrewdly call their wives in this situation, the maintenance and programs connected with church or synagogue. Directors' decisions are often made in parishioner's kitchens. The Sisterhoods and Ladies' Auxiliaries frequently supplement the treasury, to the extent of fending off ruinous deficits. Increasingly, the lady of the home sanctuary is the leader of God's sanctuary.

But I doubt that an animated talk with a lissome woman can be altogether antiseptic and devoid of sexual undertones. The original definition of the verb "converse" included sexual intercourse. Save in periods of profound grief or crisis, mine or another's, I scarcely ever chatted spiritedly with a pretty female in a state of mind hermetically sealed against the intrusion of a moment of erotic fantasy, and the swift hope that it was being duplicated in her mind.

In the decades of my rabbinate, male-female dalliance in elite society was an artful contest of wits undertaken as a convivial pastime. But such harmless flirtations vanished together with the age of innocence. Rather than being light fun for its own sake, blithesome banter now can easily become a prelude to heavy fun in bed. In every place where boy meets girl, from a lonely pickup bar to a high-minded culture salon, the range of options has broadened.

The symptoms of maximum permissiveness or controlled promiscuity in the sociosexual mores of that larger world penetrate the smaller world of the clergyman. United with the "new freedom" of women, they spell danger for his emotional and professional security.

"Charity is more important than chastity" and "premarital experience is necessary in some cases," were time bombs dropped on the Church of England by two of its vicars not so long ago. They illustrate the traditional proclivity of that staid Establishment's clergy for shocking pronouncements about traditional sex conduct. Similar dissident opinions by spokesmen in the United States seem confined to the "closet," as matters not for public revision but rather for private reinterpretation. Forthright renunciations of threadbare shibboleths surely do not often issue from the parish pulpit! Not to say that adherence to the chastity code is exceptional, but there is much talk about it today. During recent visits to a sexuality workshop for Lutheran pastors, I was astounded by the almost universal support of a complete overhaul of an "irrelevant" sex morality. No one on the panel denied that two-thirds of the wedding pairs waiting to be blessed at the beginning of a life together had been together for some time. Yet the white gown worn by the bride was matched in duplicity by the virginity implications in the service. "Are we not accomplices in 'mumbo-jumbo' for the propagation of a code visibly headed for extinction?" it was asked. A dust-laden tape recorder cassette is all that remains of that panel discussion. . . .

Can the man of God, who by training and temperament is more responsive to the human condition, avoid the possibly demoralizing impact of radical change in sex standards and the level of what is acceptable in his private conduct? Indeed, the statistically proven deflation of the Protestant and Catholic clergy's attempts to attract young men who seek careers may be caused, in part, not only by their unwillingness to embrace a celibate life, but also by their feared inability to cope with a decidedly non-celibate environment. A Catholic priest once told me that the same fear operates in reverse: "Some men enter the church to solve their sexual problems; mandatory celibacy relieves them of the burden of choice; it's all decided in advance."

That some unusually sensitive, strictly indoctrinated young men of all denominations resort to the ministry for contrary reasons has been confirmed by individual revelations. Instead of recoil from sexual decision, this push into the pulpit comes from a sense of guilt for having *made* a (wrong) decision. A revival meeting, a moonlight stroll with the current girlfriend, a dormitory party or a hot summer night had led the youth astray. Because of an intensely virginal upbringing and his church telling him to cleanse his soul and obtain repurification, what better medium for Divine forgiveness and personal rehabilitation than service of God through the ministry? Within the general pattern of a "call," the pulpit converts common, sinful clay (as he sees himself) into a man of God. Once immured within the church's domain, its servant, swathed in a gown or cassock, assumes an aura of holiness. The moment he ascends the pulpit, it weaves around his head a penumbra of Divine association. A novitiate may wear the exalted state, at first, in flustered embarrassment and with lowered gaze, but he soon learns to anticipate it and walk with more measured strides; the lofty physical setting of the pulpit alone enshrouds him in a splendid altitude approximating heaven more closely than the haunts of ordinary men.

All is well and good, even if the cleric turns the pulpit's luminosity into pomposity, carrying it everywhere he goes, because intrinsically his apartness from flesh-and-blood men will do him no harm except that it may turn him into an insufferable bore. The real danger arises from the image he creates in the minds of some of his female devotees who may glide from faith in Divine law to fantasy about a Divine lover.

Masters and Johnson have noted that women who are deprived of normal sex outlets may exhaust themselves physically in conscious or unconscious efforts to dissipate accumulated tensions. They may cast themselves into religion to find fulfillment by observing the pastor's upright stance, his deep voice and his heaven-bent gaze. All this may sketch for them a dream-like world of romance, an Atlantis devoid of pots and pans, diapers and family budgets, replacing a husband crammed into a cage by day-long business pressures that leave him too devitalized for love at night. Does not the preacher's bearing connote a shift from the domain of action to a poetic realm of intuition and feeling? The self-revelation of medieval mystics, hypnotic pulpiteers and pre-Billy Graham evangelists hint at a linkage between God-intoxication and non-ejaculatory orgasms. . . .

Were the truth told, a legion of intuitive clergymen heading large urban congregations would dub themselves less than imperturbable when dealing with the necessarily congenial proximity of personable female co-laborers in God's vineyard and pretty hedonists in the front section of the sanctuary below the lectern. How often when pausing a few seconds before beginning to preach did I scan those first few rows to catch an eye and direct my sermon to its owner, invariably with heightened panache!

Although Judaism's naturalistic, life-affirming *leitmotif* may have blunted the shock effect of the sexual explosion on rabbis, there are signs that the proverbial Jewish tolerance of ideological non-conformism, the flexibility and awareness of educated parents and the deepening fissures in the family structure are beginning to impinge on the cool sexual detachment and devotion of rabbis. No less than other clergy, they too are becoming targets for luscious sensuality. Rationalizations stream thick and fast from a theology-oriented mentality, especially when they are refined by talmudic hairsplitting, known as pilpulism. "We can do God's work better when we're happy and relaxed." . . . "Sex is not the province of religion. It's a matter of what's best for people." . . . "Isn't it a good deed to make a woman so happy she radiates it to her family?" . . . "Lying with a woman gives me faith

in life and in myself." . . . "Our profession shrinks our authenticity as complete persons; we have no freedom; sex gives us back
our male identity." . . . "Our congregants' indifference will
castrate us, if we allow them to." . . . "The old morality is dead."

Lest it be assumed that woman bears the greater guilt, I quote
a letter to Dear Abby:

> Since I am a pastor with 43 years experience, I'd like to offer
> this suggestion to the young inexperienced minister who
> didn't know how to handle a very bold married woman in his
> congregation who had designs on him. Whenever I noticed a
> romantic twinkle in the eyes of a woman in my congregation,
> I always checked to make sure it wasn't caused by a reflection
> from the gleam in my own.

Historically, rabbinic ordination did not impose extra moral
obligation on its recipient; "purity" had no claim on him beyond
faithfulness in marriage expected of all Jews. A professional,
separately identifiable, elite "rabbi" class did not emerge into
prominence until about the thirteenth century; throughout the
old ghettos of Eastern Europe the abbreviated folk-title "Reb"
used to label a man respected and honored for his learning and
integrity. The official rabbi acted as *dayan* (judge) in all disputes
of Jewish ceremonial and ritual law. If a chicken purchased by a
near-penniless family for the festive Friday night (Sabbath Eve)
dinner was found to have a blemish, it was unhallowed and either
barred from the sacred table by the Law or condoned out of
compassion for the poor. If a husband neglected his wife's
conjugal rights, only the Torah, in its interpretation by the rabbi,
could decide. But pulpit dissertations on sex irregularities were
not his wont; he preached only twice a year, on the Sabbath before
Passover and on the Sabbath of Repentance. Yet anthologies of
Jewish humor would not be complete without their quota of
ribald jokes about the rabbi's sexual lapses.

Perhaps uncharitably we have always held "saints" in
suspended judgment because of our millenial bruising contacts
with human cussedness. The rabbi no less than the Christian
pastor might be welcome as a scapegoat, a kind of "sin offering"
similar to the animal sacrificed on the altar in the ancient Temple
of Jerusalem. Ferreting out or fabricating his "misdeeds" may
also be a vent for envy of his revered status. Similarly, non-
observant pseudo-Orthodox Jews often demand that "our rabbi"

keep the dietary laws meticulously; through *his* avoidance of ham they are cleansed and cleared to eat it without guilt. Any modern spiritual leader of Orthodox Jewry in North America, nevertheless, must be a paragon of ritual practice and purity; he will be monitored no less attentively than his Christian counterparts.

But watching the clergyman to *prevent* his "fall" is less obnoxious than watching him to *provoke* it. Bold females have been known to compete for the raunchy ministrations of "that sexy preacher-man" and then boast about their conquest.

During my sojourn in San Francisco, I remember volunteering my services at Delancy Street's innovative rehabilitation center for drug addicts and ex-convicts, at the same time participating in Synanon-type "attack" games and after-lunch lectures. Barred from driving a car by my sight-impairment, I relied on "inmates" to take me home, often at night. The most interesting chauffeur I ever had was a lithe young woman whom I would have dubbed garrulous had she not been so abrasive in her speech, incisive in her thought processes and provocative in the swish of her derrière. She offered to cook dinner for me. Instant assent brought her and a barbecued chicken to my lodgings. The dishes washed and put away, she languidly stretched out on my couch to embark on a series of maneuvers so transparent they might have sparked distaste in any male not too aroused for rational assessment. The following day Delancy Street was buzzing with the glad tidings that Bonnie had "scored" with the rabbi.

Colleagues who specialize in counseling often tell me that married women seeking guidance about strained or unsatisfactory sex relations frequently venture beyond oblique propositions to broad hints implying that a close and intimate "interchange" would raise their positions among their "bosom friends." A prominent Methodist churchman once confided to me, "You'd think some of these women would want to go back to ancient fertility rites when sleeping with the temple priest was considered tantamount to having intercourse with God." He added, "I wonder how Catholic priests manage at confession."

What is the value of this ecclesiastical quarry in the female fox-hunt? Is it the same celebrity lure that crowds groupies into the arms of rock stars? Or the same thrill as savoring a new exotic dish? Could it be a challenge to sportsmanship, because "it's there," as Hilary explained his fixation on Mount Everest? Perhaps the urge to prick the envy of one's rivals, like the primping and panting of courtesans outside King Louis XIV's bed-chamber?

It is possible that Mother Nature has endowed the clergy with a wondrously saturated quiver of testosterone and an awesome coital apparatus. I have heard such rumors about black males, and Eldridge Cleaver in *Soul on Ice* has not been loathe to confirm them. However, similar surmises about ministers must be dismissed.

I am aware of only two exceptions. According to a reportage in a reputable news magazine, Jim Jones of Jonestown is said to have complained to his flock about the size of his penis; apparently, it was so hefty and magnetic that women clamored for it. One female supposedly explained, "He *fucked* me. I never was fucked like that before." It was said that at times his claim to have the only right to unlimited coitus was enforced by meting out humiliating punishments. Father Divine, a forerunner of Jim Jones, was the charismatic mahdi of a mystic cult of Harlem zealots. Although he proclaimed an imperious reign of unrelieved chastity over his idolaters, a host of female "angels" would chant hosannas to his body and perform gyrations that belied their ample white robes and his ethereal aloofness from "carnal sin." During my New York ministry I saw the black demigod being carried on a throne in a procession led by his angelic choir.

Journalists frequently refer, with pen in cheek I'm sure, to a clergyman as a "divine." But when a group of tourists boarding a plane for a distant destination turns to "the reverend" on the same flight and quips, "You'll get us there safely; you've got clout with the Man up there," there is a hint of facetiousness that scarcely hides the underlying vestigial assurance, born far back in time, that a clerical presence and his prayers will find favor in the sight of God.

The invisible, ineffable, incorporeal deity principle clamors for a body. Even Judaism's ancestral creator in Abraham's biblical vision of the unseen God was incarnated, given a *corpus* in the sacred scroll of the Torah. That Jesus Christ became the supreme embodiment of the Father does not, I suspect, fully exhaust Christians' preference for the concrete; His humanness leaves his Divineness intact. Who can better close the gap than the minister? Rabbi, pastor and priest are elevated to the altar, whether it is dominated by the Cross or the Ark of the Covenant. The stigmata of supernatural mystery that glisten from the Pope's ring and from his miter also cling in some degree to the somber gown of the lowliest parish pastor and the smalltown rabbi. In fact, virtually all religious disciplines except Satanism take for granted that "spiritual leaders" are without sexual taint. But history has recorded many examples to the contrary. In feudal times, monks of noble birth enjoyed priority right to a bride's passion on her wedding night (*ins prima nocte*) and exercised it diligently until the French Revolution, if the textbooks tell us the truth. Wide-ranging erotica about other Roman Catholic prelates are doubt-lessly blazoned in the archives of the Reformation. Pope Alexander VI, unlike Nicholas V, Julius II and Leo X, who were kindly humanists, was the medieval "godfather" of the Borgia clan. His court was the scene of a sexual license so orgiastic that only the account of papal historian Burchard makes it credible. In October 1501, it is related, the Pope ordered the procurement of fifty prostitutes, and in the presence of his son Caesar and his daughter Lucrezia they had to strip and dance with fifty male guests. Prizes were awarded to those guests who had intercourse with the largest number.

The sexual accomplishments of a parish priest are recorded in the trial proceedings by a fourteenth-century bishop's tribunal held in the tiny French hamlet of Montaillon. The priest had seduced countless married women by declaring to each one in turn, "I prefer you to any woman in the world," then threatening to turn her over to the Inquisition as a "heretic" unless she submitted. The tribunal acquitted him as a true man of God, although it is not known whether the objects of his adoration were burned at the stake for heresy, or whether they subsequently burned in hell for having committed adultery.

Father Tom, a Catholic colleague of mine and an engaging theoretical hedonist, once told me the following story: "A young woman was praying to a statue of the Virgin Mary: 'O thou who hath conceived without sinning, help me to sin without conceiving.'" I, in turn, spoke to him about Jacob Frank, a Russian Jew who, in 1726 after studying the mystic Hebrew Kabbalah, proclaimed to the devout, wretchedly poor and harassed Jews of Eastern Europe and the Middle East that he was the incarnation of the Messiah who would bring them redemption through purity. "He persuaded thousands of learned Jews that cerebral talmudic scholarships must be supplemented by promptings of the heart, to buoy up the spirits of the masses with ecstatic faith in the future. He laid down guidelines for daily conduct, albeit obscure, with kabbalistic allusions to God's sexuality; his religious seances turned into orgies and he exploited for profit the erotic fantasies of wealthy rabbinic intellectuals. Later he was excommunicated for licentiousness."

When I had finished my story Father Tom remarked, "Hell, Rabbi, Jesus *was* the Messiah, and he was not a fake. And didn't *he* want people to use the tools God had equipped them with for happiness? He didn't go around telling folks in Galilee and Jerusalem not to have fun. What a congenial guest he was at parties! He even turned water into wine, to gladden the heart as your Bible says it does. And think what *he* said about Mary Magdalene! His concerns were not laws and rules, but people! The Protestants say they seek the truth in the Bible, not in Rome. But Jesus Christ is unknown to them; they don't really understand Him."

Bless you, Father Tom. Yes, Jesus did celebrate with wine and loaves occasions for the body's joy, at wedding feasts and when a son returned home. He recognized human needs as he moved easily and amiably among simple men and women. But he made short shrift of hypocrisy, reserving his most savage barbs for the posturing of saints and the kind of piety that protects itself by shying away from involvement in human frailty. Nowhere did he curse sexual indulgence as such or indicate his views on the matter. In displaying tenderness toward Mary of Magdala, the Nazarene's attitude did not show a grain of puritanism.

Father Tom and I also talked about Paphnutius, Anatole France's true-to-life cenobite who joined myriads of godly priests in the early Christian Era, fleeing from city temptation into the desert for prayer and meditation only to burn and melt under the mocking gaze of courtesan Thais. . . . We spoke of Rasputin, the Russian Orthodox monk who seduced the last Czarina of the Romanoffs into a hypnotic cult and of John Knox who brightened his twilight years in the companionship of several ladies. Then there was King David who, abusing his royal perquisites, dispatched Uriah to certain death in battle so that he might lie with the hapless Hittite's beauteous wife Bathesheba. . . . Reverend Henry Ward Beecher, a most formidable nineteenth-century pulpiteer, and brother of Harriet Beecher Stowe, soothed his aching heart in the boudoirs of countless female torch-bearers. . . .

Paul Tillich, the Protestant German-educated theologian and a luminary in the loftiest echelons of Harvard University and

Union Theological Seminary, may be said to have experienced a private career of unchecked sexual promiscuity save for the fact that his wife shared his predilection for coitus-at-will. In her poetic autobiography *From Time to Time* she alluded to their countless liaisons, noting after a detailed account of his illness and death that these were "obscene signs of real life that he had transformed into the gold of abstraction."

The avidly cultured, erudite air of the Tillich menage is in sharp contrast to the leonine roar of controversy that surrounds Rabbi Stephen S. Wise, whose voice and upraised arm in defense of the people of Israel, Zion and sociopolitical justice gave Americans the alternative of putting him on a pedestal or into the pillory. He figured as a sex-predator gone berserk in *Strangers at a Party,* the sensational memoirs of a lady journalist who at nineteen, as a fledgling reporter, had ventured into his office for an interview. With ill-concealed relish she revealed that he "threw her on the table," although she later conceded that he had merely "knocked her hat askew." In her exposure the "enterprising pseudo-nymphette," as she has been described by a distinguished columnist, boasted of other sorties against her honor by a veritable coterie of celebrities, among them Bernard Baruch and Charles Lindbergh. However, they all suffered one common disadvantage; they had died before the lady wrote her story and could not defend their reputations with the unvarnished truth.

In fairness, I am bound to state that my tearing away of veils over sexual dissonance among individuals in the ministry of religion stems from my sympathy for their plight. Rather than perpetrators of unconscionable evil, they are, with the rare exception of high-profile psychopaths, the products of a dehumanizing, unnatural system of religious organization that subdues reality in favor of an obsolescent and irrelevant code of sexual behavior. Intense resistance to and trauma from that code induced me a half century ago to lash out in fury and frustration at colleagues of all faiths. Here is what I wrote about my New York rabbinical brethren: "Frocked flunkeys twining silken phrases; fawning courtiers to moneyed trustees; go-getters proclaiming their humility; mystic busy-bees clustered around God's feet begging for honey; sacred beneficiaries of special privilege palming off gown and cassock as credentials of cosmic revelation; fashionable friars pandering to somnolence."

In the extreme, I attacked the faith that had nourished me. My most unkind act of all was to satirize preaching, the art that seemed most deeply and most dearly shaped to fit my genes. I compared it to standing in fantasy at the center of the universe in a somnabulistic trance, lost in lonely monologue. I also came to the conclusion that the less I knew about a subject the more brilliantly I could talk about it. When speaking on the meaning of life and God I would ask myself whether it was ungrateful of me to yell unpalatable truths to the pew sitters who pampered me while they assumed that my sermonic fire and brimstone applied not to them, but to someone else. I suspected that homiletical *tour de force* belonged in the realm of entertainment, and found that Ezekiel had summarized it well when he said, "And lo, thou art unto them as a very lovely song of one that hath a pleasant voice, for they hear the words and do them not." A friend told me that he had heard one of my admirers explain, "Our rabbi throws every bit of himself into his sermons. Wonderful! When he finishes he can barely walk back to his altar seat!"

The minister, because of the general semi-religious dogma, finds it especially hard to handle guilt. Here he encounters greater risks in admission, and it is not likely that his brothers will "restore him in a spirit of gentleness," as Saint Paul advised. Daniel D. Walker in his book *The Human Problems of the Ministry* puts it this way:

> Driven underground, the cleric develops the art of sinning piously. We pass off our sins as virtues and because of the residue of "respect for the cloth" that still exists in our society, few people are brazen enough to call us on it. So we go merrily on our way, scrambling for the top of the greased pole of ambition by accepting God's call to a larger field of service, enjoying more of the company of attractive widows than would be discreet if we were not there to comfort them in their sorrow and flaring out shamelessly at our opposition who are inhibiting "the progress of the Kingdom."

Lest Daniel D. Walker be denigrated as a compulsive iconoclast, it should be noted that Bishop Gerald Kennedy refers to him in the book's foreword as a "friend of many years, gifted preacher and pastor whose book will do us all good." And Walker's preface acknowledges encouragement and assistance by a long list of clergymen and religious educators.

In Hawthorne's *The Scarlet Letter* Reverend Dimmesdale

was wracked by merciless conscience in his conflict with passion for Hester Prynne. . . . Bradley Smith, in preparing his tome *The American Way of Sex*, pored over old Massachusetts records where he found a lot of sinners, hypocrisy and cant among the clergy. . . .

Guilt feelings are easily dulled by the sophisticated weapons of rationalization and frequently denounced by health-centered psychiatry. I firmly downgrade these feelings as counter-productive, because they can neutralize one's aspirations to sexual sanity. Yet, strive as I might to deracinate guilt without a trace, the filaments of the roots go so deep in my "ground of being" that no effort of will can reach them. Though portentous cadences from the pulpit may suggest that the preacher is auditioning to play the Almighty, they don't altogether drown out the whisper of conscience that seems to wax louder for the clergyman; it confronts the chasm between what the world expects of him and what his normal flesh and blood is able to deliver.

Another chasm in the pulpit occupant's psyche stretches between its two gender components: the masculine and the feminine. That all human beings are bisexual is a biological truism; that clergymen portray a larger complement of the feminine appears to be a professional trait. For the average woman, the special gentleness and perceptive tone that mark the cleric's manners and envelop him in a nimbus are an attraction. They reflect that kind of superior sensitivity I associate with femininity. Whether in accordance with scientific fact or sentimental fancy, their linkage and interaction speak to me unequivocally after decades of woman watching. And I have never met a trained and qualified cleric of any denomination in whom that same sensitivity does not operate. Is it hormone dysfunction, deficiency or a genetic imbalance? Not at all! Rather than freaks of nature, clergymen are framed after the nature of their job. "Spiritual leader" is a term with an unsavory smell when it connotes disbarment from "important" nonspiritual matters such as big business and power politics. Nevertheless, it pinpoints our function: to lead people through the space that *really* decides their well-being, that unmarked, unmapped maze known by default of language as the spirit. We are designed neither to lead a football game, a deer hunt or a beer brawl, all requiring physical prowess; nor can we conduct a corporate or political campaign with hardness of heart and mind. Rather, we must summon insight, imagination and humane wisdom for guidance to nurture man's soul.

The deployment of a soft voice and solemn movements does not displace or replace masculinity; it supplements and enriches it. The New Testament's representation of Jesus is an excellent combination of masculine forcefulness and feminine delicacy. Historic church imagery, it seems, has introduced an imbalance by feminizing him both in appearance and in manner, perhaps to stress compassion in a violent and rapacious world. No more than a limp wrist and a so-called "mincing" gait mark the homosexual does a tender stance stereotype the man as feminine in the context of his virility. The authentic pastor is not a "he-man" father who rejects a son because his long hair poses a threat to his own masculinity; he is a human being to whom all persons and causes may come when in need of the strength that comes from his spirit. Could one describe this protective mentality in terms of the maternal? I think so, because it seals the bond between the minister and his somatic feminine patina.

By an odd quirk, the maternal flowering of the adult clergyman's role begins in his childhood. Most of the ministers I know and with whom I have conversed about their beginnings tell me that they turned to the pulpit because of their mothers. Catholic priests almost to a man traced their ordination to the life-long dream of the devout woman who brought them into this world for the service of Christ.

Similarly, U.S. presidents have been molded by matriarchs who in some instances sought to fulfill through a favorite son a secret ambition. Mary Ball Washington left George a legacy and example of implacable determination; Rebekah Baines Johnson embarked on a loving mission to make her special baby "a great man"; the same applies to Sara Delano Roosevelt, who shaped the career of her son Franklin, and to tragedy-starred Rose Fitzgerald Kennedy, who wanted to see at least one of her sons in the White House. I recall that Richard Nixon, at eleven, once wrote a letter to his mother signing it, "Your faithful dog." The saga of "Miz" Lillian Goudy Carter, born to rear and advise Jimmy, will be a richly rewarding vein of hidden nuggets for future biographers. I gather from Doris Faber's book *Mothers of American Presidents* that most American presidents were mama's boys, usually firstborn sons imbued with flaming zeal. Some of the mothers had originally visualized their sons as preachers during the decades when the pulpit topped the totem pole of desirable careers.

In a more serene and bucolic era than our own, the not-so-bright son often got the nod to become a rabbi, a priest or a pastor. The basic requirements were that he be amiable, predictable and malleable. We Jews had an all-encompassing word for such a prospective paragon: *schlemihl.* On the credit side he could comfort the afflicted, but it never would have occurred to him that he might afflict the comfortable.

The feminine mystique breeds an identity crisis in the pulpit. As a little boy, the preacher, like any other youngster, is taught to love and obey his mother. At home and in school his world is geared to female discipline and care. Once grown up, the masculine mystique takes over, and the boy must break the apron strings—to become a "man." Thirsting for approval from a newly enthroned father-boss, he may twist, turn and cram himself into an alien shape to confront a world suspicious of intellect and emotion, in which a thick hide and a thick tongue are proof of belonging. The model macho of the legendary Old West rode out on his horse with a chaw of scrap tobacco in his cheek and contempt for everything feminine in his heart. Now he drives a pickup truck with his hairy dog in the back, a shotgun at his side and a six-pack of beer on the floor. Sexuality? It's mathematics—with how many women, and how many times can you come?

Does "the masculine protest" explain the dubious stories and jokes that freely rotate at ministerial and rabbinical conferences? Are they but a coward's verbal substitute for the real thing and more acceptable than homosexuality? In my salad days I used to grumble on occasion at the feminine syndrome that boxes in a clergyman and even tags him "one of the girls" at Ladies' Auxiliary fetes. But I can't remember a single snippet of smut from the numberless host of bathroom tales I heard at rabbinical meetings. Perhaps I favored a more purgative and pleasurable way to say "I protest."

A friend of mine, on reading the outline of this book, commented that spiritual leaders may rebound from gruelling work schedules into bouts of profanity to let off steam. His remark led me to ponder about overwork as a complication in the diagnosis and treatment of pulpit neurosis. Nowadays the minister is not only God's servant, but also everybody else's. For example, he must not show ill temper, even when a Sisterhood lady phones him at midnight to ask where she can buy or borrow a Jewish cookbook because she wants to show off with a good matzohball soup to her prospective Gentile dinner guests. A brief compendium of clerics' job roles, drawn up by a tired pastor years ago, came to mind. Although my memory recovers only a percentage, I recall that they all began with the letter "p". I managed to add a considerable number of my own. Through the years I have plugged in to all these various slots: pew-filler, pen-pusher, prophet, pastor, priest, poet, patriot, pietist, philosopher, purifier of morals, patron of the arts, professor of geriatrics and pediatrics, prognosticator of national and world politics, psychiatrist for maritally troubled and troublesome brats, public relations expert, photogenic parson, personality kid, property overseer, panel pilot, philanthropy fund-raiser, party hell-raiser, post-prandial rib-tickler, protocol specialist, pacifier, punster, piscatorial prize-winner, pedagogue, pamphleteer, paladin of the young, paladin of the old, paladin of the poor, prop to the bereaved and sick, platform orator, pontificator, pin-up boy of radical causes, and protector of the Establishment.

Gruelling daily schedules can bedevil the clergyman. In addition to the demand of moral perfectionism come demands of professional perfectionism that can block his vital channels of buoyancy and joy; both saddle him with guilt, giving rise to a permanent sense of "unfinished business" and nagging inadequacy which clamors for replenishment at a woman's breast. My wife Ruth used to remark that I always found hours for the problems of everyone in town but could only spare minutes for the people at home whom I loved. Quite recently my son Jonathan reproached me that the education I gave him was fine but it need not have precluded a father's chance to get inside the skin of his children. Daughter Sarah Jane once wrote me a letter from Smith College requesting an appointment with me during her next vacation. A Protestant minister's daughter told me how she would storm into her father's study, slam the door, and shout, "I need to talk to my father, not a minister, so take off your robe and lay down your Bible and let's start." Not until my wife's doomed struggle against cancer did I forego all outside aims so that I could devote my total attention to her needs. And only now my children and I are dispelling the shadows of resentment against the rabbinate and the narcissistic "fulfillment" I, in common with most clergymen, sought from public visibility.

The Boston University School of Theology and other research centers have named the problems shared by many church wives. First on the list was jealousy over the amount of time their spouses gave to other people's troubles. One quotation is typical: "My husband is everyone's pastor; I have none."

In preparing this book, I have been astonished by the frankness and multiplicity of complaint letters from wives of the clergy. Excerpts from an epistle addressed to Ann Landers seem fairly typical:

> There are 500 members in my husband's congregation and 500 ideas on how a pastor's family should live. He puts in at least 70 hours a week, yet there is never a free evening just for us. We must visit the sick and bereaved, the couple who had a new baby and the old woman who broke her hip. (Note "*we*"!) The phone rings in the middle of the night. Mrs. So-and-So's husband is an alcoholic and hasn't come home. A widow's son took the car without permission and must be dead in a ditch. A hysterical neighbor's daughter has locked herself in the bathroom and threatens suicide . . . The dress I wore last Sunday was too short, someone wrote my husband, and I had on too much lipstick . . . It is assumed that I am to pour tea and stand in the receiving line of every civic and social affair . . . When I married my husband, I wanted to help him serve God, but in the 18 years I haven't seen one life changed by our efforts . . . I hope you won't think I'm mercenary, Ann, but I bitterly resent the fact that we'll never own our own home and we'll always have to scrimp to make ends meet. Living in a parsonage can be awful. Run-down and faded. My husband's salary is the same as it was before the cost of living skyrocketed.

The pathos and sincerity of this message pierced the dispassionate research attitude with which I had begun to read it. The reference to salary had a familiar ring. I remember when a normally considerate trustee at Holy Blossom Temple in Toronto shrugged off my plea that I could not afford to send my children to college with the remark that in my "spiritual" profession I was not supposed to be interested in money. When I sought to supplement my temple earnings with modest honoraria for hitherto free services, rumor had it that I was mercenary. It was the intervention of my *non-religious* friends, whose wise financial advice helped me pay for my son's and daughter's education.

Since the rabbi must never be officially classified as an "employee," "emoluments," not "salaries," have spiraled since my retirement. Now, some Jewish communities admit a slight obligation; their spiritual leaders must be empowered to live in well-groomed dignity as a compliment to their generosity and a symbol of their status vis-à-vis the Gentiles. Yet, the average Christian pastor's indigence causes me acute discomfort. It also worries me that hoisted salaries and other perquisites may heighten a rabbi's vulnerability to his flock's expectations because it wants to get its money's worth.

What paradox is more glaring than the demythologized clergy? We are paid by our flock to lead, exhort, cajole and press them into a way of life they reject because it runs counter to the basic grain of our society. Is the captain of a company of soldiers hired and fired by his men? Is he dependent on their favors? Unless a minister is willing to forfeit his family's livelihood, he must please and appease the pew before he can embark on his God-ordained mission, much less accomplish it. A Catholic priest must answer to the bishop and the hierarchy of the church with the same alternative. He too is committed to overturn the dominant values of the very people who feed his house. To reward him, he must make them think, feel and act according to principles that deny their worldly self-interest and nature. That same anomaly is the rock on which founder the economic security of the Protestant minister's family, the emotional serenity and stability of his person, and whatever healthy and joyous sexuality he and his wife may wrest from their religious code.

"Can we have close friends in the congregation?" was the subject of a rabbi's panel debate some years ago, revealing the keen awareness of the endemic ministerial problem—the impediment of the "cleric's holiness" which deters laymen from entering into a free-flowing, deep friendship with a clergyman. It makes the layman feel uncomfortable and timid, afraid of being too forward. Contact with the man of God freezes on a superficial level. Trapped between the snooty and unapproachable label and the compromise of his dignity, the conscientious clergyman will usually draw a line beyond which neither he nor a congregant may step; *Nec plus ultra*, "no farther!" One cardinal principle, however, remains steadfast: never confide anything to a layman, and rarely to a rabbi, that might tarnish repute or tempt even inadvertent betrayal. The net result of this "holy man" albatross is that clergy and their spouses are barred from sharing their own sexual dilemmas with persons in the church. Years ago an exit from marriage was a sure exit from the pulpit. Today, the marital canopy does not always provide a snug harbor.

It seems self-evident that sex life at the parsonage may be denatured by the "sin" label of conventional Christianity and its attendant guilt feeling. One answer to a general survey of ministers' wives reads as follows: "Our search for sexual compatibility is not over. We married young, and were subjected to a long close relationship before. The *guilt* I felt from heavy petting and the emotional block . . . after our marriage was not surprising, but tragic." Another complained that her husband was so involved with teaching the purity of marital life that sex for her was relegated to a lower level, "as unimportant or unclean."

The book *Ministers' Wives*, by William Douglas, the Boston University savant in the psychology of religion, credits dozens of top-ranking academicians, including Margaret Mead, for assistance in a project sponsored by the Ely Lilly Foundation. Six thousand ministers' wives from twenty-seven denominations candidly responded to questionnaires or interviews on almost every aspect of their place in the home, the church and in society, except that scarcely a dozen sentences in 265 pages touched on the subject of "sexual love." Just over six pages dealt with a bland section entitled "Minister Husbands: Saints, Companions and Lovers." On the second page of the text, "realizing that the minister's family will ever be regarded as the model on which the families of the parish are to be framed," the minister's wife is bidden to "converse with her own heart and inquire into the state of her individual progress heavenward." Indeed, not a promising start for a life of naturalness and earthly joy in the marital boudoir! A homily is quoted from "Hints for a Clergyman's Wife; or Female Parochial Duties" wherein her goal should always be "the advancement of her husband's ministry, the salvation of the souls committed to her pastoral charge and the alleviation of their temporal wants. Let her feel . . . that she has wedded herself to her husband's parish and to the best interests of his flock" (authorship anonymous, 1832). William Douglas' contra-Kinsey report came out in *1965*!

In another paragraph, a certain Charles Smith defines the ideal spouse of a minister as "a good, plain-looking wife whom you like and about whom you can think with affection, but *without passion*" (italics mine). . . . Charles Merrill Smith authored "How to Become a Bishop Without Being Religious." In it he advised the aspiring cleric to calculate with care before selecting "the most important one-piece of equipment he will have in his career—a wife."

In light of these traditional portraits of a minister's wife, should it discomfit us that since none of the fifty-six questions on the Douglas list relate to sex, she—being the free "one-piece of equipment" for the parish—has no identity as a woman? Need we be astonished that 71 percent of the respondents did not hold outside jobs, 64 percent were involved with their husband's work in a "supportive" way, and only 2 percent thought of themselves as individuals for whom others could not decide? As a general rule they did not have close friends in the congregation because of potential confidence betrayal and because of the danger that charges of cliquishness and snobbery may be laid upon them.

Douglas cavalierly deposited the sex issue in the lap of "someone else who will want to study it." Yet he admitted that there appeared to be no significant difference between sexual relationships of ministerial couples and those of couples in general, as revealed by Kinsey and others. But the fact that he rests this conclusion on "*the data available*" (his italics) *does* have significance. With funds at hand, his survey's extension into sex, unchallengeably a matter of importance to churchwomen no less than to others, should have been a matter of elementary logic.

According to *Ministers' Wives* the fact that most Protestant pastors are married men with attendant responsibilities is rarely mentioned in literature. The guiding image, even after the Reformation, still seems to be a celibate priest who gives undivided fealty to the church. We therefore can conclude that the Protestant Reformation continued the sexual mendicancy of prelates' wives at the same time ending the mandatory celibacy of their husbands.

The Care and Feeding of Ministers is the redemptively humorous title of a liberating book in which the author, a minister's wife, titillates us with "how to unbend without falling on your face," "your husband's ego-problems," and "how to prune and groom your husband."

For most of us, only healthy, shameless bed intercourse with a responsive wife will forestall obsessive fantasies or physical involvement with other women. Conversely, it will open channels for healthy, non-physical association with them, thereby preventing the tension-creating jealousy of a deprived wife who likely suspects and even may resent that her husband spends the greater portion of his time on chores that require the company of other women. I also have observed that the "plain-wife-who-arouses-affection-never-passion" formula has not been honored by the Protestant clergymen of my own acquaintance. In overwhelming majority their wives are strikingly desirable. Nor have I found that years ago my Jewish colleagues heeded Harry Golden's counsel. In his bestseller *Only in America* he urged rabbis never to wed luscious blondes because they might pose a threat to their synagogue's women and stir envy in the men. Ministerial neglect of mate cannot be a product of a mate's flat face, bust or figure. As primary objective the interpersonal husband-wife connubial contact must be enveloped in a cocoon that will fructify and bring to maximal flowering a healthy sexual relationship.

However, stirrings of revolt can be heard. Its time has come. A survey of the United Presbyterian Church has revealed that the spouses of young preachers are less likely than their older counterparts to assent and consent to compulsive participation in congregational affairs and to pattern themselves on old models. Some even seek outside employment, manifesting a definite thrust toward personhood, a separate self-image outside of their husbands' profession. In an age that equates "eternal verities" with the validity and permanence of a Gallup poll, this may be comforting to remember.

Sexual naiveté and illiteracy are the root cause of much trial and error in eccelesiastical behavior. I derived that dictum by closely scrutinizing many of my colleagues. The anterior responsibility is traceable to the theological school that trained (or mistrained) us for the wearing of the cloth. That conviction comes from eight years of traumatic experiences in a seminary marked by faulty nutrition (twenty-two dollars monthly for a freshman's room and board, and a landlady who locked the ice-box); homelessness (I rotated around four different chilly attics during one semester); gruelling academic chores (two full courses, mornings at university, afternoons at Hebrew Union College for the first four years and gargantuan knowledge tests); intellectual and political goose-stepping (students cashiered for "radicalism"); sexual hunger (laceration by celibacy or expulsion by decree). Whereas in my time the regular course duration could have been as long as nine years, the program now has been adapted to accommodate post-graduate studies.

The change in "lifestyles" also are striking: from proletarian to bourgeois, from dimly lit attics heated with small gas units to bright apartments with electric refrigerators and television sets; from a cold, lonely bed to a double or king-size one warmed by a wife.

The student body is thoroughly "American," in large proportion, scions of families removed by several generations from their European origins. They are more closely akin to Middle America in their conservatism than to the poor immigrants whose history and situation had evoked social and political dissent. My cronies were a "bunch of neurotics" and life was risky, venturesome and, yes, exciting; whereas the new breed living in an atmosphere of prosperity, security and perhaps complacency strike me as bland, predictable and briskly professional. Sex? Probably where it was before—underground, despite the presence of a growing number of female rabbinic aspirants. The classroom silence on sexuality that governed it sixty years ago has not abdicated its near-taboo status.

Christian seminarians—what is one to say about them? An incorrigible skeptic may allow himself to be nudged to surmise that Roman Catholics, being tooled for life-long celibacy by an unyielding papal decree, might be tempted to pay off the Devil and their biological urges with pre-ordination or post-ordination homosexuality and grapevine gossip about the priest's housekeeper. Protestants have without hesitation bored an excellent peep-hole into seminary sexuality. In 1963, John V. Monro, Dean of Harvard College, warned his students that their sexual conduct in dormitories was "getting closer and closer to downright scandal." Other university officials commented that religious teaching seemed to offer students little guidance in sexual behavior. That furor came shortly after British Quakers recommended that traditional Christian sexual ethics be totally overhauled by sanctioning sex relations before and outside of marriage under proper conditions.

In 1964, only one year after the Harvard Dean's blast, the official stance toward sexuality in a major New England seminary was still compounded by bland unawareness, blind unreality and blundering authority. Cleric informants have assured me that this martinet principle governed most other theological centers. The assumption, in their words, was that pulpit trainees were illiterate about the church's doctrinal heritage. Therefore they required instruction, above all in analysis of concepts related to God, Christ and the soul, along with thinly veiled hints on dress and social etiquette. On the other hand, the same fledgling minister for whose mind and manners the faculty designed a huge curriculum of neophyte teaching was deemed to be fully mature, in control of all his adolescent hangups, and beyond the need to get acquainted with his own emotions, least of all his sexuality. Credentials of sexual normalcy were conferred with the title "Reverend." In truth the vast majority of the ordained, according to my informants, were ill-nourished, unprepared and tenuous about their sexual identity. They asked, "How are we to guide parishioners through marital breakdowns caused by sexual dysfunction when our own sexuality is distraught and dismembered?" Yet faculty and students were inclined to disregard this loaded subject in classroom sessions.

The not surprising effect on many Protestant seminary students was conflict and despair. They felt dragooned into "irregular" vows of chastity and saddled with implicit coercion to marry post-haste after ordination. Bachelors often did not get agreeable assignments and were thought to be tainted with homosexuality, a willful indulgence so leprous in the view of seminary nabobs that decent Christians had to be shielded from contagion by stripping from indiscreet practitioners all pulpit training, placement opportunity and personhood.

In 1968 my sources checked out the same New England seminary. Initially the surface changes gratified them. There were encounter groups for freshmen, with weekly sessions under theologically reliable supervision; a small group of male and female homosexuals had come out of the closet with strident "hallelujahs"; boy-girl couples proceeded after classes to their off-campus apartments for rest and a taste of forbidden raptures; rumors were rife of dormitory body smuggling and draughts of nectar laced with marijuana.

Had a change occurred in the constellation of denials, avoidance and flight? Their familiar ghosts still haunted the ritualistic sanctuary of sexual decorum. "Sex talk" was still guarded, the responses were reluctant, the style clinical and abstract. During one encounter session a reputedly jittery student, obviously uncoiled by the promise that "anyone could feel free to open up the inmost chambers of his heart," remarked, "I can't get it on with my lady." When the attending psychologist invited him to be more specific, the first-year innocent plunged, "The fucking I'm getting isn't worth the screwing I have to take." Only the psychologist's curt reply cracked the silence. "You're not married. The subject is irrelevant and out of place."

"By their fruits shall ye know them." A more persuasive evaluation of seminary sex teaching than that afforded by this tragicomedy can be gleaned from the careers it launched. Most embryonic ministers end their studies as they began by addressing their struggles for sexual integration according to their respective competence to learn from pain and bafflement. Sparse insights are relegated to experimentation. Stifled feelings, stilled tongues and neutered sex enable some to perform their allotted duties in workaholic frenzy. "Like non-smokers avoiding tobacco for Lent, they surrender to a confused sexuality," I was told. Others leave behind a trail of broken marriages, alienation from hearts and genitals, records of professional abandonment and, in not too rare a case, an escutcheon aflame with profligacy.

I have consulted other estimable Christian colleagues as to whether "normative" sexuality was provided for in Protestant theological schools. One of them sat down with me for a talk and, in summation, confessed, "We are all responsible for our own actions, misguided or not. But surely seminaries could pay more attention to the life and precepts of their professed Lord, who seemed to have displayed extraordinary and warm compassion for those attempting to find and affirm life in its corporeal dimensions. Schools and congregations must some day discover that clean houses are neither made nor kept by forcing the clergy into mannequin-like postures of inhuman purity where such are defined by sexlessness. . . . Each person is a unique blend of body, mind and spirit. Since sexuality permeates this whole, one should be willing to celebrate the gift of a fully explored and rigorously accomplished life as co-partners in creation, thankful for the chance to touch the universe with our life and breath and sex."

So much for an overview of mainstream male Protestant seminaries. A look at sexuality in schools where women are enrolled for ministry preparation has been provided by a clergy-woman who attended courses at a seminary whose standing and standards are among the most enviable in America. Her own candor and character are beyond reproach. She told me that cohabitation arrangements are prevalent, not only for unmarried heterosexual pairs but also for homosexuals, the majority of whom are engaged in lesbianism. Lesbians appear less culpable and visible than male-male tandems. Did lesbianism flourish at the reported seminaries because it combined less guilt feeling with more protection against detection? Do the girl-girl "crushes" so prevalent in female childhood and early adolescence ease the path to lesbianism in such an unlikely place as a training school for women clergy? I wonder. Females are nurturing people, males are competitive. Is such a generalization arguable? During my four years as volunteer rabbi-in-residence at San Francisco's famous Glide Memorial Church, I officiated at a lesbian "covenant" ceremony between one of the gentlest and most unmistakably sincere couples ever to stand before me. It was not a formal marriage; my function was to witness their mutual troth. I had also helped them write their declaration and promise to each other. The ritual I had devised gave emphasis to the universal components of the Jewish nuptial rite: the sharing of a beaker of wine, the exchange of a simple statement of mutual self-consecration and the ancient priestly blessing of peace. The pure intermingling of those young women, communicated by a subtle sense of total union, left me with no guilt.

Due to mid-life career changes, or because of other delays for seminary entrance until the students are in their late twenties, many of them are married. There is also a growing number of single female parents. Chastity cases have declined; that reason for entering the ministry now is rare indeed.

Women's entries into the ministry have brought the sex issue into critical focus. Changing attitudes toward eroticism outside the seminary do not fully explain the revolution within it. Men and women headed for the pulpit do not tumble into bed without a centripetal force drawing them into a center. That center melts and catalyzes all hindrances to union, like the heat in earth's core. Men and women dwell together in a small, isolated, emotionally intense community of shared goals, values and philosophies under the sign of religious faith. These ingredients, stirred by carnal nature and positive chemistry, produce a potent mix for falling in love and/or entering into a sexual liaison.

Yet, I have been told that seminaries are no less mute on the subject of sex now than they were in the puritanical past under Middle America's tutelage. In the addresses against nuclear armament that I often delivered across North America in the sixties, I likened the danger of atomic cataclysm to lighting a match in an ammunition factory. A match ought to be lit in the theological clergyman factory to shatter the bonds that stifle sexuality.

What level of sex health can be forecast for future graduates of seminaries? My concern is not with evidence of what these institutions call "violation of God's moral law." Rather, I am shaken by the penalty visited on the psychological, emotional and professional well-being of ordained seminarians for whom the only guidelines offered in the area of sex are evasion, secrecy and compromise. *That* is immorality!

4 ∅
Is Christian-Jewish
Sex Negation Dying?

Morality is a virtue, but when carried to extremes it becomes a vice. Like patriotism, it can be the last refuge of a scoundrel, and like my aging, tobacco-caked meerschaum pipe that can only stimulate the olfactory nerve, it can become obsolescent. No wonder, then, that inordinate morality has littered time with a mishmash of contradictions, confusions and craziness. Under its sponsorship the words spoken, the actions taken and the emotions aroused have been astonishingly high in number and scope.

Need that spotlight on morality astonish us? Has not ecclesiastical moralizing riveted its enraptured gaze on the genitals, the most prized property of the corporeal person for two thousand years? All that time man's destiny beyond the grave has hung on the erect penis and the vibrant vagina. A hymenal rent or penile thrust under certain circumstances of time and partner was a one-way ticket to paradise or perdition, to heaven or hell. Has the Creator centered all his moral commands in a hirsute cleavage between the legs? Is He a celestial voyeur who builds anatomical trivia into the linchpin of man's eternal fate? I find that an absurdity beyond my ken. Yet scholars of the church for centuries accepted it as revealed truth—*credo quia absurdem est* (I believe what is absurd). Sacrifice the intellect! It was an act of blind faith.

Concentration on coitus as the criterion of openness to Divine grace also becomes the basis of church power. The logic is clear; by equating sex with sin, the church made all humanity sinners, for carnal desire cannot be evaded—it is universal. How may mortal men and women forfend Divine punishment in hell everlasting? Only through the church, chosen by God as His representative, agent and repository of His truth. And people can obtain felicity only through its intercession. The final stop in this reasoning was inevitable; the church would save those who serve, support and obey it.

Obsessed and often tormented by sex, some Church Fathers would employ the energies of bottled-up libido to monitor every sign of sexual interest or activity in others. And the most committed hunters of sexual deviance or dalliance seemed more likely to attain hierarchical positions of authority.

Since ancient days many books containing moralistic phrases, explicit sin warnings and descriptions of sex positions have been written. All floundered in their attempts to pull our fragile species through the miasma of its bestial instincts. Composed by and for the clergy, who were the only people who could read in that early era of pagan-Christian society, they probably were the first form of literary pornography.

Today one huge, inert mass clutters the road to our humanization with age-barnacled ecclesiastical sex codes. These religious compendia had the jump on today's sex manuals; they told people not only how *to* do it but how *not* to do it. For example:

> In case of involuntary seminal pollution (wet dreams) or menstrual flow, you must rise up from your bed at once and sing seven psalms; if it occurs in church you must recite the whole psalter according to the early Church Fathers' penitential books.

Sexual intercourse was declared illegal by the early church on Sundays, Wednesdays and Fridays during five months of the year, forty days before Easter and before Christmas, three days before attending Communion, from the time of conception to forty days after a child's birth, and during penance. At one period in the Middle Ages abstention from sex was ordered for no fewer than five days in the week: on Thursdays in memory of Jesus' arrest, on Fridays in memory of his death, on Saturdays in honor of the Blessed Virgin, on Sundays in honor of the Resurrection and on Mondays in honor of the faithful who had departed.

Coitus frequency was also spelled out in the Talmud with mathematical exactitude, all according to people's work schedules. Ideally, gentlemen of leisure could do it every night; laborers working in their hometown, twice a week; camel drivers, every thirty days, and sailors every six months. Scholars, rabbis, donkey drivers and men working away from home could have sexual intercourse once a week, and all men, preferably on Sabbath Eve, to honor God's creation and, even when the wife was barren, for pleasure. The Talmud omits similar arithmetic for women, in all likelihood because their role was considered to be passive and therefore didn't count.

For centuries bride and groom were barred from church for thirty days after their first act of intercourse, and neither a menstruating woman nor a woman who had just borne a child could enter a church without previous cleansing rites, an extension of the Jewish requirement of ritual baths. In some early religious paintings the Holy Ghost is seen descending in the form of a dove carrying a sperm in its bill; in others the seminal words pass through a lily on their way from Gabriel's mouth to the ear of the Virgin Mother, in order to remove the slightest trace of sexual contamination in the supernatural drama of the Divine birth of Christ.

Christian ascetic rules were in part a reaction to the prevalent merely sensual view of sex. For example, certain monks observed "a cult of filth" by refusing ever to take a bath because of the lascivious antics formerly connected with the practice in the lush days of the Roman Caesars' bath-house opulence.

In nineteenth-century England the death penalty was advocated for adultery. The Society for the Suppression of Vice, that counted among its members not only six bishops but also the Duke of Wellington, had the power to close newspapers and ban books. The basic goal of all these rules and regulations was to cut the joy of sex to the bone, to a point where it was merely consistent with reproduction, and even that permissiveness was granted grudgingly.

Literature records ardent outpourings of passion from "beautiful" women whose avowed chastity found vent in spiritual congress with their Divine spouse. Here are the words of a nun canonized in 1925: "Ah, how sweet is the first kiss of Jesus. I said to him, 'I give myself to you forever.' Nothing can detach my ardor from the divine being who ravished me."

Friedrich von Schlegel and Friedrich Ernst Daniel Schleiermacher, two German theologians who lived in the early part of the nineteenth century, held that the perfect mate combines all three functions the ancient Greeks assigned to three separate women: slave girls for sexual satiety, hetairas, similar to the Japanese geishas, for companionship and wives for children and homemaking. In quest for this perfect mate, premarital celibacy was abandoned and Plato's theory revived that we are all one-half of a sphere. Somewhere on earth the missing other half exists—

the one individual in all the universe who can fulfill our personality. Here, in the labyrinthine crania of two famous clergy philosophers, was seeded the sentimental notion of the "only girl in the world," the mushy mirage that triumphed in the twentieth century. This is the stuff that dreams, art and tragedy are made of—the apotheosis of sex.

Are we too aware and too self-conscious about our sex vibrations? Does the sight of a nude man cause another man more discomfort than the sight of a nude woman? A friend of mine who had joined a mixed group in the outdoor hot bath at Esalen in Big Sur, California, told me, "At first, I looked obliquely at the women after holding down my gaze for a few minutes to take a deep breath. Then I turned around toward the women and faced them. My mind organized itself at once, focusing vagrant thoughts on their potential. No problem! Finally, doing what my subconscious seemed to dread, I looked at the men. Instantly, homosexual feelings never entertained before swept over me, fright dispelled relaxation, and fear that the others would detect my terrible tension seized me!"

Had my friend fallen into an atavistic relapse of some long-forgotten and primitive fear only superficially erased in his genes by evolution?

In the Middle Ages witches (always female) were accused of sodomy with the Devil. Sodomy is now in some places considered a "crime against nature," and laws prohibiting it are still on the books in thirty-six states; these laws automatically classify a sizeable segment of the population as criminals, thereby permitting bigots to enforce orthodoxy under the pretext of morality. (Legal usage is not always precise; "sodomy" here points at the homosexual; it is a loosely used word covering a long list of sexual abnormalities, including oral and anal sex. Strict enforcement of existing sex statutes could keep about 99 percent of men and women out of circulation.) Kinsey surveys reveal that such forms of intercourse are not shunned by at least two-thirds of the American public. Oral sex lightens guilt since, technically, it is not coitus. Yet in California it was outlawed even in marriage, until the law was changed in the late twenties because legislators realized that prisons could no longer hold all the malefactors.

The Hebrew prophets blamed lechery for the victories of the Philistines; in World War I French chaplains attributed military reverses to sexual promiscuity, and in 1935 an Anglican canon wrote to the *London Times* that the increase in blasphemy and violations of marriage laws were more dangerous to national security than aerial bombings. We may judge our own land and time immune to similar crudity. A corrective to such complacency is the recent refusal of the American Space Agency to adopt Carl Sagan's proposal that information about earthlings' bodies be beamed to the universe and other forms of life in space by showing photographs of nude human beings. NASA however, seemed averse to over-stimulating the Martians!

Hawaiian native girls would romp in sheer joy and hospitality on the decks of Captain Cook's vessel to give his sailors some release from the celibacy of a long voyage at sea. But missionaries stopped the fun and instead founded five companies to reap and sell the sugar cane. Their conversion of the natives to "sinlessness" ultimately replaced what comes naturally with alcoholism, drug abuse and depression.

Experts such as the National Council on Alcoholism estimate that one in nine nuns are prone to alcoholism—the same rate as the general population. Sister Doody, a "recovered" Dominican, has been trying to tell others among the 130,000 American nuns that they can and must get help with a problem that existed long before Vatican II—which some contend sparked the upsurge of alcoholism by relaxing rigid rules such as the wearing of habits. Another recovering alcoholic said, "Catholics still want to see a bunch of giggling nuns sitting in a car licking ice cream cones." Will these minor but meaningful signs of advancing liberalism lead to a climatic confrontation with mandatory chastity?

On placards posted in the super-Orthodox Jewish section of Jerusalem, the word "prostitutes!" is applied to bare-armed and short-skirted women. Rabbinical students often shout the same word at passing female tourists—all in the name of their version of Judaism's God. . . .

Reverend Spencer W. Kimball, president of the Church of Jesus Christ of Latter Day Saints, announced in 1975 that the Mormon Church would not join a World Council of Churches that does not share puritanical sex standards. "There isn't any situation that justifies a woman giving herself to a man. . . . Sex between a man and woman, husband and wife, is to bear children. It isn't just for the fun of it!"

Remembering that the Mormon Church has, in its ideology and in the minds of its rapidly growing membership, a direct, incomparable channel to the Supreme Divine will through God's self-revelation to its head alone, the power of Messrs. Kimball and Ezra Taft Benson, his intended successor, looms limitless. If adopted as the absolute and literal credo for sexual behavior, the Kimball-Benson manifesto would reduce the schedule of coitus to a frequency commensurate with a pair's numerical planned parenthood. It might have been a composite xerox of the Mosaic law-giver's Sinaitic syndrome (except that whereas Moses was denied admission to the Promised Land, Mormon leaders are certain of Paradise)!

Not long ago Mormons were persecuted for the polygamy they espoused in imitation of Old Testament patriarchs and for the replenishment of the human resources that had been lost on their trek to Missouri and Utah. Their enemies, by charging that the exponents of Mormonism were licensing immoral sex, stimulated their own sexual appetites at the same time by imaginative transports to Mormon "harems." They envied Mormon males their access to women of diverse sexual aptitudes, just as the Ku Klux Klan lynched blacks for usually unverified molestation of white women to sublimate their own guilt. In that way they eliminated rivals who were, in their hate-sick minds, endowed with bestial sex potency. . . .

The lone words "honesty or poverty" in the Kimball polemic against individual choice, freedom or responsibility might have touched off some allusion to the ills that beset the world wherein these Latter Day Prophets dwell. Perhaps such a reality did not engage the thinking of a religious system whose vast properties and investments—all tax-free—are, as a matter of policy, withheld from the scrutiny even of its own constituents. Is not the Mormon artifact an archaelogical relic polished and refined for current consumption? What is their particular message if not the inflexibility of church-oriented sex in a world dedicated to change? The Mormon President is rivaled solely by the Catholic Pope. When they coalesce, as actually they do in their categorical imperatives on human sexuality, who can discern with open eyes the imminent or eventual end of the mainstream church's implacable hostility to reason, common sense, realism and gut-compassion in the decisive domain of sexuality?

During the Nevada Legislature's open debate on the Equal Rights Amendment, in which I participated, one "proud" Mormon housewife after another stood up as if in military drill, breathing opposition to ERA because "the elders of my church have been told by God that it is not His will." A Mormon-Catholic alliance finally defeated the Amendment.

The Ten Commandments, Old Testament narrators assert, were graven on stone, impervious to sun, storm and winds of change. Are the negations of our sex code similar stuff, changeless and fixed, to withstand the corrosion of time? Once accepted within a religious framework, sexual attitudes are calcified or petrified by laws that penalize deviation; then attempts are made to find philosophic, scientific or theological proof to make them an impregnable fortress of our untouchable Western culture, which compared with others has been hostile to sex expression. It seems clear that the Western world has been dominated by the folklore and theological concepts adumbrated in the earliest Christian centuries and come to flower in Europe during the Middle Ages, when the dominant view defined and deplored sex as sin. The roots of that enmity may be tangled around a primordial fear of woman in a man's breast.

Long ago a cagoule, or heavy night shirt with a single suitably sized perforation at front center, was recommended to husbands by priests so that the wife could be impregnated without further contact. The hard root of the orchid, thought to resemble testicles, used to be eaten by women for fertility; nuns preferred the root of the lily to buttress their hard-pressed search for an easy path to permanent chastity. To avoid bodily exposure, some cloistered nuns used a doll to tell a physician where it hurt. Cold baths, hard beds, religious exercises and abstention from reading French novels was the regimen imposed on young men of the Victorian age, both in England and in the United States. (The same was subtly recommended but soundly ridiculed in my own seminary days.) Did that recipe for virginity foster masturbation and homosexuality? A positive answer would not be an astonishing discovery to make. The origin of the Victorian diatribes against masturbation (e.g., that it caused blindness and lunacy) was attributed by some sociologists to acute feelings of guilt. The same applied to the adage that "good" women had no interest in sex. Husbands, therefore, had an overflowing surplus of gonads and *carte blanche* for seeking it from "bad" ones. Prostitutes were favored to provide an opportunity to pious males for doing the blessed work of moral and social uplift. Like Henry VIII, Winston Churchill's father died of syphilis, and in 1866 Bishop Matthew

Simpson calculated that London had more whores than Methodists. . . .

In New York City prostitution episodes still occur at the rate of 100,000 daily, often characterized by police harassment of the women and always by total benevolence toward their male customers. This estimate was made by a Roman Catholic priest who consecrated his life to the succor of juveniles who were ensnared in the sale of human flesh. Who are the clientele? Chiefly middle-class, middle-aged, married men. One of them, when questioned, had this to say: "Sex is what you do with a woman you don't like. Love is for your wife, whom you wouldn't want to spoil with sex!" In the pre-Civil War South of pseudo-chivalry, the white woman was calcified on a pedestal, her chaste limbs enveloped by a billowing crinoline that protected her from masculine crudity, while her husband puffed up the bellies of black slaves who did not deserve such solicitude. This dual contrast is not really a disavowal of Eve, the original image of woman the temptress, the sex-exuding instrument of Satan! Secluded and glorified, the white wife was protected from her own carnal self.

Seneca, a pivotal Stoic philosopher of the first century, cautioned men to love their wives with judgment, not with affection, asserting that nothing is fouler than to love a wife as if she were an adulteress. "Be a commanding husband to your wife, not a coddling lover," was the advice quoted by St. Jerome; it became a central prescription of early Christian scholastic. . . .

Leviticus 20:16 links women with bestiality. "If a woman approaches unto any beast and lies down thereto, both shall be put to death." Talmudic writers worried about women who were denied proper sexual partners, for they may be driven to contact with animals. Therefore, a widow was prohibited to keep a pet dog or acquire a slave. Based on the assumption, known only to be false, that female sexuality could always be satisfied by the husband, alternatives only were occasionally mentioned. Evidently it never occurred to the sages that women could do anything among themselves. As a consequence private interfemale association went comparatively unregulated and lesbianism was ignored. Cross-dressing transvestism, however, talmudic authorities linked with pagan idolatry of the sex goddess who liked to exchange garments between men and women. To drive home the "difference" men were enjoined from growing their hair long, applying cosmetics, wearing bright colors and shaving the hidden parts of their bodies; women had to keep their hair long.

It is said that New England Puritans damned bear-baiting not to ease the bear's pain but to end the baiter's pleasure. But when an issue had its locus in the genitals, the Puritan allowed himself latitude. Married men who emigrated to America unwived could woo and win without disclosing earlier ties. Most of their new female mates died in their forties from overwork and overbearing children.

In revolt against church repression, social reformer John Humphrey Noyes set up a community around the middle of the eighteenth century in which all men were potential husbands for all women and the children belonged to everyone. Often youths were initiated by women beyond menopause and older men were paired with females of tender age. . . .

Harvey Cox, a bulwark of the contemporary church, notes with apparent sadness that, whereas the Puritan lifestyles including ankle-length dresses, compulsory psalm-reciting and listening to long sermons, have vanished, the Puritan ethic remains and still affects conduct today. He quotes the German thinker Friedrich Gogarten, who maintained that the two most serious dangers to the Gospel were its being dissolved into myth or hardened into law. Thoughtful young Christian adults, in talks with me, show symptoms of viewing the Gospel not as an offer of freedom for personhood but as an assortment of confused conventions with preachments that are muddied by odd bits of sexual folklore.

The history of civilization is a record of long warfare between the applecart-tilting forces of education and the inhibitions fashioned to neutralize them. The battle ranges from Norman Vincent Peale's positive thinking that sexual laxity portends the collapse of Western civilization, to Alex Comfort's "Ode to Sex" as "the healthiest and most important human sport." Liberals credit intercourse to be rewarding both in and out of marriage, destructive only when coercive or distorted by eighteenth- or nineteenth-century Puritanism. Conservatives point and pant with alarm to carnality on college campuses "and the cosmic proportions of the copulation explosion."

Rabbi Gordis, writing in *Love and Sex*, states that organized religion has demanded adherence to specific codes of conduct in which restraints play a basic role. The first traditional logo I learned at seminary was "613," the number of religious observances or *mitzvot* designated in the Bible—365 negative commandments for every day of the year and 248 positive ones for every bone in the human body. Such a pattern of discipline, Gordis admits, is repugnant to the modern mind and mood.

I believe that theology lost the battle with biology long ago but was persuaded to reduce its losses by doctrinal stratagem, hold-fast reticence and militant mobilization of fundamentalist followers. Time-encrusted codes have been exhumed as weapons in an ideological war; these codes merely emphasize that celibacy and self-denial are no less proof of sex preoccupation than profligacy. While the VIPs of the church, those who formulate policy, are stymied in a do-nothing, know-nothing limbo, their "lower" clergy are caught up in a maelstrom of personal doubt, temptation and stress at a time solicitous of sexual appetites. Advertising presents the most subtle and attractive assortment of aphrodisiacs since African tribes first began to poach for elephant tusks. . . . The current resistance to and impatience with sin orientation creates a need and an opportunity for the church frankly to confront and terminate the sex-versus-religion vendetta which has been superimposed on their basic life-affirming harmony. Clerics should be enabled to combine their integrity as preachers doing God's work with honesty as human beings.

"Church" is honeycombed with internal contradictions, just as the Greeks were taught to abhor incest while regaling one another with incestuous myths about their gods on Olympus; Christendom gave leadership to the abolition of slavery but sanctified it in South Africa as the will of God; Jews demanded family "purity" and almost deified polygamous Old Testament patriarchs. If the church refuses to compromise with the twentieth century, the penalty for its paralysis will be chaos. In pagan times religion fondled the genitals; now it holds them in a vise. I believe that in our greed-ravaged, war-hypnotized, Cain-Abel society, kindness, understanding and charity are more vital than chastity.

Renovations of Western man's "spiritual" makeup, a fresh start in his intellectual and emotional development, is long overdue. His "soul" is smothered under the cumulative growth of dust-laden handouts of religious authority often itself ruled by lust for power. Insofar as I can unravel the theological gobbledygook of "natural law," it means that God created man complete, whole, without benefit of evolution. The church is so positive

about the spiritual specifications of man—"original sin," etc.—
that the Lord may have leaned excessively on heavenly prelates.
What was implanted in the Divine masterpiece remained without
change. Driven deep into teachings on sexuality, that concept of
changelessness hardens the protean, venturesome creatures we
fondly think we are into pieces of sculpture on exhibit in a
museum. Its name is inflexibility, the blueprint of a massive,
forbidding structure: the morality of sex negativism, religion
frozen in the act of saying "No!"

The Rt. Reverend James A. Pike, former Bishop of the
Episcopal Diocese of California, whose brilliant forays for
updated Christian doctrine and taxation of church property
landed him in a heresy court, was a close friend of mine. Led by
dissident young ministers, he said the church had made a belated
commitment to human rights and social reform. In the realm of
sexuality, however, traditional churchmen have for the most part
staunchly resisted change. According to Pike, "no religious
morals are fixed and permanent in terms of historical development. At one time it was sinful to lend money; but my diocese lent
money to churches. The only sin was when they didn't pay it back.
Slavery was once accepted by the church; there were rules within
the game on how to be a good slave or a nice master. At the 1920
Lambeth Conference—our modest Anglican version of the Vatican
Council—any form of contraception was held to be sinful; by
1958, family planning was declared a moral obligation. . . . The
church's sexual norms have been totally wrong, even within
marriage. . . . I can't buy the codifiers that say we've got a set of
rules telling us what is right and what is wrong under every
circumstance. Decisions must be made contextually, situationally,
responsibly, and religion should help individuals do that, if at all,
by rational, open, free, unbiased discussion."

Father Herbert Rogers, a member of the Fordham University
faculty, entered the Catholic Society of Jesus in 1930, taught
English literature, drama and philosophy, and wrote and lectured
on a variety of other subjects. That he would welcome a Catholic
trend toward change is evident in his remarkably ascerbic criticism
of the church's sex imbalance. "Roman Catholics have often over-
emphasized chastity to the neglect of honesty and social justice.
For many Catholics, the word 'sin' immediately suggests sex.
Many Roman Catholic moralists were wonderfully adept in
explaining away statements of Jesus about almsgiving and non-

resistance to evil, but what little Jesus said about chastity was taken with the utmost gravity—selective retention of texts on sex and comfortable exclusion of others! Sins against chastity are always treated as *per se* mortal sins, in sharp distinction to sins against justice, honesty, human dignity. Always very definite in condemning sexual sin, but wonderfully vague and accommodating about racial justice or war."

An even more forthright challenge to religious delight in things as they are came from Dr. Harvey Cox, the ordained Baptist minister, Associate Professor of Church and Society at Harvard Divinity School, author of *The Secular City* and of articles in leading magazines. His attacks mince no words. "Morality must always be a living, organic thing. We must be constantly rethinking our morals, not on the basis of rigid law but on the basis of human needs. It is wrong to insist that always and with every unmarried couple intercourse is wrong. There are instances in which it would be not only permissible but advisable before marriage. Any action that expresses affection between two consenting adults in private is something that lies outside the range of my moral condemnation."

Insurrection against the mummified sex code was an inescapable moral necessity for another clerical spokesman. Dr. James Luther Adams, Professor of Christian Ethics at Harvard Divinity School, said to be the world's most prominent Unitarian, stated, "The Christian tradition on the whole has a poor record—of devaluation, prurience, secrecy in talking about sex. Its extreme asceticism is theologically unsound; it makes sexual intercourse as such sinful and belittles an authentic aspect of human experience." According to Dr. Allen J. Moore, a Methodist minister, Dean of Students and Associate Professor of Christian Education at the School of Theology in Claremont, California, "We're moving into an era of uncertainty in which all aspects of life will be much more open-ended. The church will have to give up its authoritarianism and emphasis on the 'givings.' Most of my generation are hung up on sex."

Dr. Martin E. Marty, a Lutheran minister and Associate Professor of Church History at the University of Chicago, is a widely quoted and prolific author. He stated, "The sexual ethic of Christianity until now has been devoted to two goals: how to remain celibate all your life, thus attaining a higher degree of 'spirituality,' or how to prepare yourself for a monogamous marriage, the only other ideal. In recent decades the church has stretched and bent within these boundaries, but I don't think anything really new has emerged."

"Really new!" For that dimension of emergence we are indebted to none other than the clergy of Roman Catholicism, some of whom are marching to a different drum than the hypnotic rhythm that has closed their ranks for centuries. The grassroots stirring against absolute obedience to the past and to precedent, it may be said, has synchronized in its birth with the sexual revolution's general disdain for the rule of celibacy. It has been dramatized by the feeling among church liberals, including several cardinals, that Pope Paul VI installed an over-authoritative governance by rejecting all easements in regard to celibacy and birth control, and later, with Pope John Paul II, by confrontation on his tumultuously acclaimed visit to the United States in the Fall of 1979. Although history will characterize the Polish-born pontiff as the most popular and, on the global scene, the most powerful Holy Father in modern times, an experienced and astute Vatican City journalist reported that he finds his (ostensibly supreme) authority questioned. Exceptionally courageous and articulate clergy speak out, ignore his will, however rarely, and even dilute his diplomatic initiatives.

Why this disaffection? The diagnosis can be condensed into a few words: total infusion into the present of a morality whose formalized development by the church began almost on the day when the Rock of St. Peter was established. Staunch bans on artificial birth control, abortion, permissiveness, non-marital intercourse, divorce, homosexuality and clerical marriage were all unequivocally demanded of bishops so that they might safeguard intact the "sacred deposit of truth" for laity to obey and for priests and nuns to incorporate wholly into the fabric of their personal lives. The unabridged apparatus of sexual repression, it seems, has been transferred to a climate far removed in spirit from the weather that long ago formed its origin.

A progression from rigidity to brittleness to fracture is inevitable. No one can doubt that Pope John Paul II lifted a lance of steel to sustain a heritage he reveres as the life-blood of allegiance to the Words. But adherence to jot and tittle cannot reverse the relentless flow of time. The self-assured Orthodox Jewish rabbinate's grand design or fantasy—to make Jewish identity synonymous with observance of the 613 commandments—would suck the juices out of the Torah we exultantly greet as "The Tree of Life" at Sabbath services. Life does not stand still. Without adaptation it is in love with desiccation and death.

The wave of the future is powered by growing pressure for change from hitherto docile sectors of Roman Catholicism: radical social-justice priests and bishops in Central America, dissenting princes of the church in the Netherlands, American nuns whose agitation for the ordination of women racked the serenity of Rome when it prompted the leader of a national nuns' organization (garbed in tweeds) to rise up in the Pope's presence and plead for an end to the discrimination against religious women.

Seventy U.S. theologians signed a statement to support Professor Hans Küng, one of the world's most prominent Roman Catholic theologians. He had questioned, albeit academically, papal infallibility, authority of bishops, mandatory celibacy, opposition to birth control, and the virgin birth of Jesus. He also had expressed misgivings about Christ's conviction that He was the Son of God, and the expansion of His teachings into a new religion. Liberal-minded, not "literal," priests even muttered "New Inquisition." The day after Pope John Paul II approved the Vatican decree stripping Küng of his teaching credentials for contempt of church doctrine, two thousand attended his lecture at his post in Tuebingen, West Germany.

The casual shrug by North American Catholic wives whenever the papal ban on artificial family limitation is mentioned has become an embarrassment. In recent years thousands of priests have quit their vocation, chiefly to marry. A married former priest in Paris, one of the many who retain their Catholic beliefs, publicly accused the Pope of acting "like a great scout-master out of the early fifties." Statistics show steadily mounting defections from church attendance, except at Christmas and at Eastertime (the Christian counterparts of crowded synagogues at Jewish New Year services and on the Day of Atonement).

Apart from teaching people how to extract maximum fulfillment from their social situation, religion *can* teach people how to harvest utmost joy, a sense of freedom and fulfillment from their intensely personal, carnal-spiritual and earthly-Divine sexual situation. Hamstrung by "don'ts" and shackled to a moribund corpus of inflexible negatives, it fails to achieve this. I must denounce this failure, not in defense of any abstruse theorem or dogma assailed inevitably honeycombed with illogic, but in defense of that "Western" segment of humanity silenced by incidental, albeit no less tyrannical, intimidation.

I am aware that many clergymen, possibly most, will not share my concern for the spiritual health of their colleagues. I have no compunction to suggest that I speak in defense of clerics afflicted with confusion and conflict by a morality they can neither honestly endorse and implement nor safely disavow. Yet we need to ask: What is the origin and history of the thing that bred all this?

Sex negativism, like the religions that have nurtured it, was born in Palestine, that geographical detail that had an extraordinary impact on its character at birth and afterwards. A glance at a world atlas supplies the clue. The plot of earth on the eastern Mediterranean littoral is a fly-spot. Three continents converge there: Europe, Africa and Asia Minor. The exodus of the Israelitish tribes from Egypt for the conquest of Canaan was the first recognition by history that in this crossroads Hebrew statelet lies a strategic road to power. The Jebusite hilltop on which David founded Jerusalem fascinated and lured empire after empire like a glittering eye. Egyptians, Babylonians, Persians, Greeks, Romans, and others from Crusader to Ottoman Turk and Briton—all fought for Palestine, sometimes with pseudo-religious pretensions. Only for an infinitesimal span, under the Hasomonean dynasty created by the valor of the Maccabees in the second pre-Christian century, did Jewish Palestine eke out a brief second-rate political empire, although Palestine was never, not even for one year, free of Jews. It is no mystery that Armageddon, the war to end all war, was scheduled to be fought in the Valley of Jezreel at the end of time. Even now, geopolitical designs reckon with the Middle East and the sentinel role of Israel-Palestine.

Why do I recall the clashes of vast armies in a recital on sex? Because these imperial phalanxes bore not only their spears and shields into Palestine, but also their superstitions and beliefs, their myths, cults, and rituals about sex, well-nigh obsessive concerns shared as well by the prostrate enemy. When the imperial cohorts withdrew their military equipment to fight elsewhere, or were replaced by a superior force, their cultural equipment remained in the imitative habits of the subjugated and became an integral part of the native way of life. Every invader left behind a residue, just as a receding flood deposits sediment, often to enrich the soil. The result could be foreseen. Jewish sexuality gradually took on the aspect of a conglomerate. Whether in positive acceptance or in negative rejection, it reflected the taboos, terrors and demonic inventions of the Middle East, that fabulously opulent breeding ground for religiosexual folklore. The daily rote of Jewish sex behavior in its formative period may be likened to an Irish stew heated in a cauldron of historic turmoil, each disparate ingredient preserving its inherent form. The core of pagan religion was matriarchal, the mother-image of fecundity exalted to sex goddess, the triumph and glorification of sex as the matrix of life in the womb. Hebraism, on the other hand, revolved around God the Father, the traditional disciplinarian—authority conveyed by law. That image, with a reverential bow to Mary, Mother of God (criticized by some non-Catholics as Maryolatry) has been the basis for Christian teaching with regard to duty, ethics, self-control and sexual austerity. In Jewish liturgy it is a constant, though challenged as male chauvinism by feminists.

The cauldron boiled over at the birth of Christianity, a time of preternatural violence. Alongside the din and death of military incursions by empire builders, crucial changes evolved without blood in the domestic pattern of Jewish living. The simple Bedouin society of biblical patriarchs, embodied in Abraham's desert solitude and his shepherd staff, flowered into communities based on the agriculture of the Canaanites, who tied the fruits of their planting to sex deities and fertility rites. It was then that the Hebrew prophets inveighed, with dire warnings of Divine punishment, against the unconscionable abominations of homosexuality, incest, orgies, bestiality, all reflected in the eighteenth chapter of Leviticus. The vehemence of speech undoubtedly was a contrapuntal echo of the lewd songs and satyric dances performed by Hebrew farmers to insure the sex gods' blessings for what was, after all, their overriding concern—the harvest. Some Israelites, victorious over pagan Canaan in battle, succumbed to the enemy in bed.

The advent of tradesmen, artisans and cash commerce, with accent on towns and cities, marked the third stage in the maturation of Palestine. Merchants, traders, their caravans laden with goods, streamed across the land bringing travelers and temptation from the bazaars and brothels of Mesopotamia, North Africa and the Grecian temples of Aphrodite, Diana of Ephesus and other sex queens of the Mediterranean. Polyglot cultures, contemptuous of the abstemious native "hick" and his Hebrew God, crowded cheek-by-jowl into Jewish cities. Cramped living space, anonymous crowds, poverty and corruption were seemingly inevitable consequences of city life in the Holy Land.

Meticulously appraising every morsel of alien culture in that seething cauldron were the Pharisaic rabbis, dedicated to the task of making the Torah work by integrating its precepts into the daily lives of the Jewish people. These rabbis were determined to shield the masses from the surrounding "obscenities." They were especially wary of Greece; their debates in the Talmud reveal anxiety about moral decay, aggravated by the free-wheeling sexuality of Hellenism. Its infiltration, unmistakably, affected even the language of the Talmud, for it contains many words of Greek origin. Whereas the Roman strode arrogantly bearing the armor and mien of a victory-garlanded soldier, the Greek was clad in the ingratiating raiment and manner of a philosopher, a poet, or a naked, strong-limbed athlete. Occasionally, even women appeared in public unclothed. Greek sculpture idealized the human body with pubic hair; Judaism insisted on modest attire for both sexes. Reacting to Greek nudity in physical sports and sculpture, Jewish scholars intent on raising "a fence to the Torah" interpreted the poetic mating calls between two enraptured lovers in the scriptural Song of Songs as an allegory portraying the love between God and the people of Israel. They identified the sex urge with the *yetzer harah*, the evil inclination, although the term can cover other sinful impulses as well. Rather than the four-letter word "evil" only, the urge also merits the four-letter word "good," because without it man would not establish a family. And Jews were called upon to serve God with the evil impulses no less than with the good. The "debauchery" occasioned by the Greek penchant for boy-love (pederasty) and male priest-prostitutes in sex goddess shrines did not evoke the counter-extreme of total continence.

On the whole, the Hebraic approach to sex stemming from commonsense can be faulted for a measure of internal dissonance and ambiguity. A study of the Bible for what *it* says, not for proof of what *"church"* says, reveals that an Old Testament absolute prohibition of premarital coitus does not exist, neither for the man nor for the woman—and non-commercial sexual contact between a man and an unmarried woman is not considered harlotry. Unquestionably, however, Jewish teaching provides no argument *for* premarital cohabitation. Rabbis of the old school played down sex foreplay in favor of rapidity, while others recommended it for full exercise of preliminary tenderness. Intercourse during pregnancy, contrary to the clear prohibition in the Bible, was permitted, but not obligatory. Tolerance of coitus between singles did not wholly decriminalize hymenal breakthrough prior to the wedding night. Legitimacy, the birthright of all newborn babies in or out of marriage, was denied to the offspring of partners who could not legally wed, such as one or both already bound by marital ties. The denial did not apply to single couples, unless the male was a priest and the female a divorcée. A bastard was barred from marrying into the Jewish fold. A wife was entitled to the full satisfaction of her sexual needs even if her husband had another wife. Married couples could explore the entire gamut of coital techniques, save pre-ejaculation withdrawal, for which biblical Onan was slain by God. A husband was free to have sex with his wife whenever he wished; another authority required her consent. In the Talmud marriage of uncle and niece is allowed, while that of aunt and nephew is forbidden. Qualified approval is given to birth control after two children (a son and daughter suffice for one faction, its rival demands two sons).

Judaism has no fixed, studiously verbalized creed or "articles" about the attributes and nature of God, only His incorporeal unity. Rabbinic writings of centuries past embrace well-nigh every possible concept of deity. Why then expect unanimity on sex from a people notoriously given to individualism? Jewish ambivalence on sex, having clogged the historic stream of consciousness to the present moment, has split the intellectual luminaries of the Jewish rabbinate until today. During one brief span, as history reckons time, one Ibn Ezra viewed sexual activity as a prerequisite for physical and mental health but considered fun sex degrading for a person of enlightenment. Maimonides, greatest of all premodern Jewish philosophers, followed Aristotle in decrying the sense of touch; it supposedly lowered our humanity. Coitus deserved nothing but contempt; this sentiment was abolished only at rare intervals. Circumcision, ordained by the Torah as a sign of God's covenant with Israel, was also intended to strengthen man against sexual desire. In a treatise on the sex act ascribed to a third oracle, Nachmanides, it is endowed with purity and holiness when performed at the right time and with the right intent, because God would not have created genitalia unless they had genuine value in His sight.

The same mildly schizophrenic condition was induced by the trauma of foreign invasion. Palestine Jewry responded to it in different moods. One of these contrasts emerged from a reprise of the final onslaught by the Roman Empire, at almost the very hour when Christian sex morality began to loosen itself from its Jewish umbilical cord. On a recent pilgrimage to the State of Israel, that contrast flashed back into my mind. I relived two polarized reactions to the mighty Roman legions that snuffed out the last flicker of national independence. Masada! My lady and I trod over remnants of siege and suffering on its sun-baked summit for hours, reading on the time-defying stones the story of a three-year message of relentless resistance beamed in blood from that mountain-top fortress to all Palestine, then already prostrate under defeat—until the Roman encampment disgorged its armored killers to breach the walls and find the stiff-necked zealots of Masada slain by their own hands. That story was told by Josephus, the definitive historian of the time. . . .

The other answer to alien defilement was inscribed on parchment preserved in a dark cave of a Judean hill. Qumran's Dead Sea Scrolls! For centuries they slept in silence and serenity. Expert scrutiny of the identifiable Temple Scroll and the scroll of the "War of the Sons of Light and the Sons of Darkness" by Yigal Yadin, Israel's famed scholar-archaeologist, brings forth the authors of those hidden archives. The Essenes, whose ranks may have included John the Baptist, were perhaps the most significant of many ascetic Jewish sects. They countered the Roman legions with intense and passionate faith, a weapon not of this world. Philo, Josephus and various Greek and Roman authors have referred to this mystic community composed of apocalyptists expecting the imminent arrival of the Kingdom of God as "revealers of the secret tidings of redemption."

The rules by which the Essenes lived in the Judean wilderness may seem unrealistic and extravagant by our standards. Granting their premise, however, that this earthly fetid domain would soon vanish and be replaced by heavenly perfection, the Essene regimen of self-abnegation has all the signs of plausibility. Sex and food were abhorred beyond the rudiments of survival; contact with the profane realm "out there," even with the family, could besmirch and thwart the Essenes' "pure" preparedness for the Kingdom. "Gospel" connoted no less than "good news." They refused to take part in services at the Jerusalem Temple because it was ritually "unclean"; they desisted from all bodily functions on the Sabbath, including defecation and urination; they abstained from sexual relations while visiting the "Holy City." Did not Jesus admonish hearers to forsake kin and property to follow him into the Father's presence where there would be "no marriage or giving in marriage"? Ernest Sutherland Bates, in *The Friend of Jesus,* in masterly biblical language traces Judas Iscariot's deliverance of Jesus into Rome's hands to his faith that Jesus would then at last declare himself the Messiah and bring to pass the "New Jerusalem."

Had not the Hebrew prophets promised that national salvation would come in the midst of despair and that a day of mourning and darkness must usher in a day of brightness and the Lord's revelation? This was a time when pessimism and instability had saturated the atmosphere, when Greek and Roman culture had undermined the old ways. Worldliness and cynicism promoted a dual split that extended to human beings, setting woman apart as a source and symbol of evil. Selfish nationalism had pitted Greece against Persia, Rome against Carthage. Humanity and brotherhood motivations were erased by merciless law; nothing existed outside of it. Jews had no concourse with Gentiles, who were conceived to have blemishes both moral and physical. People sought a Messianic Deliverer; every Jewish woman with child hoped that the Messiah would emerge from her womb. A cosmic transformation was at hand that shunned all carnal appetite. By avoiding the very remembrance of woman, man would be purified to await the splendor—the end "day of the Lord."

Born of hostility for the world, these flights to a kind of life denial zeroed in on sex, the summit of all desire. Many early Christian writers even flirted with the idea that sex had never been permissible by extending and intensifying the ascetic laws of the Essenes. In the New Testament, Matthew castigated men who merely looked at women, lustily extolling celibacy over marriage for a people to whom the wedded state had been God's command. Adultery was to be exiled from the mind. The Law of Moses had provided for divorce; in the Book of Mark, Jesus barred divorce and remarriage.

Even the Essenes' rigidly codified flight from the world was moved a giant step farther by the pioneers of the newly born religion. Wild-eyed monks fled to North Africa's desert, lashing their loins with chains, dashing naked into mosquito swamps, applying hot irons to the skin, to black out every bodily craving for woman, all the while aflame with the "fire of lust" for bevies of beckoning beauties fashioned by fantasy. These mad things were not done by madmen out of madness. Rather, they externalized the central concept of the infant creed then seeping into the pagan world; by mortifying the flesh, these born-again ex-libertines would punish it for the sexual proclivities, thereby sentencing mankind to eternal damnation. And the saints and Fathers of the newly risen church confirmed and blessed their mission.

Castration was honored and envied. A priest's tonsure, his skirted cassock to simulate female garb, certified his genital-shorn membership in God's elite. Thousands underwent or performed on themselves the gory ritual, thus topping circumcision. The scholar Origen was merely the most celebrated of all castrates. But since the anatomical excision cut off the source of reproduction, thereby reducing the reservoir of future converts, the church finally forbade the practice.

Zealous Jewish laymen in moments of inter-faith ebullience occasionally "remind" their Christian friends, with deference, that Christianity arose out of Judaism. Since that sweeping proprietary gesture must include sex ethics, the point where Christian doctrine meets the most powerful component of man's personhood, this is a gross error. The life-denying cults that proliferated in Judaism during the "doomsday" decade around the beginning of the Christian Era were like mushrooms growing in dank cellars unheralded and unsung, marginal to the mainstream of Jewish life.

Paul, of course, was a Jew by birth, Saul of Tarsus, a Greek city in Asia Minor; by belief no more Jewish than Karl Marx, despite a suspiciously condescending claim to being "a Pharisee, son of a Pharisee." He was, in contrast to Jesus, a spiritual child of the synagogue whose outlook had been molded by Hellenism. Eager to win recognition of the new faith, he advised the Jews to resign themselves to the brutal tyranny of Rome. From his Greek mentors, he had derived the concept of two warring elements in human nature: body (gross, corruptible, matrix of sin) and soul (immaterial, perfect, eternal). The highest goal was to transcend or root out the physical and live wholly in the spiritual.

Unmarried and, by deduction, presumed to be unbedded, he elevated himself to the ideal state of celibacy. The achievement afforded him such euphoria that he wished all men were "as I," strong enough to attain his lonely and exalted peak. Since humans were of mortal tissue, it was better to let them marry rather than "burn." Weddings therefore, instead of generating joy, sounded a message of sadness and surrender, a grudging concession to the couple's lack of self-discipline. Later, when the church realized its failure to prevent sex altogether, it proceeded to "invent" marriage by clothing it in religious vestments.

An old talmudic legend asked: "How does the Almighty occupy His time now that He has created the world?" And the sages answered, "He sits all day and night arranging marriages." So, quite clearly, matches *are* "made in heaven." That Paul made them in hell is equally clear.

Sex, in reverse, created Christianity. Paul's look at sex and marriage has remained central to Christian faith. He devised a scenario for the drama of salvation; the Fall of Man in the Garden of Eden left on all future generations a taint that is medicable only through acceptance of the Savior. In the writings of the Church Fathers and of medieval theologians, sin was concupiscence, i.e., sex desire. The word occurs over and over again, although the full technical meaning seems hazy. The seminal infection was Paul's fission of the human principle into body-matter and soul-ethereality. To realize potential divinity, it was believed human beings had to cherish and cultivate the soul and purge the body's stench. Like the fission of the atom, this split can and does have potential power by chain reaction; it shatters the psychosomatic holism of the Old Testament, thus marking the spot where Christianity irreversibly departed from its parent Judaism, whose nuclear affirmation is the unity of God and of Man. Paul's dichotomy had antecedents. That a school of historians finds a source of sex negativism in Asia Minor's disenchantment with the Olympian gods of ancient Greece after the death of Alexander the Great in 323 B.C.E. and in the search for certainty during those troubled times does not alter the fact that Christians, indeed Western civilization, has been profoundly influenced in every sector by the Paulinian ukase.

The primordial Jewish and Christian focus on the physical, despite spiritual pretensions to the contrary, is a stubborn fact, as a recent incident illustrates. An eighteen-year-old girl, raped at fourteen, was engaged to a man who, contrary to prevailing male casualness about the subject, insisted that he wanted a virgin wife. He asked a sexologist whether her hymen could be restored, and was advised that operations had been performed in Japan by inserting an artificial hymen of a sheep's membrane. To recreate virginity by such means is illusory, he added, because some women are born with little, if any hymen and even strenuous exercise can break it. It's like granting a divorce only for adulterous *penetration* of the hymen! . . .

Holistic medicine reaffirms, with remarkable therapeutic dividends, the interrelationship of body and mind. "Soul" has become a hackneyed term, often vulgarized into a prefix to "food," "song," "kiss." Does it possess a separate entity? Primitive *Homo sapiens* linked his dream-inhabiting man to a "double," a kind of twin soul, or with his breath. Sex-negative theology has not allocated the soul to any physical place. Is that an improvement? If soul means intuitive subtlety and sensitivity toward all people it is native to and often quickened by sexual intercourse. In rare moments of total aloneness, I have deliberately tried to send through my brain one master thought: my body is *me*, homogenized and intermingled with mind and person, not some thing apart, to be fed, washed, warmed, stroked and cared for. There have been times when I said to myself that I had partially succeeded in the experiment. Was it auto-suggestion or self-hypnosis? I don't know. But I felt wonderful!

To St. Augustine (354–430), greatest of the Latin Fathers and one of the most eminent Doctors of the Western Church, Adam's fall presented an overwhelming certainty of human depravity. Actually, before his mother Monica nudged him into Christian priesthood (in the most illustrious example of maternal cleric making) he had leaned toward the Manichaeans, who saw man as a creature of the Devil. According to Augustine, God's free grace alone can cleanse man of the original sin, perpetrated by Adam and Eve's initiative and transmitted to generation after generation through the procreative act of sex.

Thomas Aquinas, John Duns Scotus, Pierre Abélard and other medieval scholars, notably the Council of Trent in the sixteenth century, tempered original sin in sundry details, but Adam's hereditary legacy persisted forever. Reformers Luther and Calvin reasserted some parts of Augustine's simplistic doctrine. Calvin even urged married men to act as though women did not exist. Doctrinal Catholicism and Protestantism, differing only in degree, eventually agreed that man's nature had been inherently corrupted by Adam's sin.

Mithraism had conquered the Mediterranean basin in the second century. In many respects it resembled Christianity, notably with regard to baptism, intercession, heaven and hell. Both religions focused on the relationship of son to father. In Mithraism, however, the son slays the father, symbolized by a bull, while in Christianity the son submits to the father and the son is slain. Whereas the Christian system idealized submission, inward aggression and masochism, finding virtue in passivity and non-resistance, Mithraism developed around action, conquest, outward aggression and sadism. In Christianity the son must deny his own sexual desires. Mithra's symbol is the sun, the life-giving energy, while Christ's cross symbolizes torture and death. It took only fifty years for Christ to drive Mithra from the Mediterranean. A similar psychological dip into pessimism about this terrestrial world is now enhancing the popularity and growth of born-again fundamentalism, with its attendant crack-down on sexual "excesses."

To the stoic, a tight rein on passion is the road to virtue. Plato spoke of the body and its functions with cool disdain. The Gnostics exalted the mind. "Salvation through knowledge!" they cried. "The natural world is thoroughly evil!" Evil had been injected into the world, they taught, when the gods came down from heaven and had sex with human females, as recorded in Genesis, chapter 6.

Tertullian, standing at the birth of Christian civilization, was the first Church Father literate enough to write in Latin. With his profound sense of man's sexual sinfulness and intense pessimism about redemption, he gained prominence for his attacks on Judaism. He castigated the Jews for rejecting Christ, causing His death, and most of all being lax and sinful. Judaism touted marriage as the only true natural state, sustained by Divine ordinance and capable of obtaining forgiveness of sin. The Talmud states that "he who is twenty and single spends all his days in sinful thoughts, if not in sin; . . . marriage protects from sin; it is the perfect expression of chastity and without it man would be overcome by sexual thoughts and have no time to study Torah."

Tertullian presented to all these views an antithesis. *Mediae-*

val History: the Life and Death of a Civilization, by Norman Cantor, tells us that Tertullian's radical fundamentalism was to remain an undercurrent in Christian thought of succeeding generations, "to worry the more sensitive Church leaders about too easy acceptance of the world and to explode from time to time in puritanical revolts."

May one cogently conclude, then, that a significant and enduring contribution to Christian theology was motivated in part by anti-Jewish reaction to Jewish liberalism? Apparently Tertullian owned up to adultery in his youth; the temptation woman had presented to him may have jeopardized his struggle for chastity and darkened his view of women and sex. I cannot evade the possibility, slight as it may be, that Tertullian's role in the evolution of sex negativism, like that of Augustine, got its steam from the need for purgation of guilt and to escape from the terrible doomsday verdict they were sure God would mete out to mankind.

The awesome longevity of sin-guilt atonement has both fascinated and disgusted me. Every year on the day before Yom Kippur, the Day of Atonement, my father would swing a rooster over his head seven times while reciting penitential prayers for his sins (females used a hen). Then the poor bird was slaughtered and the meat given to people who were poorer than we were. The practice, known by the Yiddish phrase *Shlogen Kapores* (enact atonement), was a flashback to a ceremony performed centuries ago in the period of the Jerusalem Temple. My ancestors would take a goat to a ravine some twelve miles outside the city after having tied a red thread around its head. Then, in the presence of priestly dignitaries, one part of the red thread was tied to a rock and the other between the beast's horns. The symbolic scapegoat was then pushed into the ravine to die for the sins of the worshipers. While all this was happening they and the high priest chanted, "Forgive us, oh God, our sins which we have transgressed before Thee!" This gory rite had originated with the Babylonians and was borrowed by the Children of Israel during their Babylonian exile. Thousands of years later, and despite scornful opposition from intellectual rabbis, my father and other extra-pious Orthodox Jews made a rooster their scapegoat. I wonder whether the sacrificial passion of Jesus Christ might have been a spiritualized enactment of the same scapegoat pattern. . . .

What a Modern Catholic Thinks About Sin is a brave book by John Shea in which he tells me that "the modern Catholic has seen a whole way of life come into question and then go out of style. In his more honest moments he confesses to a mild case of disenchantment. If many Catholic beliefs were shaken in the sixties, sin was positively devastated. Sin has gone underground. Furthermore, according to Shea, the suspicion is that under the pressure of some Freudian law of psychodynamics it will surface again in a bizarre and twisted fashion. The final sentence of his report wrenched me: "What image will help the modern Catholic make sense out of the disordered experiences of his life, which will allow him to think about sin?" This is the cry of a man fragmented in spirit by the ghosts of Augustine and Tertullian. Has Pope John Paul II's indefatigable rescue mission toughened the fiber of his flock for the reinstatement of "sin"?

The most far-reaching of all the Jewish-Christian differences lies in the concept of sin's basic nature. Actually, the nub of Judaism's answer to universal human frailty is that sin, far from being inherent, has no connection whatever with the moral structure of persons. Sin does not emanate from what we are but from what we *do*. The Hebrew word for sin is *het* (guttural "h"), derived from a root meaning "to miss the mark, to stray from the path"; "repentance" is *t'shuvah*, "*return* to the path." By abolishing sin as a fixed state of being shared by all mankind and replacing it with sin as an individual act, we introduce the corrective of personal diversity—and choice. A *condition* of sin is the same for everyone; the *act* of sin, and one's attitude toward it, are exactly the same for none.

Some modern Christian thinkers seek to reinterpret and circumscribe the mandates of an ancient heritage by emendations such as the Protestant surrender of celibacy and the relaxation of the stand against divorce, even for clergymen, although some denominations continue to bar remarriage for the "guilty" party. (Does making matrimony indissoluble increase the security and dignity of the wife and encourage patience born of hopelessness? Maybe!)

Millions of the laity quietly scuttle the lore and law learned in Sunday School. Yet it would be a grave error to dismiss classical Christian sex teaching as antiquarian, inoperative and irrelevant. That categorical note of caution to the radicals is the gist of numerous conversations I have had with church clerics. I often remind them that the Christian conscience has been soaked in the briney juices of that teaching for almost two thousand years, two-fifths of the literate history of mankind. However insistent and loud the assertions of the "liberated" may reverberate, a different message is being sent from the subconscious level. Shea's reference to Freudian pressure is interesting in this connection. The conviction that sex is socially immoral, if not theologically sinful, survives in an inordinate array of legal restraints and conventional gestures as religion in all its principalities still consults the past for moral judgment and ordinance. When economic, social and psychological changes occur, it limps behind. Now the church heroically shores up a sexual code that technology in its ever-growing cycle of dissolution and reconstruction has doomed. I deem it more than plausible that choices are made no longer by institutions, injunctions and individuals swathed in an aura of authority.

What does this augur for a sensitive, open-eyed clergyman? Release from the onerous duty to uphold a theological-sexual credo tied around his neck by a church paralyzed and mute before the prospect of change? Clerics must participate in the struggle for their own liberation. The ministry of organized religion stands bewildered between a world that is dead and a world powerless to be born. Let's bring it to birth. As Lord Byron wrote, "Who would be free, himself must strike the blow."

5

The Sexual Revolution: What Thou Hast Wrought!

Life is a hospital in which each patient believes he will recover if he is moved to another bed.

—Baudelaire

Life in our time has become a sex frustration treatment center in which each patient thinks he or she will find a cure in still another's bed. Bed-hopping seems to be the main achievement and sign of the sexual revolution, although bedroom peregrinations always have been the prerogative of the upper classes in every society.

A revolution can be measured by its radical changes and the areas in which they were wrought. The American Revolution converted dependent colonies into one sovereign state by political-military action; the Industrial replaced individual handiwork and cottage labor with mass production by costly mechanical inventions, thus by necessity creating investment capitalism; the Technological delivered manufacture and communication into the keeping of an electronic maze through scientific research, thus computerizing people and hastening their robotization. The Sexual profoundly altered a most private, personal and portentous world by changing human behavior and attitudes. Not things and money are its province, or artifacts of stone and steel that move on the surface of man's realm, discernible to the senses, but rather the underground, elementary forces beyond his ken or control which shake and shape his life. Powered and manipulated by a mass media scarcely imaginable in past generations, these sexual phenomena, in contrast with the mood and mode of the erotic in my youth, are truly "phenomenal."

Freedom is the code word and banner of the sexual revolution. Freedom of the human being from millenial control by the church of his/her most intimate and crucial relationships. That control was attained by a simple recipe: take sexual passion-performance, and irresistible desire in practically all people, call it "sin" punished by God throughout post mortem eternity, claim exclusive access to God as proved by Holy Writ, then offer God's forgiveness and salvation in return for obedience to the sex laws transmitted by Him to the church for enforcement and full support of its ordinances and activities. Such a formula puts guilt into men's souls—and into every bedroom the admonitory presence of preacher, policeman and psychiatrist.

A typical scenario of the fifties, enacted during my routine consultation with a couple to finalize wedding arrangements, proceeded at once to vital statistics. After the prospective groom had given me *his* telephone number, I would lower my head, and keep my eyes glued to the marriage license and mumble, "Now *your* phone number, Miss?"; then I would shrink into my chair to give her time for a whispered "Shall we tell him?"

In the sixties that delicate *pas de deux* was no longer relevant; they shared the same phone and residence; I took it for granted. Often the imminent bride, who usually planned to be clad in a white wedding gown, a symbol of virginity, proffered the information herself in a tone she might have used to comment on my study's decor or the weather.

Whereas the first cannonade for a free non-marital alternative to marital rectitude was heard with horror, now an explosive burst for it would be termed an antedeluvian relic. Cohabitation of the heterosexual young has joined the "old hat" category. One mother who interviewed me about her daughter's nuptial plans was wracked with anxiety. "They are *not* living together, rabbi, and it bothers me! She can't really know the man until she has slept with him!" I reminded her that the Hebrew verb in the Bible for having sex meant "to know," asking myself later if the future bride might have skirted premarital cohabitation just *because* it was the "in" thing to do. The worried mother was a spiritual cousin of another who booked a hotel room for her daughter and boyfriend so that they could have sex together, she for the first time. "With dignity and security, not off somewhere in her car," she said, adding, "They'll do it anyhow! Why not give my girl something nice and decent to remember?" Even the elderly are doing it, although in the United States social security benefits of widows are no longer substantially reduced by remarriage. The economic incentive therefore has disappeared to make way for more fundamental drives—despite opposition from children who may resent the possible loss of inheritance or refuse to review the apparent premise that their own conception had been immaculate.

Contrary to pietistic belief, cohabitation without a paper certificate or priestly blessing is not doomed to be casual, shallow, easily begun and easily ended. The tearful tales of a partner's walk-out I have listened to were no less devastating than a session in the divorce court. Sexual congress does not necessarily rely for its mystic meaning on legally automatic security. And even the pretense let alone the substance of moral opprobrium has been abandoned.

Recently, a thirteen-year-old girl wrote a letter to a newspaper question-and-answer sexologist. "My boyfriend wants sex," she said. "I love him and don't want to lose him. Should I try it?" Here is the answer she received from the columnist: "I want you to realize sex desire; it's a wonderful part of nature. But your first experience should be a gift of shared love, not a surrender to pressure and fear of losing a guy. Learn about contraception methods and use one or more every time you have intercourse. And there is much to learn about sharing totally: your physical need for release can also be taken care of by self or mutual manual stimulation." Sage counsel, but nary a word to a girl in early adolescence about saving herself for Mr. Right, preserving her virginity—or morals!

A correct estimate of the sexual revolution's direction must lead me to Sandstone, a project started not long ago in Southern California. Affluent couples were ushered into a thickly carpeted oriental-style seraglio for group sex. The leash of restraint and suburban respectability was cut, libidos liberated, inhibitions shed. Do what you want, with whoever is willing; anything goes, all together. A high weekly fee assured elitism. In "decadent" Greece and Rome the participants might have been blasé, sex-wise patricians and talented prostitutes who knew the joy potential of every muscle. Sandstone's paying guests were nervous tyros who soon learned from one another.

Alex Comfort agrees with psychiatrists that "non-exclusive monogamy" in which a couple condones each other's extramarital adventures is healthier than jealousy and subsequent divorce. A woman who suggests a threesome with a second female fancied by her man actually gives him a present, not the least the assurance that she is secure and has no need for jealousy; both enable the third party to share their intimacy and sexual know-how. A foursome creates a closer, more sensual bond with one's mate through the presence of another couple. In arithmetical progression we arrive at "an attempt to revive interpersonal relationships in a world short of kin, where the extended family is confined to Jews, Italians and Chinese."

Dr. Comfort expatiates further that the former fear of sensuality has now shifted to "the re-examination of fidelity, religio-social dogmas, personal feelings, fantasy needs and the deeply proprietorial attitudes enjoined on husband and wife by the priest, the neighbors, folklore and the attorney." During my sojourn in Berkeley and San Francisco I was presented with numerous bids to "private, quiet parties for group sex" from young, middle-class, often college-bred white-collar comrades I had come to know and like. I was never bored enough, nor sufficiently emptied of aesthetic sensitivity, to succumb. But fantasy has occasionally emptied my mind of all else except the far-out release group sex might offer, a thorough mental house cleaning reminiscent of pagan fertility rites. . . .

In my high school days I never saw a pregnant girl and I don't think anyone of us could have coped with the sight of a classmate's distended belly. When pregnancy did occur, the bearer of so dramatic a message, having fallen into disgrace, would quietly withdraw from school. The boys in the poolroom never seemed to tire of jeering about "the thin girl who swallowed an olive and had to leave town." Now the one-million-a-year mathematics of pregnancies that occur between fifteen and nineteen are a massive and scary blot on the revolution's image because of their accompaniments: statistical upward leaps in venereal disease (the female's pill having displaced the male's protective condom), infant mortality, still-births, congenital defects, maternal deaths, school drop-outs and soaring welfare costs—not to speak of premature fathers facing broken careers, emotional trauma and parental guilt-tripping. Little research has been directed to the frequently demoralizing problems of these young men. Another risk was recently imposed by the U.S. Supreme Court's edict that an eighteen-year-old boy can be charged with statutory rape if he and a fully cooperative sixteen-year-old girl make love on a secluded park bench under moonlight. Eighty percent of sexually active North American girls frown on contraceptives for various reasons, chiefly because, as one said, "I don't want the boy to know I expected it"; nearly three out of ten become pregnant (and a few of them think it's "wonderful"); marriage vows precede the crèche for only 35 percent; patrons of the "educated guess" further reckon that 59 percent carry the fetus to term; in Nevada, from 1975 to 1978, there was a 34 per cent rise in adolescent pregnancy and a 5 per cent increase in adolescent population.

These statistics define a critical problem of which teenagers are high on the totem-pole of *victims*. Topping the list of perpetrators of this problem is our American society. High school students in America's affluent suburbs view their lives as empty and meaningless, get their kicks from sex and drugs and consider school "unpaid labor." This is the thrust of a 259-page report released by the Oxford University Press in late 1979 based on interviews at a high school in a town some thirty miles from New York. The author of the survey, Professor Ralph W. Larkin of Rutgers University, furnished the following additional details: Watergate made the kids of both sexes suspect authority and each other; both sexes regard virginity as less than a virtue for girls and a stigma for boys; they are being forced by default into the next generation of cogs in the corporate structure, learning what they have been taught is the supreme "good": to consume, keep their eyes on the ball and get ahead in a world where all that counts is money; they are apathetic about everything but their desires because "there's nothing to look up to."

At the other end of the socioeconomic ladder, jobless black teenagers (the largest proportion of unemployed in the United States) may turn to an assortment of sexual acts to wrest some sense of identity from the hopelessness of their situation. I cannot forget one remark made to me by a black teenager shining my shoes on on a street corner in New York not long ago. His finely chiseled features allowed me to ply him with questions. "How do you spend your time when you're not working?" His eyes seemed to draw closer to each other, and the laughing voice slipped down into his chest. "Workin'?" The word had the snap of a challenge. "Workin'? Man, I ain't had a steady job in my life. If my ma wasn't a maid in a house on Park Avenoo, we'd all go hungry *all* the time! I dropped school to shine your shoes. The only time I feel really good is when I'm fuckin'. Then I don't care about nuthin', an' it don't cost nuthin'."

Will sex education soften the acerbity and peril of sexual anarchy at either end of these extremes? The pupils it would instruct already know more than they can healthfully absorb. Besides, sex education is being shunned like the plague by sections of our community who will not come to terms with an environment that pours sexual stimuli into every cranny, cranium and crotch. Nor can the flood be held back by sonorous and censorious "platitudes in stained-glass attitudes." Clerical exhortations to tailor teenage sexuality in the chastity belt design of the old morality cast the preacher in the role of King Canute shouting "Halt!" to the ocean tide; it is scarcely more relevant than the Colorado footprints of a dinosaur. I recently heard a minister orate at a Conference on Delinquency, "These youngsters must be taught discipline! That'll stop 'em!"

Teenaged girls founder on the rock of ignorance, defiance of parents, delusions of grandeur, romance of motherhood, instant ecstasy, peer group pressure—and the stale, shallow, Hollywood-style apotheosis of "love." How often have I heard these bemused young creatures say, "It's all right to go all the way when you're in love." Yet the same forces whose alliance against flexibility and liberalism in any form have helped swing the pendulum to revolt now refuse to condone a practical, competently devised and supervised program of sex teaching in the elementary public school curriculum. Middle-class parents, as a rule, are woefully inept to cope with the family crisis; in many instances they find themselves unable to engage in frank communication with *each other*, possibly because they are confused about their own sexuality. Don't castigate the young—educate them before they are old enough to learn on the street! The lethargy, or worse still the conspiracy, of self-chosen defenders of our youth's innocence— already corroded by society—must be challenged by the clergy. It is the entrenched bigotry of church fundamentalists that preserves the blight of teenage know-nothing-ism. The damsel who pops the pill into her mouth a split second before she pulls down her panties may be more than an invention.

Ann Landers, speaking at a meeting arranged by a temperance society, and realizing that the day had passed when teenagers' chastity could be urged on moral or religious grounds, reasoned from concern for their well-being when she said that an intact hymen is a safeguard against venereal disease and prevents loss of the thrill of marriage. (Why, Ann, do jaded ex-prostitutes often make excellent wives?) Despite charisma and celebrity, she did not convince her youthful audience, most of whom were church-affiliated. In reply, the kids took the offensive by arguing that young people risk being forced into premature marriages by their need of physical sex blocked and aggravated by protracted virtue.

I recall reading an exchange of letters in Ann Landers' column that revealed support, rather than doubt, of the sexual revolution. A woman of thirty-six had been dating a married man, but she refused to bed with him. Then he was transferred out of town. Although she had rebuffed him because "I did not want him to think I'm a tramp," she was tired of a state unleavened by coitus. "I want to know what it's like to have a man—before I die, I want a little fun." What should she do? Ann, not wanting to be the prissy moralist, replied, "It's wrong only if you hurt yourself or someone else, or if you think it's wrong." Bravo! Ms. Landers.

What has the sexual revolution done for or to the mystique of intercourse? A campus incident may offer an answer. An "I love you!" gasped by a college swain to his girl in the throes of orgasm had pushed her to the edge of a nervous breakdown. They had lain down in a meadow at the edge of town. "It was a perfect sun-lit day and all was unbelievable joy until those three little words shattered the spell," she subsequently related. "I shoved him away and ran. Now I can't study or sleep. The emotional involvement was too much for me; the physical act alone made sense."

Here is an unconditional option. A formula formerly despised as sheer carnality now has become the guiding credo for those devotees of the sexual revolution who wish to dedicate their talents to the perfection of sex as an art. The Christian theological tenet which exalts love without sex is, for most mortals, futile; sex without love, or something near it, is dehumanizing. Emotional entanglement, they say, can dislodge sex from its pleasure pinnacle and encumber it with extraneous considerations. Isn't that the ultimate degradation of sexuality wearing the mask of freedom?

Sex lives and burns for itself alone. The passion for freedom from sex control by powers outside ourselves has reached out to freedom from our own impulses. "Keep your cool" is more than an idle, admonitory piece of slang; it has become the code word for a "Me" generation seeking to side-step the pitfalls of getting involved while threading through the morass of interpersonal relations. Instead of a vertical relationship with one, there are horizontal relationships (in both senses) with multiple partners in the art, literally, of *making* love, not the art of *loving*. In a single-purpose determination to fend off even pleasurable enmeshment with someone outside the self, an obsessive individual actually *sacrifices* freedom to enjoy sex maximally for the "security" of enjoying it only moderately, below the top-most rung: a sharing, caring, full-bodied relationship. Lovers who traverse the *total* spectrum cast such cowardice into the ash-heap; the sexual revolution has fished it out. The growing reluctance of a cadre of militantly independent women to marry may spring from a resolve "to be free," which when achieved often translates into "being lonely."

A diverting by-product of and commentary on the sexual revolution during the 1976 race for the Republican presidential nomination was Betty Ford's admission that she would not be surprised if daughter Susan had an affair. Whereupon Nancy Reagan took the tack that non-marital liaisons and cohabitation were a superficial escape from intimacy, which is the fruit and apex of a marriage. That Nancy's politely tangential riposte to Betty's casual speculation about Susan's sex life did not balloon into a political issue between Jerry and Ronnie can be credited, I surmise, to the alarmed vigilance and political sagacity of the Republican National Committee.

In 1979 a bill to reduce the age of consent from sixteen to thirteen was submitted to the law-makers of New Jersey, after official testimony had been obtained that the vast majority of females of that age group share sex activities with peer males rather than with "older" men who may be accused of exploitative seduction. Bitter controversy ensued as parents, evidently spurning the very thought of their young daughters' sex indulgence, were impervious to and stood steadfast against data recording its rapid upswing among kids below sixteen. The legislative body's aim was to remove the onus of illegality and its statutory offense complications from both the girl and the boy. The sixteen-year age of consent had applied only when the male was not more than four years older, to keep out "older molesters" (an outdated and discredited cliché). I would not have believed the thirteen-year figure had I not been told by an eleven year old that her social set liked to roll on the floor in darkened rooms of their rotating home sites—boys and girls exploring each other.

We preachers tend to overlook the fact that sexual precocity is preceded by physiological precocity. The average age of puberty for North American girls drops about six months in every decade, some reaching it on or before their eleventh birthday. Judaism assigns a boy's maturity to his thirteenth year by celebrating the Bar Mitzvah rite of passage. A similar ceremony for girls has become traditional in non-Orthodox circles to avoid pre-playing, thus down-playing, Confirmation at fifteen. Sheri Tepfer, Director of Planned Parenthood, notes that new pressures overtake early breasted young women. A century ago puberty normally thrust little girls into womanhood between fifteen and seventeen, and marriage often followed within two years in every echelon of society. Between 1972 and 1976, by contrast, 25 percent of women under twenty-five who got married already had borne a child or were pregnant on their wedding day. Is marriage at thirteen not utterly irrational in a developed industrial economy that places no premium on the multiplication of young farm hands? On the average, North American girls say "I do" at about twenty-one; that early teenage females are supposed to postpone marital deflorescence for a whole decade instead of a couple of years is a fiat of arithmetic, combined with the immovable fact that sex stimulants purr seductively from every pore of their social ambience.

In a book entitled *Sex With Love—A Guide for Young People*, Eleanor Hamilton advanced a daring proposal to plug the dikes against the teenage pregnancy flood. The author is loaded with credentials: sex therapist, marriage counselor, licensed psychologist and author of four previous volumes on sexuality; she also is a grandmother. Her proposed method to improve on the old "necking, petting, not going all the way" customs of the young is by seeking parental collaboration. She maintains that parents must accept the sexuality of their children and *encourage* them to have the right kind of sex in the right kind of environment by allowing teenagers non-coital sex up to and including orgasm in protected surroundings safe from muggers, "Sons of Sam," nosey cops and feckless contraceptive-neglecting haste in the back seat of a parked car. She stresses, in fact, the necessity for security, seclusion and uninterrupted time of *home*, with the knowledge and consent of parents who are expected to trust their teenaged children to handle themselves and each other. Mrs. Hamilton concedes that complete intercourse is too great a responsibility for persons under seventeen. But if the conditions of the contract are clearly stated in advance—an essential requirement that might try the poise and patience of the most urbane parents—the pressure to "make out" will be considerably lessened. Biological determinism—orgasm and detumescence—can be relied on, I surmise, to do the rest, bringing the action to a relaxed and satisfied denouement.

A positive response to such radical innovations would mark a miraculous overturn of American sexual fixations, and general acceptance of the Hamilton program could reduce to a minimum teenage VD, pregnancies and peer pressure. The teen years accumulate a storehouse of sexuality, coitus or not, and the ten years between female maturity and marriage *are* too long for any bodily process to go on without functioning; no one *should* have to lay his or her sexuality in cold storage for a decade. Masturbation may be an ugly word for a pleasant thing; some teenagers may find it a more acceptable outlet and feel a deeper sense of relief. Teenage graduates of the Hamilton course might be better prepared for good-lover full-scale status with a number of partners at seventeen. They *deserve* to enjoy the fun and tenderness of sex without the worries; hugging and touching *are* good for them.

Forty percent of the non-chaste kids in the thirteen to nineteen bracket (estimated at 52 per cent) lost their "innocence" in the parental home, as reckoned by one researcher—without the benefit of a familiar, beloved environment or the wonder and sensitivity parental cooperation might have engendered. Robert H. Rimmer, well-known apostle of the new era, links sex and sorrow as hand-maidens for youngsters; he advocates the creating of an environment in which restraint would be the norm until approximately seventeen; after that age they are to be assured the opportunity for full sexual expression with social approval. "Then," Rimmer avers, "we could finally relate chastity and virginity to the physical facts of life. Instead, we flounder and try to reconcile the reality with outmoded values that never can be re-established in a technological society!"

Whether Hamilton's or Rimmer's schemata for teenage sex are so naive or so far removed from the middle-American mind that any attempt at evaluation is irrelevant, only the future will tell. I regret that Margaret Mead has departed the arena of debate on the subject. In her classic *Coming of Age in Samoa,* based on the first of her many expeditions into primitive cultures, she proved that the Samoans' easy attitude toward adolescent sexuality made the passage of their teenagers to maturity far less turbulent than teenagers in the barren bosom of civilization must experience by default.

Although revolutionaries such as Hamilton and Rimmer tread far ahead of their times, there are clergymen who do think far in advance of church doctrine and laity. In March 1980 a task force on sexuality authorized by the United Church of Canada, that country's largest Protestant denomination, announced the completion of a 100-page guide that could become the basis for official policy by 1983. It was to be debated at the church's General Council the following August before being sent to individual congregations. But Reverend Robin Smith, the chairman of the task force, ruefully warned, "We'll get clobbered. Insecurity has its final focus in religion. People want iron-clad guarantees." The report's departure from unqualified adherence to the rules explains his fears. "Christians who don't believe in emergent norms (*viz.*, changing moral standards) don't believe in the Holy Spirit who guides the church into all truth. Sexual morality has to keep up with the social sciences. God speaks to us through them as well as through the Bible. . . ." What did the social sciences tell Reverend Smith's task force? "People should take responsibility for their own sexuality. . . . All sexual relations must be liberating, mutually supportive and joyous. . . . Mature, self-accepting homosexuals may become ministers if they meet the usual requirements. . . . Masturbation is a normal part of human sexuality as long as it does not harden into a preoccupation with one's self. . . . Sex-intercourse may be right for singles under certain circumstances. . . . Everyone has sexual fantasies; to deny them completely is unhealthy." The brave reverend was right about the "clobbering" the task force would receive. More than 150 letters poured into church headquarters, 95 percent of them hostile. Summary immasculation, if not total demise, will probably be the fate of his report before the General Sessions take place.

The fact that private clerical views on sex outrun the dubious, respectability-haunted semi-liberalism of congregants is clearly shown in interviews conducted by a University of Nevada student with leaders of the three faiths. This opinion gap became a public scandal when Dr. Charles Trentham, the senior minister of First Baptist Church in Washington, D.C., was fired for dating the not-yet-divorced daughter of Jimmy Carter's Sunday School teacher. (Jimmy avoided the scheduled after-services wordbout by absenting himself from worship at the church on that acrimonious Sunday.)

Ruth Carter Stapleton, Jimmy's sister, an evangelical practitioner of "theological therapy" (faith healing), is a charismatic blend of Southern-belle pulchritude and piquancy with Southern Baptist piety. Her pronouncements can qualify as authentic symptoms of change in the sexological views of Christian clerics. Some interview excerpts from the lips of the prestigious clergy-woman emit a strong scent of dissent; she defends almost belligerently her departure from denominational roots. "Sensuality is a God-given thing. . . . Jesus wants us (women) to be beautiful for Him. . . . The sex drive is ultimately the power of God. . . . Sometimes affairs are the product of the fact that after you have tasted of God's love you become more aware of your need of love." About ministers who criticized her she snorted, "Many of them are borderline homosexuals who fear all women because they never did develop strong male images."

Evidently, if Ruth speaks for it, the "church" shows signs of awakening to the need of change for the survival of its oft-emphasized mission to influence human conduct. The Lutheran Church of America, in its own words, "seeks to respond understandingly to persons who enter into relationships which do not demonstrate a covenant of fidelity." In some churches premarital counseling sees in conjugal intercourse a source of pleasure to women as well as to men, and an enrichment of their relationships apart from procreation. Under church auspices, explicitly erotic films produced by San Francisco's National Sex Forum, founded by a United Methodist minister and launched at Glide Memorial Church, have been shown at sexual attitude reassessment seminars. An inter-faith statement approved by acknowledged representatives of Protestantism, Catholicism and Judaism warns that sex education must be shaped and guided by our Judeo-Christian teaching of God as the source of values in human behavior. Leon Smith, Director of Education for Marriage and Family Life of the United Methodist Church, glowingly pictures the endeavors of church bodies to develop full curriculum resources for sex education. In 1975-76 United Methodists planned to reach six thousand young people and parents, but Leon Smith in his optimism did not reckon with a host of Bible-thumping Protestants; these phalanxes of the "only true faith" are rapidly expanding in numbers, influence and aggressiveness, while church liberalism limps behind with lassitude and inertia.

The tradition-bound church legitimized sex only for procreation. Bowing to almost universal opinion and practice, some progressive elements grudgingly condoned pleasure as a supplementary aim. We live in an age of sexual affluence never before enjoyed by any living species. The Damocles sword of impregnation has been broken by the wide use of medically approved contraceptives; endless opportunities for genital excitement and expression have become available, and the miracles of electronic communication have not allowed this coital abundance to languish in obscurity and disuse. Now test-tube babies proclaim procreation without coitus, limiting pleasure for the doner to the incidental masturbatory sensation of providing semen. One of the many revolutionary effects of this breakthrough has already surfaced in a highly publicized project to produce a master race by fertilizing the ova of carefully selected females with the sperm of Nobel Prize winners. The ultimate reverberations of the test-tube baby's whimper are unimaginable. . . .

Although a hopeful trend away from rigid rules of sex behavior can be discerned in liberal clergy circles, the church has shown no convincing sign of compromise with its assurance that sexual intercourse can be invested with sanctity solely insofar as it reflects and implements their respective concepts of God's inhibiting will. Despite ecclesiastical manifestos to the contrary, however, sacredness is imparted to the junction of penis and pudenda by the degree to which it mirrors an authentic, mutually exalting relationship *between two persons.* That is the appropriate setting for and the basic justification of sexual intimacy at every level. Does moderation in official church policy declare an armistice in their ministers' conflict of interest? Evidence of that is not discernible. The cult of individual self-expression, the blurring of distinction between cleric and layman, tightly reined contempt for desiccative "articles of faith," widespread familiarity in once-sacrosanct church premises of sin-loaded words, startling statistics of almost extinct campus virginity, the relativity-of-morals principle retrieved from ethics class at college, the awareness of ecclesiastical power ploy in the guise of pietistic "don'ts"— all exacerbate the cleric's unease. Yet, whatever the apologetic, tenuous, official moves toward elasticity may be, the clergy still will be expected to "make like" a stonewall for the old virtues.

Many questions must nag the church. How to interpret "loving the other" when a bewildering variety of totally new erotic postures and alignments are being bred by the removal of barriers to make fun sex the center of maximal intention? When is love that "Christian love" the church has been fervently expounding for almost two thousand years? For Christians who espouse a love ethic, I would suspect this is a problem.

How does organized religion propose to deal with unmarrieds? Is abstinence or sublimation to be its only advice for the singles in our culture? Single females are victims of gross neglect by agencies claiming to assuage loneliness and isolation. Can non-celibate communal living arrangements win favor as acceptable alternatives to church-mandated deprivation? A statistician has charged that church sex guidance programs spend 95 percent of their energy on the five premarital years and 5 percent on 95 percent of the individual's sexual lifespan. Rustum and Della Roy in *Honest Sex* contend that in the coming years patterns will have to be found that are consistent with the highest Christian values, yet lead to "the expansion of the erotic community *beyond* the married pair."

The church's once-unexceptional policy of ostracizing homosexuals has been replaced in some instances by studied efforts at "understanding" them without condescension. Catholicism's hard-line attitude toward sex was flouted in 1977 by a task force of the Catholic Theological Society of America. Its report, entitled "Human Sexuality: New Directions in American Catholic Thought," published by the Paulist Press, practically reverses church standards by denying that traditionally outlawed forms of sexual activity are "intrinsically evil," and by spotlighting personal decision in all sex relations. Although the report does not claim to be the official policy of the CTSA, presumably it does reflect the judgment of most of the society's one-thousand seminary and university professors. In a Catholic context the specific positions that were taken sound like a tocsin-call to all out theological war. Here they are: There is no objective "natural law" confining sex to procreation; the purpose of sex is creative growth and integration of the human personality; the criterion of sex morality is self-liberation, enrichment of others, honesty, faithfulness, social responsibility and joy; contraception, sterilization and artificial insemination are justifiable after careful study; close, stable friendship between homosexuals is a positive good; intercourse need not be restricted to marriage; couples themselves must learn to draw the lines defining the morality of extramarital sex and condemnation of every departure from premarital chastity.

Predictably, the task force report evoked a storm of anger. In New York City a coalition calling itself Catholics United for the Faith petitioned bishops to revoke recognition of the CTSA until all the theologians who supported its demarche had resigned or were expelled; the Provost of Notre Dame dismissed the study as the "work of persons who lack real scholarly standing"; Catholic University theologians labeled it a weak effort to free people from guilt. CTSA's president, Sister Agnes Cunningham, defending the manifesto, said, "Because it saw procreation as the primary purpose of sexual intercourse, Christian tradition has denied the sexual nature of anyone who was not married."

In 1976, on papal order, the Congregation for the Doctrine of the Faith issued a six-thousand-word declaration criticizing theologians, psychologists and churchmen who challenged traditional sex morality. That peremptory polemic against all and sundry who challenge Catholicism's tight rein on sex might have been launched selectively with an aim at priests who, with sporadic lay support, have dared to articulate the most formidable and visible internal male discontents in modern church history. Mandatory celibacy is high on the agenda for sexual revolution. Remonstrance against the ban on priestly activation of their sexuality in any form may be said to have received impetus, as I view it, from Pope John XXIII, the spiritual titan of this century. He once confided to Étienne Gilson, the distinguished philosopher, "Would you like to know what distresses me most? . . . The thought of those young priests who bear so bravely the burden of ecclesiastical celibacy causes me constant suffering. For some it is a martyrdom. . . . It seems to me as if I were—hearing a kind of plea . . . many voices demanding that the Church free them from this burden." This statement still fills the hearts of many Roman Catholics with astonishment and delight. After pointing to celibacy as neither a dogma nor something imposed by Scripture, he remarked that with one stroke of the pen he could change a practice that was a sacrifice the church had freely imposed on itself.

Unfortunately, the beloved Holy Father ascended the papal throne thirty years too late (not only to brake Hitler's ascent to power and perhaps prevent World War II, as I believe he might have done) and died too soon to prevent celibacy from becoming an item of unfinished business among the church's consecrated servants. His successor, Pope Paul VI, on the other hand, told the fourth session of the Vatican Council that celibacy is non-negotiable, and Pope John Paul II insists that it remain the central identity-creating lifestyle of every man ordained to the priesthood. In a thirty-five-page letter dated April 9, 1979, addressed to priests throughout the world, he wrote, "A priest must be unique, apart, a father to all. . . . He must obey vows of celibacy to death," affirming that Roman Catholics had the right to expect this fidelity from their pastors, who commit themselves to that renunciation of sexuality "with full awareness and freedom" after long training. . . . Efforts to "secularize the priesthood and bring it up to date" must be denounced. Against the slogan "Let us be first of all women," recited by recalcitrant nuns in Baltimore, he posed a password, "Let us all be Christian." Pope John Paul II thus rebuked all attempts to lift, or at least to loosen, the celibacy edict. At the same time, Vatican officials issue bitter attacks on the evasive "Third Way"—conjugal relations without marriage—adopted by some priests (Jesuits particularly, I am informed).

There have been mild evasions, usually offering a gain for the church. In the Fall of 1976 Pope Paul VI appointed an Eastern Rite bishop as Auxiliary in Passaic, New Jersey; but the publicity accompanying this appointment omitted all reference to the bishop's family. (The Eastern Rite does not require celibacy of priests.) A year later two married Anglican priests from California, who had broken with the Episcopal Church over its 1976 decision to ordain women, were admitted to the Roman Catholic priesthood with the provisos that they would not be permitted to remarry after a wife's demise, that single men had to take the customary vow of celibacy and that no married priest could become a bishop. This startling Vatican decision clearly breached the ramparts of Anglicanism for the long dreamed of ingathering of its neo-Catholic contingent and ultimate reunion. But a spokesman of the Sacred Congregation for the Doctrine of the Faith angrily brushed aside interpretations of Rome's gesture calling it a "precedent-shattering breakthrough with enormous implications." That interpretation was made by a spokesman of Archbishop John R. Quinn, president of the National Conference of Catholic Bishops.

Whatever the ramifications of two married men welcomed into the Catholic priesthood may have been, I think Archbishop Quinn's commentary has great significance as a barometer of the underplayed stormy weather swirling about the celibacy issue within the church. Dutch Catholic hierarchy members under

Bernard Cardinal Alfrink dared suggest that celibacy imposed a downright sinful condition for priesthood; priests should be able to choose between it and marriage. . . . Nearly one-third of the entire Capuchin order, the largest in Catholicism, stated in replies to a questionnaire that they would welcome "intimate relations with women"; they approved violence, if necessary, to foster social justice. . . . *The National Catholic Reporter*, published by laymen, carried a priest's article blaming celibacy for "neurotic and twisted lives" among clergy not suited to it and called on Pope Paul and the Vatican Council to permit marriage. America's powerful Jesuit magazine had charged that discussion of celibacy by a discontented minority created the impression that celibates were neutotic and could only bring moral confusion. Several theologians argued that vocations to priesthood and to celibacy do not necessarily coexist in the same person and that a married priest can more fully enter the life of the parish. . . . Groups of priests in Italy and Brazil asked release from an "intolerable burden" which, they said, had no basis in Scripture or natural law. . . . An Indiana state-wide questionnaire even revealed a division between the two camps on celibacy. . . . Latin American padres often marry and have families: it's a way of life. . . . In Los Angeles 315 nuns of the century-old Immaculate Heart of Mary Convent were offered dispensation from their life-long vows of poverty, chastity and obedience (as the lesser of two evils) by Pope Paul VI so that they might continue to serve the church in a lay status with their extensive properties and the freedom to implement their own ideas, including marriage. . . . The vice-president of the National Coalition of American Sisters exulted, "The days of starched wimples and downcast eyes are behind us. Look up! Don't wait for orders at every stop." . . . Thousands of applications for exemption from celibacy vows, it is claimed, are on file in the Vatican. . . .

"The Church will not take a look at celibacy until or unless it is forced to it by empty pastorates," was the dictum of an exemplary Catholic periodical. Estimates of the resignation tally are variable. Are sixty thousand, a frequently quoted total number, enough to warrant a review of celibacy's effect on the church's health? I count a half-dozen resigned Fathers and several Sisters among my profoundly admired friends. Most "religious" refugees presumably have doffed cassock and habit to marry; many requested and received laicization that allows them to retain the status of priests in the church without permission to perform the specific functions of priesthood. Pope John Paul II instituted a policy whereby petitions to be laicized are inspected with such minute attention that comparatively few pass the test. The Vatican, the grapevine tells me, asks priests applying for laicized status to write letters confessing sex perversion, "evidence" that they were neither true priests nor unfrocked by their own volition.

In my pre-seminary days, every Irish Catholic mother in my home town boasted a son, or at least a nephew, who was studying for the priesthood. According to a recent survey 66 percent of Roman Catholic families would be "disappointed" if a son were to enter the church. A white-haired priest with decades of consecrated service behind him lamented to me the scarcity of young priests. "Men of sixty, widowers, are taking the vows to keep the church alive!" "Why the crisis," I asked. He clenched his teeth in obvious discomfort, then replied, "Well, it's . . . sex! Today most youngsters in high school and college have experienced sex, and can't visualize doing without it. They even can't believe *we* can! One of them said to me, 'Father, you *must* be getting it! You *have* to.'" That Catholic youth's diagnosis of his priest's libido may also explain why Dr. John B. Wain, a Catholic physician with a wide convent practice, reported that there was "too much neurosis among the 'religious' (nuns)." Shall we attribute the malaise to the supposition that the religious life has a certain appeal for the emotionally and mentally unstable, as Joan M. Laxan suggests in *Convent Life*? Although my acquaintance with nuns is limited, I believe they are persons of remarkable poise, maturity of spirit and humane values. Yet, one said to me, "Respect our womanhood without the necessity to be sexually active." Not so long ago, nuns teaching in high school, I am told, used to advise girls to shun patent leather shoes that reflected their underwear, to sprinkle talcum powder in the bathtub and to remember that white reminded men of bed sheets. In some orders the consecration ceremony for a nun includes a ring and other wedding appurtenances to seal her conjugal marriage to Christ.

An ex-priest, now happily married after two marital collapses due to his "sexual immaturity," regaled me with details that almost outran my capacity to believe about the warnings "crammed into our guts about sexual crime and punishment in parochial school. Transfixed I would sit and stare for hours at a statue of the Virgin Mary in the hope that her purity would sink into my soul and help me stop masturbating."

Jesus obliquely acknowledged individual choice in the phrase, "Let those accept it (*viz.*, celibacy) who can." Certainly everyone *can't*! Some servants of the church, male and female, seem unable to handle it. Symptoms of that congenital "defect" (absence of a gift for celibacy) may assume radical proportions, e.g., homosexuality and alcoholism. If the widely rumored retort of a highly placed Catholic prelate in Toronto was more than incidental pique, the church has been myopic. When asked by a reporter whether he thought celibacy was a potential cause of alcohol addiction, his response did him neither justice nor honor. "There are drunken men out there who *do* have wives!"

The Apostles were all married, it appears, except perhaps John, and so were bishops in the early stages of Christianity, if credence can be attributed to Paul's advice (in Timothy) that a man who is to be a bishop must be faithful to one wife. Enforcement of the edict against sexual activity in any form, first issued in 386 C.E., has met with resistance through the years. For example, the Second Lateran Council in 1139 found it necessary to invalidate the marriages of clergy in sacred orders. Though now enshrined in Canon 1072 of the church law code, it is *not* immune to papal revocation.

Does a shadow of doubt hang over the celibate state of Jesus? The lack of indisputable evidence in the New Testament has freed literary imaginations to speculate. D. H. Lawrence in *The Man Who Died* wrote that the resurrection of Jesus was his awakening to sexual love. Kazantsakis declares the Temptation of Christ to have been the struggle to overcome sexual desire. Tom F. Driver, Associate Professor at Union Theological Seminary, in the Union's *Theological Review* contends that to dismiss Jesus's sexuality is to fall into an ancient heresy which deemed Christ's body as a mere phantom, and to accept the unbiblical notion that sex is sinful. . . . One thing seems clear: the Nazarene Jew did not see sex either as a barrier to salvation or as a condition of spiritual blessedness; he saw it as a fact of life.

What logic has impelled Roman Catholicism toward a policy uncertain both in its philosophy and its fruits? Some likely motivations have unarguable pragmatic value. A celibate priesthood is automatically an untouchable caste, shielded from the cares and chores of family, but also from the experiences that equip him for wise counsel to families in crisis. . . . Does eunuchism also conserve the vital energy drained off by frolics in bed? Is intercourse the thief of male strength? Biologically, semen is stored and restored in the testes; psychologically, life has taught me that it quickens the mind. Modern scholarship gravely questions Freud's generalization that bottling up the sex drive has been the architect of civilization by sublimating the libido into building art, science and industry. The economic advantages seem tangible enough; church coffers bulge with the funds saved by non-family ménages, paying meager salaries to priests and not paying nuns in teaching, administrative and janitorial positions. An historically older money incentive derived from the fact that Catholic clergy were endowed with a "living"—land-property which supplied personal income. These "livings" would be lost to the church through inheritance by a legitimate son, contingencies eliminated by the interdiction of marriage. . . . A conspiratorial, intriguing motivation for celibacy was flashed out to me by an angry priest who, I gathered, was engaged in a battle against the hierarchy. Over lunch one day he mapped out the church's strategy to me. "In the fourteenth century," he explained, "the church instituted the no-sex rule to nail down its control over priests by emasculating them. Physical congress with women bolsters male ego, self-assertiveness and energy for challenge. Once a man beds a woman, he finds out that he has balls. So— none of that. Then they wrap his flesh in a female-style robe—and he's as tame as a pussy-cat!"

These traumas inflicted on the Catholic clergy barely stir a tremor in the councils of Judaism. Granted, the Dead Sea Scrolls revealed that the ascetic Jewish sect which had inscribed them barred persons who had experienced sex or even a seminal emission from entering the "Temple City" of Jerusalem. They may have been the original inventors of celibacy. Such abhorrence of the flesh was an excrescence on the main body of Judaism, however, and had only negligible input to its ever-flowing stream of ethical development. Both Bible and Talmud repeatedly affirm the right to pursue happiness through sexual activity; compulsory disavowal of sex would have been waved aside as an insult to the Creator.

In place of Paul's wish that every man "might be as I," celibate, Rabbi Simeon, son of Azzai a talmudic sage, felt constrained to apologize for not marrying because he was prevented from doing so by his complete absorption in the study of the Torah. The high priest in the Jerusalem Temple was not permitted entrance into the Holy of Holies on the Day of Atonement unless he had a wife. The ancient slogan "No man without woman, no woman without man, neither without the *Schechinah* (Divine Spirit)" appears in Hebrew-English text on the marriage certificate read and presented to the bride and groom at every wedding ceremony.

Is not mandatory celibacy for clergy in essence, if not in form, a directive for their self-castration? A marginal unobtrusive comment on this pervasive principle is embedded in Jewish annals. It seems that extramarital relations were not uncommon among intellectually and aesthetically sophisticated Jews in medieval Spain, before Catholic Ferdinand and Isabella expelled them and the entire Jewish population from the Iberian peninsula (except those driven to baptismal safety in both worlds by the Inquisition.) Was this sybaritic libertinism of affluent Jewish males an acculturation to the behavior pattern of the Moslem patricians who bestowed on them the "Christian love" denied by the rulers of Christendom? It seems that the rabbinic authorities of the time reacted to such elegant pecadillos with deferential ambivalence, burying their eyes in the talmudic debates that ended a thousand years before.

Rabbi Robert Gordis, in his book *Love and Sex—A Modern Jewish Perspective,* throws some light on Judaism's critique of the complaisant permissiveness in America today. He eloquently argues from tradition and history, rarely referring to the unaltered stance prescribed by orthodoxy. The Torah teaching revealed by God is inexorable, in his view, and must be obeyed even if it is not in accord with reason or worldly felicity. A talmudic sage attributed the Ten Commandments to God's plan that they be instruments of human purification. Another wise man stated their primacy in the following homely parable: "One must not say, 'I have no desire to eat pig or have intercourse with a woman whom I may not marry.' One must say, 'I would like to do these things, but my Father in Heaven has forbidden them.'"

Gordis laments the demeaning niche assigned to women by Judaism and pleads for their sexual rights and dignity. Yet the equivocal note implicit in his general view of sexuality is sharply focused on the major issue facing the conservative sector of

Judaism, namely the ordination of women, at present blocked by the dalliance of the Jewish Theological Seminary Faculty, on which Rabbi Gordis serves.

The adamant refusal of Catholic "keepers of the flame" and the hesitancy of their Jewish counterparts to tamper with a sexuality system supposedly reared up by God, and the recalcitrant fundamentalism of a probable majority in Protestant church echelons, testify to the still-operative momentum of the past. Their physical edifices may be primped for the architectural race into the solar-heated twenty-first century, but their pulpits still echo liturgical ceremonies fashioned in huts of straw! Can we expect an overnight transvaluation of sex rituals set in motion two thousand years ago?

From the early fifth to the late eighteenth century, the church's governance in matters of morality went unchallenged; then the power to shape sexual behavior and attitudes gradually underwent a transfer to science; psychiatry, fiction, mass media and, in general, to a renascence of individual hedonism. Secular society took many years to realize that sexual etiquette had been the artifact of a religious establishment to which it was no longer bound. The desperate, autocratic and prolonged attempt to suppress sexuality did not wholly succeed; irregular sex was pushed underground. But genuflection to the tyranny of "no!" continued until the human being got off his knees and stood on his feet. What powers arose within us to incite us to do that? None that were demonic, mystic or manic; simply the unfolding response to reality in flux. Not a frantic effort to "push the river," but rather a willingness to join its flow. The stream of life is freighted with a number of powerful influences. They are scientific knowledge about sex, rejection of a body *versus* soul conflict, the tentative emancipation of woman (hitherto "protected" from sex outside marriage by terrible penalties), but above all, three incandescent insights: humanism, hedonism and individualism. Supplementing these winds of change, certain "events" have conspired to disrupt the established norms for the activation of sexuality. Recognizable by everyone, they are progressive disdain for the authority of church and state; popular over-simplification of Freudian psychoanalysis; protest against the "unclean" sex syndrome; peril of nuclear annihilation and the impulse to have a fling before a holocaust; personal anonymity in the city crowd; glamorization of Hollywood harlotry; prurient commercial adver-

tising and entertainment; a porn-exploiting press; pocket paperbacks with incendiary intent; penicillin as an antidote against VD;
ponderous immobility of tradition-bound religion; and, of course,
the Pill. Change began with attitude; it is now action. Churchmen
who had relied on "conception, infection and detection" to
dissuade people from "sin" found sin itself rusting in their hands.
Whereas pagan fertility rites ruled by the fear of hunger and
church rites exploited the fear of hell, the dominant fear today can
almost be said to be the fear of zero orgasms.

Does the current revolution portend future trends? Although
the implications are not yet visible, the young, women and
freedom fighters can see sweeping changes that will grow and last
forever. Sexuality, however, is linked up with all the multiple
issues that confront Western civilization, and their outcome will
affect, in varying degrees, the sexual configuration of every citizen.

One thing is sure; the era of silence has ended. If Nora's
slamming of a single door in Ibsen's *A Doll's House* could echo
through Europe and America in the latter part of the nineteenth
century, how are we supposed to take the crescendo of slamming
doors, creaking bedsprings, screaming liberators, bawling extramarital babies, obscenity-spitting rock stars and proudly marching homosexuals? How many North Americans can consider their
sexual mores or their lives stationary during such volcanic years?

Many of us are asking, "How much liberation?" Is the sexual
revolution being betrayed by noisy vulgarians who inject the
angers of infancy and childhood into the ever-present play of
deliberately unleased eroticism? Are some vociferous paladins of
total license the conflict-of-interest purveyors of smut? Did not
the upsurge in popular sex interest build a $200-million *Playboy*
enterprise and its many imitators? *Playboy* had been deodorized
by the Jimmy Carter interview and its sponsorship of a panel
discussion on sexuality shared by an elite circle of the nation's
clergy. And its female crotch gallery has lost shock value, as rou-
tinized nudity eventually must. I suspect people are getting tired
of two many books, speeches and stories telling them how, where,
when, why and how often. Possibly society has become accustomed to and now feels at home in the jungle. A fever of pent-up
tensions and reticences born of previous sexual curbs has been
released on the world scene, aggravating the need for a binge.

The Decline of the West by Oswald Spengler prophesied the
dismal realities of our time. No footsteps on the moon can

medicate or mitigate the disappointment of contemporary man, his loneliness, his inability to cope with a callous, crushing and computerized economic system, his fear of violence, terror and nuclear war. More and more children grow up without faith in anything but their genitals' gift of instant gratification. With "bed" becoming the single certain refuge for revitalization of zest and transcendence of worry, nothing else beckons. It does not require a ticket, a bank deposit or collateral, it bears no price tag, except in minuscule currency transactions with a prostitute. Boredom, a by-product of mankind's complex nervous system, is doubly trying in the absence of a job or some creative activity; it therefore seeks an outlet in drink, drugs, Ku-Klux-Klan-type infantilism, elaborate religious shindigs, political crusades and sexual pastimes.

More urgently than the quality of a relationship, the search today is for the ultimate in boudoir accomplishment: the ultimate orgiastic experience. Freedom in this form becomes corrupted not only by an internal malaise of hyperactivity but also by commercialism. Madison Avenue has long resorted to sex for the stimulation of a consumer appetite blunted by satiety.

These negative features of the sexual revolution derive from the exploitative nature of our society. Should we negotiate with Eros from strength or from fear? The ideal is to transmute sex into a constructive force. But our society provides little scope for the free flow of soul into feeling, for the replenishing of vital energies in the quiet regions of the spirit whence will emerge both creative force and sexual tenderness.

A backlash from the inevitable extremism of a revolutionary frame of mind has begun to stir in the more perceptive and pragmatic sectors of a generation now on the verge of self-awareness. Joyce Brothers, the eminent counselor-columnist, sees a strong swing toward commitment and a happy home and family life as a reinstated top priority for young people. Monogamy and conventional marriage seem to be recovering some prestige; the free spirits who bravely had illegitimate babies as a matter of "principle" a few years ago now consult ministers on wedding plans. Occasional allusions are even made to a revival of romantic love and sentimental poetry. Rehabilitation of the marriage license might well put a brake on the sexual revolution. Are we easing into a conservative trend? The sex scene can never be wholly stabilized; waiting in the wings are the props for the next act.

Religion and sex are the two roads into the subconscious where what we do so often originates. Today may North Americans have abandoned the quest for religious experience. The road of sex therefore must be opened wide enough for religion to walk beside it toward freedom. Sexuality can take many forms, but a rational, tolerant sex code can come forth not so much from a "sexual revolution" as from a rational, tolerant—and mature— people. Can our society produce them and put them into positions of power in the church? I wonder.

6
Male Chauvinism: Bitter Fruit of Religious Tradition

"My husband was recently cured of impotence; for a long time we couldn't have intercourse. Now, with me on top, he performs better and enjoys it more. But he told me last night he won't do it that way again because being on bottom hurts his dignity. He says the man must be in the superior position, on top."

That plaintive letter was sent by a distraught wife to a San Francisco newspaper columnist who gives free medical advice to the sexlorn. If the sexual revolution has generated little more heat than the anger that boiled over in the feisty breast of that San Francisco protester, it has earned credentials as a red badge of rebel courage. A decade or two ago, what spouse, however outraged, would have pressed her case in the press with the bill of particulars related to a dispute over anatomical posture in coitus?

Only recently have women dared to demand publicly the satisfaction of their importunate sexuality—except for isolated cases such as Virginia Woodhull, who about a century ago ran for the United States presidency on a free-love platform, proclaiming that she was its practitioner and, in reverse, Mormon wives, who tirelessly proclaimed how glad they were to share a husband's erotic resources with the rest of his ménage before legal, moral and militant harassment induced the Latter Day Saints to abandon polygamy.

Male chauvinism goes back to the universal image in primitive religions of prone Mother Earth being fructified beneath passionate Father Sky. The female's nether niche on the totem pole is therefore coeval with human history, beginning with the nature-mandated difference in musculature that made males stronger of limb. Her lowly state's reflection of his brawnier physique, however, does not extend to all creatures of the forest.

Female lions and she-wolves often outrank males in hunting skill and leadership of the pride and pack; they will even join forces to chase off or chastise a male annoyance. At a sign of danger a buck deer, on the other hand, may send his doe harem ahead to take the risk, while he hides in the bush. That men preen themselves with knottier sinews cannot yet be completely dissipated by evidence, despite the increasing penchant of women for a policeman's badge, a fireman's hat or a truck driver's lingo.

Edward O. Wilson traces the difference in physical prowess to the ice age. In his grand reprise of that time, he states that it was rooted in the genes. But did not the macho male stride into history as the primordial hominid's response to a simple economic need—the provision of food in which the energy-supplying protein of animal flesh was a prime ingredient? During the long span of evolution, the imperative to track down and slaughter produced the physiological equipment to effect it. Did not the fish finally develop fins out of a need to swim and spend its life in water?

Muscle conferred on the male the role of hunter; in turn, it associated him with cunning, courage and leadership, traits greatly feared and respected by predatory tribes. Today the hunt's call of the wild still retains priority among Indians living on Canadian reservations, just as machos pour forth from executive suites into private planes for the duck hunt, lug rifles every fall to shoot deer—sometimes blinding a Bambi-like doe with their auto headlights in the name of sportsmanship—and British redcoats ride to the hounds, all nostalgic enthusiasts for the kill.

Years ago Bertrand Russell, inquiring in a magazine article "Why Men Fight," proposed the following answer: men go off to war because they no longer go off to hunt. Adherence to the strongman syndrome is so stubborn that he must find in wood and stream a compensatory expression for the killer zest. The importance of prehistoric man's war on meaty beasts has been downgraded by Richard E. Leaky, world-famous anthropologist, in his fascinating account of the African *People of the Lake.* Though not denying that our forebears were hunters, he contends that it was the cooperation of both male and female, forcing the brain to enlarge, that transformed apes into humans. Man owes his evolution to a uniquely intense social contract in which the nurturing *woman* played a crucial role.

I envisage Russell's brilliant hypothesis in relation to male chauvinism, starting with a personal observation. I have yet to meet a clearly non-chauvinist man who at the same time is a zealous hunter of deer, ducks or dollars, the last being as much the obsessive pursuit of a "hunter" label as the coonskin cap and musket formula was in the days of Daniel Boone. After I spent some years in the "Wild West," that formula revealed only one true exemplar: a pistol-totin' critter-huntin' female who had declared war on rattlesnakes.

Any society or era given to physical violence, riven by acute antagonism, psychically geared to war, hypnotically dedicated to aggressive competition and/or exploited as a captive audience by religious imperialism is subject to the symptoms of a grievous inequity we now call male chauvinism. Isn't that a portrait of the 1980s in America? Norman Alcock, an internationally respected Canadian researcher into the causes and cure of war, has reported that churchgoers are decidedly more susceptible to war-mindedness than people who have other things to do on Sunday morning.

The evolutionary role of the female has been cast in anthropology textbooks; she is the gatherer of nuts, fruits and herbs, the cave-keeper, the child-bearer, the repairer of her master's animalhide jacket. The Eskimo woman who still chews a seal's skin into a parka and into a pair of boots for her man is reincarnation. Woman may have dropped the fruit of her womb unattended in field or forest—a happenstance that may overtake luckless females in tribal societies today—but in all likelihood the subsequent months of weaning a breastfed infant were a period of physical and emotional dependence on the male, who probably growled and grunted in savage, mercurial mood changes, even hostility, toward the wriggling bundle of flesh and bones that competed for his woman's care. As Hamlet's apostrophe "Frailty, thy name is woman!" began its misleading course down the corridors of time, her reservoir or authority was further depleted.

The comic strips and cartoons of my youth made "caveman" a synonym for brute mayhem toward women: today's "battered wives," a tragic reminiscence, pay dearly for that model syndrome. These male-invented cartoons appeal to the masculine ego, intimating, often not too subtly, that the "little woman" actually likes the heavy hand. Habitués of a saloon next door to my home in Ohio used to babble between hiccups that the "reg'lar Satidy night beatin's" they administered to "the wife" were expected and appreciated as proof that "we love 'em, by God."

I suspect that the weak, docile image of the woman in a cave setting has been one of history's oldest frauds. We have been conditioned to picture the male as he might *then* have been—hirsute, chunky body, bulging muscles, predatory shuffle, gripping a club, while the female throughout many religion-ruled centuries has been presented as she is presumed to be *now*: soft-spoken or silent, submissive, flaccid, always aware of her inferior rank. As I see it, the frail, frightened stereotype of prehistoric woman and her carbon-copy successors in the brief period of our civilization have been a public relations triumph for male chauvinism.

Suppose that the strong, valiant, guileful lady combatants highlighted in human history—from the biblical matriarchs to mythic Amazons, from the Greek Olympian Hera to Joan of Arc and Bella Abzug—are merely isolated and exceptional attempts by an embarrassed Providence to apply a poultice! What about the fact that the shrinking, shrieking females of the caveman cartoons have survived? If *they* were the authentic image, could they have mothered the future? And why assume that in this instance the Darwinian law about survival of the fittest was ignored?

Like most mammals, it benefited the male in early human tribes to court one female after another, thereby increasing his chances to own many offsprings. At the same time, women became more selective about their sleeping partners. Coyly they learned to refrigerate their procreative urge until they could identify the male with the most powerful torso, giving precedence to the quality of strength in the weeding-out mathematics of evolution. Females even now yell "sock it to 'im" in front-row seats at boxing matches; their number does not suggest flossy delicacy. And I wonder whether the prehistoric male had enough self-restraint to make him wait upon her choice. . . .

The geological periods of natural selection have deposited hereditary tools in the American woman of the 1980s for the comeuppance of social and sexual sadism—and perchance the attainment of a notably longer life expectancy. Most effective of all these tools is an increment of superior insight, intuition and native intelligence—misogynists might say "pragmatic wiliness"—the outgrowth of sheer necessity, to compensate for social, sexual and bodily handicaps. While happily observing the half-flirtatious, artful "come-on" of a girl baby, my own and others, directed by some arcane plan toward *males*, I have been tempted to pontificate that "a girl child is born a woman; it takes a boy child all his life to become the simulacrum of a man." At the risk of being charged with pro-*Jewish* chauvinism, I submit the proposition that the continued existence of the Jewish people through successive periods of normally devastating harrassment might be ascribed in part to intellectual acuity acquired by way of redress, protective shield and self-reimbursement, a sort of indemnification paid by history. Perhaps nature also has been redemptive for women in that it has endowed them with a greater capacity to endure pain.

Sexist patterns are transmitted across the generation gap by a tribal communications underground, in the automatic response of the young to the adults in their environment. Youngsters imitate gender stereotypes and continuously build up the cultural sanctions that maintain and exaggerate role distinctions. The result is a male-centered society that compels a ranch lad to risk being maimed by a bucking bronco rather than face the shame of being called a sissy for refusing to ride him.

Do women have an innate aptitude for and trend toward the interpersonal areas of the marketplace, a bent fashioned by their "feeling" for people? The apparent preponderance of females in such jobs might clue a positive answer. Or, ironically, this alleged inclination is being exploited by corporate bureaucrats perfunctorily to tap female employees and freeze them in public relations and personnel slots. Social work orientation, the science of relating to and caring about people, news hens, who are given human-interest assignments considered peripheral to the "really important" reportage of politics and the economy, secretaries schooled to handle the boss's appointment book, phone messages—and sometimes "himself"—all these may well be manipulative devices of the male-dominated system to cabin women in nurturing positions—"what they do best"—instead of setting them free to seek what they *want* to do.

Children note differences not only between themselves and adults, but also between men and women, and they take on their respective roles as observed. Even in egalitarian Israel's kibbutzim (agricultural settlements) where the sexes are theoretically free to choose whatever roles they wish to play, women like, or are persuaded to like, the nurturing occupations such as overseeing education, recreation and ceremonies, while men actively gravitate to defense, security and economic planning. The divergence of interests is purely a matter of social conditioning and has no origin whatever in kibbutz philosophy. From the start the Israel kibbutz movement inaugurated male-female parity in status and function. It was a calculated program arising out of the Socialist ideal that everyone is to have an equal share of responsibility and benefit, without prejudice. The art of military defense, including the use of arms, became a deservedly renowned part of the female's training for kibbutz life. This collective experiment in human relations, organization and economic commonality, not to be confused with Communism, was remarkably innovative and suited the urgent and austere requirements for the conquest of a desert. The widely disseminated photo of an Israeli "with child" on guard duty near the Syrian border with a rifle at the ready is the authentic logo. But equality of the sexes, along with other radical measures such as the early abolition of the marriage ceremony (although that was later revived), were a consciously recognized departure from the long-regnant Orthodox tradition of Judaism.

That tradition is most vividly exemplified in the diametrically opposite views on female military service held today by Israel's National Religious Party, a clerical-political alliance dedicated to the permanent establishment of a hierarchical state ruled by Yahweh (e.g., His clergy). Under coercive pressure, a minority government (almost inevitable in the Israeli multi-party system), whose continuance in office would be jeopardized without NRP support, has to exempt all Orthodox women from a stint in the armed forces, even in non-combatant categories; claimants to such exemption need only state that they live in accord with Orthodox law. This pietistic blackmail ploy imposes heavy penalties on the state by depriving it of desperately needed defense resources, as well as on non-traditional women who must sacrifice higher education and employment plans during the term of military service. It also strains the integrity and patriotism of those who honestly confess to a non-Orthodox lifestyle, and encourages dishonesty among those who don't.

Beyond its practical effects, this arrogant assumption of totalitarian authority under a religious umbrella is an inexcusably pejorative, insulting slur on the sexual morality of every woman. The basis for the virtual exclusion of presumably innocent Orthodox females sheltered from contact with military installations and men is that females eligible for military duties must be protected from *themselves*. Intermingling the sexes in military quarters might subject them to sexual temptation beyond the "feeble" self-control capacity of Israel's potential lady paratroopers or any other physically mature females. Nubile girls? They should remain at home; if single, in the proprietary care of father, if married, in the protective and possessive care of husband! In 1980 Rabbi Menachem Porush of the all-cleric Agudat Israel Party, with 4 Knesset (Legislative Assembly) members out of 120, boldly asserted that "the girls are not strong enough to resist temptation," i.e., sex. Evidently he has no qualms about their resistance to lying to escape defending their beleaguered country; an Israeli girl need merely sign an affidavit that she keeps kosher and does not travel on Shabbat (the Sabbath).

More than an ambitious tactic to resurrect the "Torah-true" rabbi-ruled theocracy of ancient times in this scenario, Israel's Orthodoxy-oriented politicians and their followers would ultimately reinstate total male chauvinism, which in my dictionary is Judaism's "original sin."

"Jewish chauvinism?" one might exclaim. "But look at the great women of the Bible!" Yes, indeed there were many. In all fairness I must summon a galaxy of distaff celebrities as witnesses for the defense. Eve lured complaisant Adam to the tree of carnal knowledge and fig-leaf obsolescence; barren Sarah gave to Abraham Hagar, a slavegirl concubine, to bear him a babe and then, after the Lord gave her an off-schedule child, had the master drive Hagar and Ishmael adrift, although he did put up a faint demurral; Rebecca made her son Jacob an accomplice and her husband Isaac a simpleton to transfer the birthright from Esau to where she had decided it belonged; Rachel and Leah determined the apportionment of Jacob's conjugal energies without consulting him; Tamar disguised herself as a prostitute to conceive a son in the name of her dead husband; Miriam cozened the Egyptian princess in the bulrushes, indulged in querulous debate with big brother Moses and danced before the Ark of the Covenant; Deborah rallied the tribes of Israel to crush their enemies with copious bloodshed at what she assumed was the Lord's behest; and Hulda the prophetess led King Josiah to read the Book of the Law for Reformation—a most laudable objective. Although Esther won a beauty contest and deliverance of the Jews from destruction, it is *not* related that, like Vashti, she refused to display her charms to the king's guests. Jael inveigled Sisera, the redoubtable foe of Israel, to a siesta and drove a nail through his skull; Jezebel got her name in the Guiness book of history's depraved women by pursuing evil with unrelenting vigor, whether to extirpate Yahweh-worship or expropriate a peasant's land. . . . The only biblical heroines untainted by husband domination, deception or mayhem were the comely maiden in the Bible's Song of Songs who shared erotic love equally with her companion-in-ecstasy, and the "woman of valor" from the Book of Proverbs, whose role as housewife and helpmeet of her husband seemed to leave her completely devoid of even a smidgen of discontent. She was the biblical stereotype of the German burghers' *Kinder, Kirche und Küche* (Children, Church and Kitchen) paradigm to whom the pious Jewish householder recites the Proverbs' tribute at the family dinner table every Sabbath Eve.

Scriptural and secular documents portray a long line of Jewish women of extraordinary ability and energy who served in trade pursuits, as breadwinners and home builders for the Jewish family. Customary law invited a mother to play a decisive part in the marriage of a daughter. Job gave legacies to his daughters together with their brothers. From Naomi in the Book of Ruth, who offered for sale the fields of her dead husband, to the extensive business transactions in the fifth century B.C.E. by formidable women of a Jewish-Egyptian military colony, we glean vague glimpses of outstanding deeds by women. In pre-Holocaust Eastern Europe, countless Jewish wives and mothers labored to exhaustion in petty trades and shops, apart from their around the clock household chores, so that the man of the house might be released from familial interruptions to his holy God-destined study of talmudic law and lore.

My mother bore and bred ten children. I once reckoned that she must have spent most of her life cooking meals, washing dishes, scrubbing floors, rubbing clothes on the washboard and waiting up at night until the last of her brood had entered the door. My sisters helped at the sink when they returned from school or work; we boys, seven by count, did nothing.

Allusion to my sisters brings to the surface a conviction that has been buried in my mind for many years: the onus of sexism in the pious Jewish family fell heavily on the daughters. Biblical lore entrusted a father with unchallengeable authority to decide a daughter's future, even to sell her into marriage or annul her vows; he also could ordain that she inherit a paternal estate in the absence of male issue. A father might substitute a daughter in payment of a debt, but not a son. The Feinberg girls, as they were affectionately called, had every endowment of personality and character for felicitous marriage, breathtaking loveliness of body and spirit; yet Nathan, their father, interdicted even minimal social contact with Gentile boys in a small town devoid of suitable Jewish male companionship. My sisters meticulously observed this ruling out of inbred respect for their father and because of their loyalty to tribe and tradition. The Feinberg sons on the other hand made the town's entire female population their province. Neither my sisters nor my mother ever complained by sound or gesture. To serve their men and to serve God was their destiny— God's will.

"God's will," always the Divine imprimatur, the president's seal, the dictator's signature, the bureaucrat's stamp, more compelling than the intrinsic demerits of an official document! That Bible and Talmud were compiled by men, save for an occasional insertion into the latter record of a brilliant commentary by a woman, can be said of religious literature in *all* ages. It is a fact of human history that creed and deed are often shaped by raw quest for power. In the so-called eternal "war of the sexes" the overwhelmingly male codifiers of doctrine wished to harvest the benefits derived from a put-down of women. That they ascribed the put-down to the will of God is verified in a voluminous stream of sacred scriptures and ecclesiastical edicts.

To see and name the bedrock foundation of disdain for women our guide must be ancient paganism's exaltation of the female principle. The pagan addressed himself to and apostrophized the deities of Earth; in their most arresting guise they were sex goddesses. The freewheeling sexuality of the pre-Israel Middle East spawned a riotous swarm of seductive shapes and shrines, all geared to Mother, the source of life, who enfleshed the grip and touch and squeeze of sex; it was she who invited her votaries to sate lust and suck life at her multiple breasts.

Abraham (Hebrew for Father of a People) at the moment of his entrance on the biblical stage blue-printed Judaism's Fatherhood of (One) God, a stern, omnipotent Ruler who would command him to sacrifice his son, and the image of the austere desert tribal chief who was Abraham himself. Whereas *matristic* paganism's law was sexual love, *patristic* Judaism centered in love of the Divine Law. The books of Kabbalah mysticism (significantly a favorite treasure-trove of the more literate sex-exploring young of the sixties) celebrate the Mother-aspect of God as *schechinah*, the indwelling presence that dissolves barriers to itself with concern for loving relationships. But the whisper of intimacy with one another and with the Divine vanished into the stentorian formula "And God spoke," a prelude to Yahweh's commands that guided the Jew in fear of punishment.

That the God-Father-Law formula opposes the interpersonal givingness, meshing and sexual spontaneity epitomized in Mother Earth seems seminal truth to me. The wrath of "Our Father who art in heaven" (a prelude to prayer in synagogue liturgy) inevitably would be loosed against rampaging sexuality—and the baneful influence of women, yoked to it by guilt of association. Rabbi Richard Rubenstein, commenting on the traditional Jewish loathing of a woman's adultery, more severe than a man's, ascribed the primary cause to the essentially patriarchal nature of Judaism and its masculine orientation. Woman aroused both fascination and fear. She had to be fenced in so that men might be shielded from her insidious power. Wherever the corpus of rabbinic statutes can be activated as in the hermetically closed enclaves of orthodoxy some inequities and iniquities are still in force. The Sanhedrin, supreme court of the ancient Hebrew commonwealth, theoretically the sole authority for change, was dismantled centuries ago. "Ethics of the Fathers," a talmudic collection of wise aphorisms on the good life, still advises against engaging in too much conversation with women because they are "flighty, garrulous, and unworthy of mature man's mind." Ancient rabbinic jurisprudence did not consider women, minors, deaf mutes and the insane competent to act as witnesses in lawsuits. Other contemptuous evaluations of the female intellect and adulthood surfaced in offhand Talmud remarks, not necessarily reflecting basic attitude but indicative of the flippant machoism stubbornly clinging to the American prototype.

"Much talk with women increases witchcraft"; "Better that the words of the Torah be burned than that they be handed over to empty-headed women"; "A pretty woman without sense is like a gold ring in a pig's snout." This pattern of denigration also was manifested in America's anti-obscenity censorship of a few decades ago, when the cry was "We must protect our womenfolk" because exposure to erotica would not only contaminate them morally but set off nervous breakdowns or mental sickness.

The Book of Genesis contains two versions of the creation— one, that man and woman were created directly by God in His image, the other than woman emerged from man's rib during his slumber. Rabbinic chauvinism utilized the *latter* explanation, a mythic fairy-tale argument for woman's subordination as integral to God's cosmic design, rather than the terse majestic pronouncement "male and female He created them."

In antiquity throughout Asia Minor, virginity was considered capable of raising to maximum level the power and spiritual rank of both genders; it therefore endowed the numerous (non Hebraic) virgin-birth gods with supernatural potency. In Judaism, a man had to wed a virgin as certification of his paternity; a priest could marry only an untouched female to avoid uncleanness before God; a Jewess who failed the virginity test was disgraced in court by the rabbinical judges who either pulled down her hair and tied it in a slip-knot or uncovered her breasts. (Young rabbinic students were barred from witnessing this rite.) Even today a Jewish woman of the old school replaces her hair with a non-ornamental wig at marriage because her natural hair is considered an invitation to lewdness. A prayer recited every morning by the tradition-observing Jew thanks God for not having created him a woman. In explanation or apology, it has been interpreted as a tribute to the Torah; because of necessarily unscheduled (or unremitting) household duties, women were excused from the supreme virtue and privilege of obeying its *mitzvot* (commands) that depended on specific performance at certain times. Skepticism about this explanation is understandable.

Thoughts on menstruation reveal the ages-old irrational dread. Blood had supernatural power; therefore the flow of blood without visible wound or pain addled and terrified ancient man; its loss suggested death. Primitive tribes in some regions had menstruation performed in the fields to enrich the harvest. Sundry tribes segregated the menstruating woman in a specially built hut; she had to bypass any path frequented by men, often risking her life in the uncharted wilderness. Whatever she touched was burned; even her food had to be served by others. The story goes that an Australian native killed his wife and then died of fright after discovering that he had slept on a couch she had used during her "period." It is still believed in some European countries that a woman in menses walking along the water's edge will drive fish away, will ruin a hunter's catch by crossing his path and cause flowers to wither. A tribe in what formerly was British Guiana did not allow women to bathe during their period because they could poison the water. After childbirth a woman had to purify herself by performing religious rites; in many regions cleansing was incumbent on the pregnant and nursing. Did women perhaps originate these bans for convenience, rest and release from burdensome sex urgency?

Strict Jewish pietism today specifically forbids sex to a couple for five days during menses and for seven "clean" days thereafter. At the end of twelve days each month a woman is commanded to enter the *mikveh* (ritual bath) before sex can be resumed. The ritual has been regulated in detail: first a thorough cleansing. Having removed her clothing and ornaments, she dips into a small pool of water obtained from a natural source, generally rainwater or ice untouched by metal, and allows the water to come in contact with her entire body. An attendant is always present to ensure complete immersion. Pious Jewish brides are expected to observe this custom before marriage and again four days later; a female proselyte to Judaism must bathe in the *mikveh* as part of the conversion process. A growing segment in the younger crop of presumably Reform rabbis recommend *t'vilah*, the purification ceremony, to prospective female converts, without (recognizable) coercion, in a communal facility built for the purpose. I have yet to meet a Jewess of any age or religious persuasion who has ever found it essential or desirable to purify herself in a *mikveh*. Therefore, even the subtlest hint of *t'vilah* to a woman sincerely seeking admission to the Jewish faith and people puzzles me—unless the convert is not deemed ready for participation until she receives a practical demonstration of the durability of Jewish chauvinism.

Some medical men believe that the actual method of ritual cleansing plus careful attention to irregularities of the menstrual cycle contribute to a lowered incidence of uterine cancer among Jewish women who use the *mikveh*. I am not qualified to assess cancer-prevention value. If it were authenticated by far-flung research, the *mikveh* would have top priority for physical health. In any case, such a benign result of the ritual would be a providential concomitant, not its avowed goal.

Aristotle and Aquinas thought that male semen contained the entire human being of *homunculus* (little man); the female had only an auxiliary function in child-bearing. According to the ancient Hebrews the vagina was merely a receptacle for the all-important male seed. A wife had the right to insert *mokh*, a spongy substance which hindered conception but prolonged the husband's enjoyment (an example of confused and contradictory attitudes toward birth control). Another ambiguity related to conjugal rights of the husband; he could have intercourse at any time in one talmudic passage, while another denied it to him without her consent.

After marriage, normally at eighteen, a man was not allowed to consort socially with women in general and as little as possible with his wife, except for sexual contact. If feasible, they ate separately. Birth of a male child renders the mother "unclean" for forty days; a female's arrival segregates her for twice that time. Since it was believed that the expenditure of semen aged and debilitated its donor, the female consignee became identified not only with life in the womb vessel, but also with death. Long-existent rites related to dying show female involvement. Even now in some cultures the woman washes the corpse, wears black, leads the funeral procession in the cemetery and may serve as professional mourner. In short, the generous rabbinical servants who are gifted with superior understanding of the way our mortal race must comfort itself toward dying conferred on woman the joyous (?) experience of close tactile contact with the cerements and remains of death and decay; priests were barred from such contact to prevent their contamination.

In the Bible adultery by a married woman constituted a crime punishable by death; not so for a man. As she was deemed the chattel of her husband, his proprietary right of exclusive possession would be violated by an adulterous act; his accusation alone that she had conducted herself licentiously provided enough evidence to convict her. An unmarried female, not yet "branded" by a husband, did not qualify for such sinful complicity.

For generations polygamy warmed the carnal parts of biblical patriarchs and their successors. Often implemented by the intriguing institution of concubinage (considered respectable), it gave the husband multiple bed partners without endangering his wife's pride. In fact, Judaism might have invented the time-rusted limerick: "Higimous hogamous, woman's monogamous; hogamous higimous, man is polygamous."

In the tenth century Rabbi Gershom of Mayence convened a synod of prestigious rabbis from France, Germany and Italy which forbade polygamy under pain of exile or excommunication, but the ban did not apply to Jews in Islamic countries. When Yemenite men immigrated to the State of Israel they often brought a second wife, if she was affordable. Not until legislation could be enforced did the practice disappear. The extinction of Jewish communities in Arab lands has totally expunged legal polygamy among Jews.

Divorces were simple in biblical times. A man would hand his wife a bill of divorcement. When Hebrew society became more complex, two schools of thought arose; one permitted divorce solely for adultery, the other expanded the grounds to include any kind of unseemly behavior; in the end this more liberal method became law. Several Talmud sages in a mood of fraternity toward males and of sly humor toward females detonated tongue in cheek shockers that need not be too solemnly interpreted, *viz.*, a man might divorce his wife "if he found her displeasing," "if she put too much salt in the soup," "if he found another woman more attractive."

In the second century consistent efforts to redress egregious injustice brought about the *ketubah*, or marriage contract; it guaranteed support to the wife in case of divorce or widowhood; traditional rabbis still draw up such an agreement before a wedding. Since the initiative for divorce had rested solely with the husband, a list of possible conditions now became available to the wife; she could present a plea for divorce to the rabbinical court. The grounds included false premarital pretenses by the husband, pursuit of an immoral profession or an intolerable trade, desertion for any length of time, incorrigible embarrassment and sexual incompatibility.

In the tenth century, the *get* (divorce decree) was held to be binding only if the wife consented to receive it. In Jewish Orthodox families a woman cannot remarry religiously until she receives a *get* from her husband, whereas he needs only a civil decree. The children of his remarriage suffer no disadvantages. Those of her second marriage (if *get*-less) are considered *mamzerim* (bastards), and although they are entitled to full privileges as Jews they may not wed persons of legitimate Jewish birth. A civilly divorced Jewish woman may have to postpone remarriage because her officially Orthodox ex-husband refuses to give her a *get*. Complainants have come to me with verified stories of extortion and occasional blackmail. When requested, I solemnize a remarriage without the *get*. The revival of militant fundamentalism in Orthodox rabbinic circles and a deferential bow to submissive coexistence with romanticized "tradition" dissuaded too many of my liberal colleagues from performing this act of simple justice and compassion.

According to Old Testament directive the brother of a man who dies without offspring must marry the widow of the deceased to continue her husband's name. She may not marry anyone else until the brother has released both of them in the *halitza* ceremony (which includes the symbolic gesture of throwing a shoe). That decision can be made only by a mature, responsible adult, i.e., when the brother has reached his majority as a Bar Mitzvah at the age of thirteen. If the deceased has left a brother of five, let us say, the woman must let eight years pass unwed. Such a case actually occurred in Israel, where all matters of personal status are governed by rabbinic law.

After years of controversy, measures were adopted to ameliorate the disadvantages imposed on Jewish women. The Conservative movement, for example, has devised a *beth din* (house of judgment), or rabbinical court, to negotiate a premarital compact which considerably mollifies the impact of historic wrongs. But both the male beneficiaries and the female victims still take chauvinism for granted wherever Jews venerate the unalterable Divine Law handed down from Sinai for male implementation.

Law and life must be jointly considered in evaluating current Jewish chauvinism. The modern temple has afforded women enormous scope not for the normal auxiliary service alone, but for leadership. The roster of women prominent in the councils of Jewish philanthropy, social agencies, education and support for Israel glows with "big names." Yet the synagogues of Orthodoxy, by far the largest though loosely knit component in North American Judaism, effectively countermand progress. Adherence to old ways looks with barely lukewarm approval on religious and Hebrew education for girls, rejects their *Bat-Mitzvah* (female Bar-Mitzvah ceremony), refuses to count women in a *minyan* (quorum for worship), is revolted by Reform Judaism's admission of women to the altar for recital of blessings, and segregates them in a more or less obscure seating section during worship to forestall the incursion of impure fantasies into Yahweh-intent male meditations.

Does the Jewish mother model of unassailable dominance in the home rebut the charge of chauvinism? The supremacy of family as the bulwark of survival during centuries of Jewish isolation and pariahship gave its maternal center a position of almost legendary honor. Regrettably, the once impregnable Jewish fortress family, like all minority peculiarities, is succumbing to "melting pot" acculturation. Its decline interjects an exception to the endurance and longevity of traditions thrown off by the wheel of history and the exigencies of the Law. The "woman of valor" now attends parent-teacher meetings, physical fitness classes, college extension courses and women's liberation rallies. She often spends intense and stressful hours in public and private sessions with psychiatric counselors in a desperate quest for guidance in the manic-depressive world of her precociously adolescent kids, the actual power structure in the household. As for the *Yiddishe Mameh*, it seems she has been reduced to an ever-reliable prop in the repertoire of standup comics.

I have descanted at length on the mother-faith's assignment of underling status to woman as prelude to the theologically deeper chauvinism of the daughter. Christianity, girding itself in sin-exterminating armor against the moral anarchy of the Greco-Roman world, exceeded its Hebraic mother, and discarded mentor, by annealing the genitals with an iron chastity belt of dogma in salute to the Divine Father. (Mary, Mother of God, in contrast to the pagan earth mothers, symbolized sex denial, i.e., virginity). Adam, as the celebrated father of the human race, did for fundamentalist Christianity what Abraham, the father of a people, did for Judaism. Both founded theologies. Abraham, in his desert solitude, envisioned a solitary God whose unity begat the tenuous doctrine of Jewish universalism; Adam, in his elysian garden, by submitting to the most famous and fateful seduction of all time by Eve, begat the timeless doctrine of original sin, the nucleus of traditional Christianity. Abraham's followers, zealous to preserve austere Yahweh's supernal Father-unity, built a "fence for the Torah" against the infiltration of sex symbolic goddesses displaying multiple-breasted femaleness. Their spiritual descendants, the Church Fathers, sought to save all mankind from eternal damnation for the primal sin of sex indulgence by purging it of female sexuality. Both were the progenitors of male chauvinism. Based on Adam's unitary aboriginal role, the creators of Christian theology, like the early architects of Judaism, made male superiority a keystone of God's grand design.

Genesis 1:27, the crucial Bible precis of creation, presents a syndrome of exegetical web-spinning. "God created man in His image; in the image of God He created him, male and female created He them." With the first part alone, the Church Father would have felt no qualms. It referred to man's soul or reason, patterned after the character of the Divine. Philo, the Jewish scholar of Alexandria, had already established such an interpretation. It was the *last* phrase, "male and female"! How reconcile the spiritual view of man in God's image with the subsequent affirmation of two sexes, both in the lowly body? God is wholly incorporeal, but this linkage of contraries implied either a sexed spirituality or a bodily God. Hair-splitting efforts to resolve this impasse engaged Christian speculation for centuries. Their solutions usually bore down on woman. She conveniently was abstracted from the male-female pairing to represent the body, thus leaving mind, soul, spirit to man—and God. Augustine, bishop of Hippo in North Africa, was the jugglery's mastermind. To him, Adam, the male principal, alone was fashioned after the full image of God. Since Eve emerged from his rib, a minor part of him, she symbolized only the flesh, body, man's corporeality, its appetites and desires. A helpmeet she was—for procreation, the sole function she could perform. Woman counted only when conjoined with the male who is her "head," whereas the "head" of man is Christ, by whose grace he can perform tasks of the spirit. Augustine, in a metaphysical excess of narcissism, sees woman's debasing carnality drag man from his heavenly heights.

Thomas Aquinas gave impetus to this female subordination. His epochal work *Summa Theologica* leaves no gap in its tight logic. Woman is inferior to man both by her lower rank in the order of nature and by her carnality in the disorder of sin. Not really a self-sufficient whole person with equal honor, she nevertheless subjects the male to mortal and moral danger through sex. Flesh must be subject to spirit, body to soul; so the female, the physical element, must submit to the male, who represents reason, rationality and righteousness. Sin enters the world when woman, the carnal principle, revolts against the ruling spirit and draws man's mind down to a lower realm.

How can a woman overcome the body? By embarking upon a monastic and angelic regimen of virginity. Then she is bound for heaven, and to get her that supremely coveted crown her male devotees will despise all real earthly females, all meditation on sex and fecundity, and etherealize Woman into a bodiless phantasm. These incorporeal creatures thus become love objects for the subliminal libido of man, never for his carnal, conscious desire.

By providing such sublimation, the virgin guards a man against the sin of physical sex with the daughters of Eve. Consequently, the natural affections of man and the natural humanity of women are both sacrificed. Once a woman becomes pregnant, her body no longer is her own; the fetus she carries belongs to the church which has jurisdiction over it.

Woman is both a man's sex object and the object he fears. A striking condensation of this duality was a bit of sage advice given by the Roman philosopher Seneca, who was so well-loved by the early Christian Fathers that they referred to him as "Our Seneca": "To love sex-pleasure is to love an adulteress. A wise man loves a woman with judgment not with affection. Let him not be borne headlong into copulation. Let the female imitate animals when her belly swells. Show yourselves to your wives not as lovers but as masterful husbands."

Chrysostom, master of polemical preaching in Christianity's infancy, ranted against woman as "a necessary evil, a natural temptation, a desirable calamity, a domestic peril, a deadly fascination, a painted evil" (consummate in evil just *because* so consuming in fascination). . . .

Modern psychiatry has added a new dimension to the civil war in the masculine ego. It began with Freud who attributed woman's sense of inferiority in part to penis envy, although a female-oriented psychiatrist might charge men with womb envy. Countering this is fear of castration. The male subconsciously may even equip that outwardly placid organ with teeth—the *vagina dentata* (toothed vagina) that threatens decapitation of his prized possession.

Polarized duality of opposites seems to be an underlying pattern discernible at the core of religious male chauvinism. Rosemary Reuther, a Catholic thinker of great distinction, declared it to be typical of a theology that exhibits misogyny, hatred of woman, while celebrating her virginity. Reuther thereby identifies the schizophrenia that bifurcated Christendom's version of femaleness for centuries and still afflicts many of its prelates. The duality is epitomized in Augustine's antithetical pairing of Eve and Mary. "Through a woman (Eve) we were sent to destruction by concupiscence and innate human depravity; through a woman (Mary) salvation was restored through her intercession with the Son of God whom she conceived."

Can anyone deplore or deny the beneficent impact exerted on

humanity by the veneration of her to whom devout Christians pray as the Mother of God? Even strident feminists are moved by the gentleness and compassion of one of their gender who bore a child without masculine partnership, and agnostics will forego importunate rationalism in the presence of her image. I have never viewed representations of the Virgin Mary in European and American churches without the intuition that I was on holy ground.

Our concern here, however, is the vassalage of women, embedded in the recesses of Christian doctrine. The long martyrdom began in the fabled sexual diabolism of Eve, in assiduously taught fear of the female's *moral* corruption, of her alleged power through sexual arousal to pervert mankind's hope of eternal salvation as revealed in sacred Scripture. Dr. Howard Moody, a distinguished leader of the United Church of Christ and a Yale Divinity graduate, does not refuse to indict the church for fostering the humiliation of women in our society. To him, the Reformation was "a masculine thing." He asks how many female theologians the church has had and what feminine viewpoints ever got incorporated in its thinking. Virtually none! A whole mystique about female evil was supported by the church; as an example of church woman-hatred, over a million women were put to death as sorcerers and witches. "The church is in large part responsible," he said, "for our traditionally distorted view of women as either vessels of sin or holy paragons of virtue."

Dr. Martin E. Marty, one of the most prolific and widely quoted church historians and a Lutheran minister, accuses the Christian church of having depersonalized women for centuries. In actual practice, he states, churchmen traditionally have been anti-sex and anti-pleasure. They have always asserted that before God women are equal to men. But, he says, you can't conclude from any of the church's practices that through most of its twenty centuries it regarded woman as a parallel crown of creation. Early Christian spokesmen saw her only as a mere receptacle for the male, describing her in almost all cases as "inferior."

In seventeenth-century Protestant Holland sporadic emergence of feminine leadership was sparked by Marie van der Ende, a teacher who inclined Spinoza, one of humanity's most intrepid and inspiring thinkers, toward a view of woman that was more enlightened than that of the rabbinical establishment which later excommunicated him for heresy. Physicians in England up to the time of Lister often refused to treat pregnant women for bed-sickness because they had "sinned."

No more than traditional Judaism could its Christian counterpart tolerate "unclean" woman on the altar. Aquinas may have permitted her to baptize in dire emergency, and a fourth-century stir of enlightenment may have borne an occasional deaconess and the adoration of Mary, but neither innovation ever eviscerated the notion that the active force in the male seed produces a perfect masculine likeness while the product of woman inherits her defects.

Male fear of woman is occasionally overlaid with a thick blanket of bluff, pretense and martial poses. What other motives might have impelled the enlightened citizens of the Athenian city-state to the use of a hetaira for intellectual companionship, a boy for pederasty and a deliberately infantilized wife for child-bearing, house-tending with severance from the outside world? Aristotle's discussion of friendship omits any positive reference to husband-wife relations. The dominant bogey—domination by females—breeds dominant homosexuality. In moderate form it still operates today, seducing frightened men into flight from mature, older, better-educated and socially more congenial consorts.

"Inferiority" of women was sanctified as the Lord's decree and formalized in countless ways to obey it. From Old Testament double standards on adultery, Mormon discriminatory "sealing" for heaven, to Catholic-Mormon lockout of women from the priesthood and Protestant espousal of Luther's priority to child-bearing, the "church" has been woman's nemesis. Chauvinism finally legitimized the "Judeo-Christian" facade in that it presented a common platform. Though clad in the sheen of tradition it is not a cosmetic; instead it lends a distinguishably dark patina to the portrait of both religions.

Rejection of women is an expensive social mannerism. One of its lesser effects is disdain of man's feminine element as a sign of weakness and a dilution of masterful masculinity. Boys have been inducted into homosexuality by our culture's assumption that certain so-called "feminine" traits indicate an innate trend.

Fear of the sexual female does not exhaust its protean variety. Do not his viscera tighten at the approach of a cerebral female—her mind? Isn't that the most plausible rationale for the hedges man has built to impede her entrance into the labor market, business and the professions? Competition is the soul of trade, vendors of free enterprise tell us. Between the sexes, male blue collars, white collars, professionals, executives and entrepreneurs commit treason against the capitalist system by an eccentric inclination to think and pray that competition is a snare and a delusion.

"Act like men," a University of Connecticut research team advised career women. Corporate big-wigs give the nod to tough, masculine personalities—the jutted chin, the assured manner, the heart that bleeds only "in the red." My infrequent forays into the oak-paneled sancta of corporate gods tell me that too many women have followed that formula. The "arrived" female vice-president may blunt the nerve-ends of sensitivity, twist her intuitive ganglions out of shape, and permanently thicken her hide into an impenetrable barrier against the love of a man or herself; the final dividend of a stance taken for career purposes can be callousness and aridity. Machismo, they tell me, is beginning to show a deficit; our computer-idolizing, dehumanized corporations could *do* with a touch of femininity.

Even women who have a desk in the executive suite, a chair in the boardroom and a high spot in the professional pecking order often have a nagging sense of unease and insecurity. The response of the pinstriped fraternity to their presence may fluctuate between the cloying chivalry and condescending courtesy of "gentlemen" toward a fragile female—and puerile attempts at sexual subtlety and finesse for which the usual American male has little talent or training. She is therefore frequently driven to thicken still further the insulation of tight-lipped reserve and impersonality she had donned in an effort to meet the norms of the business world.

Discriminatory evaluation of female executives in big business extends even into the always fertile field of inside gossip. Examples can be chosen at random. "*She* slept her way up," when a female makes it; "*he* climbed (or clawed) the steep road to success." This oscillation of judgment—from businessman to businesswoman— occurs in a variety of other linguistic packages, but the content is the same: He's aggressive, she's assertive. He never says die, her ambition is killing her. He dresses with charming informality, she's a slob. He's a sexy he-man, she's a conniving slut. He's a man of the world, she gets around. He knows how to delegate, she has others do all the work. He never shirks details, she nags everyone with trivia. He's a perfectionist, she drives herself nuts. He says what's on his mind, she talks too much. He never stops being a man, she's no longer a real woman. He acts with authority, she's a know-it-all. . . . And on and on.

The word "promiscuous" is a widespread sample of linguistic chauvinism. Who would paste that term on a boy? Everyone takes *his* sexual hijinks for granted. Frantic parents are more likely to push daughters into the arms of the law for exercising sexual options reserved for sons, possibly because they fear a "bad girl" name will remove her from the marriage market. Juvenile Courts in general interpret *any* sexual activity by a single young woman as tantamount to promiscuity—and the mere suspicion is often all they need to arrest and convict an unmarried girl of a "statutory offense," such as victimless crimes limited to legal minors. Have these "promiscuous" children—for such they are—been summoned to the prisoner's dock and possibly to institutional incarceration because they summon something from far antiquity: fear of Eve's unbridled sex that is the primal source of male chauvinism?

Revision of chore responsibility in the household toward a more equitable balance has been allotted an important place on the practical agenda of anti-chauvinist strategy. Some men have chosen to be house-husbands as their wives take on an earning function. Since a paternity leave policy went into effect at New York's Board of Education, a growing number of men interrupt their work for child-care. Will the American male universally achieve enough release from machismo to become homemaker fathers? A Harvard-based project on Human Social Development questioned four hundred parents in Cleveland with children between three and eleven. More than half believed that men and women should share housekeeping and family chores—but the followup survey revealed that only 5 percent actually did. The final count showed 90 percent of the wives and 85 percent of the husbands unalterably conditioned by habit, familial custom or religious tradition to regard "the house" as a territorial imperative of the "little woman." A spokesman for the research team thought the statistics reflected the popular view throughout the United States and Canada.

In my young parent stage, endemic chauvinism blinded me against the pleasure and closeness to one's child that more enlightened fathers now derive. Rare indeed was the pater familias who bothered his head or hands to learn how to fold, pin up and exhale the smell of a diaper. As to the handyman role, we were too important for any house chore except perhaps inserting an electric cord into its destined plug. So I am all the more proud to see new, young fathers who have disengaged themselves from these primitive taboos. Whether married or in cohabitation, they have sloughed off the ploy that cuddling a baby in public is an act of treason against the male of the species.

That these young husband-fathers of the new breed gladly share household cares is a dividend of their liberation from paying homage to retarded adolescence. I have watched them with admiration outdoors and at home. In most instances their dress, ideology and general lifestyle designate them to be fully emancipated and freed from machismo.

The query "Do you work?" addressed to more than half of North American women over sixteen could be answered in the affirmative—and the average workwoman earns only 58 percent of a man's wages. When the question is addressed to a housewife it may evoke, deservedly, a cold stare. She *does* work! But our North American value system denies the noun "work" to activity, however strenuous, when it draws no paycheck. Statistics Canada for 1977 disclosed that if homemakers had been paid they would have earned $74 to $84 billion, and a special study reckoned that the fiscal amount credited to unpaid housework by Canadian women was between 35 percent to 40 percent of the gross national product. The estimate is 32 to 36 percent in the United States. Yet only paid housework by persons outside the family is counted in the GNP, and then only when earnings are reported to the tax department. . . .

"A modest woman seldom desires any sexual gratification for herself; she submits to her husband only to please *him*. But for the desire of maternity, she would rather be relieved of his attentions." That quotation from a nineteenth-century marriage manual can serve as a precis of the gross, unconscionable inconsistency that distorts even now our cultural view of feminine sexuality. Along with the Augustinean image of carnal woman in league with the Devil and equipped with sex to pervert man's reason surfaced her antithesis: the female whose crown of glory was frigidity. In the Victorian Era, upper-class ladies meeting for tea primly paraded their sexlessness with an air of self-congratulation that almost matched the multiple-orgasm recital by women today. The Victorian apostles of female purity were duplicated by the white plantation lovelies in the pre-Civil War South, pedestalized in crinolines and childlike isolation; their surrogates for coitus were black slave girls.

Warrior knights of the Middle Ages worshiped and the troubadours serenaded their ladies with scrupulously non-sexual ardor. I have long suspected that the exaltation of chivalry then as now was phony blather and decorative fustian to conceal the denaturing of women into toy dolls devoid of passion or cerebellum. A considerable segment of the older female population today still hanker for the hat-tipping, door-opening, curbside-walking, dinner-check-paying swain whose obsequiousness was not wholly free, I suspect, of snide contempt. History seems to show that the souls of women were most revered when their bodies were desexualized. Chaucer's *Wife of Bath* did not evoke a high opinion of her character, but she had fun. Females received least honor during periods of heterosexual lustiness like Chaucer's time in England.

From the most ancient to the last word in modern erotic art, the female has been portrayed on occasion reading a book, munching a tidbit or occupying herself with other diversions during coitus. No artist ever portrayed a male in such extraneous postures. Feminine reaction to phallic frenzy apparently swings from painful suffering at one end of the spectrum through complete indifference to orgasmic ecstasy at the other. Her pleasure is often derivative, born of delight at giving rapture to the man. What would the reproductive record of mankind have been if sperm ejaculation had provided no more fun than ovum extrusion? It is no insult to womankind to doubt that they would have undergone voluntarily the rigors of parenthood without the pleasure-bonus of sexual intercourse. Judaism recognizes the ebb and flow of female sexuality. On the one hand she may reject her husband's sexual overtures, but on the other she is encouraged to take the initiative, being promised a reward of fine offspring.

As I see it, men have utilized their political and economic advantage to overcome the sexual spontaneity advantage of women. But do-it-yourself livelihood options for the "weaker sex" have begun to stiffen the female spine. Training for economic survival on her own should be part of every girl's formal education.

What is the clergyman's first obligation in an endeavor to which he must consecrate himself in awareness of religion's past disservice as progenitor and preserver of male chauvinism? He must exert maximum leadership clout to uproot it from our respective turfs, our individual base of operations in church and synagogue. The terrain of battle discloses many strategic objectives. For every sortie against male chauvinism and all forms of gender injustice, the basic strategy was epitomized by Dean Hoge of Catholic University in Washington, D.C., who stated on April 22, 1981 that there will be no turning back from the sexual revolution for college students; their views on sex and other issues of personal freedom are as liberal as their counterparts' in the sixties. How can the pulpit help shape the enduring fact of personal freedom? In that seminal truth's light, the clergy can seek and find what God-centered religion *really* should believe about the relative status of men and women. These two lines, written by George P. Winship, Jr., are a signal of hope:

> God chose the humblest role that Godhead can;
> For our redemption SHE became a man.

7

Second Thoughts
on the Superwoman

"If we're fragile, supportive, not too spunky and remember that boys don't make passes at girl smart-asses, the prize
will be a king-size bed and the privilege of patting down the sheets
every morning." This is one of the caustic sneers by an embattled
libber at the prospects, expectations and strategic requirements of
pre-emancipated woman. A second and more sanctimonious
version that "God created woman to keep her womb open and her
mouth shut" is followed by one from that arch-chauvinist "Bill"
Shakespeare: "Frailty, thy name is woman." Yet, many of his
major female characters (Lady Macbeth, King Lear's Goneril and
Regan, Hamlet's mother, Kate the Shrew and the witches of
Endor) were strong-willed, ambitious, passionate, greedy and
cruel often to the point of plotting murder.

Shakespeare's predilection for base women comported with
his illustrious penchant for dramatic composition; these harridans
were excellent props to an unparalleled genius for exciting narra-
tive. This is not a peripheral detail, however. We cannot overlook
the fact that the most creative and scintillating literary imagination in the Western world conceived the human female in terms of
such legendary opprobrium. The Bard of Avon in his contempt
for the female of the species distilled for theatrical perfection the
patterns, symbols and representations of the daughters of Eve that
impinged upon him not only in the womanizing environment of
his own time and place; they also were the cumulative inheritance
of countless centuries.

Trendy historians attuned to today's feminist movement hint
that the Eternal Woman bestrode the human race about eight
thousand years ago through the enormous power of sexual desira-
bility concentrated in the clitoris. Social order was then unknown,
they say; the sole authority (or anarchy) resided in the tiny
repository of rapture at the top of the orifice between the female's

legs. Not until the male shifted the center of action and attraction to the less volatile vagina did a semblance of civilized discipline enter the world. (Sigmund Freud, according to militant paladins of feminism, aborted a promising switch back toward clitoris preference and feminine ascendancy—in his era at least—by centralizing the vagina.)

Be that as it may, the alleged, possibly non-existent period of woman's dominance under the sign of Queen Clitoris was at best only a momentary interlude in the ageless annals of woman's humiliation. The first battered wife cowered in a prehistoric cave—and her successors have never left the domestic tableau, wherever it chanced to be. Woman was the original persecutee, at the vagrant will of her mate's brawn; subjection and fear were built-in appurtenances of the narrow domain she dwelt in. Primitive woman, however, was not a sickly vine encircling her mate for protection and paying for it with servitude. To estimate the cave-woman's physical hardihood by the standards of today's sheltered urbanite is to lack perspective. Ancient woman *had* to be strong to survive and assure the future of the race. She was no match, however, for the male. And, whether we like it or not, sheer brute muscle tipped the scales in the millenial man-woman confrontation. The war of the sexes is more than a phrase!

Leopold Zunz, a prominent nineteenth-century Jewish scholar, epitomized the historic martyrdom of his people in a classic statement: "If suffering at the hands of others is reckoned by duration and intensity, Israel has experienced travail beyond all others." I am not one to deny his dictum. The people of Christ is the Christ of peoples. Nevertheless, on the scale of time, no ethnic or religious group can equal the repressive, belittling, the subtly contemptuous dole meted out to women by the irrevocable fact of their gender. Sporadic incidence of matriarchal societies interrupted the otherwise unbroken continuity of perfunctory, well-entrenched chauvinism that was always exalted by the "church" to an article of faith. In protean forms, in a broad gamut of refinements, the lordship of the male was taken for granted as an edict of the Lord.

The woman one loves—mother, wife, sister, lover—is the end product of the response made by her mind and spirit to the condition of inferiority in status and power imposed by her ancestors over a time period coeval with the cultural evolution of mankind. Despite aeons of change in the manner and means of human existence, the imbalance of power in man-woman encounter has shown a constancy different only in degree and violence of expression from the hunger for food and sex; the genus female is the oldest victim of continuous oppression by the powerful against a class unable to resist by arms.

Considering organized religion's mathematical infatuation with myths in direct proportion to their longevity (how else can one explain the centrality of Adam and Eve in church doctrine?), it is not astonishing that Woman prostrate and powerless, a million-year artifact of male mentality, was assumed to be a fixed item in the grand design of God. Organized religion hugs the big success story. Ecclesiastical circles could not be expected to recognize either the need or the possibility of women's liberation. Less than two decades ago I did not exclude myself from sporadic addiction to the state of smug and wilful blindness.

Academic interest in woman's psyche and social situation has touched my curiosity no less than her sexuality has quickened the gonads. My first venture into print on the subject came in 1924 during my first year in a rabbinate at Niagara Falls, New York. A full-page article on "Women" appeared in the press and I delivered a learned lucubration on their significance before the town's literary club. In 1963 I wrote an article for the Toronto *Globe and Mail* on "Twentieth Century Woman." I allude to it now as evidence of male myopia and frivolity:

> Woman is the most successful American revolutionary. To many students of the war between the sexes she may be comparable to the praying mantis who consumes her mate as a reward for impregnating her. She is over-privileged, over-dynamic and over-dieted. The favorite types are: Mom, who smothers her child's soul with a love both carnal and lethal; glittering encircler of fashion salons; do-gooder bully of mayors and boards of education; gigolo-companioned survivor of terminated tycoons; bright-eyed siren who lures a hypnotized swain into the nuptial noose; lady executive who with tinted finger-nails pries open the oyster of big business. Rarely in history has the human female been so expansive, expressive and expensive.

But the shameless parody goes on. The prevalent patter about women's equality is vaporized into wind by the brute fact that she has a biologically permanent monopoly on parturition. Equality of the sexes is nonsense as long as child bear-and-care is the prime responsibility of one and, at most, an auxiliary condescension by the other. During pregnancy and the weaning cycle the female is emotionally dependent and deprived of mobility. The resultant superior competence, by sheer necessity in intuitive human relations, will enrich her character and contribute to her spiritual growth; that is definitely not equality of power. She may be less susceptible than the naive, incurably romantic male to mob illusions about national honor and fantasies of military pizzazz, less likely to be fobbed off by the glory of fatherland or the divine destiny of race (albeit ferocious enough when the nest is imperiled)—but such healthy cynicism devoid of decision-making confers more grace than aggrandizement.

Why do I encapsulate the aeons-long, universally accepted, inextricably impacted presence in human reckoning of women's inferiority? Because it underscores the phenomenal magnitude of the surge toward women's liberation that began only a few seconds ago on the scale of human evolution. The course to full liberation has barely overcome the first hurdles; nor can it be said that the advances are positive, irreversible or even unflawed! Yet the burden of a thousand of years old cultural suitcase on humanity's shoulders is now being examined. We want to know what the actual contents of this sack of anti-feminist notions are that we have been carrying since we crouched in caves on a primordial hillside. Are they the cumulative clap-trap of the ageless night? If so, let us empty the sack and fill it with ideas that reflect a peerless challenge: God made humanity but only humanity can make humanity human to proceed unencumbered, no longer wobbling up the next rung.

The once plaintive beeps of feminine remonstrance by suffragettes, free-love tribunes, heroines of the incendiary word (Margaret Mead notwithstanding) have been absorbed in a piercing trumpet sound of advocacy. Disruptive changes in North American social structure and attitude have tilted the familiar immobile applecart. The domino theory of successive national conquests by Communism so beloved by American hawks crying havoc for the Vietnam War has at last justified itself: one bastion of chauvinism after another has fallen to women's liberation. From the din and clatter a "new woman" has emerged. Is she truly liberated? Where shall we find her? Where is she most visible?

The single exclamation "Super!" has become a linguistic commonplace in the younger set's lexicon of extravagant exuberance. It is applicable to hamburgers, "joints," the team's quarterback or someone's current lover. Freud affixed it to "ego," Nietzsche to "man," showbiz press agents to "star," real estate developers to "market"; a musical even tagged it on the name Jesus Christ! "Super" marks the absolute; beyond it no further garland of excellence can exist.

"Superwoman" was added to the pantheon of higher beings around the first year of the seventh decade of the twentieth century. She embodied both the achievement and the dream of the movement for women's liberation—a combination of TV's "Bionic Woman" and Whistler's Mother! Conceived in the heyday of "doing my own thing," gestated in the self-relying, self-improving (and self-serving?) Me-Too generation, brought to birth in the inflammatory glow of the new passion to "prove myself," the job prospectus of Superwoman is so taxing that she may *do herself in.*

A television commercial's jingle in Madison Avenue style ballyhooed an "8-hour perfume for the 24-hour woman," for a woman who "can put the wash on the line, feed the kids, pass out the kisses and get to work by five-of-nine—'cause I'm a wo-man." But there's a hasty brush mark in this portrait. Being a denizen of the middle class, she dumps the laundry into a washing machine, the clothesline having been banished to the terrain of the work-woman proletariat. She rushes from, not only to work. En route to work, she drops off little Allen or Dorothy at school, at the day-care center (if there is one), or with a non-resident baby-sitter. En route home, she takes them to dancing lessons, the orthodontist, music lessons, Cub Scouts, etc. She cooks (or supervises radial oven dinners), establishes peace among siblings, reassembles the kitchen and the dishes, with an occasional assist from a reluctantly liberated husband, unless she's one of the divorced singles who also helps her son or daughter with homework; she vacuums the rugs, shops for groceries, cajoles the kids to bed, throws the wet laundry into the dryer; grades papers if she is a school teacher, worries if there is trouble at the office or the shop. She dresses for VIP social functions, conducts morale building chats with her husband, who has been reading or watching television to escape worrying about *his* day at work.

Self-liberating movements must fashion a fantasy ideal to fascinate and galvanize the zeal of the followers they seek. Christianity filled its dream with world-abjuring saints, Communism was enamored of the self-obliterating proletariat, women's liberation conjured up Superwoman. At her most glamorous she is

what the pent-up self-suppression ground in by age-long sub-
missiveness can be expected to produce when it meets an historic
moment of unprecedented opportunity provided by an electronic
age that throws off miracles with the regularity of an assembly
line. Tailored to the sexual revolution, she unleashed a surge of
romantic excess that envisaged a female writing the great American novel or researching a cancer cure in one side of her brain and
using the other side to rear the ideal American family.

Granted that this cosmic Superwoman inevitably must be
shrunk to the pots and pans, diapers and drudgery, paychecks and
parsimony of a daily work-home routine, does she exist at all?
Every female who draws a wage on a job outside her home is a
potential Superwoman. That the North American image of True
Womanhood has moved from Supermom to Superwoman needs
no explanation, except to introduce a truism from our national
scene; the girl who was told that growing up meant husband,
kids, keeping house is now a grownup being programmed for
man, kids, keeping house, job (or a "career"). I suspect that guilt,
the goals and the grind are achingly familiar to most of the
women who chance to scan this page, for the simultaneous
pressures of home, family, job, and the relentless contemporary
ukase of heightened consciousness require the adroitness, skill,
imperturbality and strength of an old-time Barnum and Bailey
"champeen" juggler. And, like the circus performer, Superwoman
receives the cheers of the feminist multitude—but her act is often a
reaction to the prod of bread: inflation in a devil-take-the-hind-
most economy.

Money-strapped life offers women no more choice about
outside employment than Pro-Life offers about abortion. For
households of the middle class, double income is on the way to
unexceptional necessity status. The poor have always prized the
"extra" pittance of a non-pregnant wife. But with a lifespan
nudging eighty-two, motherhood is no longer a life-time job—
and grandma's baby-sitter slot has shown severe limitations in
feasibility and endurance.

Another vital statistic: 40 percent of all marriages end in
divorce. It is irrelevant whether the breakup is the cause of
woman's entrance into the workplace by forcing her to go it alone,
or whether it is an effect by expanding her self-confidence, her
male contacts and courage to end an already deteriorating union.

Workwomen figures suggest a staggering tide, the twentieth

century's most far-reaching social change: 51 percent of North America's adult female population; wives working solely in the house, outnumbered by two-job wives, one paid on the outside; 5.5 million are mothers of pre-school children. Of all married moms with kids under six, 43 percent have paycheck employment and 7 million children, of whom only 1.6 million get day-care in public, private or commercial facilities. The huge remainder are kept in tow by expensive baby-sitters, in improvised nursery schools by mothers' rotating co-ops, by house-key neck pieces, or nothing. This is in an ultra-rich country resonant with religious rhetoric, honeycombed with free-spending government agencies, dedicated to "the family"—and untouched by the need to build a serious child-care program for mothers who apparently have been "liberated" to the privilege of choosing economic deprivation with their kids or "benign neglect."

The "decadent" French have created an extensive crèche system, a free kindergarten network, agencies for volunteer-sitter placement and about 200,000 professional nannies. Communist Russian centers enroll infants as young as two months. The government puts practically every woman into a labor spot, from street cleaner to physician. Universal day-care is political policy, although frustrating shortages have dampened maternal enthusiasm for the system. The socialist Swedes provide day-care through the ninth grade and 90 percent of the parents' salary for a year to keep mom or dad at home. The 60 percent of women with kids who work earn 87 percent of men's salaries, instead of the 58 percent paid in the United States. Sweden's welfare-state generosity, one must add, had been faulted on several counts. Tots may be nudged toward the state's ideology, and some harsh critics have charged that even the Swedish system no less than the North American overly stiffens parental authority. Only 10 percent of Sweden's fathers take advantage of the state's generous paternity-maternity leave; they are sufficiently intimidated to fear that such leave may damage their standing on the promotion list.

Women's liberation American-style is far from its goal. Equal pay for equal work—or better, equal value—remains to be fought for. One of the new subtle gimmicks to bar women's entrance into top-salaried frames is amendment of the job's title. Time-Life was accused of hiring male "writers" while females with the same education and responsibilities were classified as "researchers," thereby relegating them to a lower bracket in the budget. The Pittsfield, Massachusetts' school board was constrained to pay female "housekeepers" the same as male "custodians." A skilled executive secretary, often the backbone of her employer's success, may rate a metal nameplate on her desk, but often her paycheck barely tops the lower amounts doled out to thousands of file clerks, typists and assistants—robot-like niches that allow no opportunity for the development of management aptitudes, dignity or self-worth. In 1976 these desk-chained, compulsorily charm-schooled, vestigial wage-slaves of American industry constituted 98 percent of the secretariat and earned less than the boiler room subattendant. Is that the fledgling Women's Organization for Employment which assembled several thousand persons for a noon rally in San Francisco to hear Jane Fonda? It was too circumscribed by its lady-like image for Teamster-like unionization.

One indictment echoes ex-President Nixon. In 1971 he vetoed a $15 billion Congress-approved grant to make quality child-care accessible to all on an ability-to-pay basis. The project was condemned and labeled as "government interference" that threatened family life—a deceptive slogan dear to the Radical Right in its crusade against federal abortion-aid to the poor.

Preference for parental care (father's included) scarcely calls for controversy. The question is not whether, but how? Some European corporations make it possible for parents to spend more time with their offspring. In West Germany, for instance, about half the white-collar workers can set their own schedules through "flextime"; in the United States, this is only possible for 6 percent of the full-time work-force. A consultant on company benefit plans has admitted to *Newsweek* that only the large socially aware firms are even talking about such progressive blueprints. Would a pressing labor shortage—a pipe-dream in any foreseeable economic situation—induce corporations to entice workers with such exotic bribes? Child-care directors, through their close involvement with Superwoman, have concern but no clout. Only 17 percent of women workers belong to unions. No tough-talking union boss to strong-arm an alternative work schedule into a contract, and no newly elevated big-time super-Superwoman will risk raising the eyebrows of upstairs males. Besides, 80 percent of the female workers are still plugged into so-called women's jobs: secretary, salesclerk, waitress, public school teacher; only 6 percent are managers.

Anti-ERA activist Phyllis Schafly's solicitude for the family is not exceptional enough to be worn on her sleeve or hammered into her platform plank, although she puts it there. Were not the women who work nourished on the assumption that their primary place is in the home? Has maternal tenderness withered in their bosoms and chosen to blossom in Schafly's breast? Motherhood and the household, the ceded turf, are as much the only seat of power and fulfillment for an overalled, grimy bolt-twister on the assembly line as for the ladies who lecture them on child-rearing obligations. The double burden of job plus kids is so heavy that some quit the one to have the other, foraging for whatever unsatisfying child-care arrangement is available to them. The alternative is abject poverty or denying themselves the luxury of rearing children rather than working to support a baby-sitter. Demographers say the declining birth rate in North America is both source and result of woman's out-to-work explosion. Is day-care a positive or negative factor for a child's upbringing? With definite research lacking, the usually clamant expertise is ambivalent, tentative and contradictory; it seems justifiable to agree with the majority view that hard evidence does not ascribe any harmful influence to day-care.

What of the second indictment leveled at the Swedish system, that participation in parental-leave benefit by fathers makes them afraid to lose their jobs? Resistance to this open avowal of auxiliary motherhood would be inevitable in any but the most enlightened male psyche. It is conceivable that such a role, however noble and necessary in straitened economic circumstances, might embarrass the father and degrade his self-image. Masculinity has fed its authoritative status and esteem on the sole bread-winner role, one might say, from the halcyon Stone Age of the caveman-hunter. I have shared in counseling guilt-stricken husbands who could not abide seeing their wives go off to work, and I have talked to others on the brink of divorce or desertion who were restive under the stress of humiliation and self-reproach when their spouses' contribution to the family exchequer exceeded their own.

As to the specific fear of Sweden's fathers, there are indications that the day-care concern of corporate bosses in the United States began to fade since the sixties, when two hundred firms undertook such projects. They were later proven unpractical because on-site centers slowed company reimbursement for day-care expense or turned eyes away when high-echelon staffers brought a kid to the plant rather than tie a latch-key around his neck. Moreover, there are indications that budgetary cuts, a drop in federal funding and an over-supply of job seekers have been responsible for a swing toward corporate apathy and indifference. Par for the course! Men in the sensitive, moderate-salaried bracket hint that the big boss now looks askance at incursion of family obligation into their terrain. The dictum does not mince words—"Your job comes first!"

Superwoman confronts a miscellany of barriers in the cold appraisal of hiring nabobs. She must make the steep, unfeminine grade of toughness, have an impermeable hide, undiluted loyalty and aggressiveness—she must stop being a woman. Once she has passed the test, she is scrutinized for total commitment. Companies want to be sure that women will buck their traditional preoccupation with home and family and back the profit sheet. They also have to assure themselves that company morale will not suffer because employees, women even more than men, may resent a female boss.

A further hazard to Superwoman in search of a good job was dramatized some time ago at a trial initiated by a stenographer who had won the right to sue her employer for sexual harassment. In those days, such a case had never gone public; there was only "sex discrimination." She pursued the case for five years, never retreating from her testimony, "Suddenly I heard him say, 'I want to fuck you. It's the only way we can have a working relationship.'" Contradictory versions of the incident underscored the difficulty in proving such a charge. The Court of Appeals that permitted the woman's suit issued a landmark decision. . . . A female Yale student charged her professor with giving her a low grade because she refused to review her class notes in bed with him. Reverse situations also transpire; girls have offered to barter a roll in the hay for an A. The "casting couch," a widely disseminated item in the Hollywood scandal market, has allegedly been a sexual ploy of entertainment moguls since the days of the bucolic silent screen. The San Francisco Women Organized for Employment have deemed it necessary to issue a guide for the wide-eyed girl enamored of the word "starlet":

1. Make certain you can't be accused of encouraging.
2. Be emphatically negative in the presence of other employees.
3. If he persists, document his advances with a list.
4. If he doesn't back-up, send a memo to management.

In the fall of 1979 Patricia Harris, secretary in the U.S. Department of Health, Education and Welfare, found it necessary to issue a memo warning chief deputies in the 150,000-member agency that sexual harassment would not be tolerated. Her memo even proposed training of certain officials in the subtleties of sexual harassment and counseling on complaints. It was a remarkable document—free of bureaucratic gobbledigook.

Perhaps only a sensitive black woman like Harris could create such a directive. On April 21, 1981 the insensitive white woman, Phyllis Schafly, "informed" a Senate Committee that *"virtuous* women are seldom accosted by unwelcome sexual propositions, familiarities or obscene talk," that a woman walking across a room speaks a "universal body language" men understand and that feminist and government attacks on motherhood and dependent wives are "the most cruel and damaging sexual harassment." At the same hearing it was officially revealed that the 130 cases of sexual harassment charges pending before the Equal Employment Opportunities Commission "may be the tip of the iceberg"; a study released by the Center for Women Policy estimated at eighteen million the number of employed women overtly sex-harrassed during 1979-80. Were they *all non-virtuous*?

A president of the National Organization for Women predicted that if sex discrimination must be eliminated on a case-by-case basis, "we'll be working on this for 3,000 years." Male chauvinism in the contemporary mass mind and media suffers from the superficial jackanapes that smear every aspect of the man-woman nexus in America. Some of its ideological forbears, however, are monstrous examples of error and arrogance. In the eighteenth century, one of Great Britain's high-caste legal commentators, whose dicta had far-reaching influence on American jurisprudence, postulated that a woman's very being is suspended during marriage. The 1856 rhetoric in the law code of Georgia named as head of the family the husband to whom his spouse is subject, her legal existence being merged in him for her benefit and protection and for the preservation of public order. It has not been substantially changed, I'm told. Instead, the Reverend John Hutcheson of the Tabernacle Baptist Church, Clayton, Georgia, recently resonated, "We believe God established the family with the husband at the head."

In 1873 the Supreme Court denied women's constitutional right to practice law. Justice Joseph P. Bradley tendered ladies a compensatory compliment: "The natural and proper timidity of the female sex evidently unfits it for many of the occupations of civil life." In 1961 the liberal Warren Court upheld a Florida statute that taps women for jury duty only if they volunteer— again for their benefit, since the restriction enables them to remain at the center of family life. This gallant concession to motherhood was reversed fifteen years later when a 1976 session of the Supreme Court allowed companies to withhold pregnancy benefits under a medical plan that financed vasectomies, rejecting the argument that would outlaw sexual no less than racial discrimination. Justice Powell declared bias against women to be not "inherently odious." Even the high court's favorable verdicts reflect prevailing anti-female prejudice. I cite the striking down of Idaho's preferential treatment of men in the administration of estates and a school board's arbitrary dismissal of pregnant teachers.

Samuel Johnson's aphorism of two centuries ago that "nature has given women so much power, the law has wisely given them very little" lends more than admiration of his wit to the ponderous legalistic roadblocks against Superwoman's advance. Perhaps the astonishing incursion of women into law schools will change the temper of the profession and its polite disdain for the puny analytical talents of soft-headed "skirts." Several challenges await the lady lawyer. Did not the Lee Marvin-Michelle Triola performance point a finger at the need for an as yet unformulated type of written contract for prospective "living together" partners, especially since the judge denied contractual status to their act of cohabitation? And why not equalize the receptivity to alimony? That flagrant example of reverse sexism should be scrapped forever by the women themselves as an obnoxious remnant of their economic debasement. The Marvin trial highlighted a salutary substitute for either alimony or "palimony": a "rehabilitation" fund for a period of time long enough to ease reentry (by the woman or man, I surmise) into the work force. The Marvin judge awarded Michelle $104,000. Such a resolution of marital or non-marital breakdown validates the women's liberation faith that today's woman can look after herself. . . . A less momentous challenge to the distaff-side researcher into the vagaries of the law might stem from the huge income, large appetite and informal lifestyle of entertainers. Whatever the sexual pragmatism or vulnerability of their female roommates, these glamour-conquered women deserve somewhat more generous legalistic consideration than that accorded the soul-mate of Peter Frampton, who lost a palimony suit because her alleged contract required in its performance the commitment of adultery, "which," the judge pontificated, "remains a crime in New York State." Or should adultery be decriminalized?

Rape! A field choked by a tangle of weeds begging for the plow and new seed. Rape has been committed by husbands, lovers, friends, relatives, strangers and by invading armies. It is probably the most frequent and least reported crime of violence in the United States and Canada. The brutality of forcible sexual intercourse without consent has now entered the domain of confrontation jurisprudence. It provides an ideal setting for the professional competence and courage of a female practitioner of law, since her gender is nearly always its victim.

In the Hebrew Bible the sons of Jacob were condemned for slaughtering the males of Shechem to avenge their sister Dinah's rape. The case of David's daughter, Tamar, and his son, Amnon, involved not rape but incest, one of the crimes Jews had to shun even under the threat of death. Rape in war from time immemorial evidently has been regarded as a reward to soldiers for victory; like all peoples in biblical times, Hebrew warriors ravished captive women. Deuteronomy records endeavors to abate and humanize the practice. The Talmud's general attitude, I must confess, invites the suspicion that it reflects the subordinate rank of woman in Jewish tradition. On the other hand, a Jerusalem district court has sentenced a man to a three-year prison term for raping his own wife. Three male judges rejected the defense plea that rape does not apply to relations between a married couple, citing the Jewish law that whereas a man is obliged to have sexual relations with his wife she is not similarly obligated to engage in sex on demand with him. The verdict set a world precedent. Since her initial moral resentment may gradually turn into instinctive collaboration, the actuality of rape was deemed by some rabbinic wiseacres to be impossible. Proof of female resistance with all her might throughout penetration and thrust could not be sufficiently absolute to remove hesitation and neutrality from rabbinic scholars committed to the principle of innocence until guilt is established beyond a shadow of doubt. Also, such perfectionist vigilance against vengeful hate conformed to the prevailing view of woman's infernal and eternal sexuality. Isn't that "old devil," the theological dogma of female carnality relayed by Augustine to the Christian Church, reincarnated in most court hearings on rape?

Historically, the main stumbling block in rape trials has been the difficulty to prove lack of consent. (It is no frivolous taunt against the judges to hint that the doubt hovering in the masculine mind about feminine refusal to honor penile attention may spring from his machismo; how can she reject King Phallus?) A women's crisis center in Salem, Oregon, has put up a sign "When a woman says no, it's rape." Is that good, realistic law enforcement? A prosecuting attorney friend of mine answered, "There are many variables and degrees of 'no.'" Unless the rapee has been attacked and brutally beaten by a complete stranger, police skepticism can be humiliating. Defense counsel may elaborately question the woman's past, as though fact or fiction of virginity had some connection with the violence inflicted on her by the assailant. Should not this egregious act of judicial chauvinism be forbidden by unequivocal statute? A society that ingests a gargantuan spread of sex and violence served up with lavish decor by television, in movies and through airport paperbacks cannot possibly deny its responsibility when sex and violence erupt together into rape.

Many rapists have been freed because physicians could not find any semen in the victim's body. Two Massachusetts researchers, Nicholas Groth of Southbridge Hospital and Ann Wolbert of Boston College, reported that jurors are inclined to rely too heavily on such evidence. A study of 107 convicted rapists revealed a surprisingly large number of sexual dysfunctions that interfere with ejaculation; 16 percent became impotent during their attacks, 3 percent ejaculated prematurely, 15 percent were unable to ejaculate at all or had difficulty doing so. The researchers' conclusion was reinforced by a survey of twelve women who had been hospitalized after sexual assault; in more than half, no semen was found.

Rape might be more accurately and practically classified as a crime of violence rather than of sex—a minuscule but authentic "smell" in the numbing miasma of organized political terrorism that now threatens to suffocate the gentle art of civilized behavior. Psychological profiles of rapists too often confirm that they were out to harm women, not to "have a ball." Tests intimate that mates who force sex on spouses are themselves bestialized by a psychopathic need to wreak "punishment" on them through beating up what is readily and visibly at hand, *viz.*, their bodies. It

is not so much lust for penile thrust as for the activation of punitive power. Aggravated assault, measured by the pain and shame
it inflicts, thus becomes a caricature of coitus, a kick in the groin
instead of a kiss. Can rape victims perceive their humiliation to
be linked in kind with and not basically different from ordinary
physical assault? Can it be, for them, desexualized? I doubt that.
The dread it engenders may be likened to a man's fear of castration.

Rape's loss of its high, special profile among monstrous
crimes, by assimilation into the huge assortment of crimes under
the rubric "violence," reflects woman's loss of identity. Our male-
dominated system of jurisprudence seems to be offering her a deal
whereby she can surrender her womanhood for the law's concession to treat her as a human being. A female by the terms of this
contract is to regard rape not as an act directed at her person
specifically. Not at all! It shrinks to just another item in the vast
catalogue of human misdeeds, listed under "V" for "violence."
Almost, it may be said, by a quirk in a man's disordered mental
processes, the vagrant impulse to break bones picks a woman as its
target.

The change from "rape" to "violence" would make the traumatized victim far more willing to report and testify; it would
curtail the dangerous and potentially imitative sexual fantasies
which lurid reports of "rape" may create in sick psyches open to
such insidious influences.

Judges themselves flounder and bruise in the rape cauldron.
California Supreme Court Chief Justice Rose Bird almost lost
confirmation for her office because she ruled that rape by itself is
not "great bodily injury" in the context of the California statutes
as they were then defined. . . . Judge Hertz of Manhattan aroused
ire by deciding that a man can be tried for rape of an admitted
prostitute if he reneges on his agreed upon fee, draws a pistol and
obtains the *quid pro quo*. . . . Judge Bryan Crofty of Salt Lake City
reversed a jury's unanimous guilty verdict in a rape case on
grounds that the victim had provoked sexual assault by sitting at a
bar in a flimsy dress with a black man, taking his affection, eating
his food, drinking his drink, thus making a case for promise of
mutual consent. Women's groups vowed to agitate for the judge's
removal. One representative said Crofty apparently gives men
the right to rape and assumes women want it. Nancy Joyce,
coordinator of sixty-nine crisis center volunteers who help
victims of rape and battering, declared, "We (women) have been

taught that we have no choice, that sexual submission is our role in life."

These tragicomic incidents spell out the opportunity for female lawyers to vindicate their own liberation. Any profession should become more nurturing and caring after the admission of women to its practice. If the feminist movement has unalloyed justification, it is that any woman liberated into law or medicine would use her knowledge and skill to transform the domains of health care and legalistic interpretation, and that she might respond to the needs of all women, people of color, children, the aged, the dispossessed—for whom law and medicine function largely as repressive controls. Certainly, she will take note of her sisters, grievously scarred by violence to their sex.

That anti-rape laws should be erased as unconstitutional until male victims also benefit not surprisingly has been proposed by exponents of the same equality principle so fervently espoused by feminists. Recently in California the statutory rape offense punishable by law was challenged by an eighteen-year-old youth convicted for having intercourse with his not-unwilling girlfriend of sixteen (under the age of consent). His legal counsel alleged that the law discriminated against males, who under its provisions and by definition could not make a case. The California Supreme Court rejected that argument, apparently motivated by the female's greater jeopardy of impregnation. . . . In a similar approach, registration of nineteen- and twenty-year-old males for military service drew flak because it *excluded* females. . . . An incident of perverse and physically laborious attack on masculine dignity was provided by two women who had abducted a man at gun-point, forcing him to mount them after precipitating arousal by manual dexterity and animated self-exposure. What catapulted the pair into such defiance of law, tradition and anatomical difficulty? Sex starvation, drug-induced aberration, zany impulse, their man's mind-boggling fascination—or an irresistible need to denounce the double standard of sexual license for females in a dramatic act of self-liberation? Or was their unique panache mere seduction? I don't think it is unbelievable that a normal male can be sexually "had" by a sturdy amazon. However, I do find it hard to imagine that a self-respecting man will contend in court that he was the object of seduction rather than its subject. In any case, the frenetic hip-and-thigh movements ordained by his virility and ageless evolutionary precedent disqualify "lack of consent." He would be reduced to charging the lady with committing violence against his person.

Bodily mayhem almost always accompanies forcible sex. After centuries that held aloft the manly "exercise of marital rights," the law now is more concerned with protecting individuals from domestic violence, of which child abuse and wife battering are an appalling expression. Public abhorrence of wife beating has risen to such a pinnacle that it occasionally condones the ultimate in violence: murder of a husband by a victimized wife supposedly rendered desperate though not insane or irresponsible.

Spontaneous applause from feminists has rippled around courtroom verdicts of a light sentence or acquittal. The accused rarely contests factual evidence, confining her testimony to an account of provocation. One wife restrained her sobbing long enough to tell me that "when the cops came at the urgent call of neighbors, they engaged in trivial chatter about football" with her husband. A New York criminologist maintains that police practice the informal "stitch rule": "make no arrest unless a wound requires a certain number of stitches." A Denver study accused police of discouraging the victim's report—of what the FBI named the most unreported crime in America. By all accounts three million beaten wives suffer in silent fear; some experts triple that figure.

Does a homicide case end with these tragic data for the defendant? Logic and justice can be invoked for the other side as well. The principle of retreat, obliging a person acting in self-defense to abjure violence and minimize retaliatory force, must not be uprooted by a storm of indignation. Capital punishment carried out by their own hand, moreover, will not substantially ease the lot of battered women. It revives "Wild West" frontier justice, in whose name lynch-law, all the more heinous because it had the imprimatur of a community, displaced the rule of law. Finally, the equality ostensibly (and at times ostentatiously) sought by libbers means equal culpability for criminal acts committed by women which, statistics show, have increased at an alarming rate in recent years. No more than they can expect to be seated by special courtesy in a crowded bus can they rely on consideration for their delicacy in a courtroom.

Big business also proposes to women knocking at its doors that they slough off their intrinsic qualities, perceptions and insights with which they have been endowed by a million years of evolution—"Only then will you belong with us!" The aspirant for a chance to climb and cling near to the top of the pyramid can be trapped by the rules of the game; man is bidden to express his supposedly decisive manliness, but a female's womanliness is "verboten!" In my "mere man" perspective, a woman who "makes it" is bound to hold her feminity no less precious than she might have held her virginity in a previous time. Independence, achievement, earned fame and fortune vibrate positively with masculine values; they can, however, corrode the spontaneous behavior and psyche bequeathed by the "eternal feminine." The actively striving precedent to lofty achievement in the "man's world" often is a prelude to discomfort, anxiety—and loneliness. The price for replacing the natural with the unnatural, I strongly suspect, can in the long run reach exorbitant dimensions. Self-depreciation, self-pity, inertia? Whenever I watch a VIP "spokes-person" present a statement on government or corporate policy via television, I seem to sense a vacuum in her demeanor. Is it vestigial chauvinism that tempts me to name emptiness as the place in her personality once redolent with grace, velvety softness and charm?

Nancy Friday in *My Mother/My Self*, the best-selling mix of interviews and excerpts from her own life, purports to trace the governing imprint of mother on a woman's behavior from bed-room to boardroom. Mama's preachment that competition is unladylike smacks of resentment about her own housebound life, if Friday is correct. Competition festers to hangup in a daughter who believes herself liberated, yet the wine of a big job promotion turns sour on her tongue; she fears success will make her unfeminine. It is mother who has taught her inferiority, passive-ness and pretense. For the first time in history, women have an alternative to the wife-and-motherhood meal ticket. As the door creaks open, anxieties rooted in early childhood may prevent them from walking through that door with faith in themselves.

Ingrid Bergman's movie *Autumn Sonata*, portraying a middle-aged parson's wife and the concert pianist mother she savages for childhood neglect, lays less painfully on my stomach than the ferocious irony of *My Mother/My Self*. Was Nancy Friday's pen guided into extremism by the mother *versus* daughter tension I have often sensed among the carefully but not altogether successfully hidden "secrets" in high-geared North American families? Feminist Gloria Steinem contends that women are not allowed to pattern themselves after their more adventurous fathers because society and teachers inhibit them. "Differences in sex, as they are known today, are based on the bringing up by mother; she is always pushing the female toward similarity and the male toward difference," Margaret Mead stated in a study of male-female relationships. "Women still seem to be underestimating themselves," was the conclusion reached by an overview of 3,347 undergraduates at six of America's most prominent colleges. "They have lower self-esteem and fewer aspirations than men, even though their grades may be the same."

Alice G. Sargent, a consultant on organizational behavior and on male-female issues, sheds further light on the timidity of women in business. She points out that a man in a female-dominated group is likely to be the central figure of deference and respect, whereas a woman in a male-dominated setting will probably tilt toward isolation and be treated as trivial or a mascot; a woman alone on a team may deny herself full contribution by a tendency to be invisible and unsupported.

Does Ms. Sargent's perception afford us a significant peep into the future? Feminine behavioral patterns are clearly vulnerable and ask for understanding. Female sensitivity will be more valued in a marketplace that appreciates concern for human relationships as well as for tasks tied to computers. It would then be as relevant for men to heighten their interpersonal abilities through affiliation and intimacy as for women to become more assertive. Perhaps Sargent envisages a kind of bisexual arrangement where *both* genders serve the well-being of the whole community and each other by retaining and leavening their own psychic heritages. Women's liberation thus can establish in the upper echelon work sector a model for females everywhere: not only freedom to be themselves as women but obligation to unite personal integrity and practical success.

The Superwoman who deliberately opts for a career and has been known to preempt wearing the maternity gown or to postpone it until her "time" has passed is a bourgeois phenomenon. Undeniably, the rush to the career-oriented sector and the overriding absorption in its goals marked women's liberation as a middle-class, if not elitist movement. Until relatively recently women's liberation has made little effort to appeal to the *poor* working woman. Thousands of women in menial, ill-paid, mind-anesthetizing jobs labor to eat, shelter themselves and shield their kids from hunger, with or without a man in the house; yet they *dream* of being fed, sheltered, cared for—and being dependent! *Poor* North American women do not differ that much from their Russian sisters who sweep Moscow's streets. The cleaning woman and the black domestic would be glad to scurry into a "housewife" ménage. Countless widows and divorcées who had never needed to earn their keep or learn how have divulged to me a pathetic readiness to marry or live with "any gainfully employed guy who comes along." They couldn't care less about their sisters' careers. On the other hand, innummerable heroic young divorcées support themselves, bring up their children as a single parent, work at a career and serve their communities beyond the call of duty. An inadequately publicized obstacle to ERA ratification has been the grass-roots disinterest fomented by the seeming correlation of ERA partisanship—true or merely apparent—with "class," e.g., high-level literacy and affluence. (Men wary of threats from the feminine intruder say, of course, that women want jobs to gather a few extra dollars to gratify their consumerism.) Career motivation has no place in the life plan of the poor. An awakening by women's liberation brass to the existence and claims of the "career"-scorning proletariat who *must* work for their meat and potatoes cannot be premature. Without a broadened base of active participation by full-time, often impecunious workwomen, women's liberation may not outlast the eighties.

Myra Wolfgang of the AFL-CIO, testifying against the Equal Rights Amendment, was quoted by Canadian journalist Barbara Amiel in an article published by *Maclean's*, the leading Canadian magazine: "It's one thing for a middle-class feminist to talk about the psychological uplift of E.R.A. She can afford a brief high. Her working sisters will have to pay for her 'fix.'"

Indifference to feminism also has been manifested by the economically secure, who are both seen and heard. The Mormon woman boasting with too-smug humility that she is "just a housewife, and deaf to women's rights"; the nostalgic dowager who longs for the gallant pre-Civil War southern gentleman who would doff his hat to his simpering wife in their boudoir; the man-eater whose cumulative alimonies supply her with gigolos— these are some of the less savory scorners of the shared freedoms and responsibilities of liberation.

The February 1979 issue of *New Woman*, a magazine for the emancipated, garnished its cover with blurbs on articles concerned with the methodology of a woman's emotionally secure relationships in a milieu which gives priority to her need of a man's love. Here are the titles: "That Special Quality that Keeps a Man Devoted—for Decades"; "Do You Have Any of These 11 Symptoms of Sexual Frustration?"; "How to be Happy and Overcome the Terrible Pain of Loneliness"; "Everybody Needs Somebody"; "Do You Have a Good Marriage?"; "Can You Make Him Love You Forever?" Nary a syllable about freedom, sex on your own, independence! A "new woman"? Hardly! Rather the old prototype with an increment of confusion, anxious to be counted with the lions of liberation and courted with the sheep who "baa" for a male's lifetime bedmate contract.

"Sex Object" self-acceptance has been repudiated by the liberated woman. Does she mean it in a shrewdly manipulated society that advertises erotic perfumes, push-up bras and exercise fads, that knows what the knowledgeable woman wants, of austere tailored suits or organdy blouses for work and slit skirts and bare midriffs for the evening?

Men, in general, also want to be considered handsome. How often in my seminary days was my feeling of total rejection by the university coeds assuaged at the shaving mirror when I recalled again and again that one of them had once told me (in mockery, no doubt) that I had a profile like John Barrymore! Most men, however, are content to regard their faces as a record of personal history; crags, scars, lines furrowed by experience lend them an aura of strength and struggle. But most women seem to shrink from letting the face write what they have been, and above all how long they have been. Experience and age are the classified archives that a billion dollar cosmetic and beauty parlor industry is paid to obliterate. Although double standards are anathema to me, this one, however, cannot be attributed to a masculine conspiracy. It may be that the leaders of women's liberation have not yet candidly analyzed the psychological, emotional and cultural condition of the average woman. There is a contradiction between the demand for equality of status and the desire to be physically attractive to men. There is a paradox in resenting the cosmetic imperative and at the same time refusing to disclaim it as narcissistic baggage. Should women who yearn to share and confront the challenge of our endangered human species give a damn how their complexions and contours appear to men?

In 1928, on my first trip to Israel (then a part of British-mandated Palestine), I spent several weeks in Tel Yosef, a new kibbutz. For the whole of one night I listened to a riotous communal debate on the use of lipstick. The female population was divided. A strong Socialist Left faction derided cosmetics, arguing that they are a concession to the bourgeois enrollment of the female as a sex object. "Women kibbutzniks must renounce rouge and lipstick if they are to build a new kind of nation and stand foursquare on the same footing as men," they maintained. That brave resolve of Tel Yosef faded with the years for the same reason that women's liberation in North America has failed even to assert it. The kibbutz lasses did not comprehend or measure the as yet immitigable imbalance in the proclivities of men and women. If the nuclear bomb boys would keep their fingers off the proliferating push-buttons long enough to give the human race time for further evolution, that tilt in genders may be corrected. In the meantime it merely impedes the growth of women's liberation.

To numbers of otherwise promising volunteers in the crusade for women's liberation, the gravitational pull away from it is the millions of years old injunction to wed and raise a family. Would the biblical author of "Be ye fruitful and multiply" have been silenced by a population explosion that symbolically plants a "Standing Room Only" sign on our planet? He conceived himself to be the spokesman for Almighty God whose command is irreversible. And his descendants in the synagogue and the Vatican still hear the echo of the command.

In November 1979 the chairperson of a task force on Jewish Women in a Changing Society underlined the women's liberation involvement of Jewish women. "Most of its leaders are Jewish," was her (unverified) pronouncement, "but we are different. Even as we push for equality, we are guided by Jewish values which place high priority on the family and make the woman the central figure in the home."

This Judeophilic citation is faulty on two counts. First, family orientation has burrowed deep into the tradition-inheritance of *all* people. Second, for most North American women of every ethnic origin—even Superwomen—the family shuts out all else, as it did in the days of their humbler ancestors who ventured beyond the hearth only to go to barn, field or market for food and to the well for water. In today's political and religious climate of clamorous conservatism, the pro-family call, whose aim I fully endorse, has been appropriated and politicized by "Pro-Life" and the Right. Their enormous money-power is shaping "back to the family" and related creeds into a single-issue instrument against any movement for women's rights. Can past records of propaganda power persuade us to write off the effect on Middle America of such richly orchestrated hogwash when bedrock reverence for the family is trumpeted by the salesmen of fundamentalist religious evangelism as a "born-again" stampede "back to God?"

Not all women are lured by outside jobs. Some may prefer to endure the guilt feelings provoked by a neighbor who berates her for dissent from the non-dependence dogma, rather than the guilt feeling stirred by real or fancied neglect of family. The full-time housekeeper may find herself in a marginal "box" outside the circle of aware men and women who attend smart cocktail parties and talk about the conflicts and commerce of the world. I clearly recall the words of a militant protagonist of the old-fashioned homemaker so happy in her little "fun cubicle," as she fondly termed it, that the local minister held her up as an ideal Christian! She whispered to me before an inter-faith ecumenical session I was to address, "The men benefit most from women in the work force. They know that their wives can support themselves so they don't feel any compunction about walking out. A God-fearing wife would never dream of deserting her family, even if she had a well-paying job."

A dogma was fostered by women's liberation in its all-out early phase that personal fulfillment for the modern woman is a dividend, primarily, of career. That dogma can downgrade motherhood and homemaking as an appanage of narrow horizons and trivial interests. Such devaluation of mother's currency aggravates a worsening crisis of her patience and endurance, induces maternal anxiety while diminishing matriarchal authority. Some women give the nod to the boredom and drabness of "just a housewife" rather than the scope and allure of liberation. Is women's liberation sufficiently sure of *itself* to nourish the self-assurance of (to them) "deviant mothers"? Despite the lure of North America's consumption ideal the wageless housekeeper need not feel put down. Even the Superwoman breadwinner often remains subject to the "little woman" stereotype. Betty Friedan, profiled as "founding mother, astute and caring observer of the women's movement" by columnist Ellen Goodman, once stood before an audience of superbly identifiable Superwomen to deliver an astonishing eulogy. This is Goodman's quote: "We told our daughters, you can have it all. Well, *can* they have it all? Only by being Superwomen. Well, I say NO to Superwoman!"

I beg to suggest that Betty Friedan interred the Superwoman *religion*, the idealization and the cult, *not* the Superwoman herself. She will exist as long as history's subjugation of the human female persists and impels women to resist. Betty preached the eulogy over a dream that she herself and subsequent igniters of the flame had kindled by believing the myth that women could dig out of themselves the answers and the energy to apply them. Career *and* children, factory *and* family, a tailor-made job for kudos and self as well as homemade jam, bread and cookies for the kids and their pop. With steely will and supreme effort it could be done by Superwoman alone! Of such brave stuff ideals are made!

Men have always realized that work can drain the zest for living. They took the rap for collapsing into a sofa at day's end, ignoring the kids and being hardly aware of their wives—but they had to bring home the bacon, banish the garbage and out-brazen the bill collector. For women there is no such job description. Neither our society nor their inner selves have kept up with equal employment opportunity. Nourishment (and nurture) and immediate environmental protection are still woman's province. I suspect, somehow, that rationalizing about principles and privileges and prejudices will not change it much. Do women *want* to effect a radical change above all else they want, and in sufficient numbers to make a difference? I sometimes wonder.

My profound affirmation of women's liberation objectives does not divert me from a position of ambivalence, at least in regard to its methods, which at times have seemed to border on the raucous, unduly provocative and slightly hysterical. Women's liberation is on probation, with tenure hanging suspended by the thread of an economic recovery. And the double-standard, driven deep into our psyche, still lies coiled there. I am tempted to correlate the status of woman in North America with that of Israel among the nations—allowed to enter the charmed circle as a sovereign entity, but denied the customary and honored prerogative of a country to retain morsels of territory won at enormous sacrifice and absolutely essential to its defense and survival. No other independent state has ever been ordered by world opinion, supposedly embodied in the United Nations Assembly and Security Council, to make such renunciations. The same double standard, likewise mortized in history, hobbles the movement for equality "as of right not sufferance," which defines the all-inclusive, minimal consummation of the Jews' age-long passion for a homeland and women's hope to dwell in equality. Both have won some triumphs. They need the chance to use what already has been achieved for advance toward the ultimate accomplishment. The vanguard of women's liberation must reach out beyond the parochial aim and horizon of an enfranchised, unapologetic woman to the place where callousness toward the endemic encroachment of corporate power, fundamentalist religion and political illiteracy is summoned to justify itself.

More importantly, Friedan's eulogy called on both sexes to pursue a practical program of social betterment. However slight the agenda may be, it marks a giant step toward the enlistment of women's liberation in the ever-renewed struggle for a society that promotes the well-being of all persons. Whether out of the impending retrogression and the need for a broader base, or out of the mature understanding that the liberation of women is an integral part of and dependent upon the liberation of *everyone* from the bonds of inequity and iniquity, Friedan's growth from the mystique of the individual feminine to the espousal of a revolutionary feminism was destined from the start. Did not women trudge and drudge at the side of men to settle the Old West? Did they not share military combat with men in revolutionary Russia and in China? Did they not farm and fight for the birth and defense of Israel like the others, neither asking nor expecting exemption from risk? Israel harbored three generations of pioneers over sixty years and five wars. Together men and women cast off the stifling ghetto subservience of Woman and tried to establish true, honest relationships as the matrix of a sovereign, secure state. That ideal means gender equality—a principle, abrogated by Israel's politically ambitious Orthodox rabbinate, but vigorously alive for the progressive majority of its people.

Why do I particularize the pioneer stage of a nation's history for its urgent need to bring women forward out of pampered seclusion into unhampered service, at the side of men or independently? Because I perceive North America to be bogged down in such a stage now—between a world that is dying and a world so far powerless to be born, between an increasingly unacceptable present and a future that eludes imagination, between political mediocrity, intellectual stagnation, moral hypocrisy, corporate avarice, religious arrogance and plastic values—in a word, endemic dehumanization! With woman's liberation, men will be liberated. The eighties are packed with portent; they will see a choice made. The struggle to bend the mind away from the dead past marks a pioneering adventure no less indelibly than the massive efforts of the nineteenth century to bend the wilderness toward the now evanescent American dream. The feminist movement has the opportunity to replenish itself and resuscitate the fading hopes of the American masses. It is the only radicalism of the Left still alive and kicking in America, and therefore the first movement named for destruction by the radicalism of the Right.

Some anthropologists maintain that there never has been a society in which men did not predominate—and they cherish their top-dog status. An ingrained habit of lordliness is not easily broken—even with a will to do so. Literature from Homer to Hemingway has exalted the male's rites of passage on the field of battle and in the boudoir. Hemingway virtually wrote the code of behavior for modern machismo; the heroes of his stories did whatever was expected of an elemental man. Manhood was a prize to be won by feats of machismo—and so it is for many males today. It was the popularly mocked "hippy" in the sixties who mounted a brave though doomed challenge to the Organization Man of the fifties. What the hippies began was a kind of unpremeditated ground seeding for women's liberation. The civil rights movement of the sixties harvested the fruits, organizing against Establishment hostility the social, often semi-mystical insights of loving, non-militant flower children. But civil rights leadership did not follow the pattern out of machismo; it fertilized the seedbed of women's liberation by flagrant indifference to its ultimate objectives.

"The black woman," Michel Wallace concludes at the end of her published work on *Black Macho and the Myth of the Black Superwoman*, "belongs to the only group in this country which has not asserted its identity." The black matriarchal Superwoman is as mythical, she suggests, and as politically helpless as the black macho stud. Yet the *black* females were the first to rebel, forging a road to freedom rides, sit-ins, voter-registration drives, even street brawls with club-swinging police. They proved that women had the brains and the guts to liberate themselves. No longer bound by groups who diluted and polluted the new social revolution with old sexual politics, female civil rights graduates began to group and grope for definition of themselves and to discuss their goals.

By that time the movement that had sharpened their eye-teeth was splintered by factional disputes, but the temper for women's emancipation had begun to rise. In its weaning by the tentative Left of the sixties the feminist uprising had begun to be radicalized. Veterans of those days faulted the National Organization for Women for sacrificing informality, exuberance and free-wheeling debate for corporation-like reports, public relations and disciplined adherence to a "party line."

J. Edgar Hoover called the first trial demonstration of women's liberation "subversive," which in his book was synonymous with "radical." . . . Betty Friedan's name was dropped from the 1980 World Almanac's list of the twenty-five most influential women in the United States because she represented the "militant faction" of women's liberation . . . and now Evangelist Bill Bright has launched a billion-dollar crusade of right-wing ministers, many of them religious broadcasters, to enthrone fundamentalist theology, the political New Right and *their* concept of God over the American people—and while doing so to unmask the ungodliness of the movement for women's rights.

"The justice that some men (and women) seek is the change others fear," is painted on a wall poster above my desk; it can be a manifesto for women's liberation. Can the Superwoman movement visualize itself as a supergadfly stinging both genders into common espousal of the goals they share as human beings caught up in a time of social decay? The air of the United States and Canada has become tensed and clogged with the flaccid, deadend conservatism of men once distinguished by prescience and probity. The exotic hothouse growths of the sixties have withered away and its former circus barkers are either in hiding or in three-piece suits. Women's liberation alone seems to promise redemptive rebirth of a serious, gravely concerned radicalism begotten by need to heighten the responsiveness of secular government and spiritual religion to a giant step toward enlightened change.

The distinction of women's liberation as the radical Left is further acknowledged by the opposite end of the North American spectrum: a cluster of neo-conservative intellectuals, America's elite ideologues. Many of them are Jews, maestros of academic learning—Nathan Glazer and Daniel Bell of Harvard, Seymour Martin Lipset of Stanford and editor Irving Kristol, the man who trod a path from anti-Communism to Trotskyism to liberalism to the Right, now a road well-marked by the onrushing feet of born-again Right-thinkers such as Eldridge Cleaver, Patrick Moynihan and Watergate's Charles Colson. Their center organ is the monthly magazine *Commentary*; its editor, Norman Podhoretz, launched it in 1970 on a stentorian crusade against radicalism on all fronts, nailing pretentious sobriety to frolicsome irresponsibility by charging that leaders of the anti-war movement were less interested in terminating America's invasion of Vietnam than in promoting a Communist triumph. In 1967 I journeyed to Hanoi and talked with Ho Chi Minh. It was a mission of peace. The Podhoretz slander is a gratuitous insult to a host of men and women who opposed the most costly blunder in the annals of our country.

Can a change in law even when formalized in the Constitution be assumed to effect a change in the realities of woman's place in our culture? A new sentence in the Constitution will not deracinate the tangled roots of hostility that have burrowed through time. To expect or hope for a detour or halt in the massive inching of history during one's lifespan gives hostage to romance; to await such a phenomenon's emergence from the sound and sight of phrases in a nation's credo is a fantasy headed for frustration. In a society that largely pours the instruments of power into the monopolistic palms of white males, the wrongs perpetrated against females will not be assuaged by poultices administered through the "personal growth" industry (e.g., Transcendental Meditation, EST, India-exported guru adoration and hot-tubs). They leech the vital force and assiduously hoarded funds of predominantly female seekers while transforming their quest for identity into commercially profitable and politically defusing narcissism. Nor is fashionable patter about a "liberated lifestyle," i.e., sexual freedom, little more than a temporary tranquilizer. Once for all time the principle of sex equality must be spelled out where it cannot be erased. The future of women's liberation cannot be calculated in a vacuum. Trends seem to be forming from whose effects women's liberation will not be isolated. I dare to mention them with considerable misgivings, allayed only by the realization that I shall not be "around" to be held to account for my lack of prescience:

1. Rehabilitation of marriage among the young, erstwhile candidates for women's liberation leadership, not to get a meal ticket or primarily to have children. Wedding bells have always been, for most females, an unadvertised priority. Now they ring as

a backdrop to almost every counseling or conversational experience in female company. The motivation for cohabitants and the few others, I am persuaded to say, is emotional stability, a "reliable bed partner," as one social agency worker admitted. . . . According to a recent educated guess business enterprises related to weddings have increased in number, magnitude and profit.

2. The health of women's liberation is meshed with the health of the North American economy. Prospects for employment are dwindling and with them jobs for women. The statistical graph for prediction is darkened by remedy-resistant inflation, reduced productivity, global tensions, government voracity and waste, foreign oil monopoly, loss of industrial supremacy—and gloom. Whatever the unfair practices in the workplace have been, having no place to work will cut the roots of independence and self-assertion that sustain the feminist progress.

3. The New Right pools vast resources to reverse the progressive turns of the last decades, including women's liberation. In such a climate the movement and all sensitive, concerned people will need the active guidance, collaboration and progressive vision of clergy who can sense the threat and can gird themselves for resistance.

8

Clergywomen:
Key to the Kingdom

The sinuous (and sensuous) priestesses who served in the ancient pagan temples dedicated mainly to female sex deities sold their bodies for the maintenance of these temples by performing the rites of intercourse in ceremonial service. They were the first clergywomen that we read about in history books, but they were also the last. For centuries the Jewish-Christian ecclesiastical patriarchs refused to even consider sharing with women their rulership of our earthly haven and control of admission to the heaven above.

Except for sporadic outbursts of pietistic frenzy by female devotees of Christ during the Middle Ages and the sacrificial consecration of nuns, the "Brides of Christ," that revered the Host, the Mass and the Eucharist without fully ministering to them, no female person has trod the Christian altar as ordained clergy. How could untaught Woman expect to reach the rank of *Rabbi* (my teacher, my master), how could she, the "spiritual carrier of Satanic sexuality," aspire to represent God's son? Females, therefore, entered the synagogue as the underprivileged, never ascending the *bimah* (altar); they entered the sanctuary of Jesus as cleaning women, penitents, altar society subalterns, or as cloistered, depersonalized Sisters.

The first major breach in the hitherto impenetrable walls of fortress-religion was the growing demand by women for equal recognition and ordination as fully fledged servants and interpreters of God's will and way. The intricate mazes of chapel, church and temple have been calibrated to examine, express and enforce the doctrines of religion and the duties of mankind. In that crucial undertaking women now demand an equal role.

Of all the truth-squads—science, rationalism, etc.—our eruptive world has sent against the battlements of religion as it was, the freshest yet is this clamor by women to share the prerogatives, perquisites and responsibilities hitherto monopolized by the "Fathers."

The fact that women's influence on politics has been far from drastic or even noteworthy has little relevance in this case. The goals and mechanics of mundane government do not evoke women's distinctive talents. The backrooms of wheeler-dealer politics is not her milieu and the women who successfully master its techniques usually seem to be mastered by its ethics. The world of commerce and trade is yet to show signs of the "feminine mystique." Female invasion of the pulpit has not been massive enough to warrant high expectations. In the meantime, women continue to knock at the gates and incite confusion among the forces entrenched behind them.

Evangelical Presbyterians have permitted the ordination of female elders since 1930 and of women clergy since 1956; not until 1978 did the denomination insist on making the election of female elders obligatory. Several conservative delegates to the General Assembly attacked this extension as infringement of local church rights. Representatives of the church's 2.5 million membership upheld the ruling, with temporary exemption for recalcitrant congregations; a hundred of them warned that they would secede unless the exemption became permanent.

A similar ruckus fractured the Reformed Church, oldest in America, I'm told. Despite its repute for possessing a well-disciplined and highly educated male ministry, some free spirits ordained women without official authorization. The chief executive visualized wholesale desertion from church ranks if such lawless custom breaking were legalized. Although in 1958 a synod found no biblical or theological justification for denying ordination to females, action to endorse it repeatedly has been turned down by regional units of the sturdy West, in contrast with the effete East which saw one Brooklyn woman consecrated in 1978.

A Southern Baptist church in Columbia, South Carolina, revoked the ordination of Shirley Carter Lee, the second woman in the history of the denomination to achieve that status, because she was three months pregnant when married. Having loyally served a year as chaplain of a state correctional institute for women, she decried the non-acceptance by the church of persons joined "in the sight of God" prior to a formal wedding. She testified that nowhere did the Bible confine the start of marriage to the marital ceremony, reminding her judges that several male Baptist clerics caught in adultery had merely been transferred to other pastorates. Evidently the double standard is more than a *bar to* the pulpit for females, but a *bane in* it!

Bishop Paul Moore of New York's Episcopal diocese ordained Ellen Marie Barrett, a professed lesbian, to the priesthood in 1978, at a time when the three-million-member church was already being torn apart by the clergywomen controversy. Disgruntled conservatives formed a schismatic alternative. The storm of criticism caught the bishop flatfooted because he had been a civil rights anti-war activist and had himself been incensed by a previous irregular ordination of eleven women in the Philadelphia district.
. . . The Lambeth Conference of Anglican bishops, which meets once every decade to discuss the spiritual well-being of sixty-four million faithful in sixty-five countries, voted decisively in 1978 to accept the ordination of women in the United States, Canada, New Zealand, Australia, Hong Kong and India. But it upheld the ban on British women clergy, despite support for a reversal of that decision by the Archbishop of Canterbury, a preponderance of bishops and members of the laity. It was the rank-and-file clergy who had voted it down. Rumor had it that Anglo-Catholics shrank from an act which might jeopardize reunion with the Vatican, while the evangelical-minded, in a strange coalition, ruled out any "warrant for female clergy in the Bible". . . . Over and over, the damning reference occurs: "Not in the Bible!"

In August 1980 the Vatican declared that married Anglican clerics could be ordained as Catholic priests. Two Episcopal priests had petitioned for that innovation three years before; they were among the seventy priests in the Los Angeles-based Pro-Diocese which broke with the Episcopal Church because it had decided to ordain women. Most Catholic scholars interpreted the Vatican's action as a reward to the Anglican dissidents for opposing female ordination. Apparently, the chairman of Notre Dame's theology department commented that the exclusion of women was far more important to the Vatican than the exclusion of married people in the clergy.

The bibliolatry that immobilizes the church's already depleted vital fluids did not freeze the United Methodists, who for years have inducted women into their clergy, having elected the first woman bishop in any major denomination. Not until recently, however, do congregants actually receive a woman as their personal pastor. A female associate minister of a towering Methodist cathedral gave me a glimpse of the various reactions to her pastorate. Some congregants gave her "looks of astonishment, quick, favorable relatedness, rejection of a doer of weddings and funerals, preference or aversion for a woman counselor, the feeling that she is a 'threat,' not only to the wife of a male co-minister but also to parishioners, who steer their husbands away from church leadership to insulate them against close contact with 'Reverend Miss' or 'Mrs.'—apart from the 'threat' a competent and vigorous 'she' may mount against male colleagues."

Church finance, another Methodist woman cleric informs me, bears a sign in lurid red, "Female pastors keep out!" She has learned to string out the skirmishes and avoid engaging in battle on too many fronts at once. Yet even a whimsical sense of humor in an enlightened, future-bent branch of Christendom could not blind her to the conclusion that the women clergy identity will remain in the pioneer stage for years to come.

By the 1870s women had gained access to Episcopal priesthood, Lutheran ministry and some Southern Baptist pulpits after having won the role in sundry minor Protestant sects. But pockets of strong counteraction have not been liquidated.

The chemistry of a male-female dual pastorate may be an explosive one. It can sanctify what Rollo May calls "the new Puritanism" that permits physical intimacy but interdicts intimacy of spirit, emotion, psyche; or it can ease the sexual revolution into its second phase: an about-face to the identification of intercourse with spirituality, comparable to the East Indian tantric pursuit of gradual progress through successive degrees of self-restraint to orgasm without ejaculation.

Will bisexual work-togetherness in the physical precincts of the church lead to the invention of new relationship models? The cumulative weight of joint experiences may alter the pattern that Christian doctrine has set down for women. I think the male cleric will learn to come to terms with his own sexuality, first in fantasy toward his female colleague, then toward female "others" in the congregation. Perhaps, at last, the four Greek words for love—epithymia, eros, philia and agape—will emerge from the shadows of ponderous ecclestical verbiage to take on life in operational terms.

Reform (Liberal) Jews are happily relieved of any official indecision or vagueness. As early as 1837 it was argued by the acknowledged intellectual leader of reform that within Judaism there should be "no distinction between duties for men and women." In 1846 a Breslau (Germany) Conclave declared "the female sex religiously equal with the male in its obligations and right," agreeing that women should receive a Jewish education (institutionally withheld from them in the ghetto) and that girls should celebrate Bat Mitzvah, a female's rite of passage to religious maturity (confined to boys' Bar Mitzvah by Orthodox Judaism then as now). Reform Judaism brought women out of the separate seating galleries to which the diehard synagogue had consigned them. They could ascend the *bimah* (altar) to take part in the Torah reading ritual. Conservative synagogues in increasing numbers adopt that new custom. (I have never seen a woman on the altar of an Orthodox synagogue during a worship service.) Not until 1922 did the Central Conference of American Rabbis officially approve the ordination of women; fifty years later, at Hebrew Union College-Jewish Institute of Religion coed enrollment reached 20 percent, 35 percent in the cantorial department. Eighty-two is now the statistic for females (1981). I suspect, however, that female rabbinical students find themselves in a men's club milieu, studying a male-oriented body of literature that is being taught, interpreted and translated by men in a language stocked with masculine metaphors and scarcely aware of a female scholar. It is estimated that by 1984 70 percent of Reform rabbis, in a total American and Canadian count of approximately seven hundred congregations and one million members, will be feminine. That seems an extravagant guess. At present about forty women have applied for admission to the Conservative (middle-ground) Jewish Theological Seminary, whose faculty has so far blocked female ordination. Thus it cancels out the favorable (11 to 3) stance taken in January 1979 by a Special Commission of the Rabbinical Assembly and the chancellor on the grounds that such an innovation would "disrupt the unity of our movement and the traditional values of youth." Some months later, the decision triggered a protest demonstration outside the seminary.

The Conservative commission sees no cogent argument in the refusal to train and induct women into full rabbinical status. It has recommended that immediate steps be taken toward that end. Trude Weiss-Rosmarin, erudite editor of the *Jewish Spectator* and so-called "guru" of intra-Jewish feminism, thinks the real issue arises from the ancient talmudic rule that interdicts witness service by women in a court of law; as a corollary, they cannot legally function in that role for marriages, divorces or circumcisions. Obviously, the time worn code of Judaism recites a formula ripe for the ashcan, that Woman is not a fully mature and rational adult. In a shipwreck, it proposes men be saved first because they have more *mitzvot* (religious rites and rules) to perform.

I rejoiced when I learned that my own alma mater will not assign a student rabbi to a congregation that rejects a female officiant; my rabbinical body (C.C.A.R.) has stepped beyond formal sanction to active promotion of women into our collegium, welcoming them as members and participants at meetings. Bravely it suggests that rabbis invite women students into their pulpits to break down the "culture shock" that afflicts laymen on seeing for the first time a female reading from and preaching on the Scrolls of the Law.

Isn't the dominant myth in Western religious systems, the (Hebraic) Father-God, an infinitely enlarged masculine anthropomorphic figure? Sheila D. Collins, a teacher in the New York Theological Seminary, prophesies that we shall soon hear "Our Mother Who Art in Heaven," perhaps in the Lord's Prayer. "Everywhere," Ms. Collins reports, "women are casting aside the veils of 'compliance, complicity and comfort,' and nowhere more than in religion." Behind the baton of the New York Federation of Reform Synagogues Task Force on Equality for Women, Reform temples have lined up to dechauvinize the language of the prayerbook. "Created, by men for men, (it) disregarded the changing role of women in social and religious practices," and puts women in the "same category as slaves and minors, outside the complete list of religious obligations and opportunities."

In Reform prayers "Lord, Father, King, Master" have surrendered to "God, Almighty, the Blessed One, the Eternal, the Creator"; "House of Jacob" has become "House of Israel"; "Fellowship" is amended to "Friendship," "Forefathers" to "Ancestors," "Shield of Abraham" to "Shield of Our Ancestors," "Men" to "Humanity," "Brethren" to "Brothers and Sisters"; "Jacob" is stretched to embrace matriarchs Sarah, Rebecca, Rachel and Leah. . . .

On November 12, 1980 the National Conference of Catholic Bishops voted to purge some of the "sexist language from church prayers, subject to Vatican approval, thus becoming the world's first hierarchy to seek such changes. One prayer, which now says at the climactic moment of consecration of the bread and wine that Christ's blood is "shed for you and for all men" would be changed to "shed for you and for all." Other changes voted would alter the phrase that God has "always done what is good for man" to "what is good for your people" and would convert a phrase saying God "restores man to your friendship" to "restores us to your friendship."

It is "a much needed step toward the acceptance of women as full, equal, visible members" of the church, said the Women's Ordination Conference, which also seeks admission of women to the priesthood. Although the Archbishop of Milwaukee asserted that many men as well as women have been disturbed by the generic use of "man" to apply to "everyone," I have heard snorts and grumbles from synagogue curmudgeons to whom liturgical modernizations are the advance agent of "Red" atheism.

Yet, after much ideological rhetoric of intent, resolutions and hyped publicity attending the first woman rabbi (Holy Blossom Temple's addition of Rabbi Joan Friedman to its staff in 1980 became a journalistic scoop in Jerusalem), resistance has protruded at many levels. Lucy Davidowicz, a widely read historian, garnered not inconsiderable approval when she charged that "the assumption by a woman of a rabbinic or priestly function in the synagogue undermines the very essence of Jewish tradition." I beg to differ. It is the assumption that tradition is the absolute and omnipotent value to which all others must be sacrificed that undermines the very essence of Judaism's viability. Ms. Davidowicz foresees that once women attain total equality men will flee from a synagogue sickened by "female power and usurpation." But she does admit that "women are efficient, they can raise funds, bring order out of chaos." A lady rabbinical student answered Ms. Davidowicz's ambivalent warning with a blunt charge that Lucy prefers chaos and poor organization in the synagogue to surrender of male dictatorship.

More inimical toward the historian's reactionary posture is the fact that almost one-fourth of all Reform temples boast a woman president and nearly all have female board members. Holy Blossom Temple's most productive contributions to the Jewish faith and people were made during the presidency of a beautiful woman. It is the women, not the men, Lucy, who squawk at the "very idea" of women on the pulpit!

Sally Priesand ignited a media blitz by being the first of her gender ever to be ordained by a rabbinical school, my own. Like most of her subsequent imitators, she became "assistant" in a large congregation. When the "chief's" illness temporarily removed him from the arena, she carried on a full tour of duty in full regalia. Sally sought her own pulpit after a seven-year unblemished rabbinate in the Free Synagogue of New York—in vain. I understand she then accepted a last-resort part-time position.

Only in America, a Harry Golden bestseller whose wit and wisdom brightened my days long ago, admonished fledgling rabbis to avoid marriage with a toothsome blonde because female parishioners would be bitten by fear and jealousy. Is the Sisterhood flock now likely to supplement misgivings about the rabbi's svelte spouse with disturbing fantasies about presentable young women pulpiteers and their susceptible middle-aged husbands? Dr. Mortimer Ostow, chairman of the Department of Pastoral Psychiatry at the Conservative Jewish Theological Seminary, avows that "men with perverse sexual dispositions would be especially aroused by the sight of women performing the roles traditionally reserved for men," just as "a male officiant in a religious service is not without sexual attractiveness to the women in the congregation and to the unconsciously homosexual inclinations of some boys and men." He adds that the urge is more easily controlled in women because they already have become accustomed to seeing the rabbi as a male. This tribute to the sexual lure of the rabbi symbol carries with it at least one negative: the rabbinical female can be reckoned to suppress her sexuality with more self-restraint than the male, if for no other reason than the intimidating impact of her public celebrity. She will be the object of stares and scrutiny until she grows ubiquitous enough for perhaps a welcome escape into relative obscurity. Aside from that brake, sexpots normally do not pant for the pulpit as a profession.

That the final verdict on female rabbis will be rendered from the pews rather than from the pulpit and by institutional nabobs is a truism buttressed by the dependence of liberal Judaism, and other non-absolutist, non-eternal salvation-bartering denominations, on the will of their dues-paying supporters.

What are the prospects? Candid confessions by women already at work in "Yahweh's Vineyard" suggest that synagogue affirmative action endorsement rests in limbo at present. Their disclosures convey more than a hint of pathos: "People see me as a *woman* rabbi rather than simply as a rabbi, while expecting me to deny being a woman and to ignore such matters as ERA." " 'Now I can finally kiss the rabbi' is supposed to be a joke." "There are 4,000 Protestant women ministers, but we are like strange critters in a zoo." "Where we serve as assistants, it's always for behind-the-scenes educational chores." "They judge us as a group. If one of us fails to please, they turn thumbs down on all of us and demand a male replacement." "I could handle sex and marriage courses without special problems, but the ladies in the Temple don't think so." "The congregants won't have me for personal contacts—weddings, funerals and counseling—not because I'm young, but because I'm a woman." "When my husband was transferred by his company, I had to quit the congregation or get a divorce, which may be OK for a man in the rabbinate, but not for a woman."

Beverly Lerner, a female rabbi stationed then in Atlanta, Georgia, branded the hesitancy to accept female leadership as an obstacle to any woman wishing to take a responsible role in a congregation or community. "Whereas a professional man can generally find another man to support and guide him in his job, a woman pioneering in the rabbinate does not normally find a role model. If a woman must emulate a man, she may lose part of her identity as well as her effectiveness. We must still seek ways to affirm our femaleness and at the same time perform our tasks in an all-male environment. According to Daniel J. Levinson, men generally regard women in one of four ways: attractive but not gifted; gifted, but sexual attractiveness interferes with work and friendship; intelligent but impersonal, pseudo-male; a little girl who can't be taken seriously. . . . It will be many years before the congregation-community and female leadership are comfortable with each other."

Mormons and Catholics find the issue cozily defused without haggling conferences or litigious theologues, the former by a President-prophet who alone of all creatures is the recipient of Divine revelation, the latter by a Pope who alone is the repository of God's truth transmitted through His Son. Their simple retort to women clergy is "No!" Paradoxically, Mormonism has no professional clergy, yet all men in good standing are members of the priesthood and eligible for elevation to bishops. No non-Mormon or non-conformist may enter the temple; therefore no murmur of dissent can be heard within the church. Any member infected by contrariness withdraws from the portals of the Latter Day Saints or waits to be excommunicated. Mormonism and a passion for Mormon priesthood cannot reside together in a female's dream. In 1978 God revealed Himself to President Spencer W. Kimball and instructed the consignee of his will and wisdom to end a century-old color ban that barred men of Negro descent (blacks) from the all-male lay priesthood—but the Father of all the living absent-mindedly forgot that He had created woman, who as a result must be content with enjoying the goodies of the priesthood only as an appendage and reflection of her husband. "The Lord said the priesthood is for men. No scriptures or teachings indicate a possible change by divine revelation"—thus spoke Elder John H. Shoberg, a high official of the Latter Day Saints.

What can a rabbi say about the Roman Catholic Church? Of all the domestic issues that plague the Catholic hierarchy, the ordination of women for priesthood has generated the most volcanic latter-day heat—a dream of verbalized revolt that touches the hem of the papal robe. Its power to shake and startle received unprecedented confirmation during the few days of Pope John Paul II's visit to the United States. On October 4, 1979, in front of ten thousand priests seated on the main floor and two thousand nuns seated in the balcony of Philadelphia's Civic Center, he reasserted that the priesthood is not a proper or acceptable calling for women. His declaration was discussed by Catholics and non-Catholics, ecclesiastics and laymen, men and women. The executive director of the National Council of Catholic Women, a semi-official conglomerate of eight thousand local church groups, said it accepted it, suggesting, however, that the matter be kept open for further study. . . . Doris Gottemoeller, a Sister of the Leadership Conference of Women Religious in Washington, an organization representing the leadership of 90 percent of Roman Catholic women's religious orders in the United States, countered that the issue had been far from resolved by the Pope's words. Her riposte underscored the "growing urgency felt by women to participate, the church's repute as a perpetrator of sexism," and denial of priestly status to women as "a kind of sacred dimension to a basically sexist attitude in society." The president of Marymount Manhattan College, another Sister, also expressed disappointment: "The issue is not going to go away." Sister Rita Jirak, who works with the Inter-Community Center for Justice and

Peace, commented that the Holy Father "has not been able to talk with anyone but the hierarchy." Sally Cunneen, an editor of *Cross Current*, a quarterly ecumenical review, ascribed to the Pope blandness toward what was happening in the church and suggested that the applause occasioned by his remarks indicates "a defensive, fearful attitude." Dr. Mary Buckley, theology teacher at St. John's University, arguing against the papal stand that the ordination of women is not one of human rights, traced the rejection of female priesthood to the dual nature understanding of the human person. This leads to the concept of women being separate and unequal and to the doctrine of female subordination. Dr. Claire Randall, general secretary of the National Council of Churches in Christ, a grouping of thirty-two Protestant and Eastern Orthodox Churches, stated that "the denial that human rights are involved only makes matters worse. The Pope is saying that women cannot have the same relationship to God that men can have, or that God cannot use them in the way He can use men—something that many women and men, both Protestant and Catholic, cannot accept." Sally Martino Fisher, president of the National Association of Neighborhoods and a practicing Catholic, voiced faith in what the Pope told her about God-made rules, but didn't think "God made the rule that there should be just men on the altar." The Reverend Robert Kennedy, a director in the Brooklyn office of Catholic Charities, opted for "local church autonomy in the choice of a minister, including women."

The above responses to Pope John Paul's snub of female priesthood were quoted in the *New York Times* of October 6, 1979. The most telling and courageous rebuttal—one that stirred North American Catholics and everyone deeply aware of women's changing role and the tremendous power of the Throne of St. Peter—was presented on October 7, 1979 by Sister Theresa Kane in Washington's National Shrine of the Immaculate Conception before the Pope and the five thousand nuns he had come to address. John Paul II had refused an audience to the Leadership Conference of Women Religious, the only organization of American Sisters officially approved by the Vatican, and led by Sister Theresa. Many nuns, correctly or not, had detected a note of condescension in the Pope's Philadelphia speech condemning female ordination—and a lack of grace in the applause of smiling priests. Certain preliminary actions such as an all-night prayer vigil outside the Pope's Washington residence, distribution of pale blue armbands, and the abandonment of a proposal to stand up as a group solely because it would obstruct the view of others were clues to the mood of many nuns assembled there. One hundred and fifty-three did stand.

What prior event could have prepared that convocation of sworn acolytes for the formal greeting to His Holiness? The co-director of the rank-and-file National Assembly of Women Religious later termed it "beautiful, gentle and reverent, yet saying everything that needed saying." It was a tableau unprecedented in the annals of the Catholic Church. A figure clad in a neat brown suit with only a lapel cross to show she is a nun (her attire proclaiming more that she is a nun in daring albeit dignified dissent, since the Pope had repeatedly remonstrated against the replacement of nuns' habits with civilian dress), Sister Theresa Kane stood almost like an apparition before the absolute bearer of Christ's truth (and before a national television audience)!

That was the scene. Her words? Clear and audibly she asked the Vicar of Christ to be mindful of the "intense suffering and pain which is part of the life of many women in the United States." They were asking him to provide the "possibility of women as persons being included in all ministries of our church." Then she knelt to kiss the Pope's ring and receive his silent blessing. Likely all the nuns gasped; half of them probably applauded. A religious who had not been a vocal feminist when chosen in 1978 to head the five thousand Sisters of Mercy in their work for the poor had crammed into a moment the feminist thinking and feeling among the leaders of American church-women. The 130,000 nuns in the United States are a divided Sisterhood on the advocacy of priesthood. The perception seems to be gaining adherents that they who have given up motherhood for service of the church should be given equal rank with male priests in the celibate life of sacrifice.

After the Pope's United States trip about one hundred and eighty members of Catholic institutions from the Chicago area issued a statement regretting "the closed model of hierarchical authority" shown by the Holy Father. No Jesuit signed the statement, the order's heads having been told by the Pope that "requisite firmness" should be used by them against dissension. Yet the head of the New England Jesuits, who had notified a brother, the Reverend William J. Callahan, that he was being recalled from his Washington post for "reassignment" because he supported women's ordination, joined twenty-five faculty members at the Jesuit School of Theology in Berkeley, California, criticizing as a serious mistake the 1977 Vatican order barring women priests.

Terse words of a syndicated Associated Press religion writer epitomized the Callahan case: "In the first known crackdown on debate on admission to the Roman Catholic priesthood, a Jesuit priest has been silenced and ordered transferred." A few months later, as reported on March 1, 1980, about one hundred Roman Catholic groups and 2,600 individuals signed a statement voicing "anger and great sadness" over an alleged trend "to repression" and silencing by the Roman Catholic Church. The statement's title, "Even the Stones Would Cry Out," had been excerpted from a comment made by Jesus just before his arrest. With the signatures it filled four full pages in the *National Catholic Reporter*, an independent weekly. Most meaningful of all, the Callahan brouhaha was cited along with the summary measures taken against the Reverend Hans Küng of West Germany and the Dutch theologian Reverend Edward Schillebeeckx—both eminent albeit dissident scholars.

In December 1979 Gabrielle Burton wrote an incisive, vitriolic commentary on Pope John Paul's visit to the United States. It was syndicated by Gannett News Service and I read it in the *Nevada State Journal*, Reno edition. The following verbatim excerpts need no exegesis from me:

> I hung on (his) every word. After all the ground kissing and baby hugging, the 12 languages and the poetry, the message is the same: No Women Allowed. . . . M is for the million times women are invisible in the Pope's language. . . . He says the Church's traditional decision not to call women is not a statement about human rights. Because women aren't human? Because we don't have rights? . . . He says that Jesus Christ's mother, Mary, stayed away from the Last Supper where the priesthood was established. Where does he get this information? I'll wager my inmost soul that Jesus and the Apostles were not cooking, serving and cleaning up. . . . He tells women to emulate Mary. Biblically Mary was nearly mute; the male writers recorded her that way. Mary is a mother who birthed without man's help, a role-model impossible to emulate. Every time women attain the goal, motherhood, we've violated the condition, virginity. . . . On the Pope's Mexican trip, nuns

tasted the papal food as a security measure. For U.S. nuns, not culturally inclined to check out possibly poisoned food, sexist hierarchy is working a week of 12-hour days commencing at 4:30 a.m. to bake 60,000 communion wafers that, once conse-crated by men, will be distributed by men. . . . It's not surpris-ing that the Pope, like most powerful men, has no inkling of women's oppression and concerns. The shocker is that he feels no obligation, let alone moral imperative, to find out. . . . Like another sexist traditionalist, Ayatollah Khomeini, he's saying, "Go back into the veil."

The Pope's reiteration of celibacy during the American tour received unreserved applause from the nuns; apparently that was not among their complaints. The virginity of Mary (adoration of whom has reached "Maryolatry" in the view of detractors, but whose love, piety and compassion Kenneth Clarke in his *Civiliza-tion* lectures called one of the greatest of all civilizing influences) has become a source of pride in nun circles. As expressed by a past president of the Leadership Conference of Women Religious, Mary had been asked to become the mother of Jesus without male intervention, and she did so as a free agent, not bound by physical dependence on a man's cooperation nor by moral constraint to seek a man's approval. (May one interpose, then, that Mary was the first Christian feminist?)

Is anything about the priestly office so manly that a woman cannot perform it? Can it be doubted that she may have a talented ear and intuitive heart for confession? These questions were asked and answered some years ago with an unmistakable negative in an article published by *Commonweal*, a liberal Catholic periodical. In no denomination would females be incapacitated by taxing muscular requirements, except, one might suppose, the athletic prowess of a devil-swatting evangelist such as once-renowned Billy Sunday. Preaching, teaching, praying, visiting the sick, marrying, burying, socializing—are they the job schedule of a Tarzan? A veritable hemorrhage in the young blood supply of priests has already persuaded the church to seek transfusions from nuns on whom the deficiency in priest personnel is conferring unwonted duties. Many parishes have contrived team ministries.

In my boyhood the only nuns I ever saw, always with keen curiosity and wonder, were teachers in parochial schools. The shortage emergency has evoked their hitherto unheralded gifts for preaching, hospital chaplaincies and for spheres of work that

198 / Sex and the Pulpit

enliven and cosmeticize personality, appearance and lifestyle. Sisters have broken out of the shell of unworldly isolation. Some even make song records, a sort of churchified rock 'n' roll. Downcast eyes, austere gown and the buttoned-up look are the relics of voiceless ages of resignation to repression. Nuns are coming of age and reaching for the rights and responsibilities of concerned human beings in a world that needs them.

It has been noted that the vestments worn by priests resemble the raiment of women. Perhaps cassocks merely illustrate religion's reliance on the antique for ceremonial display. Was it not the conventional masculine dress in ancient times? That a case more scholarly than the above can be presented for the revisionist position received convincing proof in a three-year study by a seven-member (four men, three women) task force of the Catholic Biblical Association commissioned to study the role of women in early Christianity. Its findings are simple and specific: the New Testament points toward a female ministry; many of the functions now belonging to the male priestly clan were never limited to the Twelve but were, in fact, exercised by women; there is no evidence that women were excluded from any of them. Women founded churches, held leadership positions, took part in public worship and were among the ministers and teachers celebrated in Romans 16:7 as "outstanding apostles."

Vatican scholars and papal pronouncements admit the absence of a scriptural basis for barring women, referring instead to long-fixed tradition. In 1210 an epistle of Pope Innocent III rested the church policy on the argument, among others, that Jesus did not call women to be part of the Twelve Apostles because it was not to them that the Lord had entrusted the keys to the Kingdom of God. Feisty Sisters are unmoved on that score. They reply that women alone stood by Jesus, who ignored the edict against consorting with publicans and women. Was not the prostitute Mary Magdalene witness to the Resurrection?

In December 1945 peasants digging for natural fertilizer near Nag Hammadi in upper Egypt came upon a clay vessel holding thirteen leatherbound papyrus books. In the light shed on the origins of Christianity, they may rival the Dead Sea Scrolls. Dating back perhaps to the first century, these books deal with Gnosticism, a religion practiced by an ancient sect that helped shape the thinking of Christian Fathers before its decline into obscurity. Belated analysis by some scholars leads to a remarkably strong speculation: some Gnostics venerated a goddess deity or one with female attributes, and the period before and after the birth of Christianity witnessed a rebirth of goddess worship as a central feature of pagan fertility rites. *The Gnostic Gospels*, by Elaine Pagels, reviewed in *Ms* magazine April 1980, posits religious sexual equality as the overall principle observed by respective branches of the sect in slightly variegated forms. One bowed in reverence to woman, consecrating the sacremental bread to Mary. Another practiced sexual equality so scrupulously that it chose women as their spiritual guides; its adherents were condemned for deviation in 340 by an orthodox Christian council. A third branch, a secret elite within the Catholic Church of Lyons, drew lots for every position of leadership, which enabled women to serve routinely as priests, deacons and bishops.

What is the line-up of logic today? Perhaps the dialectic of confrontation can be encapsulated by stating the church's thrust and then the riposte.

One: Jesus selected only male apostles, to which one may reply that he had other characteristics which did *not* require imitation. Was not Jesus a Jew and unmarried? Yet clergy are Gentile and married in most Protestant denominations.

Two: Since Jesus was both divine and male, God, His Father, had male attributes and only males can "represent" Him to the world. A reasonable answer might propose that Jesus was one in *Spirit* with the Father; in earthly manifestation, the *humanness* of Jesus was more important than His maleness.

Three: Of all the anti-female passages in the New Testament, three can be cited here:

> "I permit no woman to teach or have authority over men; she is to keep silent." (Timothy 2:12)

> "Women should keep silence in the churches. If there is anything they wish to know, let them ask their husbands at home." (I Corinthians 4:34, 5)

> "The head of every man is Christ, the head of a woman is her husband and the head of Christ is God." (I Corinthians 11:37)

Churches that already ordain women dub these passages typical of first-century patriarchal society; they are hardly normative for our time.

The Pope's suzerainty over all he surveys requires no assertiveness; it has been "here" for almost two millenia. Unmatched power over seven hundred million Catholic faithful has been conferred by unitary control over the world's most far-flung and opulent religious monolith; it is made impregnable by the undisputed belief in his infallibility. The Vatican insists that this credo originated with Jesus Christ to preserve His vicar from error and keep intact the unalloyed truth transmitted to Him by the heavenly Father. It is to remain for all time resident in the keeping of the popes in apostolic succession.

Infallibility in matters of faith and morals evoked mixed reaction among Catholic clergy from the day it was confirmed as a definite doctrine of the church in 1869-70. A number of bishops withdrew before stamping it with their approval. Many theologians choose to regard the doctrine as peripheral rather than central to the Catholic creed, even hinting that Catholicism would be stronger without such far-reaching concentration of authority. Despite subdued internal tension, investiture of the pontiff with divinely ordained infallibility has general acceptance all the more firmly because of Pope John Paul II's stern imprimatur. Thus all discussion, debate and polemic about female participation in God's worship on His holy altar stops at the Pope's forehead and what dwells behind it. But there is a hitch; the incorrigible humanness of popes cuts deep into carbon-copy sameness of judgment and roils frozen dogmas with wide disparities in personal temperament. Like Supreme Court paragons of abstract justice who render fateful verdicts by a 5-4 vote, papal cogitation may come to rest on opposite sides. Pope John XXIII's warmth, wit and innate response to his fellow pilgrims on this planet remain sparkling gems in my memory from the day in 1959 when my late wife and I were granted a private audience with him. Humble parish priests still talk about an incident that occurred two days after his accession to the papacy. While at daily chapel service he paused for a split second after reciting the prayer for God's mercy and a favor unto "all men," then murmured, as if in quiet meditation, "and to all women." Beyond the spontaneity of this unannounced liturgical departure, it was a peek into the trend of his mind—and what could have been a pronounced future leaning toward recognition of women in the church.

Technically, my source has explained, the ban of women priests does not rest within the discretion of the church, in the light of the Vatican's traditional interpretation. Its repeal might be a betrayal of Christ's intention. Yet, were the occupant of the papal throne ever to advocate a radical change as vigorously as Pope John Paul II opposes it, the interpretation would be geared into reverse. (Celibacy, it seems, can be abolished by papal fiat because it is situated on the "softer" level of custom.)

Personally, I am inhibited by semi-cynical realism and a temperamental list toward suspended judgment from crediting any creature of flesh and blood with infallibility. If by some misadventure or failure of sane judgment I were to be the recipient of such an accolade, I would be frozen in acute embarrassment, paralyzed in terror at so awful a responsibility. I belong to a religious community that vehemently denies to anyone partnership with God in power or wisdom. The synagogue grants the rank of rabbi, "my teacher," to knowledge, integrity and devotion to the Jewish faith and its people; it grants to everyone the right and the duty of individual reason that God has given to all human beings, created as they are in His image. No Jewish thinker ever recommended the *Credo quia absurdum est* (I believe even though it is absurd)—motto of the medieval church—as a guide to the good life, or *sacrificium intellectus* (sacrifice of the intellect), the dictum of illustrious churchman Novalis, as a penchant to be treated with reverence. Also, as every rabbi knows, his authority and that of any version of Judaism are always "on the line," subject to challenge by any Jew with a categorical imperative to disagree.

Abolition of Catholicism's lockout of female clergy would hearten and strengthen women's liberation around the globe. Despite today's wintry wolf cry of the pack, I have no doubt that ultimate expansion and triumph of religious liberalism, with the impetus provided by a remarkable upsurge of candor and courage in the ranks of America's nuns, will persuade a Holy Father that the interests of the church, always paramount in papal strategy, can most effectively be secured and advanced by bold, reasoned advance into tomorrow.

Sister Theresa Kane and her less daring but like-minded followers are of course a minuscule enclave within the church. Outstanding figures in the Women Religious community link militant feminists who have plighted their troth to the church with pejoratives such as "impertinent." Mother Theresa of

Calcutta and of Nobel Prize fame—a formidable foe—pointed to Mary, Mother of God, who had no further ambition than to serve Him in humility, as the role model for nuns. . . .

A beloved ex-priest, during a chat with me about his parochial-school-bungled psychosexuality, unveiled a "hunch" that the adamant negation by the hierarchy of any compromise on the female priest issue emanates from the Establishment's "understandable" fear of radicalized nuns. On being permitted to infiltrate the strongholds of priestly authority, they might burst into the decision-making process, even to dictate the choice of a pope, and ultimately uproot the monolithic product of a two thousand-year-old power ploy programmed for eternity.

Methinks I hear the thundrous pulse-beat, the feverish, sweating nightmare of aboriginal fear, fear of the demon in woman, of her hypnotic power to arouse and be aroused, which if unleashed would soak the Godly "Ground of Being" with the offal of carnal excess. Is the church's shackle a chastity belt after all? Did the rejection of female clergy emanate from the terror-haunted fantasy of Augustine and Aquinas, who believed that the sinfulness of Eve would till the end of time endanger the salvation of all men and unless expunged would cast us all into hell?

The Leadership Conference of Women Religious object to subordination to monks, who they charge are given greater scope. Their quarrel with hierarchical conservatism has been gathering steam for centuries; it spurts out in all directions and against all abuses of power, weighty or trivial. Essentially what they want was spelled out by one of them in a casual remark: "We want recognition as adult human beings, as volunteer members of a religious community that is not amenable to coercion." Is that not the credo and quest of any demarche for radical and rational change in our society?

9

Is the Penis
Expendable?

After my return from Hanoi in 1967 I addressed many anti-Vietnam War meetings, one of them in Atlanta, Georgia. I remember well a conversation I had with a college student as he drove me back to the airport. A comment he made about sex pulled me to the edge of my car seat. "Lots of my friends on campus are fixin' to have a nervous breakdown, Rabbi," he said. "They're gettin' psychiatric treatment; some even have whispered to me that they're becomin' impotent. Know why? 'Cause the women on campus are makin' demands on 'em. Nice girls, old families, goin' wild on sex."

A few days later I saw a newspaper story on "Man-Watchers," an organization that makes it OK for women to stare at men. The members hand out cards to attractive males, signed with initials only or with their full names if both are single. Man-Watchers got its big start after a poll had shown that women like to look at men's fannies. One bottom-watcher even said that was the only reason she liked football games. . . .

"Rabbi, I need to talk with an up-to-date clergyman." That came from a bank executive who took me aside at a United Way luncheon. The next evening, across a table in a dimly lit, elegant restaurant, he explained it all. Would I help him start an organization to protect *men* from sexual harassment? "The females in my office invite me to come over for a swim in their pool they say, 'when my husband's out of town.'" His voice rose, "Sometimes they want me to have a pickup drink with them after work. Before you know it, Rabbi, they lean down and brush my arm with their breasts, or swish a slit skirt into a subtly provocative peep-show as soon as we are alone." I wondered. Is the man hyper-imaginative and ego-massaging or a lecher? I've shared office space with secretaries—but beg to suspend a verdict to plots to share my bed.

Some time ago I attended a Conference of the National Organization for Women. There were speeches, motions from the floor and resolutions; then one high-pitched shout, "Look, everybody! Here's the message that'll beat the men." A red-lettered placard shot up into the air: "Don't fuck! Masturbate!"

Similar to the mail-order brides who helped lonesome cowboys and miners settle the West, or the Japanese brides of returning American GI's after World War II who, as the boys boasted, "treated you like a king," there is a magazine in a little town in Washington that caters to men yearning for docile Oriental wives who make neither sexual nor any other demands on them. The publisher says that a lot of American men are turned off by aggressive women. His magazine includes a picture album of Asiatic maidens; there is an extra charge for addresses. Business was so good he gave up his job as a college professor.

One of California's largest high schools conducted a survey of its male students. A remarkable number of them wanted to get a girl pregnant just to prove they could. They complained, "the cards are stacked against us by the Pill."

Another survey, by the Harvard-based Project on Human Sexuality, in which 1,400 parents were questioned, clearly showed that women prefer strong, masculine men. In the coordinators' unanimous opinion men were being made painfully conscious of their own inadequacy or fear. . . .

The aforementioned happenings are widely disparate—from limitless female lubricity and lofty contempt for male genitals to the growing ranks of men who have been scarred and are scared of women. The examples I quote have three traits in common:

1. Authenticity. The first was confirmed to me from the trembling lips of religion-ruled campus males shaken by coed taunts for their "she-men purity."

2. Women's liberation ancestry. The genealogy line of lyrically free-spirited women is easily traceable to forthright feminism. Its markings are as clear in substance to men as were those of the abominable snowman to the fevered imagination of Himalayan sherpas some years ago.

3. Abrogation of sex control by the penis. He whom I have crowned King Phallus some chapters ago seems to be drooping his head, no longer ramrod straight and proud of his long reign. It is a lament over the rod god's decline, in a tripartite motif: Insatiable Woman, Obsolescent Penis, Man in Retreat.

Insatiable Woman

In *The Nature and Evolution of Female Sexuality* Mary Jane Sherfey declares women to be sexually insatiable and civilization to have emerged from their forcible suppression. Masters and Johnson had already voiced that idea. Some thousands of years ago, on the threshold of recorded history, it is said, the sexual appetite of the female of the species focused on the clitoris and cast human habitations into anarchy until the males in desperation enthroned the vagina (or penis urge) and began to institute order. Brigit Brophy, tilting a lance against monogamy, contrasts the man's erotic need that can be satisfied by one woman and the biological imperative of woman for multiplication of her lovers— a natural dictate choked off by marriage. Such a vaulting measure of woman's sexual voracity scarcely meshes with the reticence and restraint of Middle America. Nor is it likely that the average establishment would agree with Jessie Bernard, who states in *Future of Marriage* that the modern woman is potentially "sexier" than her predecessors. What then can be the response to Kinsey associate Wardell Pomeroy's bland observation, "They (women) seem to have lost their inhibitions about sex and want their pleasuring," and the widely influential *Hite Report*? The extensive survey taken at random on which it was based led Dr. Mary Calderone, venerated head of the United States Sex Information and Education Council, to affirm that the sex potential of women is almost infinite.

Such theories about women's capacity for sexual congress (notably promulgated by that gender, who should know) are beyond my competence to judge, save in the light of "strictly private" experiences which permit no conclusion but unequivocal endorsement. That these estimates may promise more than life can deliver is a second certainty. Visions of grand and continuous sex indulgence belong in the realm of hyperbole. How often are all of us frustrated by the limitations of physical and emotional endurance? Maybe a New Woman is being born who is faintly adumbrated in a 1976 *Redbook* survey showing a host of wives who, following a rendezvous with their lover, returned home to a husband with whom they consider themselves happily wed. The survey also includes cumulative data on extramarital liaisons by wives who shatter the double standard with gusto after initial but quickly overcome unease.

Women's erotic stamina has frequently engaged the interest

of ancient Greek mythology. When Zeus was reproached by his spouse Hera for numerous infidelities he defended them by arguing that when she shared his couch, she had far more enjoyment than he. Teiresias, who had been both male and female, was summoned to settle the matter. His answer would probably have gratified the champions of the gentle sex: "If the parts of love-pleasure be counted as ten, / Thrice three go to women, one only to men."

Literature offers us a lengthy compendium of ladies whose raging fires could not be quenched. The Latin bard Juvenal's Sixth Satire sang of the "foul longings inside each girlish breast"; there was Chaucer's Wife of Bath, Joyce's Molly Bloom, Shakespeare's Desdemona (according to Iago), the lusty inamorata in Boccacio and Rabelais and, at the receiving end, Mozart's Don Giovanni, Byron's Don Juan and Henry Miller, whose hero, a tireless stud, assigned himself the delectable task of slaking the ravenous thirst of "uterine hysteria" at the giving end. Today, magazines such as *Playgirl, Cosmopolitan, New Woman, Ms* apparently feature not how to copulate (the manuals having already been memorized) but how to secure and enjoy the most glamorous opportunities. There are guidelines worthy of Madame de Pompadour for recovery from an affair, for achievement of orgasm (simple or multiple), for sleeping around without a sense of promiscuity and guilt, for saying no without turning him off, for turning him on when he seems about to say no, for easy and ecstatic seduction, how to initiate a male virgin, and lastly, tips on opening the mind to wonderful fantasies.

Is the insatiable vampire stereotype a male artifact engendered by the fascination and dread that occasionally center around his fevered image of beauteous, beckoning call-girls or nubile nymphomaniacs? Has the constantly lengthening catalogue of sexual hellions been fabricated by men? That is possible. Therefore, let each man peer deeply into his own erotic experiences and let each woman delve into hers. Mark you, it is worth repeating: the gurus of sexuality who cast ballots for the unquenchable sexual thirst of woman at the beginning of this chapter were women. One thing seems certain—this generation of mothers will not tell their daughters that sex is a dirty, disgusting, dismal duty performed solely to please "hubby," or because the Creator in His wisdom has devised it as the only way to have a baby.

Judeo-Christianity carved the first lustful woman out of its demon-terror as well as its own lust for power. The Hebrew Bible led Eve to seduce Adam into knowledge of the joys clumsily hidden under a skimpy fig-leaf, then punished her initiative with both sexual passion and subservience. "Unto him (Adam) shall be your passion, and he will rule over you." Exodus 21:10 prohibits deprivation of a wife's food, clothing and the conjugal rights that are her due; Deuteronomy exempts a recently married man from military duty for one year that he might bring gladness to his bride; the Song of Songs celebrates the carnal rapture of a young woman rejoicing that "I am my beloved's, his desire is for me." Biblical Judaism did recognize female sexuality, but in the dark shadows crouched Lilith, demonic ancestress of the wicked witches, all female, who allegedly roiled the scabrous imaginings of men throughout the centuries. And earth-women of the Bible bared their bosoms even to the sons of God that the mighty ones might stoop to sin and beget children upon them, thus provoking the Great Flood. Finally, the lush and varied zestfulness of female lubricity which had flowered in matriarchal paganism succumbed to the rigors of a patriarchal, father-dominated Hebrew morality. It bound women in iron safeguards against their presumed God-defying eroticism. On her marriage a Jewess had to part from her cranial hair—a component of the sexual armor that could lure men into sinful thought. Out of Eve's wickedness, Christianity wove the tangled web of a monumental theology; without her lust-propelled conquest of Adam's naive virtue, there would have been no Fall, no Original Sin, no need for salvation by grace—and no increment of enormous power to the church as the sole instrument of Divine forgiveness.

Thenceforth, with few deviations and a potpourri of theological minutiae, the vaginal ferment was placed under lock and key. The ordinary citizens of the classical world restricted the sexual horizons of women to the marriage state, while men were allowed supplementary intercourse with concubines and prostitutes. This lopsidedness of opportunity has been largely prevalent in the Western world until today. The ruling male power contrived law and precept to curb woman's erotic spontaneity and depth—but short of blocking illicit impulses of a man who had the means to exploit them. . . . In brief, penile sovereignty; King Phallus was never seriously challenged or endangered.

The supreme, solitary male-genital scepter of King Phallus was reinforced in the "winning of the West" period of American history. Was not machismo nourished by the call to conquer a wilderness and span a continent? For women, in the sexual connotation, it meant abdication from every shred of sexual initiative; indeed, the rigors of shaping a new world forced them to dim the very consciousness of sex. After the American Revolution men dedicated themselves to building a society worthy of the new freedom. Women and sexuality could have become a distraction, if not a threat. Have not Americans romanticized the man who works alone, the cowboy, the hunter—his physical prowess and his exposure to peril—the James Fenimore Cooper man?

Ernest Hemingway made warfare come alive in novels, but he did not live it. The only person he killed was himself. Aside from crossing streams and mountains, clearing forests and cozening weeds into harvests, the original made-in-America macho slew Indians in well-nigh genocidal frenzy. His women shared the perils and the promise—at the price of their womanness. They were treated for the most part as men—equal partners in the crude conditions and tough asperities of life. That was not a mean or degrading slap at the women's self-esteem; it was grim acceptance of a way of life that did not allow backwoods women to receive tenderness; nor were they encouraged to give it. The overriding goal—to bring to birth a new nation and progeny who would preserve and enlarge it—brooked no other. Now the macho who once trussed up a continent for ordered human habitation is poured into fancy handtooled boots and buckskin, sports a cloying drawl and appears in shootout movies. *He* denies women tenderness out of arrogance or its twin: a sense of cultural inferiority.

Believe it or not, nineteenth-century medical pundits, of all people, fostered extravagant notions about female sexuality. J. Marion Tims, a preeminent gynecologist at that time, saw sexual intercourse as a mechanical process for the male manufacture of kids wherein the female supplied minor lubrication. In a case of severe spasmodic vaginal contraction which prohibits penile entry he recommended an anesthetic. A certain Doctor Augustus Kinsley Gardner warned that a woman in arousal can have a destructive effect on her partner in copulation and on society. In the second half of the nineteenth century, removal of the clitoris or clitoral hood (circumcision) was sometimes performed to keep women from masturbating, which it was believed could spring a female's ungovernable passion. A woman "in heat" could corrupt, enervate and divert a man from his mission to build and govern a land "from sea to boundless sea."

John's obsessive brooding about the loss of sperm arose in that period from a stark, incorrigible fact: a man's capacity to come to orgasm is limited and no stimulant can goad it into "supernatural" accomplishment. Jane, however, is not prevented by anatomical or physiological limitations from having any number of climaxes, a boon whence she may draw bliss until the end of her life, years after the bed mates she knew ceased even to hope for a fully operative erection. A woman can experience repeated climaxes without relapse in arousal while her partner awaits the completion of a refractory period following seminal emission, i.e., his biologically appointed span of time that must pass after ejaculation before he can be aroused again. Aeons ago, in the sexual economy developed by evolution, evidently the prime objective was maximum fruitfulness of the womb during a female's period of fertility—not gender equality in performance. That obvious evidence of woman's sexual primacy may afflict laggard masculinity with a fear that can still further unman it. When allied with anxiety sharpened by age over a low sperm count, the tragic sense of built-in disadvantage sends a stream of hyped remedies rolling down the years.

A nineteenth-century reverend, true to his pulpit calling, preached against masturbation, considered as an unforgivable squandering of sperm; many other advisers on morals counseled couples to curtail copulation to contain excessive expenditure of the vital juices.

That woman's desire is more easily suppressed can be vouched for by an endless file of rebuffed womanizers; that her potential for wantonness when cooling influences vanish is immeasurable can be attested to by nocturnal exhaustion of the successful. Viewing penile incompetence in contrast with vaginal-clitoric bedmanship, is it logical to charge a normal woman with penis envy? Freud's theory that women are gnawed by such envy is countered in Phyllis Chesler's book *About Men* with her thesis that sees men traumatized by "womb envy." Instead of the little girl rendered "less aggressive, defiant and self-sufficient" by her lack of a penis, Chesler brings forward a man hostile, insecure, incapable of love and hating women because they alone possess that most prized gift of nature—a womb. The debate seems somewhat academic, except for the rash of ultimately unprovable theories fought over by psychoanalysts. In any case it appears to me that womb envy, if it exists at all, is only a secondary reflection of vagina-clitoris envy—a hopeless yearning by hapless men to emulate the erotic, endlessly orgasmic demi-urge coiled like a steel spring in eternal Woman.

Does *she* accept that accolade for the power of her inherent sexuality? Not in overt verbal affirmation perhaps. A social phenomenon of recent years, however, signals unfettered, joyous acceptance. I refer to the status symbol of up-front breasts. A generation ago or less, large breasts, along with buttocks, ranked low on the aesthetic scale; their concealment enhanced whatever their owner had of the daintiness and remoteness supposedly marking an attractive female. Small, pear-shaped bosoms muted sexuality; they were a gentle murmur of hidden delights, scarcely heard; that was all. Now the young, in the vanguard, seem to pine for and even falsify a well-stacked top. Their mature sisters, having achieved the freedom they have worked for, are still not sure about its expression. So they fall back to the stereotyped definition of femaleness, now more brazenly flaunted—opulent breasts moulded for maximum display short of obscenity.

Exaggeration of the body responds to women's need for sexual identity. On a panel with several clergymen the publisher of *Playboy* stated that "many women walk around as though wearing bodies outside clothes." Bosoms revealing size, shape and points favored by contemporary fashion, with the warm approval of the average girl-watcher, may better serve as a faint suggestion of the emancipated woman's refusal to repudiate sexual insatiability, or her sweetly savored delight in the abdication of the penis from centuries-old control of sex.

The accounting in terms of male felicity spells crisis. Threats to masculine sex sovereignty assail him from many quarters. His working wife meets other men, possibly with common job interests, in contact beyond his surveillance. Liberated single women with an expanded frame of reference "rate" their lovers. According to a Los Angeles feminist, "Men are aware they are being graded and by God they try to measure up!" At the insistence of their mates they are turning up in numbers at psychiatrists' offices, plagued with worries about impotence or premature ejaculation. Is the under-thirty huntress scorning young blades into impotency, neurosis, aborted tumescence and humiliation so severe that the men lose their taste for heterosexual congress? Is Phallus in retreat?

An official of the American Institute of Family Relations puts the blame on the unreasonable demands of women who come in with requests to "fix my husband up and make him give me an orgasm." A steady trickle of letters from wives addressed to "Dear Abby" questioning the sexual adequacy of their husbands might lead one to conclude that regardless whether some women are unsatisfiable, indubitably they appear to be *unsatisfied*. A placebo from the gods is that any man blessed with a loving zestful bedmate knows that *her* peak pleasure can be derived from giving in to *him*.

I am inclined to believe that in order for sexual freedom truly to benefit woman, she must become independent, capable and self-actualized. Doesn't our social structure engender the opposite? The radical discontent of so many women may be the direct result of the contradictions between the ideal of feminine equality and the reality of deprivation. The crusade for women's liberation has promoted a quantitative broadening of the "space" for their sexual fulfillment—heralded by near-collapse of the double standard, cultivation of multiple clitoris-orgasms and "decriminalization" of masturbatory release. Contemporary North American women are more affluent in sexual opportunity than any previous generations—but I think they want qualitative, not quantitative change; their sexuality must be under their own control in a milieu that no longer is trivialized by the disdainful scurrility "All she needs is a good fuck!"

Consummation of that dream coincides, of course, with the renunciation of masculine control. Casual talks with college students, the bellwether for the middle-class male populace, have convinced me that only a tiny percentage of men are real libbers. "My wife's career is OK, as long as it doesn't interfere with mine." How much greater is the discomfort when the common variety he-man sees himself forfeiting control not of careerism but of carnality? The struggle for adaptation to role reversal in a sexual relationship can catapult him off balance. To Harvey Cox, one of America's top-ranking sociotheologians, it seems evident that men like to have women in a dependent role; that's part of the art of seduction. Now women no longer care; they are as free to be predatory as men always have been. Men must adjust to that, whether they like it or not! Howard Moody, another famous cleric, after admitting that women are obviously engaging in premarital sex no less than men, volunteered this striking observation, "They are not (being) seduced, coerced or hoodwinked."

In moments drenched with the rose-tinted light of simplistic dreams not alien to the clergy, I wish division of the sexes could be subordinated to human unity. Like race and religion—both precious values in themselves—sex has been misshaped into an instrument of power so formidable as to dilute its incomparable gift of joy. The sexual union of man and woman can be the nuclear cell from which vibes of affection and mutuality ripple out in ever-widening circles. What more clearly symbolizes the human potential for loving embrace?

Free Men, a group of largely middle-class professionals, was organized in Columbia, Maryland, in early 1977 to ponder the male's dilemma. Its seminal credo was Herb Goldberg's *Hazards of Being Male*, wherein was celebrated the resurgence of scientific opinion that the male is biologically destined to remain aggressive and that the female is best suited for nurturing.

Will irreversible sexual advantages of the female apparatus lead to a new male asceticism, resort to homosexual relief, an antiseptic woman-free "brotherhood," non-theological conversion to celibacy—abject capitulation of the penis? Will the removal of King Phallus from his centuries-old throne lead sex-hungry women to yearn for the macho's restoration? With its passion for equality the liberation movement would be well advised, I believe, to counsel moderation of women's imperious sexual demands. To rescue essential masculinity for a growing male-female approachment would be a plausible, productive course that will surely be positively scrutinized by lib leaders who have been schooled in realism after many years of only partial success.

Obsolescent Penis
On a T-shirt devised by the feminist revolt, there appeared this pungent message: "A woman without a man is a fish without a bicycle." What is its cryptic meaning? A fish without a bicycle is not deprived; it doesn't need one; it can swim. Nor is a woman without a man deprived; she doesn't need one; she has alternatives. Smothered under the reticences of female submission during the centuries, the dream of self-sufficiency, of at last cutting the

umbilical cord that has kept woman an infantile prisoner in the womb of time, can become a viable reality. In the most crucial confrontation between the former vassal and her master, namely the sexual bond, that reality is enfleshed by the formula I saw printed on that placard: "Don't fuck. Masturbate!"

The phrase, "Love is to man a thing apart, 'tis woman's whole existence" can ignite a feminist's anger to fury, whether it's an arrogant posture of macho condescension toward the female or the rubric of an elaborately neutral research into female susceptibility. In *Lysistrata*, a drama of ancient Greece, the women devised a ruse to strike a blow against war by denying themselves to men until they ended the clash of arms. It was a harbinger of the Vietnam dissent slogan "Make love, not war." Is not this twentieth-century penis boycott a rebellion against enforcement of millenial coupling, an attempt to open up the whole question of human sexual relations beyond the confines of a male-female role system?

None of the gifts bestowed on women by nature rationalizes the determinedly manless woman. It is her will to act out sexuality on her own. In polarized contrast with insatiability, outright and total abstinence from male-female congress is the vaginal version of penis withdrawal. Has not self-direction in sex behavior nestled, usually without overt acknowledgment, at the innermost checkpoint of the ultra-liberated North American woman? It is being attained by libido activation to the limit of man's tumescent capacity or, at the opposite end of the gamut, by summary deracination of lust for the entrance of the rod into her body. She alone makes the choice. The effect of either, however, is to reduce the scope of penile prerogative. *Both* bring to a close the hitherto unarguable dictatorship of King Phallus.

What does a woman feel during intercourse? I used to wonder. D. H. Lawrence was for me the most acute male chronicler of her sensations. However, one fancy has taken shape in my mind— namely, that a sensitive, high-spirited woman must associate her partner with exigent physical imperative and herself with its insistent "thing." Yet it is not beyond comprehension that she might consider renouncing sex and thus free herself from the tool of its violence?

In medieval times chivalry had an honored place. Women could find in the religious nun's life an option more desirable than marriage and motherhood because a husband was not considered a prerequisite for personal fulfillment. A christian woman was acknowledged to have an independent life; she could be something other than wife and mother. Sainthood was the one permissible agency through which a demand for emancipation from the male's disdainful arrogance could be answered. Günter Grass in his epic *The Flounder* offers the incisive opinion that the penis-degrading phase of women's liberation bears a not outlandish resemblance to a convent.

Sex understood as a coming together of two autonomous consenting male-female adults for mutual pleasure and advantage is said by some ardent feminists to be an entirely male concept useful in the economy of sex to keep him supplied with intercourse. Any woman who endeavors to be sexually attractive to men is thus meeting an unfairly troublesome demand; she is doing violence to her own humanity. Offering herself without resistance to opportunity for erotic appeasement by a man entails risk to pride and vanity, and surrenders the one small bit of her bargaining power. The ensuing transaction is rigged against her. Members of the feminist movement are bound together to protect themselves and one another from further exploitation. Each ventures out alone into a world of sexual encounter and is left alone to bear the consequences. According to one arch-feminist, a modicum of security resides only in belonging to a group in whose chaste society woman can find support.

Other equally involved evaluators of feminism are more gently disposed toward the essential worth of heterosexual indulgence. Germaine Greer sees danger in a revolutionary strategy that opts for shying away from sex because conditions under which it is available make it "inauthentic and enslaving." She contends that sex is the principal confrontation whereby men and women can create new values. Rather than advocating a severance of relations with men, she would welcome a change whereby both sexes can be liberated in a joint venture. The target should be not men as they are intrinsically accused of being, but men as they may well become under the aegis of new values. In my view, once the masculine ego no longer has to "prove" mastery, a man's sexuality possibly might be relieved of the pressing, importunate drive worked up in part by the dynamism of woman's vented resentment of injustice. Mastery and injustice must both be retired from the stage.

I have observed the birth of such positive trends in what has been called an "adrogynous" relationship; both partners, man and woman, are homogenized products of both intuitions. Nothing is stipulated verbally or in writing. Young, educated couples share everything. Instead of the traditional pattern of barter—his need of sex for her need of protection—a true companionship develops extending into full-scale adult conjugality an asexual affection such as sometimes blossoms between school chums. Perhaps this is not an exciting, tempest-tossed kind of connubial bliss, but it may stand on solid ground and would require far more "give and take" mutual self-discipline than most couples normally bring to a union.

The "Women Only" sign of the penis-eschewing sorority may have more impact on the future. Midge Decter, whose prestige in the counter-feminism camp is validated by her association with *Commentary* magazine, upholds the freedom of women not to be sexy, the freedom not to be free. Freedom in the broadest sense, she argues, must include the right to abjure the right to freedom in the explicit sense of unabridged sexual choice. What, then, is the status of lesbianism? For the lesbian, flight from King Phallus does not reach its goal in barren chastity but in the pliant body of a loving sister. Far from a resurgent impulse back to maidenhood, for the lesbian the liberation movement moves forward; it is the sesame to pure love, a corrective to the Hollywood-style romance that despatches mad swains on a competitive race to *get* love—a ritual in the American worship of success. Lesbians only want to *give*, they say. A woman preening herself on her passion for and with a person of her own sex often boasts that she is the most precious jewel in the hilt of liberation's sword. Whether lesbian or not, the main issue of an authentic women's libber is to find some ground on which she need not be a participating partner predicated on presenting her private parts to a suitable male.

On the masthead of the Declaration of Independence against penis imperialism is the word "clitoris." Until some decades ago, I wager, it was for many people a detail of nomenclature in a gynecologist's vocabulary. Clitoral usage would end reliance on the not always trustworthy penis. The clitoris can provide for the elderly and handicapped an effective substitute for penile shortcomings; it can above all help eliminate the female partner's sexual frustration.

The popular *Hite Report* concluded that while most women

have moderately satisfying sex, they achieve it not through coitus but via masturbation. Because it seems to make them feel guilty they yearn for a definition of sex encompassing a whole gamut of physical contacts and activities—not necessarily leading to intercourse. The women are casting aside the concept of sex as reproduction plus pleasure. Since according to the *Hite Report* only 30 percent of the vast number of random respondents achieved orgasm regularly from King Phallus, his regal command alone is but a feeble simulacrum compared to the self-service that almost always guarantees full orgasmic gratification. Among the correspondents, 82 percent of the total, many equated masturbation with orgasm. In the words of a Catholic woman who chatted with me after a workshop we both attended, "Mary had a baby without a man! Why can't I have fun without one?" I advised her to address the query to her priest during confession.

I rather guess that Masters and Johnson still treat certain sexual problems by teaching people how to masturbate. The initial step, I surmise, is to unlearn the prohibitions that mothers used to enforce with whacks and shouts of "dirty" and "nasty" whenever they saw or suspected that the tykes were fondling their genitals. Old wives' tales, such as the one that warns people of masturbation because it causes insanity, will be an occasion for ridicule. That myth was born in the eighteenth century via the Marquis de Sade who, on seeing asylum inmates assiduously busied with crotch-exploring fingers, theorized that such preoccupation had caused their madness.

Do some liberated women regard man as the enemy? This question has repeatedly flashed through my mind. "I Hate Men" is the title of a song in the musical comedy *Kiss Me Kate*. As a ditty on stage it is rollicking entertainment; when spat out in fury it can be a declaration of war. *The Female Eunuch* lashes men who don't trouble themselves to see women in their individual identity. "Breasts are not part of her person but lures slung around her neck to be kneaded and twisted like magic putty, or mumbled or mouthed like lolly ices!" What more need be said to express full-blooded revulsion toward men? Once women are freed from compulsory docile silence, a new breed of militants who have shucked off timid self-effacement will emerge. Should we require that they stuff into a textbook footnote the evasive double-talk inflicted upon them by smirking churchmen and supine statesmen—an unholy alliance masquerading as the elite servants of God?

I regard the North American woman as an underprivileged, over-constrained minority no less palpable than the blacks, the very poor, the very old and the very young. Sexism differs from racism and anti-Semitism in that it started earlier, will probably last longer, does not pinpoint a numerical minority and is lodged deeply enough to be pooh-poohed until its victims raise their voices. Wrath festering beneath a lacy blanket of restraint can surface in odd forms once the reins have been loosened. "Overweight women," a therapist once stated during a panel discussion on marriage and family, "are really angry women, who flail a macho-ruled world that commands them to be attractive sex objects on the one hand, and on the other hand, orders them to refrain from satisfying an appetite for something sinful and sweet."

A Crossley Survey in 1977 purportedly found that 95 percent of the men it reached did not object to the demands made by their partners during sex; therefore, women need not be afraid to suggest how men might improve their performance. (Crossley also unveiled a phenomenon which dimmed whatever confidence I have in the qualifications of its respondents: many of them professed to be "unnerved rather than turned on" by a beautiful woman!) Yet women interviewed for the *Hite Report* rasped that men were interested only in their own satisfaction, made no effort to please in bed and didn't want to be told how.

SCREW, the Society for the Chronological Role-Reversal of Emancipated Womanhood founded by an elderly matron, is another example of eloquent if futile gestures by the wrathful woman. Also, in a novel entitled *Some Do* the central character leaps to her feet and tells a group of women that the only way any of them can be free is to give up sex altogether because it is stupid, ugly and essentially rapacious. Whatever sense that pronouncement makes is engulfed in the nonsense that follows. The speech riles up some of the women to vengeance. A businessman with an occasional inclination to rape is gored through the anus with an outsized dildo. . . . A review in the December 1978 issue of *Ms* stated that the book describes its female personnel to be varied and memorable; the men are all callous, brutal nitwits.

Marilyn French's *The Women's Room*, a bestseller in print, a "rave" movie on television, skillfully dramatizes the bleak view that men have the clout, women bear the cross, and happy marriages are made only in heaven. The author allocated no character dimension to any of the men; they shout, strut, fornicate—never to the sexual satisfaction of their wives. Indeed, French said as much that her women see and feel men as "impediments in their lives." The TV version might have been billed as a medieval morality play climaxed by a rousing apotheosis of womankind.

The heroine of Marilyn French's later novel, *A Bleeding Heart,* is an English professor on leave who writes a book on "Lot's Wife: A Study of the Identification of Women with Suffering." She resents sex as slavery to the body, and laments that love makes you betray your principles.

In *Fanny* novelist Erica Jong aims a direct broadside at King Phallus. The heroine is a 1980 reincarnation of the "Woman of Pleasure" Fanny Hill, whose derring-do *Memoirs* were published by John Cleland in 1749. Jong's *Fanny* scans the "ins-and-outs" of an untethered woman with *her own* eyes. She scorns the original eighteenth-century record scripted by Mr. Cleland. "Only a Man would dwell so interminably on the Size and Endurance of sundry Peewees, Pillicocks and Pricks. . . ."

With psychologist Phyllis Chesler the turn-about of carnal passion against men comes full circle. Her tome *About Men* has been called "a hatchet-job on the male pillars of modern thought." The first eminent scalp is that of Sigmund Freud, patriarch of MCPs (male chauvinist psychologists). In rebuttal of his revelation that penis envy produces "masculine women," Ms. Chesler unveils the horror of womb envy that supposedly produces murderous men—wife beaters, infant stranglers, war mongers. She states that "male science, rooted in uterus envy, has carried us all to the brink of planetary, genetic and human destruction."

That the putdown of woman in the centuries of Augustinean blight might make a mockery of conventional Christian teaching and send the pendulum swinging toward retaliation and even vengefulness is an axiom of human nature. Such psychopathological aberration, however, must be distinguished from the Chesler madness at two points: First, the Fall of Adam and the consequences that have emanated from a primitive theology. For today's woman on the rampage, the masculine principle is brought down by a barrage of sweeping generalizations disguised by mock-historical and pseudo-scientific "facts"; thank goodness they are not blamed on God! Secondly, the Church Fathers of antiquity feared the sexual *power* of woman. Amazons of modernity who bludgeon man the enemy rather seem to be anta-gonized (and agonized) by *his sexual weakness.*

Punishment for past abuse of absolute power can become no less an enslavement to the tyranny of the human condition than ecclesiastical adherence to letter of the law strictures on the dignity and freedom of woman. War of the sexes about sex, like war of nations about nationalism, leaves no prize for the winner; in both cases "that for which we have fought" is destroyed. It is true that the woman liberated in mind and goal must be *militant,* but to be *belligerent* will lead her nowhere save to non-productive rhetoric. The liberation movement cannot afford the spendthrift extravagance of hate-indulgence.

When Adam and Eve left Eden they walked together, I imagine, locked arm in arm to meet and match their common fate. If the church has any salient role to play to make it easier for man-woman to find the way through the labyrinth of their sexuality, that role must be to erase from its teaching and practice the bale-ful influence of nonsense chimeras about female inferiority. Only then can Adam and Eve leave the outgrown innocence of an unreal paradise *together.*

Retreat of Man

Picture a man and a woman in bed. He is curled up under the covers, comatose; she is holding up a report card marked "D-Minus." That cartoon at first impressed me with its wit; now it has become deeply imprinted on my mind for its truth.

Another cartoon follows across my mental vision. A hairy brute, club in hand, dragging a blissful woman naked like himself by the hair into his cave. When we were boys we loved the "cave-man" image and pounded our chests in approved gorilla style. That macho syndrome, now feebly reincarnated in the American Rifle Association and male strippers, gave man physical domi-nance, allowing him a double standard of sexual behavior. How he loved to call his Missus "my little woman!" Perhaps the cave-woman was not as fragile as the cartoon proposed. Its male crafts-man saw her after the manner of a frail, wispy drawing-room "lady" of his time. *Now* that would be derided as a caricature, for the female form streaks in the swim meet, serves on the tennis court and strikes in the welding shop while the erstwhile member of the master race is denatured into flabbiness by urban life's sedentary occupations and the mechanical substitutes for brawn.

The report card cartoon, however, might be filed away as an authentic sign of the times by a loyal archivist of women's liberation. It lends reality to that alert mail-order entrepreneur from Oregon who offers to procure for the scared male a docile wife from the Orient.

Ever since the human species became sufficiently released from total concern with elementary survival to savor sexual intercourse as the apogee of all pleasure, the female was allotted the responsibility to bestow that pleasure and the male the privilege to receive it. The myth of male sexual imperialism today lies crumpled like a bundle of frayed, old clothes in the closet, and the specter of frigidity, once a favorite ruse of sundry wives repelled by a husband's bumbling ignorance, has been replaced by his terror of sexual *inadequacy*.

As might be expected, the role of man as predator and of woman as willing or unwilling prey is being questioned. Faking orgasms to please the other and headaches to extricate oneself no longer apply. *The Sexual Sensitivity of the American Male*, Karen Shanor's nation-wide study of four thousand men over a period of two years, reported that many men were reluctant to end a sexual encounter before the final climax because they feared the partner would think there was something vaguely wrong with her or, more emphatically, with him—that he is not quite a man. Among seventy men interviewed at length, a considerable number characterized sham orgasm by a male as something relatively easy and successful. Ms. Shanor herself pronounced women unable to identify the moment of ejaculation, especially when its agent was sheathed in a condom. Since even control of pregnancy has been transferred to the female by the Pill, I would guess that "the rubber" has almost vanished save as a precaution against venereal disease. That the Pill increases loathsome infection seems irrefutable.

Ms. Shanor discerned variations in male response to role reversal; some liked the aggressive approach and were tired of taking the initiative, while others recoiled into near-impotence. However tentative and hesitant the direct male responses may have been to the Shanor survey, Natalie Gittelson displays no such timidity. In *Dominus* she analyzed interviews with men of every type and from every locale to gauge their feelings about renouncing traditional prerogatives. Her conclusion? Men are in a sad state of psychic health; in adjusting themselves to the demands of women's liberation they have bartered away their own mastery for escape from manhood's responsibilities. The enormous price they are paying for compliance with new-fangled living arrangements sponsored by the feminist movement is evident in the discussions by men's liberation groups. Gittelson presents as testimony an assortment of casualties: "house husbands" squirming in a peon role so that their wives may realize themselves outside; single swingers of ambivalent sexuality and chary of involvement; blue-collar men frightened by the brassy presuppositions of their newly emancipated women; couples who turn their functions around full circle in conformity to the latest ideas.

Gittelson's adroit use of comic relief and irony would be more devastating to the feminist cause had it not been a source of delight to one interviewer, whose euphoric estimate of her attack was published with obvious enthusiasm in *Commentary*, a consistent enemy of the "radical" women's movement. Here is an example of the bizarre parody of a couple who have discarded the old role definitions. "Thelma was square and her hair was short; Benjamin was round and his hair was long. Her hips were narrow and her shoulders were broad; his hips were broad and his shoulders were narrow." Another vignette was about a men's group. They listen to a lecture on their burdens, after which they form a circle, are bidden to hold hands, then decide to hug; finally they think it may be interesting to explore homosexual relationships. This progressive process warms the heart of the guest guru lecturer, whose expertise on the trauma of men was born in the matrix of it all, namely in women's liberation.

Does the role reversal fostered by feminism bear the seeds of homosexuality? The question obliquely solicited by *Dominus* cannot be skirted. Women repeatedly strung out by their partner's inept bedmanship and/or incapacity for intimacy and the cuddling of body and spirit sensitive human beings reach out for have told me they flirted with, then fled into lesbianism (solitary masturbation being devoid of interrelationship). Why, then, would *their* alternative not beckon to men debased, depressed or outraged in their own sight by failure to perform with suitable panache? The Crossley Survey of 1977 calculated that 98 percent of men blamed themselves when their partners did not achieve orgasm. Orgasmania is the neurotic obsession with a non-essential experience inflated by fantasy. One wife, admittedly prone to swift arousal, casually informed a counselor that she "would rather have three orgasms in a row than three cars in her garage." In such a bind, the cumulative experiences of mortification and chagrin might understandably lead men to Japan via the mail-order salesman from Washington—or to a same-gendered paramour.

Fear also enters into premarital planning. Young men are more terrified than women of permanent relationships with the opposite sex. A generation ago, prior to a marriage ceremony the groom usually would show in body language more signals of ineffectually stifled nervousness and fear than his bride. After years of tactful questioning on my part I came to the conclusion that the impending marriage sent economic qualms cruising in his viscera; he now had to make a living for at least two. The bride, a virgin (then), oscillated between eagerness for sex and trembling before the untried. Today's Jane knows what to expect—and John knows she has a paying job. But *he* is worried about making it in bed.

Perhaps John's sexual energy, no longer fettered by the female animal's "in heat" seasonal schedule, was released for aggression in the materialistic cockpit of free-enterprise capitalism. Was Jane's released for guile, a trait rarely applied to men? Its repeated linkage with women has commended itself to male chauvinism's cavalier disposal of their claim to intellectual equality. Given the muscle-mastery wielded by the man, his mate honed shrewdness for protection, how else could she survive the onus of motherhood?

From my perspective the larger canvas of history discloses an end-to-end vein of *masculine* guile. Woman as woman was endowed with superiority. Being closer to nature in that she carried the only prospect of species renewal in her belly, she seemed born to taunt and, worse, to threaten King Phallus. Man, being closer to the seats of political and social power served by the lackey church he had created, drew tightly around her the noose of moral and cultural restrictions, letting the reins slacken for his own playfulness. The eyes of Jane were led to the Virgin Mary and to celibate Jesus, while those of John looked to Mary Magdalene and to rakish Casanova.

King Phallus even suborned the muses: sentimental poems of love-sick swains, "Moonlight and Roses" music celebrating female allure, epics of vast armies and armadas locked in combat for a woman's favors—all portraying the heroine "giving" herself to the man bent on "winning" her—and bewitching starry-eyed ladies with the pretense that *their* wish or caprice directed the play of love, while men trooped off to the *real* business of war.

Now art has swung across the spectrum from bosomy curves to geometric planes; literature from apotheosis of "style" to unequivocal analysis of the man-woman equation; science from mystic speculation about cosmic forces to microscopic concern with the human body and mind; philosophy from catching ultimate meaning to snatching clues to happiness, and the popular song from "Love Me and the World is Mine" to "Where Have All the Flowers Gone?" Instead of pretending to be gulled by the romantic fustian of Lord Byron, they hearken to his bugle call: "Who would be free himself (read *herself*) must strike the blow." And while tough feminists amass sophisticated data and harden their demands, many men go progressively soft. Being under pressure, they must become more responsive to the intimacy needs of their mates. Many marriages come to grief because men don't know or don't care about their woman's sexual pleasure—at least not enough to divert the phallic monster from the sheer act of thrusting to the art of thrilling. I often heard it whispered in strictly private seances of research-minded amateur sexologists that Chinese and Hindu men are preternaturally skillful practitioners of libidinous intercourse, perfecting every possible permutation and combination of the human body. Must these options be despised as degenerate by fastidious or envious North Americans?

To the familiar orgasmic physiological handicaps of male eroticism in relation to the female's, a sexual infirmity endemic, it seems, in all civilized societies has been added. That infirmity is sacrifice of the pursuit of Eros to the pursuit of affluence, status and political power over women. Work and sex are enemies, and the more personal commitment work requires, the more inroads it makes into sexual life. Man puts into a profession what woman invests in a relationship.

Sexual anorexia, a lowering or loss of appetite, may further impede male gonads. The nerve connections that control phallic alertness to sexual opportunity are extremely sensitive to emotions. The penis is a barometer; its somnolence is one of the first signs of mental stress. Dr. Helen Singer Kaplan, clinical professor of psychiatry and head of the Human Sexuality Program at New York Hospital-Cornell Medical Center, ascribes "highly prevalent" sexual anorexia to stress and fear of intimacy and success. She reports that patients with such problems usually accept therapy at the request of a spouse or lover.

Is the root of masculine bedroom bungling planted in childhood? The first five years of life are subject to and supervised almost totally by Mother, and the following five years or more usually by a female schoolteacher. A girl can continue for life in the feminine role conditioned by the maternal model, but before a boy approaches puberty he must make an almost 180° turn toward masculinity and repress the feminine component evoked by the women who molded him. Mother's apron strings? Teacher's pet? There is no disgrace more dire in the North American code. The result is contempt for frills, swaggering tribute to machismo, compulsion to chest-beating heroics, helmetless motorcycling— and finally the swift speedster, the five-minute stud whose hide has been thickened against any tiresome, sissy impulses to show tenderness to his mate.

Whereas woman's grievances are concrete and specific, man's confusion and uncertainty have no clear contours. Actually, he dares not even define them to himself—much less proclaim them in a protest meeting or a mass demonstration. Nor can he find solace in a sense of historic martyrdom or in the sympathetic fellowship with a group of peers banded together by similar experiences. Sporadic, short-lived liberation movements are not taken seriously, as a rule. They cannot match the workshops, discussions, polemic and the endless stream of literature that have signaled the feminist movement. Men have nobody and no gender to blame. Theirs is a sense of failure all the more keen because, unlike the opposite sex, they have basked in a self-esteem which is no longer a male's exclusive possession. Also, when a man feels inferior at home, inadequate and degraded in bed, the tremors are felt in every area of his life. Only inordinate love and tact of his *spouse* can deliver him from becoming undone.

Despite the statistical increase of women who shun the marital state, even choosing single custody of illegitimate offspring, all that I have observed rivets on one inescapable fact: most women prefer official and presumably permanent validation of a not-intolerable union; this applies especially to divorcées who are torn by pangs of loneliness and those co-vivants who begin to sense the restlessness of their partners.

When "love's" frame of reference is reduced to its common denominator, namely, the intrinsic primal fuck, the old wheeze that long ago filled my vagrant heart with roars of machismo can scarcely evoke a whisper. "Love is to man a thing apart"? Hardly! Sexual competence reckoned by *her*, no longer by him alone, is one of his life's pivotal, yet always only potential achievements—and it may be the measuring rod and determinant for all the others. Fulfilling her demands in bed provides him with some visceral reassurance of meeting the demands of the outside world.

What does the coital encounter, its inmost essence, say to woman? I have long foraged in and plundered my brain for some elusive answer to this fascinating mystery. In lieu of the direct personal experience barred to a male, I have tapped the skill and candor of Midge Decter, who in *Toward the New Chastity* has interpreted female in coitus. Other introspective female writers, too, tell me that for a woman coitus is isolated, dispensed with at completion, an end in itself. She enters each sexual happening with no further pressure than that of her willingness or unwillingness, and with no compulsion to produce firm proof of readiness; for her the degree of arousal need have no observable effect on the enactment of the scenario.

A virgin may become a heedless glutton once her initial resistance, social for the most part, has been overcome. There is no obligation to impede or impel her sole bit-part, namely just being there, exposing herself to his exertions. She may dissemble and pretend a response not felt, even to climax, without risk of inability to carry off the deception. Or she may wantonly take the initiative, fairly burying him under an escalating array of entanglements, postures and embraces. The option between these two extremes, and all the stages that separate them, is *hers*. Therein lies one salient reality; the other, little recognized but enormously significant, is this: beyond the trauma of guilt, currently evanescent as a rule, attendant upon her "first time" termination of chastity, the success of an act of intercourse is on the whole irrelevant to *her* success beyond the bedroom; to *his* well being in life's competitive market it is *crucial*.

That Jane doesn't realize how much of John is at stake has been rendered more lethal, and less visible, by her infatuation with orgasm, the "Big O," the absolutely, almost "divinely" ordained apogee of terrestrial existence—and by her assumption that coming must be synchronized to the split second with his. That man and woman are meant to share equally and simultaneously the same rhythm of arousal, action and release is a counsel of ideal perfection beyond the capacity of a mortal male to guarantee. Can the biological differentiation which establishes a time-gap between the respective male-female ejaculations be erased by his delay and her acceleration? Very rarely, I suspect, and only with mathematical monitoring so assiduous as to destroy all pretense of spontaneity; and spontaneity is the quintessential ingredient in the chemistry of sexual, unmeasured, unrationalized "yes."

Female sexuality awaits liberation not so much from penis tyranny as from the powers that dehumanize the sexual activity of both male and female. The agents of this corruption are at large in every twist and turn of our perpetually whirling world, perverting sex into a merchandising gimmick for cars and perfumes, a means of livelihood and financial self-aggrandizement, a weapon of rebellion against parents or teachers, a rationale for sense titillation, a path to the right clique, career or centerfold, an ostensibly mystic, semi-religious exploitation of eerie "self-awareness," a certificate of conformity to what is "in," and an excuse for ecclesiastical mind control. Sexual liberation means to be free from all these forms of dehumanization. Emphasis on shaping the man's sex urge to feeling a revival of gentleness might be one antidote to the reverse, *female* machismo.

I am unable to absorb the fact of instant, casual sex. Whether it is a remnant of my horse-and-buggy-era upbringing, vestigial romanticism, retarded-adolescent veneration of Woman, I confess to that stigma of inconsistency. Perhaps my compulsive recoil may be an echo of a vagrant male asceticism that, I believe, is not exceptional. Long ago I discovered how easy it was to deny myself sex enjoyment in the absence of a pliable and desirable accomplice. And the alleged deprivation brought me a welcome mood of release from an exorbitant sex-motivated forfeiture of time, energy and mental turmoil. As a test, I spent two months in a Catholic rural retreat. The womanless air did not stir the slightest zephyr of self-pity.

That experience conveys an incipient warning to the vanguard of women who downgrade penile status. Men may not be loathe to seek or unable to find a not-intolerable adjustment to their lack of heterosexual intercourse. Besides, a psychiatric commentator in an article entitled "Why Women Are Depressed" has made a strong case for a theory that female depression, more prevalent than male's, reflects her greater need for relationship bred into the genes through the long stretch of evolution. The bond tying her to the man reaches beyond the physical to the essence of emotional and psychological relationship. Wives are more tolerant of spousal infidelity; they often "hang in," loathe to discard the male factor altogether from the marital couch.

Rising divorce incidence does not mirror woman's lack of interest in male bedmanship, but her growing insistence on improving it. As I wander about our cities, I see that they are swarming with lonely divorcées and widows. If one-to-one talks with a stream of them who left unsatisfactory spouses are admissible for a deposition, my judgment cannot be side-tracked. Many of them, enamored by the freedom and self-reliance, their banners raised high by the feminist insurrection, have been traumatized by an awakening to the stark fact that the exchange rate for an intrepid life is possible economic penury, lifestyle disarray, sporadic periods of brooding regret, a series of transitory live-in trial candidates and the bleak prospect of empty years ahead. I call these broken dreams casualties of the feminist struggle. Should not the movement for women's liberation reckon with the unfathomable depth of their relational and sexual dependence when assessing the success quotient of "equality"? "Expendable Penis" is an epithet and battle cry surfacing into shrillness from humiliating centuries of coerced reticence. Is it futile?

The scepter of King Phallus is being wrenched from him by a massive sociopolitical uprising whose force may eventually shrink the clamor of dissident women to a sleeptime soliloquy. Are the million corpses of starvation-destroyed children strewn across the waste sands of Africa a fetid foretaste of human fate in the next century? Penile power must be curtailed. The halcyon days when King Phallus rode erect and bedizened in Christian-pagan religious processions celebrating fertility are now a hollow charade. A Damocles sword suspended over humanity has been forged on the anvil of famine, the atomic bomb, missile war and pollution of air, ocean, land, water—and the compulsive urge to do what comes naturally, *viz.*, augment the earth's overpopulation.

An astonishing source—the revered and authoritative sovereign of Catholic Christendom—has lent formidable though unpremeditated support to the image of penis on an ascending course of expendability. In October 1980, at a weekly general audience, Pope John Paul II, discoursing on the words of Jesus about adultery, said that adultery in a man's heart is not only a concupiscent look at a woman *not* his wife, but also *at* his wife. Aside from the absence of moral differentiation between *lustful* desire for any woman and *loving* desire for one's spouse, and the apparent omission of any allusion to the possibility of a woman's all too-human response to man's lewd appraisal, the Holy Father—I take the liberty to wonder—may have opened a logical sequence to negation of male reproductive autonomy. Without a signal from the optic nerve connections to the brain in reaction to a female's hypnotic nearness, there can be no brain-instructed readiness in the penis for intercourse and its impregnation sequel. Unless technology becomes so elaborate that intercourse can be computerized, monitored and mandated simply as a mechanical means to continue the *Homo sapiens*' career on earth, the ages-old cycle—optical nerve, triggered by the sight or thought of a compliant female body, to brain, to penis—must be traversed before the quiescent penis springs to attention. *Concupiscence* provides the motive power. As the Hebrew Talmud reminded us, there would be no home, family, community, no stirring of life, if God had not created in mankind the *yetzer horah* (the evil impulse).

Far more portentous for the future regime of King Phallus than the pontiff's pronouncement is a blond, chubby tyke who saw her first birthday on July 25, 1979. Her name? Louise Brown, commonplace enough to be lost in a crèche. Her fame? She is the first test-tube baby, born after her mother's ovum and her father's sperm were combined in a laboratory and then reimplanted in her mother's hitherto barren womb. Louise's squall on her entrance into existence was heard around the world, but not because of her immediate effect on that world. We need only look down the road to read the story of possible "future shock." For King Phallus, the principal actor in the renewal of the human species, Louise's arrival can be an invitation to his retirement. When the male sex apparatus is ejected from its mission of elevating women to rapture and is confined not merely to impregnation, as the pristine church, ironically, had ordered, but to seminal emission into a test tube, King Phallus will join the mummified rulers of long-buried empires, finding recognition only in melancholy monuments to his life-force that governed sex from the dawn of time.

Atomic fission-fusion and a crop of scary technological breakthroughs may bring to a halt the career of our human species long before Louise's test-tube tribe will be augmented by numbers. Millenia hence she may be classified as the original mutation that finally added a new branch to the family tree of human evolution. At my age I find it more comforting to foresee aeons than years. But the galloping pace of technology and its potential can telescope centuries into a few weeks. The most blasé scientists are awestruck. When tiny silicone chips half the size of a fingernail are scratched with enough circuit power to book seats on jumbo jets, keep them flying, cut complex fabric swatches and teach children how to spell and play chess well enough to beat all but the grandest masters, we may well ask, "What next?" or "What *not* next?"

In June 1980 the U.S. Supreme Court ruled that new forms of life sired in the laboratory can be patented. Validity on the highest level was thus given to the most revolutionary of all scientific adventures: genetic engineering, which has already brought into being forms of life beyond current existence. Its potential in multitudes of new creatures is beyond imagining. The court's decision clears the path for corporate enterprises that could multiply as rapidly as microbes.

Recombinant-DNA technology is the genie the U.S. National Institute of Health released from its test tube in the autumn of 1979 by relaxing some of the guidelines fear had imposed on it. How else except with trepidation should men approach a life-creating formula capable of condensing into scores of months what Darwinian evolution could achieve only in thousands of years? When Dr. Stanley Cohen of Stanford University first implanted foreign genes in bacteria to produce a unique life form, he called his new bacteria "DNA chimeras," after the terrifying three-headed mythological beast.

Alvin Toffler, to whom "Future" connoted "Shock," alluded in his book to the current of change, so powerful that it could overturn institutions, shift our values and shrivel our roots. In an age of routine moon walks and spaceships, may we dismiss as impossible the surprises technology can evoke from the *inner* universe, i.e., the structure of man himself? A gradual *devolution* of the penis into an organ earmarked for feeding seminal fluids to sperm banks and artificial insemination centers may have snuggled into the crèche with Louise Brown.

10

Homosexuality: Salute to a Gay Friend

Of all my fellow-students at seminary, Gabriel Altman came nearest to being a male I could truly love. His gentleness, sensitivity, spiritual and physical grace, imaginative mind and unflagging zest for life set him apart by temperament and choice. But not from me. He played the piano with tremendous gusto, abandon and talent, drawing from it the songs I liked to hear and sing. We made music together, and when I sat on the piano stool next to him, his flying fingers fascinated me. Sometimes he screamed with delight. Always vibrant, actually talkative in a shrill, piercing tone, Gabe instantly scattered the cloudlets of *Weltschmerz* that too often enshrouded me. We never conversed intimately and quietly, but his hand would graze mine at times, then abruptly pull away. He was older than I, and the initiative was his to take; when we were alone at the piano I found myself surprised by the vagrant thought that he was, somehow, afraid.

In my third year of rabbinical study Gabe's parents moved to Cincinnati and bought a big house, primarily to make a home for their son and break the cycle of cold attics and survival dining to which he had been enslaved. They took in seven of his friends, myself included. When the double rooms were assigned, Gabe told Ma Altman he would like to share with me. I felt flattered.

After barely a month I awoke one night to the damp presence of human flesh panting full-length at my back and the clasp of sweating fingers around my genitals. My mind froze. A few pages of Havelock Ellis grabbed at the university library were covered with academic terminology about same-sex "case" episodes. That was all I knew. The Levitical ban on such "abomination" studied in class touched me personally not at all; it was a boring lesson in Bible exegesis. Homosexuality belonged to *terra incognita*. I was totally absorbed by a consuming interest in male-female union; for me awareness of deviation from that alluring pattern lay far down the road. The "corn-hole" frolics of our gang of nubile kids on the hills above Bellaire had not an iota of boy-boy motivation. They were exercises in defiance of adult authority with a bonus of delicious penile arousal—a bravura step toward the ultimate breathless boy-girl mystery. A tangible, touchable "fairy" (the term used in those days) had no greater place in my fantasy than the Neanderthal Man of Darwinism's evolution taught in my Varsity anthropology class. I didn't even know the full anatomical mechanics of a "fairy's" art.

As befogged as my mind became during those seconds of sudden sensation, my body reacted in reflex to an unwelcome intrusion. I squirmed away toward the wall on the far side of the bed and lay still, my eyelids pressed tight, until a swish of sheets and the creaking bedspring announced my visitor's departure. Then the mental log jam broke and my thoughts ran riot. No single spurt of curiosity, dread, speculation or puzzlement emerged to take command of the helter-skelter. I was, in fact, neutralized by a balance of equally strong emotional forces, strangely calm, with one notable lack: revulsion; there was no disgust. But a surviving whiff of rationality warned me that future nocturnal visitations must be aborted without delay.

At breakfast I whispered to Dave, a senior soon to be ordained, that I had to have a confidential talk with him. He was a man of sagacity and trust. As an accomplished violinist he had often accompanied my amateur vocal efforts. In short, Dave was a friend. "First, we must find out who it was," he said.

That night I retired early to my room. We tied one black thread along the near side of my bed, and after Gabe had put out his light Dave tied a second black thread across the open door leading to the stairway. Meanwhile I prepared for siege by curling up tight and lying motionless toward the wall. I was resolved to make no response nor risk frontal encounter and possible recognition of my wooer, who I reluctantly sensed to be Gabe. Early the next morning Dave's hushed tone and stern mien brought me the report; the thread across the door was intact; no third party had entered the room. But the thread along my bed was broken. Someone had crawled stealthily to my backside, depositing an unmistakable message. . . . We now knew; it *was* Gabe. That day I skipped forenoon classes until Dave, honing his acumen for future rabbinical diplomacy, negotiated a change of roommates by persuading Ma Altman that a general reshuffling of personnel, at intervals, might be "good for group spirit."

At the time Gabe and I never exchanged a word about the incident. Nor did anyone else, except Dave. I have never ceased to thank him, especially for his agreement with me that I would act as though nothing had happened. Only in that way could I shield Gabe from inner hurt, guilt or shame. Affection for Gabe was intensified, if anything, by pity for his plight. At my prompting, save during semester exams, our after-dinner songfest became a daily fixture in the Altman house, with Dave often joining us on his fiddle. I managed to vocalize my zest for life more lustily than ever before—standing behind Gabe, my hands resting lightly on his shoulders. (However, I could not steel myself to resume sitting beside him on the piano bench. In retrospect, I think I was afraid. My feeling for Gabe had a quality I could not quite define or side-step.)

Before the end of the academic year, my mini-ordeal came to an abrupt end. Gabe was expelled from the seminary. The faculty let it be known that he had violated an administrative rule—one we all knew was routinely honored in the breach rather than by observance. I was shattered. Had over conspiracy of silence failed to conceal the Gabe-Abe affair? Had the faculty got wind of it? Dave swore that Gabe's involvement with me had had nothing to do with it. Soon a grapevine report revealed Gabe's dismissal had been sealed following an exhaustive probe and after the Board of his biweekly congregation had sent a committee to complain about his effeminate pulpit mannerisms, his erratic social behavior and the frequent reference in his sermons to sexual love, as well as his voluptuous, seemingly compulsive habit of "pawing" people. The seminary president, a relentless moralist, insisted on psychiatric interviews. The diagnosis—"homosexual-type, erotic instability."

The Altmans returned to their home town and Gabe vanished from my sight. He would have made an ideal specialist-rabbi, bridging the gulf between fearsome and myth-ridden middle-class Jewry and its marginal gay enclave with a rare combination of sensitivity, brilliance and humanistic concern. . . . A pulpit colleague he never became. In my mind, however, Gabe and I never stopped celebrating our love of life at the piano.

This chapter of my book is being written with empathy and truth to the utmost limit of my ability to express them, because I knew and loved Gabe. Had I been as familiar with the stereotype "homosexual" sixty years ago as every teenager is now, I easily might have been able to link Gabe with the gay tribe. Volatile gestures, upper-register speaking voice, plump frame, agile hips, artistic sensibility, complete indifference to women, apparent compulsion to touch men—they all belonged to Gabe. Even this identification chart, however, has been summoned to close scrutiny in our time. Masters and Johnson and other sexologists stoutly aver that these "signs" of homosexuality, being slightly underscored traits associated with the universal male's nipple-breasted bisexuality, are only a threadbare membership card. The "in" garb for a chic homosexual today is a cowboy hat and boots, a tooled leather vest, tight, well-faded jeans, a handkerchief of specific color hanging from the correct pocket (to denote sexual preference), a string tie and a swagger-stick as if to wipe out the womanish myth with machismo.

Gabe. Was he gay? Some sexologists draw a line between the authentic homosexual condition and activity in which homosexuals engage. Kinsey graded them from men who never were anything else, to occasional seekers for easy self-indulgence, to dysfunctional misfits, to those who want out. A prisoner in a penitentiary or a sailor who has been long at sea usually reverts to his previous heterosexuality. The gay state may tempt by its deliverance from the need to self-adjust to a supposedly "other" kind of human being, *viz.*, a woman. "A mode of thinking and feeling, not merely of acting," someone called it. In fact, D. Sherwin Bailey in *Homosexuality and the Western Christian Tradition* introduced me to a gem of shrewd wisdom: neither the Bible nor Christian tradition knew anything of *intrinsic* homosexuality as such; they knew the homosexual *act*; in itself, because it involves no responsibility, it is morally neutral. Did not the panel of psychiatrists that analyzed Gabe's stance and substance pronounce him a "homosexual type"?

It was the British writer Christopher Isherwood who condensed into one sentence my musings about Gabe: "You just *know* you're a homosexual when you fall in love with another man." The shivering and quivering of Gabe's flesh during those two unforgotten nights do not equivocate. It was not an impulsive whimsy but a focused, all-mastering passion that had led his feet to tiptoe across the carpeted floor between our beds. Even if I wished to follow "Papa" Freud into the fiat that homosexuality is a defective personality development, the intervening years of tranquil reflection on my relations with Gabe and his tragedy, as well as subsequent contacts with gay acquaintances, have etched a clear portrait onto my brain. Gabe was a believing homosexual who had affirmed himself before God in faith, accepting constitutive apartness from the ordinary without regrets, self-pity or the self-depreciation imposed by society. He had sought a good, full life of rabbinical service in keeping with his powers.

We witness today the struggle of homosexual men and women for self-knowledge and for transcendance over the weight society lays upon them. Their ideal values in sex are mutuality, responsible sharing and sustained friendship. Gabe's gayness was not a response to involuntary and tormenting heterosexual deprivation—an oft-repeated rationalization by devotees of the trivial—nor was it a bit of by-play in the bitter drama of possessor-possessed whose denouement may be sado-masochism. It was a quest for friendship that enables partners to grow and become more truly human.

For years, every night before sliding into sleep, Gabe was reborn in my silent meditations. He still loads me with unanswered questions. Intermittent pondering across the time-gap has nudged me toward tentative and vulnerable insights about which little can be assured—other than that nothing is really known as let us say one may know the chemistry of a virus or the potion concocted to curb it. There are riddles even more intractable than those concerning the role of Gabe's homosexual patina among the central constructive elements of his personality, and they refuse to gather dust in the attic. For example, the matrix, the *source* of his gay bent. How did Gabe get that way? This succinct query, like a whisper, releases an avalanche of didactic opinions about the roots of an individual's homosexuality.

My odyssey to find the answer threatens, at times, to fragmentize Gabe into splinters of interscholastic controversy. When experts disagree, what is a clerical amateur to believe? And I need to know! To the nondescript physician the homosexual is a sick person; to the lawyer who judges only "by the book" he is a criminal, or at least illegal, and in Nevada he's a felon; to the churchman who moves and breathes by the Bible he is wicked. To me, the homosexual is a mystery.

The alignment of contenders for the key to Gabe is essentially an encounter between two basic concepts of the human psyche: nature *versus* nurture. Do the springs of our thought processes arise irrevocably from inborn, deeply lodged concentrations of potential energy, or do they flow in upon us from environmental sources subject to change? Is sex inclination voted by the genes within us or by the conditions and circumstances that surround us? The contention began with the first person wise and worrisome enough to scratch his head in puzzlement over the vagaries of human behavior. Let's hear some of the voices in the debate. First, the case for the position that sexual lifestyle is a response to the external facts of life.

In 1905 Freud suggested that a man with a weak, indecisive father and a strong-willed mother is apt to become homosexual. In 1962 Bieber's New York study of 106 male homosexuals recognized in the background of a majority a detached father and a domineering, over-protective mother. Gabe's parents modeled the syndrome: a warmly demonstrative, nurturing mother who got things done, a dimly visible, somewhat bewildered father. Like most of the seminarians of all faiths, I know the maternal dream had guided Gabe to rabbinical studies. That had been the final influence for me as well. I adored my mother. Pop was a frustrated rabbinic scholar in a land whose focus on business enterprise made him a marginal, hopelessly alienated, penniless American. Prone to chastise me as the most rebellious of his ten children, he was no less remote from my world than the planet Mars. Not until maturity gave me understanding of his tragedy and of the pride in his piety did empathy and love reach out to unite us. By contrast, did the infinitely gentle, all-loving kindness and sturdy intelligence of my mother sway my tentative eroticism toward males? Adolescence for me was more likely to brook over fantasies of incest and even bestiality than over homosexuality. Gabe reached out to men from his individual, self-directing center of volition; there the die was cast. I have watched innumerable boys grow into lustily heterosexual manhood under the vigil of an adoring "Jewish mother."

Abraham Kardiner in *Sex and Morality* finds some men so overwhelmed by heightened pressure to meet the demands on their masculinity by liberated women that they flee from a sense of inadequate resources and the challenge to selfhood into a compromise haven that offers pleasure without impossible obligatory clauses, *viz.*, their own gender. Many of my boyhood cronies quailed at promoting or even permitting positive relations with the complete "otherness" of girls who, as a supplementary shoo-off, grew faster, had social aplomb and seemed to anticipate the "assertiveness" admonitions of the later feminist movement. Might not adult gay experimentation promise delay if not permanent avoidance of further maladjustment, a delay all the more appealing to men flayed by continuing social awkwardness and sexual urgency? Gabe used to shun our bull sessions about the astronomically distant, sexually desirable girls at Varsity and in our suburban neighborhood; he never went to the temple dances and left the room when a garrulous would-be Lothario began to brag about his dates.

Fear of homosexuality may trick some men into irrational behavior patterns. By joining the 101st Paratroop Division a World War II veteran traced his nervous breakdown to "masculine protest," the compulsion to prove his manhood and conquer his fear of becoming gay. . . . I always kissed my daughter on leaving home for a professional engagement. My son? I sometimes nervously patted him on the shoulder and then hastily reached for the doorknob. By this omission I implanted in him a jealousy and resentment that surfaced many years later. I have explained my tactless and dull-witted action as a laudable effort to avoid a sentimental "feminine" gesture calculated to embarrass Jonathan. Was it instead my underlying fear of homosexuality?

"I believe that homosexuality is the product of experience, not genetics. We're born man, woman—sexual beings. We learn our sexual preferences and orientations. They are not inborn," said William Masters in a television interview prior to publication of *Homosexuality in Perspective*, the first book by the husband-wife team in nine years. Their clear implication is that men and women choose their sex-style and can change it—a logical necessity for a lifestyle, centered as it is on therapy. Only in a situation caused by environment and conditioning is the Masters and Johnson remedial treatment applicable.

This perspective on gayness seemed to zero in, however, on data assembled from medical measurement of such reflexes as blood pressure, respiration, heart rate, muscle tension, lubrication, uterine enlargement and tumescence during sexual acts performed by volunteers judged capable of psychologically free intercourse while wired for beeps, gyrating needles and photographs. They were often adulterous by legal definition, traversing the entire gamut of manipulation from the masturbatory and oral to the anal. Furthermore, it may be fruitful to note that the monitored subjects did not represent a cross-section of either gays or straights; most of them had a college degree and a comfortable socioeconomic status. Yet the Masters and Johnson conclusions deserve deference, if for no other reason than the impact such heavy-weight celebrities have on general opinion. I am moved even more to report their findings because of the favorable light they shed on the emotional dividend in terms of *happiness* of gay sex. I hope Gabe's "bedtime story" brought him sufficient reward to counterbalance the harassment he had to endure.

Dr. Robert C. Kolodney of the Masters and Johnson Institute, in reply to the charge that homosexuality is a dysfunction and that its practitioners are impaired or less adequate in their responses, cited the *Perspective* research: "It just isn't so." Gays have mutually satisfying sex, they excel in foreplay and relaxation, moving slowly through excitement and lingering at plateau stages. They postpone stimulation for full-body play, taking turns in orgasm, and are able to communicate more freely their feelings about amorous activity. Ms. Johnson evoked an approving pat from me by her lament that heterosexuals have been loathe to accept their sexuality and "sex is still being taught as sin." No difference in physiology between gays and straights can be detected, as the penis doesn't know whether it is plunging into vagina or male anus, but the subjective mental attitude apparently does vary in the two groups.

The chillingly scientific purview of *Perspective* embraced a project to convert homosexuals into heterosexuals at their own request. Out of a group of fifty-four men and thirteen women, it reported 65 percent success, lasting up to five years. Can a crash two-week treatment course reverse a gay of long-standing involvement? Some psychologists tag the mutation "superficial."

Dr. C. A. Tripp, author of *The Homosexual Matrix*, denied that anyone can "cure" a gay since his condition is not an illness. As to changing him into a straight, no such case has ever been validated, and none ever will be, he bluntly asserted. . . . A dozen articulate, obviously clear-headed male and female gays revealed on television that although they had been programmed for marriage and children, they sacrificed reputation, security and freedom from harassment by police and parents (who sometimes committed their gay "brats" to institutions). Why did they renounce these advantages? To resume again and again the lifestyle for which nature had designed them. The men and women I saw and heard on television that day had obeyed an *inner* compulsion from birth. . . . Anita Bryant and her clique of clerical swordsmen vowed to rid the land of criminal "perverts" who *deliberately* picked and hugged their vice; a Mennonite minister scoured a gay rodeo in Reno for men sunk in sin whom he would "save" from eternal punishment. Their premise, that homosexuality is chosen, has not been verified by protracted, dispassionate research that is not muddied by the tyranny of impersonal mechanical gadgets.

Was Gabe diverted from conventional sex maturation by the example and influence of gays in his early development? Gynecologist Masters estimates that at least 10 percent of Americans are "reasonably active homosexuals"; children cannot be insulated against *any* "vibe" around the neighborhood. They *may* learn "it" from anyone in the environment, as they learn other habits. But *do* they *borrow* "*it*" that way?

Pretenders to the Messianic halo who stride forth into battle to save the world from gay "Satanism" arm themselves first with the fallacy that people become straight or gay in adulthood. On the contrary, as readers of Joyce Brothers know, it is children who cross that line. In myriad, highly complex, different uncharted ways, a small child develops sexual orientation—and it is not likely that it will change much throughout life. Gabe's childhood was spent in a society centered around the family, when parental power to shape the mind of a son had not yet been replaced by peer dictatorship. Gabe's parents were heterosexual; they showed no symptoms of quirks or funkiness. Preoccupied with livelihood and love of offspring, the mere thought of homosexuality in their son, much less its possible "taint," would not have entered their minds. And if they had the barest inkling of their son's gayness they would have dedicated the entire arsenal of parental status to safeguard his future with no less abandon than the mother who once reserved a motel room for her son and his girlfriend "to make sure that he gets the right heterosexual start."

What about teachers in public schools? Dr. William Cameron, a clinical research fellow at Johns Hopkins University, maintains that "we have no evidence whatever that gay teachers can affect a child's sexual orientation." My own pre-high school teachers were all "old maids," a label which then stuck to any unmarried female over thirty; some, I am sure, leaned in their loneliness toward lesbianism. My daily alertness to the behavior of girls in my class brought to light no portent whatsoever of permanent maidenhood or lesbianism. Quite the contrary! Few Catholic kids taught by nuns take the veil of celibacy. Today gay teachers are likely to position themselves at a distance from their pupils, abjuring all personal contact, however innocent, because of their vulnerability to gay-baiting bigots. Heterosexuals are not thus constrained.

Within the limits of my experience, I have found gays to be among the most decent, law-abiding and peaceful people in a community. The drag queens of San Francisco's Polk Street are the comic clowns of the gay world, cruising flesh-hunters in rest-rooms and bath houses are its tragic casualties; rather than pariahs and predators, they are the wounded in a society at war with its own sexuality. The preponderant proportion of child molesters are heterosexual in their adult connections. A study by the former director of the Massachusetts Center for the Diagnosis and Treatment of Sexually Dangerous Persons looked at 175 random males convicted of sexual assault against children. The majority turned out to be heterosexuals using a child for gratification or pedophiles who had always been drawn to children.

Many adolescents have some doubts about the direction their sexuality is taking them and get crushes on kids their own sex. Is not homosexuality "latent" in everyone, as the experts are fond of reminding us? Everything ever done by human beings, no matter how absurd or inhuman, becomes a potential for all of us, under similar conditions. No woman with normal anatomical equipment is immune to "latent" pregnancy. The combination of male and female, psychosomatic grooves in the brain of universal mankind, does not confound or menace school children with some arcane peril. If role modeling were a dominant factor in the making of homosexuals, how can they achieve a substantial niche in an environment of heterosexual parents and the negligible probability of homosexual contacts?

These to me are among the commonsense arguments against paranoia concerning the alleged bacilli injected into our school kids by gay teachers. They did not prevent a California State senator (who had previously advocated the death penalty for gays) from introducing Question Six, which would permit school authorities to dismiss homosexuals from teaching, administration and counseling jobs. It would also permit a vicious, neurotic child to shape innuendo and rumor into weapons for destroying a teacher it hated. Lillian Hellman's play *The Children's Hour* was a gripping psychological searchlight on a rotten little girl who ruined the lives of two teachers of her school with a lie about their lesbianism. It might have been an effective vote-getter against Question Six. In any case Californians rejected Question Six at the polls. I rejoiced.

Judd Marmor, widely respected University of Southern California pundit, after a superfluous notation that few experts agree about the cause of homosexuality, considers the public school grade one to be the watershed for the "set" of sexual orientation; after that it does not easily change. He states that "it may be determined by prenatal factors, a hypothesis especially cogent in types with symptoms of effeminacy." Although gender is not psychologically differentiated at birth, it becomes a habitué of the mind (as well as the genitals) in the course of growing up. Many scientists posit a critical point in the uterine male fetus when its brain must be sensitized by male hormones; if not, they will behave in an "effeminate way" (whatever that is!). Others breathe the word "predestination," which supposedly decides at a certain checkpoint what an adolescent's sex-style will be.

All this modern-day, "scientific" advocacy of the "inborn" theory is *ex post facto,* after the fact. Following Gabe's trek across the carpet to my slumbering body, I had consulted Havelock Ellis, who believed that homosexuality could be trailed to genetics. In his finality lay my will to believe and Gabe's absolution from guilt. Gabe might have echoed the riposte of a gay teacher-friend sixty years later: "Rabbi, none of us chooses our sexual orientation any more than we can choose our first language or the color of our eyes. How callous can people be to punish us for being what we unalterably are?"

Another voice spans the six-decade silent void between this moment and the day Gabe muffled his goodbye to me at the Cincinnati railway station. "Abe, I couldn't have made you love me as man loves woman. There is no evidence, Abe, that occasional exposure to such love will make a boy its lifelong acolyte. What nature God has stored in your *genes* is the Divine word! If God had written it there you would have stretched out your arms and belly to me, beloved friend, instead of curling up against the wall!"

Did the black thread Dave had strung along my bed in the Altman House decide my future? Would I have slowly sunk (or soared) into gayness under Gabe's tutelage? The issue rests on the polarity of nature (genes) and nurture (environment). Would affection for Gabe, who inhabited the realm around me, have outweighed the absence of a gay predisposition within me? The horns of that dilemma do not easily crumble before logic. Recently, identical twins adopted soon after birth by two far-removed sets of parents were reunited after thirty-five years of incompatible upbringing. Exhaustive study unearthed astonishing similarities in behavior, psyche, habits, taste—and also some glaring contradictions. Geneticists chortled over the resemblances—proof that they were right; environmentalists rejoiced with equally blinkered sight in the differences—a proof that *they* were right.

Is, then, gayness a matter of sexual preference, or is it predestination? Many traditional concepts of sexual behavior are grounded on *culture*, the standards and assumptions that reflect the interests and prejudices of those in our society who are in power—and "in." Becker, in *The Outsiders*, presents a novel thesis. "Social groups," he says, "can create deviances." How? By creating rules whose infraction constitutes deviance, then applying them to people whom they label "outsiders."

Like a squalling babe, the enigma of gayness-genesis cannot easily be put to rest. I am reduced to a pair of pacifiers. First, homosexual fantasies—day-dreams common to men of both persuasions—do not spell commitment. Second, I am always incurably, at times ecstatically, in action unreservedly, heterosexual, but also permanently dedicated to pursue and publish the truth about gays, to promote equal fellowship with them to combat the injustices under which they labor.

My vendetta against homophobia began when Gabe's dream of serving God in the pulpit was brought to an end by the governing board at Hebrew Union College. In my opinion justice had been cast overboard. Why was Gabe cashiered? If the psychiatrists' verdict "homosexual-type, erotic instability" was his conscious choice, teachers of religion, it seems to me, would have been moved by compassion to ask that the physicians of the mind recommend and administer remedial treatment for such a fixation. If Gabe's idiosyncracy was innate, beyond his control, summary punishment without appeal could not escape the familiar phrase "cruel and unusual," if not "cruel and inhuman."

The seminary had always taken pride in its flexibility and liberalism. During that same time-span, on the heels of the Soviet Revolution, another student had been expelled for his missionary agitation on behalf of atheistic Communism. From the vantage point of conventional, dogmatic theology, such zealotry for a creed that had eliminated deity constituted a foray against the seminary's foundation. In the star-chamber session at which Gabe preempted the agenda, did his interrogators panic with similar fright? His digression from normality was considered a clear danger to the seminary's bourgeois standing of Jewish rectitude and propriety. It shared that dubious distinction with other regrettable upsurges of student "imbalance," such as kabbalistic seances, Hasidic frenzies, soap-box harangues, Zionist aeschatology (pre-Holocaust) and sermonic paens to a universal Community Church religion. It was a time of intense turmoil, the legacy of World War I and its inevitable disillusionment.

The sober minds who directed the seminary, a hallowed shrine of Jewish wisdom, knew that the anarchic flurry would pass. But *this* Gabriel Altman kind of deviance seeped poison into the vitals! It might spread throughout the student body! How many of Gabe's intimates may already have been infected? In my imagined (and at this late date unverifiable) reconstruction of the mood and events that led to the faculty's expulsion of Gabriel Altman, the fateful adversary was moral revulsion. Sex? It means "wife and children," "be fruitful and multiply," as the Bible says. What *else* can it mean? I can hear the indictment: Man-to-man intercourse deliberately practiced for non-reproductive pleasure is a stench in the nostrils—in a Jew of *any* station, the ultimate stain. In a rabbi, an irreconcilable contradiction. Leviticus 18:22—does it not call the unmentionable thing an abomination? Again, two chapters later, in the context of sexual sins, including incest and adultery, are we not warned, "They shall surely be put to death"?

Sheketz (Hebrew noun: "abomination") goes beyond failure to observe the 613 legal statutes in the Torah. It is more than a negative or positive misdeed; it is a ravenous corruption. Judaism sprouted in the Eastern Mediterranean littoral, notorious then, as now, for its practice of, indeed its euphoric panegyrics to homosexual "love." Yet the Talmud took pains to claim that the Hebrew nation was not under the suspicion of homosexuality. In classroom Talmud sessions, reference was made to the neuter (*tum-tum*) hermaphrodite and transvestite. I do not recall any oral, open allusions to homosexuals. Did that lacuna indicate a lack of concern or of forthrightness to avoid a disturbing subject?

Of all the "substance abuses" of the written word perpetrated since men first put chisel to stone or brush to papyrus, few are more unconscionable than the misappropriation of the first five books of the Hebrew Bible for the purpose of thought control. That Scripture is the story of an ancient Near East people's stubborn quest to know God. It carries no final authority on anything save that the search for truth about the Divine Being and Will, about the meaning and purpose of human existence, is fraught with unconquerable difficulties, not the least of which arise from the spiritual weakness of man himself. More than the revelation of God's Law to us, the *Humesh* ("Five," as the first five books, the basic Torah, are commonly called by traditional Jews and all rabbis) is the revelation by man to God of his (man's) schizophrenic, divine-bestial quality. No more and no less! Divided in his essence and astray in a cosmos not of his making, man sought spiritual guidance. Scripture became his refuge, a do-it-yourself guide. It is a miscellany of legendary lore and laws, often repetitive in detail. Like the sex rules in Leviticus, it was composed by men of spiritual genius so that their people might be led to a godly life, as they in their time defined it. The first five books were a mass of heavenly prohibitions mediated through a self-perpetuating priesthood, to definitely disprove, for example, evolution in favor of a currently rehabilitated Creationism. They contained rigid regulations on pain of death on the sex-style of adults, even when no coercion or injury to others were involved. This last preoccupation in the Levitical section is the burden that crushed Gabe.

What then was the meaning of the anti-homosexual verses that named my friend unfit for the rabbinate? They were a spin-off from the vulnerability of the all-too-human Hebrew people who were being corrupted by sex-deity worship and its practice of male prostitution glamorized in the rites of Egypt and Canaan. Homosexuality therefore arose in, and was a part of, idolatry. Among human sins, it was the worst abomination and became the prime target of the great Prophets. The late-vintage portions of the *Humesh* had been composed under the tutelage of the Prophets for whom homosexuality was transgression in its most reprehensible form—bowing the head to and thrusting the penis in worship of idols centered in sexuality. It would stir Yahweh's wrath and lead the Hebrews to national destruction, they said. It was the collective homosexual *act*, not the *condition*, that drew the death penalty.

In several biblical references gay practices and the pagan cult of male prostitution were synonymous, for they posed another threat to the survival of the small Hebrew community: non-procreation violating the first commandment, to be fruitful and multiply. Hints of the "taint" may be drawn from the curse laid on Ham, Noah's second son, for uncovering his father's nakedness; David's bond with Jonathan that "passed beyond the love of woman"; Ruth's adherence to Naomi. Of all the religions in antiquity, Judaism and Zoroastrianism were distinguished by the total denunciation of homosexuality. The post-biblical Talmud distinguished between wanton homosexual transgression, theoretically punishable by death (although no such penalty is recorded), and an inadvertent act expiated by a sin-offering in the temple.

In the so-called "Holiness Code" of Leviticus, eating shellfish or performing marital acts with women during menstruation were also forbidden and invited banishment from the ranks of the living. Desecration of the Sabbath was another crime punishable by death. Yet these ordinances got short shrift from the Reform Judaism then taught at my seminary. Why did homosexuality alone remain on the critical list?

Finally, were not the words "Sodom and Gomorrah" integrated into the English language as typical examples of homosexual corruption? They are even now being invoked in the virulent epithets of bible-exploiting fundamentalist gay-baiters. Destroyed by the wrath of Yahweh the legendary sin cities received their well-deserved punishment, thereby exonerating the pietists who hated the sinner more than the sin.

Sodom and Gomorrah—can we squeeze into a footnote the twin by-word for depravity? Only to avoid "a sin of omission," I summon two witnesses to testify on the true cause of the sin cities' debacle. First, the Bible, escorted by a host of jaunty, self-confident churchmen whose case has been upheld, they think, by Judeo-Hebrew Scripture, comes forward, sacred and immune to profane meddling. A familiar verse that has confounded the skeptical for countless generations is again intoned: "Bring them (Lot's guests) that we (the Sodomites) may know them." Does not the Hebrew verb *yoda* (to know) mean sexual intercourse, and were they not all men? Therefore, it must have been homosexuality that swallowed up Sodom and Gomorrah in fire! Now *yoda* does not necessarily mean *sex* in this passage. Out of the hundreds of appearances of the word in the Bible, only a tiny number convey such meaning. And when *yoda* does appear, it is always in connection with heterosexual coitus. The homosexual kind of coitus, as well as bestiality, are denoted by the word *shachav* (to lie with), a physical posture far more germane to the subject. Besides, Lot's status was that of a *ger*, the Hebrew word for a resident alien. Lot had received into his home two strangers who were possibly hostile; fluid, intertribal warfare had fomented deep apprehension. Lot, therefore, might have ventured beyond a *ger's* province. The Sodomites wanted, literally, to *know* them. In demanding that right with peremptory violence, however, they had disobeyed the traditional Near Eastern tradition of *hospitality*. Narrated in another Genesis passage, such hospitality was typified by the warm reception Abraham had given to three strangers. That, in effect, was the Sodomites' iniquity—and not the alleged crime to which they gave a name.

As further testimony, no biblical allusion to homosexuality mentions Sodom and no Sodom reference mentions homosexuality. A later period, around the beginning of the Christian Era, seems inclined to link them together. Philo Judaeus, an assimilated Alexandrian Jewish scholar who lived at the end of the first Christian century, left vivid descriptions of the men of Sodom mounting each other in wild disregard of fixed top-bottom active-passive roles. Still later, the Jewish historian Josephus again connected Sodom with homosexuality, which had not achieved top-rank as a God-cursed crime until the second century before the Christian Era, when the "Sin of Sodom" was defined in sexual terms for the very first time. Since then Sodom, it seems, had been broadened into a general catchword for whatever the religious establishment deemed wicked.

Another witness for the defense arose, identifying itself as

Reason, and its argument was brief. Chronology and conditions, therefore, point to one conclusion: "Sodom-Gomorrah" spells "polemic" against idolatry. Like the death-penalty verses heretofore examined, the interpretation of "Sodom-Gomorrah" as a homily against same-gender sex does not hold up; instead it belongs among the Pentateuchal narratives, shaped under prophetic influence to drive home their single-issue message: the Hebrews must uproot from soil and soul the already burgeoning seeds of Egyptian-Canaanite *sexolatry. Not* homosexuality! Propaganda for a return to Yahweh who was being offered up as a holocaust to sex deities served by male whores within the sacred precincts of the temple! *Kodesh* (male prostitute) is alluded to specifically with disdain and fear in biblical invective that bears the names of the great Prophets.

Archaeology allies itself with Reason. Around 1900 B.C.E. a great disaster, possibly an earthquake—as excavations seconded by history and literature reveal—leveled the cities of the plain. They now lie buried under the southern expanse of the Dead Sea.

Catholic scholarship has not been mute. Jesuit John J. McNeill in *The Church and the Homosexual* declares that the prohibition of homosexuality in Old Testament legalism, notably Leviticus, is not binding on the conscience. (Vatican interdiction delayed the book's publication for two years, banned its author's further discussion of the subject and denied the church's imprimatur to any further editions.) Five Catholic professors drew immediate fire from the American Conference of Catholic Bishops for their paper, "Human Sexuality: New Directions in American Catholic Thought." Sensual behavior, including homosexuality, is said there to be dependent on circumstances and personal conscience and intention; Scripture is said *not* to be a "text-book of ethics giving absolute prescriptions with regard to sex." A hefty boost for these Catholic liberals came from—of all places—the Second Vatican Council. In one of its documents we find a most impressive but down-played view of the Bible: "Since God speaks in Sacred Scripture through men in a human fashion, (its) interpreter . . . should carefully investigate what meaning the sacred writers really intended and what God wanted to manifest by means of their words." A far cry indeed from the "closed" mentality which would forbid probes of the Bible's seminal meaning because its message is so unchallengeably clear that discussion becomes superfluous!

Was Christianity's Bible (the "New" Testament by edict of its theology) among the plaintiff's artillery against my friend Gabe? Not likely. Sixty years ago Gabe's prosecutors could not be classified as exegetes at home in that text. The Gospels contain not a word about homosexuality. Had a text been quoted, Chapter 1 of the Epistle to the Romans would have got the nod; there Paul (Saul of Tarsus) lashes out in the strongest terms stating that homosexuality is against "natural law." Some Christian scholars are not able to ascertain exactly what Paul meant by the phrase, and modern readers, I am told, associate "natural law" with diverse sources: Freud, later philosophic speculation, scholastic theology, social taboos and personal fears, to name some. Paul's intense concern had its source in the fact that most of the converts to Christianity, in his time, had been reared in paganism, an environment drenched in homosexuality. Did he not further extend the spiritual lineage of the Hebrew prophets by condemning homosexuals as idolaters? (Loyal to his male chauvinism, he assigns the lead in these "shameless passions" to women; "their men," he said, followed "in turn.")

A church's view of the Bible can color the lens it directs at homosexuality. Whereas the Southern Baptist Conference *praised* Anita Bryant's joust with the homosexual dragon because it bore the imprimatur of biblical law, the United Church of Christ *deplored* the use of Scripture to generate hatred and violation of the civil rights of any gay or bisexual person.

The dictatorship of "Holy Writ" over the whole realm of human thought has blighted intellectual growth, social change and moral enlightenment for centuries. This has seldom been more eloquently attested to than by the ongoing power of a few sentences in the Judeo-Christian Scripture to make the homosexual an object of derision in slang and social attitudes, in leers and legal codes, in jokes and job discrimination, in whispered nudges at cocktail parties and crude taunts hurled by street-wise teenagers, in the way we automatically think and feel and deliberately choke off knowledge.

Michael Goodich, author of *The Unmentionable Vice: Homosexuality in the Later Medieval Period*, had not yet published the tome when I read a preview. Its bold historical sweep showed dimensions of grandeur; there was no widespread persecution of sexual deviants until the thirteenth century. At that time the agenda of the church was still preempted by measures to

eradicate adultery, blood-relatives' marriages and clerical violation of celibacy. Same-sex union was not a (stake-) burning issue.
But the thirteenth century altered that ecclesiastical perspective.
The sinfulness conclusively proven by the fire and brimstone that
had erased Sodom and Gomorrah now demanded the extermina-
tion of homosexuals. These "accursed minions of Satan" were
subjected to a genocidal program whose ferocity matched the holy
war of extinction against apostates, heretics, judaizers and dabblers
in magic. . . . In other words, the anti-homosexual stance of Christianity reflects the sociological and psychological state of the
religious authorities who interpret it; there always are periods of
paranoia, submergence and revival.

Actually, homosexuality did not see the light of day until
Kinsey's monumental work. "Gay" was on the road to becoming
a cliché when he found that at least a third of all males were gay-ly
engaged one or more times in their lifespan; that 13 percent "were
predominantly homosexual"; that six million men in America
would be isolated if gayness were institutionalized. Kinsey finally
concluded that homosexuality has been "a significant part of
human sexual activity ever since the dawn of history, primarily
because it is an expression of capacities that are basic in the
human animal."

The deflation of the Bible-centered reading ritual in the
American family, the respectability, if not the glorification of
non-procreative sex, the engulfing tide of scientific secularism,
permissiveness toward new patterns of erotic outlet—were they
not factors calculated to introduce an era of benign unconcern
about gayness? Yes, a new era has dawned for *all* Americans. It is
unconcern about the poor, the young, the elderly, human rights
of women, minorities and out-of-step dissidents—but *not* unconcern about groups whose behavior, political and social philosophy
or sexual preference "offends." What once earned the breast-plate
"Military-Industrial Complex" has now become the "Moral"
Majority: a newly soldered, potentially omnipotent Rightist
alliance of a budget-bloated military class, corporate conglomer-
ates hog-wild for profit and electronically equipped and money-
sinewed clerical *servants of the Lord. They* believe in and are
determined to establish an American theocracy under a Constitution that is amenable to their amendment and under a Bible
whose God-revealed Law, as they "understand" it, is considered
no less eternal than the everlasting hills. A historically unpre-

cedented, vociferously "religious" lobby has formed, whose strategy would capture the seventy million or more Americans who call themselves born-again Christians. It may draft them into a political right-wing army for the deracination of any movement, program or idea that contravenes selected biblical injunctions. Can such a lobby omit homosexuality from its prime hitlist? *Christian Voice* has already "declared war" on homosexuals; they are being baptized in unholy water as the only persons in our land whom everyone is permitted to hate without apology, secrecy or guilt.

During the sixty years since Gabe's ejection from seminary, I have noted with mounting disgust and fury the social, economic and psychological torment heaped on persons whose sole march to a different drummer is their personal and private sex partnership. Like Gabe, they bear no ill toward anyone, and usually rise above their barriers in ethical awareness, artistic innovation and commitment to social service. In every class, color, creed, occupation, profession, the one thing they have in common, and the one thing that differentiates them from the mass, is the right of sex preference that would be unchallengeable in an enlightened society.

A lifetime of brooding about the millenial martyrdom of the Jewish people has immunized me against tears over the god-versus-beast bifurcation in human nature and the "church's" moral inconsistencies. Jew-baiting has cosmic dimensions, spurting forth from unfathomable depths in the human psyche; gay-baiting, for me, still swirls around Gabe. So I take note of its more noxious manifestations. Shall the miasma be uncovered? Gabe, I suspect, would ask me to spare myself the disillusionment and pain attendant upon a full recital of the wrongs perpetrated by "Judeo-Christian civilization." I shall, therefore, restrict my remarks to a minuscule smear of the latest social disease: psychotic homophobia! Here are a few random specimens of the virus:

"Homosexuality will ultimately lead to the disappearance of our country as a great power. Where are we going to get our armies to protect us? Homosexuals don't want to fight. We're not going to maintain the will of our normal people to breed children to be turned into that lifestyle" (interview with a member of the United States Congress by Robert Scheer, in the *Los Angeles Times*). . . . A California Supreme Court ruling that a public utility may not bar gays from employment without first proving that gayness made them unfit for the job reversed a more typical contrary verdict by a Superior Court in San Francisco, where gays supposedly have clout for self-protection. . . . Here's a pearl of wisdom dropped in my lap at a party: "I like Jim a lot. He says he's gay, but he must be pretending. How could a decent guy belong to that despicable gang? I'm sure he's acting like a queer to conceal his affairs with women." . . . Miami, St. Paul, Wichita, San José and Eugene, Oregon, have rescinded, by popular demand, ordinances for gay rights. . . . A Rhode Island High School student was beaten up by his classmates because he pressed and won a court battle to escort his boyfriend to the senior prom. . . . Under fierce maledictions from Orthodox rabbis, homosexual Jews from several countries holding their first convention in Israel, having been turned away by hotels and collective farms, not only were forced to meet and tour secretly, but also were asked to accept a refund of their $9,000 donation to plant trees in the name of the International Conference of Gay and Lesbian Jews. . . . Homosexuals from foreign lands have been barred from entering the United States even as tourists, in conformity with a 1965 federal law excluding persons "afflicted with psychopathic personality or sexual deviation." (In 1979 it was conceded that immigration and naturalization officials would no longer ask, "Are you homosexual?" and the newcomer would not need to volunteer a statement.) Only an act of Congress can nullify the law. . . . The Fort Myers, Florida, branch of the Gay Metropolitan Community Church goes underground in members' homes every other Sunday after having been ousted from five different meeting places over five years. . . . A desecration of fundamental Christian teaching was incited by a Baptist minister, head of Fort Myers' fundamentalist Moral Majority, who quoted "God's word" to substantiate the view that "they can't be Christian and homosexual." "Also," he boomed, "they are recruited; to say they are born that way is against Scripture." . . . The network of Metropolitan Community Fellowships in scores of U.S. cities and seven counties reports harassment by death threats, fires, cross-burnings and vandalism. . . . Harvey Milk, a gay elected to the San Francisco Board of Supervisors, was shot to death by a former colleague on the Board who had cast the only vote against strengthening gay civil rights and, according to the evidence, deliberately sought him out in his office for slaughter. The punishment meted out by the court seemed so absurdly tokenish that thousands of gays and straights besieged city hall in riotous protest. I had admired Harvey Milk for his gentleness and generous relations with people, and had fostered acquaintance with him at Glide Memorial Church; I also supported his political campaign. (Threatening letters and telephone calls had led him to expect an attempt on his life and to leave word on a tape recorder that he wanted no church service at his funeral because organized religion was an enemy of homosexuals.)

Is the pulpit the enemy? Anita Bryant's biblical wolf-cry against gays put the match to a national hate conflagration. It was merely an echo, however, of the cassock-coated venom spewed forth by a Baptist minister from whom she had received the benediction that "we are facing the Devil himself in these homosexuals!" Later, Dean Wycoff, a pastor from Santa Clara, California, sermonized, "I agree with capital punishment and I believe homosexuality could be coupled with murder and other sins." Only a narrow time-gap separated these pietistic perversions from a distribution of fliers in a Los Angeles suburb by a group called the National American Party for Manhood, who demanded that homosexuals receive capital punishment. A cause-effect relationship links the vociferous cannibalism of clergymen and N.A.P.M. Is it partisan on my part to whisper that the provocative spotlight on "manhood" in the group's flamboyant name bears out a theory expounded by a psychologist friend. He told me that "crusaders who launch a nation-wide campaign of defamation against a large group of non-criminal citizens are probably in the process of compensating for homosexual inclinations they can't openly confront."

Gilbert Chesterton, one of this century's most brilliant literary champions of Catholic conservatism, once quipped, "About sex especially, men are born mad," adding, "and they can't reach sanity until they reach sanctity." He probably meant that men will not be sane about sex until they attain sanctification in Heaven. A cloudy forecast! The vengeful gay-haters of fundamentalist religion, however, wear the halo of holiness here on earth, and therefore I consider them all the more insane.

Ironically, Carl Jung, the anti-Freudian luminary in the psychiatrist world and a favorite of conservative believers, wrote in his *Collective Works* that the homosexual is endowed with a wealth of religious feelings which help him bring the spiritual church into reality, with a receptivity that makes him more responsive to revelation. A less abstract contribution by gays to a better world might be their assistance in freeing males from lopsided emphasis on violence as an essential proof of masculinity. Although they occasionally imitate the worst aspects of heterosexual excess, violence in general is remarkably absent from their behavior pattern, although particularly prevalent, if some sexologists are to be believed, among men striving to stifle their latent gayness. Were the reality of universal gay tendencies and fantasies accepted, the heterosexual could stop damning "the queer" and would no longer need to play the "tough guy."

Rabbi Richard Rubenstein, the creative and controversial theologian and renowned author, attributes the hostility toward homosexuals, in part, to the fact that practically every human being has some latent homosexual feelings. Not wanting to recognize it in themselves, they turn with anger against those who acknowledge or glorify it; it's their defense against temptation. Author-sociologist Reverend Howard Moody of the United Church of Christ recalls that the marines in his unit who beat up gays showed clear symptoms of questionable sexuality in themselves; the strong heterosexuals were not ridden by such hobgoblins.

Despite pulpit-pounding threats of annihilation, devotees of the "gay life" were sufficiently heartened, for a time, to come out of the closet; that was when I began to think of Gabe with lessened pain. In 1969 a police squad raided the Stonewall Bar in New York's Greenwich Village, precipitating the birth of the gay liberation movement. Rather than submit to the usual brutality, the patrons quickly took up battle positions and fell upon the foe, with results still recounted in raucous celebrations of the first physical resistance by homosexuals against oppression. And for a while, at least, the tensions of homophobic neuroses seemed to relax in the cool shade of the sexual revolution umbrella, as hedonistic pleasure and humanistic interpersonal freedom were legitimized to be at least supplementary priority goals of sex intercourse. Church resolutions began to decriminalize homosexuality and to decry discrimination against its adherents. Civil rights burgeoned. The U.S. surgeon-general refused further to examine prospective immigrants and certify that they were without homosexual sickness, in view of an American Psychiatric Association's clearance. The U.S. civil service ruled that homosexuals could not be fired on account of their sexual persuasion alone. A dozen large corporations announced a policy of equal opportunity for homosexuals. Almost a score of states repealed restrictions on sex between consenting adults, although some still punish "sodomy" (an offence subjected to variable definitions) with a five-year jail sentence. Forty cities and counties in the United States passed anti-discrimination ordinances; legal reforms were supported by official ukase of the American Bar Association, the Y.M.C.A., the American Federation of Teachers and other clout-carrying bodies. A gay rights group petitioned the Federal Communications Commission to halt the broadcast of such gay stereotypes as child molesters, murderers and simpering fruitcakes. A federal court ordered the reinstatement in the U.S. Air Force of a much-decorated Vietnam War veteran who had been booted out after openly proclaiming his homosexuality.

In San Francisco, flagship of soaring self-esteem, a Gay Community Liaison was the first governmental agency designed to work specifically with homosexuals; having achieved a degree of accommodation among churches, parent-teacher and business groups, they now sit on many "do-gooder" boards and in city hall, and melt into the San Francisco scene in a seamless pattern—delivering mail, selling securities, healing the sick, walking the beat on the police force and representing clients in courts of law. Occasionally, they "raise hell" like *any* human being, but *without* hoopla, press headlines or staged excitement. It is the kind of casual acceptance which, in my opinion, provides the ideal climate for nurturing a free, unstudied mutuality, one that reflects a semblance of progress toward "civilization."

Yet, we ought to question the rootage and stability of the homosexual paradise. Obviously, there are flaws and flecks in the pastel portrait. Gays miss the joys of child-rearing—and taking the blame for the population explosion. To some it may be selfish or short-sighted, but that's their choice, and they have a right to it!

Unwillingness to find anything alien or objectionable in gayness is common among its practitioners and theorists. *Word Is Out*, a documentary of twenty-six interviews with gays that describe them as individual human beings with variegated attitudes toward themselves and one another, is a moderate and welcome exception. *Faggots* by Larry Kramer, a book about a large class of New York gays, takes an almost debunking approach to the subject; it discusses the rarity of lasting relationships, excessive drug use, distasteful sado-masochistic bouts, bus terminal seductions and desperate, artificial gaiety. Flaunting self-assertion does not always respect the canons of good taste or, in the long run, the minimal code for survival. The drag queens and their supporting cast of mincing, prancing transvestites are, I believe, expendable, because they reduce moral protest to the degrading, personal exhibitionism of a burlesque show; San Francisco's Polk Street is the pits! *The Joy of Gay Sex* analyzes the causes of sado-masochistic antics, then cautions that some statements are "intended to belittle it" (gay sex) and can be dismissed as concessions to "hopelessly narrow-minded bourgeois and amateur psychologists." In my judgment, these machismo-celebrating excesses play out a master-slave relationship I have always thought inhuman. The standard treatment of habitués of "tea-rooms" (flesh contact restrooms) is another illustration of lack of balance. Such activities totally divorce sex from love, affection or even elementary personal acquaintance.

Homosexual *hutzpah* got unparalleled expression at the 1980 Democratic Convention in New York. The Lesbian and Gay Caucus of the Democratic Party appeared in the conventional comic-opera regalia of delegates to nominate as a candidate for the vice-presidency a mild-mannered black woman named Mel Boozer (hardly a vote-drawing moniker). At the same gathering eighty-six gay delegates proudly affirmed their sexual allegiance (compared to four in 1976), claiming to represent twenty million Americans. Whereas the 1976 shindig had openly shunned and secretly reviled its four "interlopers," the eighty-six generated headlines and VIP headaches in 1980. But the dream was soon shattered by the results of that November election. It brought a new arch-conservative air and new faces to the center of power, a new Rightist coalition that assisted and claims reward for the main push in the change of government. New lackey hordes, new phalanxes of servitors of churchianity and new messiahs such as the Californians for Biblical Morality have appeared on the scene. Lesbian and Gay Caucus indeed!

The destiny of gays in the foreseeable future can be verified by the ominous tone and temper of Moral Majority and other anti-civil-liberties (read "anti-homosexual") groups already gestating since November 1980. Their pronouncements and plans posit battle lines. On the one side are the "humanist devils" who espouse atheism, evolution, self-centered autonomy (read "individual freedom"), socialism and amorality, and on the other side are their millions of members. The "solid gold" trumpets' sound of alarm did not wait long. Damning San Francisco "the arm-pit of this homosexual perversion" and, for the umpteenth time, "Sodom and Gomorrah," an alliance of "good, old-fashioned" church groups announced the immediate expenditure of three million dollars on a media and mail blitz to be directed against homosexuals. A task force bearing the name In God We Trust, Inc. is spearheading the campaign with an appropriate bow to the motto on the United States silver dollar. Seventeen states in the East, notably the New York and New England strongholds of sophisticated modernism, are the target. A massive drive is being started to save the skeptical from unbelief and the sexually tempted from hell, while the founder of Moral Majority, Jerry Falwell, and his lieutenants press law-makers for legislation purporting to criminalize the renting of lodgings to unmarried couples.

Ah, but there is an escape-route for the homosexual miscreant! A leading advocate of the holy war emphasized, "We want to minister to homosexuals and win them to Christ and stop their sinning. Convert to Christian heterosexuality, or face the wrath of God; your sex-style is against His law revealed in Scripture!" (This is verbatim copy, similar to the choice given to Jews before they were tortured and burned by the Spanish Inquisition!) Coincidentally with this gesture of tender benevolence, warning letters were mailed to firms that advertised in a gay newspaper. Most alarming of all the signals was an item published in the February 2, 1981 issue of *Newsweek* under the heading "Who's Who in the Right: a Short Guide to the Political Right." It sets out in frames the leading lights, priorities, action groups, publications, financial angels—and *bugaboos* (*Newsweek*'s word, not mine)—of the respective Rightist constituents. Among the *Bugaboos*—demons of sick fantasy—that obsess the *Religious Group* in the Rightist camp, the *first* ones are "Homosexuals!" Do we need more proof? Gabe, by my reckoning you would be eighty-six years old in 1982. Forgive me for wondering if you are still alive. If you are, avert eye and ear from the next rotations of the wheel of history. Withdraw into your shell, relax—and outlast the storm.

All across America men and women who discover themselves to be homosexual will be marked for contempt, villified in vulgar or subtle language of exclusion, judged sick, immoral and perverted in a kind of collective psychosis. If economic doldrums deepen, gays may find themselves cast for a scapegoat role, cheek by jowl with suspect minorities. Some victims will swallow the hostility and sink into self-rejection. We Jews are well acquainted with the self-hate syndrome implanted by a ceaseless tide of ancient and contemporary slander. That we forged persecution into an instrument of survival is one of history's salutary lessons learned by acquiring, nurturing and replenishing an intellectual tradition and value system. The crematoria of the Holocaust cradled the State of Israel.

Homosexuals across the globe would do well to lift a page from the saga of Jewish survival. Sigmund Freud's analysis of Leonardo da Vinci, named by some biographers as the most creative mind of all time, can be an auspicious beginning for a coordinated campaign by the North American homosexual community to sift their history-laden, never fully explored spiritual and intellectual heritage. Freud's oracular authority has faded. In "Leonardo" he certainly did not intend to gird gays with courage, but he makes da Vinci's gay bias a unique, dazzling exception. With exultation in his discovery, the Doctor points to the very fact of Leonardo's homosexuality as the force that enriched and directed his genius!

Gays, make Leonardo da Vinci your model! Bore into the millenial past of our species, and dredge from it the art, literature, science, religious symbols, original intonations and accents in the language of idealism, all the enduring cultural conglomerate with which you have fortified the human condition. Let your souls walk *straight*, shattering the verbal monopoly of that adjective by the others. Let none lower your self-esteem! Build a library culled from the best writings of men and women, inside and outside your ranks, who care for and about you. Don't be afraid to converse with your environment, friendly or hostile, in the language and practice of love, a word over-preached, and under-practiced.

Dr. Harvey Cox, whose lustrous career in church leadership and scholarship has been interpolated with pride into these pages, declared, "I would be in favor of a society in which there were no legal restrictions whatever on the private behavior of consenting adults." Fordham University professor Father Herbert Rogers, a prominent Catholic writer, recommends the same treatment for both homosexuals and heterosexuals, because he sees anti-gay laws encouraging much worse evils. Methodist minister Dr. Allen Moore, Dean of Students at the School of Theology in Claremont,

California, regards homosexuality as one of many styles of sexual expression, subject to the same defects as heterosexuality; he's ready to adopt more liberal laws regarding gays, to get rid of widespread police brutality against them. Dr. James Luther Adams, Harvard Professor of Christian Ethics, said to be the world's most prominent Unitarian cleric, doubts that all aspects of morality should be subject to investigation by the law; he invokes the right to privacy guaranteed in the American Constitution.

My antennae to Christian clerics who reject the anti-gay "Children's Crusade" alerted me to Roman Catholic dissent; despite hierarchical regimentation, it demanded and received an outspoken voice. Two theologians stand tall among the many to whom common report assigns a role of discreet silence; their concern is the traditional church admonition to homosexuals: "Accept counseling aimed at your change to the approved sex-style or totally abstain from interpersonal sexual activity." The first one is Father Henry Fahrens who, in the September 1972 issue of *U.S. Catholic*, dubbed that policy brutal, self-righteous, prejudiced and un-Christian, and called on the church to witness the "celebration of love between two people of the same sex." Then a *Commonweal* article of February 14, 1974 riveted my attention on its byline: Gregory Baum, a name both famous and familiar, a world-acclaimed leader of the liberal wing of the church, and a creative Jewish-born theologian whom I deeply admire. I surmised that he had written in support of "Dignity," a growing national organization of gay Catholics formed "to give witness to the Catholic Church that it is possible to be Catholic and gay, to help men and women homosexuals find a mature and self-accepting life of faith." From its first national meeting on Labor Day weekend 1973 in Los Angeles, "Dignity" underlined its seminal credo that gays can express their sexuality in a manner consonant with Christ's teaching. Baum was impressed not only by the tone and sincerity of the "Dignity" statement—"a challenge" to Roman Catholic theology—but also by the courage of the men and women involved.

Would Gabe be reinstated as a rabbi today? A baker's dozen Orthodox leaders in the ranks of Judaism may permit themselves to enter the Moral Majority camp on the issue of homosexuality, while on others they hold their noses. Rabbi Robert I. Gordis, a widely hailed Conservative-wing leader of broad scholarship, conceding to gays a just claim to be released from legal penalties and social disabilities, brands as perhaps "unwise" the removal of all restrictions directed against them in some areas. Reform Judaism does not equivocate. The Central Conference of American Rabbis, representing almost a thousand members, at its 1977 convention resolved "to encourage legislation which decriminalizes homosexual acts between consenting adults and prohibits discrimination against them as persons . . . and towards that end to undertake programs in cooperation with the local Jewish community." Gabe has, at last, been absolved of crime! And wonder of wonders, Hebrew Union College-Jewish Institute of Religion has publicly affirmed that it will not deny admission or ordination to a homosexual otherwise qualified. A superlative triumph for Gabe.

"I personally know forty gay rabbis afraid to 'come out,' and I hear from more of them every week! . . . I would believe that there may be as many as a hundred gay and lesbian rabbis in America." This astounding estimate came from Allen Bennett of Temple *Shalar Zahar* (Golden Gate) in San Francisco, the world's only openly gay rabbi, in a formal address delivered to the Board of the Union of American Hebrew Congregations on November 20, 1980 at the invitation of U.A.H.C.'s president. Yet it has come to my knowledge that a Hillel Foundation rabbi was fired for erotic advances to male students on the campus of the university he served. More disheartening to me is the fact that his rabbinical colleagues repulsed his desperate pleas for counseling.

That the pulpit enfranchisement of a gay rabbi would be violently attacked as blasphemy can be deduced from a statement from a New York task force composed of rabbis, sociologists and psychiatrists. On the day of its scheduled presentation a spokesman announced cancellation of the meeting and dismissal of the task force. But the report still exists. It is a definitive version of homophobia recorded for the history books: "Jewish tradition opposes any form of unnatural sexual practices; homosexuality, as of old, is a form of idol-worship." The statement concludes that in American society pleasure is idolized; it is not indigenous to the Jewish people, but part of a basically "hedonistic sociocultural setting." The Jewish community cannot yield to the pressure of so-called "enlightened" progressive opinion, and sanction all kinds of sexual practices for pleasurable gratification. Finally, the document calls for "uncompromising and all-out opposition to any legitimization of homosexuality." The establishment of a gay synagogue or any other gay institution is an act of "spiritual self-destruction."

I suspect the suppression of the report was triggered by fear that a gay synagogue might be located in New York. The first one, *Beth Hayyim Hodoshim* (House of New Life), made its debut in Los Angeles in 1972 after heated rhetoric, under the championship of the Pacific Southwest Council, Union of American Hebrew Congregation. In view of the frenetic reaction to a gay temple, who can calculate the rise in communal blood-pressure at the thought of a gay rabbi?

Of eighteen Jewish gay groups in large urban centers of the United States, ten are synagogues; two have been allowed to join U.A.H.C., after acrimonious debate. Eight groups are scattered in England, France, the Netherlands, Australia and Canada (Montreal and Vancouver, not Toronto—yet). Gay synagogues embody and reflect their own concept of worship and their own definition of togetherness—not blatantly different from the conventional, but their own. Jewish families kiss after *Shabbat* service. The same-sex symbol of affectional attachment is apt to cause problems for gays, and cardiac arrest for non-gays, in the decorous and respectability-gauged ambience of a Reform Temple. At this date, one may not expect the average synagogue-goer to recognize this gay social rite, and right, as anything more than a silly mite of trivia, or stubborn exhibitionism.

Allen Bennett, in his earnest talk to the secular leaders of global Reform Judaism, pleaded for an ingathering to the temples of the half-million or 600,000 American Jewish homosexuals. He calculated that figure on the basis of Alfred Kinsey's arithmetic: a 10 percent estimate of the gay proportion (probably growing with the advent of the Gay Liberation Movement a generation after his volcanic report). Only one-twentieth, Bennett conjectured, are invited into the organized Jewish establishment. "They should be encouraged to come home."

Far more self-discipline, intellectual receptivity and compassionate understanding are required for the average congregant to accept a spiritual guide whose life pattern negates biblical law, who ordinarily does not have the right to marry, adopt children and show joint property insurance. Besides, the influence on the erotic behavior of "our susceptible youth" would, in the congregants' mind, be a loathsome source of contamination, even though he may embody every grace of Jewish life except the begetting of new lives.

Protestant synods wrangle to weariness about the ordination of homosexuals. In 1980 one thousand delegates to the quadrennial General Conference of the United Methodist Church, America's third largest and most liberal bastion of mainline Protestantism, ranged themselves squarely on opposing sides of the gay issues which have plagued their organized consciences since 1968. The outcome was a standoff, liberal and conservative decisions balancing each other. Among a miscellany of carefully hedged ballotings, they refused to add specific language to a general order prohibiting gay ordination and then approved language that conservatives claimed could lead to trials of homosexual clergymen. . . . United Presbyterians in the General Assembly of 1976 created a task force of nineteen members or so; it met seven times, held four regional public hearings, collated a two-hundred-page report and suggested that the matter of gay ordination be left to local presbyteries. At the same time it recommended an outreach program for gay membership. Sara Bernice Moseley, the first woman moderator of the Presbyterian Church in the United States, underlining the inconsistent policy and existing anti-gay bias, agreed with a study paper's stand against homosexual ordination: "It affirms our concern for homosexuals as persons and for their rights as citizens. But I believe their lifestyle is not of God's interest." (*Isn't the Christian God interested in all people whatever their "lifestyle"?*)

There are gay ministers in churches—secret, clandestine, hidden—who lead a double life in a poignant and rending form. Theirs must be a harrowing existence, dreading detection, disgrace and dismissal. For them no support system exists within the church. Heterosexual sinning by a pastor in some Protestant denominations, a church report intimated, is occasionally penalized by transfer to another parish. Why transfer a gay minister to limbo or, ultimately, to purgatory? Are we to rate adulterous hanky-panky with the organist on a lower scale of depravity than a roll in the hay with a gay? "Only a fool would deny that we have homosexuals in our clergy," exclaimed the chairman of a task force on human sexuality appointed by the United Church of Canada, that country's largest Protestant body, "and they succeed admirably in ministering to their flocks, although placing them officially in clerical positions would be difficult, since congregations are not ready for it."

Reverend Troy Perry founded the Los Angeles gay Metropolitan Community Church which has proliferated into a national network of homosexually oriented congregations seeking to offer gays the opportunity to worship among their own. This fills the vacuum created by the irreligious unwillingness of mainstream congregations to welcome them as persons. "Reconciliation of gay and straight Christians can arrive," he declared, "only when an enduring same-sex marriage is recognized as a valid God-given form of human sexuality"—a conviction and a hope repeatedly voiced by clergymen who reject out of hand the notion that any church should shun anyone.

Lay homosexuals have been able to live within the Roman Catholic Church since medieval times, as long as they do not engage in gay actions or lifestyles. The confessional does open a channel to God's forgiveness; masturbation and sodomy are condemned as sin. For priests the regulations regarding celibacy and chastity prohibit not only marriage but any overt sexual act or even the desire for such acts. Catholic clergy are bidden to sublimate sexuality and thus *exclude* it. As to homosexuality, there is maximalized prohibition with maximalized opportunity in a same-sex community. The chemical retort can be foreseen.

The *Nevada State Journal* of September 23, 1979 carried an interview with Father Robert Gerard, a Jesuit theologian and former professor at Boston College. Himself a homosexual, he is the author of an unpublished novel about gay priests. He writes under a pseudonym because he fears that openly admitted gayness would bring him harm. The interviewer was Philip Nobile, a syndicated journalist. In reply to direct questioning, Father Gerard said:

> Gays should be ordained. Sexual preference is hardly a qualification for the priesthood. The true tests are theological competence, spiritual development and counseling ability. . . . Eighty percent of Catholic priests are homosexual. Traditionally the priesthood has been a refuge for sexually unsure men with homosexual leanings; they are drawn to this all-male society. If that percentage seems high [*It surely does, Father!*] remember that many straight priests left to get married. The 80 percent figure holds true for my Jesuit class-mates. . . . The hierarchy knows the situation. They were once priests. Some

bishops, cardinals and maybe even popes are bound to be gay as well. . . . About 10 percent of gay priests accept and express it, with a single lover or several men. Maybe a majority occasionally—with guilt and fear. . . . Young Jesuits in any seminary who were caught got expelled or just a warning. It depended on who caught them. . . . John Boswell, a Yale history professor, will soon publish a book on the church and sexuality. [I have since confirmed that the book, *Christianity, Social Tolerance and Homosexuality*, was published in 1980 by University of Chicago Press.] Boswell found that the church actually celebrated homosexuality during certain periods in its history. He came across a document from the Middle Ages which purports to show that a pope granted adjoining dioceses to two Spanish bishops who were lovers. [*Note:* I am unable to check the veracity of this possibly apocryptal tale.]

The interviewer's name, "Philip Nobile," is unknown to me as a byline for any article I can recall. My quest for biographical data has elicited only the information that he writes a column entitled "Uncommon Conversations." This intriguing discourse is beset by two unknowns: the priest who allegedly replied to queries and the journalist who asked them. Some readers, I surmise, were confirmed in their prior opinions (or prejudices); others fumed at the mendacity of a pseudonymous priest. The supposition that sundry homosexuals work and have their being in the Roman Catholic priesthood need not be waved aside as illogical or challenged as libellous. No more than the clerics of other religions are they immune to whatever attractions gayness offers mortal flesh.

Gregory Baum resigned from the priesthood, has married, and at this writing retains his professorial post at prestigious St. Michael's College in Toronto. He finds the argument that gayness is against human nature fallacious. What has been assumed to be "human nature" in the past is a human *creation*—not a given thing or a "noun" (my analogy)—but a product of people's interactions and symbols bound together by custom over a long period of time—in short, a "verb." "Human nature" has dehumanizing elements. The crucial moral question is whether a homosexual relationship can ground a friendship that enables the partners to grow and become more human. If so, homosexuals should acknowledge themselves as such before God, accept such inclination as an aspect of their calling and explore its meaning for the

Christian life. (I rejoice that my own core predilections press me to join unreservedly in Gregory Baum's counsel to clergymen who tilt toward homosexuality. Gabriel Altman embodied his spiritual formula for the Jewish life.)

The positive ideal for clergymen (and for *all* people), I believe, is the integration of sexual powers into the total personality so that the erotic urge can serve and invigorate the spiritual urge, to reach union in love with a human being and with God. Why couldn't two men build a temple of love for *their* togetherness? Their relationship may differ from the "normal" only in the format of carnal expression. For a lonely and isolated person, it may offer a redemptive break-out from self-absorption. A multitude of unheralded and unsung men and women have entered the same-sex conjugal pact with another person in fidelity and mutual respect, without becoming entrapped in promiscuity and depersonalization. A gay clergyman could respond to a special challenge, as a corrective to the endemic anti-individualism that threatens to convert North Americans into mindless automatons. That would be a mission worthy of a man of God.

Confused ambivalence—tolerance of gays without approval, civil liberties without the freedom to be and live one's self, gays equal in the eyes of lawyers and politicians but degraded in the eyes of the Lord, same-sex devotees in the pew but not in the pulpit! With the exception of whole-heartedly positive Unitarians and some peripheral sects, the vision of homosexuals crowding into the vestry still causes acute discomfort, and full recognition of their clergy seems dependent on the Second Coming. These social attitudes toward gays reflect a life-long gripe of mine. It is the *generalization* in our response to and judgment of minorities we don't bother to know as individuals. Identification is immediate; the slightest sound of a minority alerts the stereotype: alien, foreign, mysterious, thus suspect. Jews have been card-indexed for centuries, as though all of them were tatooed on the wrist like Hitler's concentration camp prisoners or branded on the forehead with the mark of Cain. "Homosexuals? They're all alike. Garbage! I wouldn't go near one with a ten-foot pole!" The one-syllable word "gay" covers everything. Among the plethora of cop-outs in our plastic society, none is more dangerous, destructive, dehumanizing—and lazy—than the failure to recognize as human beings those who are "different."

Like playing the one introductory chord phrase of Beethoven's

Fifth Symphony, or hinging America's political destiny on the anti-abortion "single issue" of Pro-Life, society finds it convenient and simple to reduce the whole tangled skein of human values to one simple datum. Concerning Jews, the Nazis asked, "Who were your grandparents," blacks have their skin color and homosexuals are condensed into their choice of sleeping partners. But shouting "I am a homosexual! See!" is not only ineffectual, but supportive of the very penchant for indolent, superficial labeling that reduces gays and other minorities to a phony, demeaning shred of personhood. The Kinsey Institute in August 1978 released a report totally demolishing the idea that all homosexuals are misfits obsessed by sex and ridden with guilt. Commissioned by the federal National Institute of Mental Health, and under the rubric, *Homosexualities: A Study of Diversity among Men and Women*, it maintains there is no such thing as a single stereotyped gay. In living arrangements, occupations, social activities and sexual relationships they are like everyone else— soup-cans on a shelf—or better still, mechanical ducks in a shooting-gallery. Psychologically they are no more at loggerheads with the world than heterosexuals, and most surprisingly, fewer than 10 percent work in so-called gay occupations such as decorating, hairdressing, nursing and dancing.

The masculine-feminine duality has over-simplified our relations with one another. Most Americans, I believe, theoretically acknowledge that human beings combine both elements. Achieving "man"-"woman" identity does not rest at an automatic, rigidly imposed stereotype as though the one had blue eyes and the other brown. The male-female parts of us are in various proportions at various times, and an individual throughout his or her lifetime may freely engage in any combination of heterosexual, homosexual or auto-erotic impulses. North Americans—Jews and Gentiles—ordinarily lack subtlety, imagination and daring to face the acute "threat" to their peace of mind implied by the complexity in human nature that bends toward being "unusual" and "different." Maybe one should approach sex the way one savors a gourmet food; some people smack their lips over a dish of escargot, for instance, while the same dish may throw the innards of another into a tornado.

Dogmatism about sex is decidedly premature. Unless it can give us an absolute insight into the human psyche, a term such as "unnatural" is a mere reflection of personal experience. Sex has been practiced in wide variations among many peoples and cultures and neither Middle America nor any other society can lay claim to represent the human species. Homosexuality is one possibility among others open to everyone. It is not an illness to be pitied, but a natural expression, for some persons, of sexual felicity, to be leveled with and accepted like any preference as long as it combines free consent, concern for the happiness of others and a modicum of aesthetic sensitivity.

I have related the calumny and threat now being perpetrated by American and sundry Canadian gay-haters to the upsurge of anti-homosexual madness in the thirteenth century. In the seven intervening centuries nothing new has been added to the minds that govern some of our religious organizations. One might deduce that in the matter of sexuality they have learned nothing thirteenth-century bishops did not know. And was not the thirteenth century also the time of the Black Plague, when thousands of Jews met death at the hands of religious fanatics duped into believing that Jews spread the disease by poisoning wells? It was a time of retrogression in humanity's struggle to become *human*. Are we caught in a similar quagmire today?

Long ago, Gabe's visit to my bed aroused in me more curiosity than cramps. Remembering that night, what have I now to say to him? I am still uncertain, as every honest clergyman must be, about the logical or factual validity of my search for truth about human sexuality. If I err, I would rather do so on the side of loving acceptance than in the direction of severe judgment. Let the God within each of us guide our consciences. We all need healing. There is nothing absolute between homosexuality and heterosexuality; no human condition or lifestyle is intrinsically justified or righteous.

Persons who differ from others in sexual orientation can be found among all classes and races, in all walks of life, in all professions, trades and in the church. The vortex of public hate swirling around a small group of citizens who want to be left alone has reached psychopathic proportions that are all the more terrible for having been instigated by leaders of organized religion. Inherent morality, the rightness or wrongness of homosexuality, as a condition or as an act, is not so much a question as a flight from *the* question; namely, whether same-gender lovers have the right to activate and perpetuate their love under the same code of conduct as lovers of opposite gender. I believe emphatically that *they do have the right.* And Gabe, in the name of civilized enlightenment I will so declare until my last heartbeat, or until the day comes when people will whisper not, "Is that person gay?" but, "Is he/she just in the marketplace, kind in the home, feisty for the poor and dispossessed, unwearied for peace—and militant for the individual's freedom to love?"

11

Abortion:
America's Armageddon

"Onward Christian Soldiers," following the Lord's Prayer, opened class on an up-beat note in my grade-school days. I often wondered why a military marching song had been chosen to augur victory for the Prince of Peace. It seemed "funny" to me until World War I put God "on our side" and history taught me that whole continents, such as Europe during the Thirty Years War, were ravaged by interreligious strife. Not to speak of the Crusaders who, clad in chain armor and broadsword, did massive blood-letting on their way to Jerusalem, and the Moslems, who conducted fierce forays into foreign lands in the name of Allah.

Old Testament exultation over the Israelite conquest of Canaan and reference to Yahweh as a "man of war" show primeval Judaism girding for battle at Divine command; yet the sages of the Talmud were loathe to celebrate the Maccabean defeat of the Syrian oppressor in the second century B.C.E. because it had been achieved by force of arms. Drawings in medieval liturgical books for Passover Eve clothe the Wicked Son in a soldier's uniform, and many Jews, myself included, today welcome the armed prowess of the beleaguered State of Israel only with profound sadness that she must rely for sheer survival of nation and people on military power alone. While self-enhaloed dictators of private morals busily monitor bedroom behavior, the faith-people which begat their biblical "authority" is in mortal danger, without their heed, from oil dictators who exploit international immorality to wage a genocidal campaign for unctuously hailed "holiness."

War is all the more brutalized by self-righteous fervor. A *Jehad* (holy war) manages to muster maximal fanaticism and ferocity because it is God's. Such a war is now being fomented within the borders of America by the skillfully organized, treasury-sinewed, monolithically disciplined and theologically inspired foes of women's right to choose not to give birth. A pregnant woman's right to control not only her body but also the body *within* her body is part and parcel of every woman's rights in the male chauvinistic world conditioned to deny them. The struggle for abortion is the epicenter of the struggle for liberation.

In December 1979 a black-bordered summons to "America's Armageddon" appeared in a Reno newspaper. Unrelieved irrationality leaves no scope for partial excerpts; its mad ingenuity makes it a candidate for the *Guinness Book of Records*. The abortion ruckus seething in American churches, maternity wards and legislative halls—and in the hearts of millions of women of child-bearing age—justify reproduction *in toto* of the words:

AMERICA'S ARMAGEDDON:

Abortion is Anti-Life and Anti-Christ

The pervasive pernicious planned parenthood propagandists persistently present particularly persuasive pecuniary profitable professional programs postponing probable precious pregnancies, preventing postpartum possibilities of present prenatal posterity per paganistic procedures, partisan political promulgations, publicized press pronouncements, and prolific publications possessing preposterous prevarications promoting pathetic parsimonius perverted procreative preventive practices, permissive promiscuous puberty peer pressures, plus perilous pathways to population perdition! Patient perserving prayers and penitence prevent punishment and procure peaceful prosperity!

Read and Heed "A Private Choice," by John T. Noona, Jr., "Aborting America," by Bernard N. Nathanson, M.D., "Margaret Sanger, Father of Modern Society," by Elasah Drogin. (Copy Dec. 11, 1979) American Conceived Helpless Infant Life Defenders (C.H.I.L.D.) of God, Box 785, Reno, Nv. 89504. Charles F. Anderson, Founder. (P.S. Help desperately needed to continue C.H.I.L.D. Crusade!)

Believe it or not, the author has chiseled this call to arms, like ancient hieroglyphics out of rock, by his solemn avowal to incinerate with Divine wrath every trace of the Devil's cloven hoof and tail centered in abortion. This mishmash differs from logolalia (syllables poured forth in ecstatic religious seizure) only in the fact that they are published. However, it is an extreme, possibly unauthorized (unintentional) burlesque of circumspect pronouncements by men in the topmost echelons of the Catholic Church who are girded with the mission to interpret and implement its centuries-old teachings.

At Cebu in the Philippines during a Mass in February 1981, Pope John Paul II issued the hardest line of his pontificate against the most controversial issues facing the church: divorce, birth control and abortion. His blasts at these oft-rehearsed dangers to the family have set off a crisis of faith in the United States, Canada and Europe among those Catholics already resigned to give planned parenthood priority over parochial piety. The Holy Father, seemingly preoccupied with the sex-related private problems of his global flock, voiced deep concern for *their* sexual health at almost every stop of his unprecedented world-wide tour. In Cebu, as in Mexico, he invited the anger of all-powerful overlords by favoring non-specified reforms to make more bearable the lives of barely existing slum-dwellers. But out of forty-nine million Filipinos the thirty million who live below the poverty level have one of the world's highest birth rates. His contraceptive ban prevents the brood-mare women in those countries from avoiding impregnation, and his abortion ban prevents them from doing anything about it. Double jeopardy! The same closed cycle of frustrations also haunts females in the developed countries of the West. Nelly Gray, president of the March for Life, told a throng assembled in Washington in January 1980 that they would push for a Pro-Life constitutional amendment banning abortion and for the opposition to the legal use of birth control pills and the IUD. Should the church feel maligned when cynics deduce from this dual birth de-control that it is a stratagem to increase the number of "little" Catholics in the world? Some years ago the then occupant of the Throne of St. Peter offered an ingenious if unrealistic countervailing project against the population explosion allegedly nourished by the church: colonization by us earthlings of the moon!

The Roman Catholic Church, Pro-Life and Pro-Choice partisans agree, is the strongest single bulwark of organizations such as the National Right to Life, which claims up to twelve million members, a budget of $1.3 million and lobbyists in every state capital of the United States. By one estimate, Catholics make up about half the national movement's membership, contributing hundreds of thousands of dollars. In 1975 the American hierarchy committed itself to organizing public and political opinion. The National Conference of Catholic Bishops issued a thirteen-page pamphlet calling for an educational and public information (read "propaganda") effort to achieve the moral outlawry of abortion. Throughout areas such as the western states, blessed with the spiritual uplift available through the fiscal and political power of the Church of Latter Day Saints, the priest-cum-politician blitz to kill abortion (and ERA, erroneously linked with it in a diabolic plot against Divine Law) has a formidable ally. In structure and policy related to this world, Catholicism and Mormonism are kin, in a relationship not at all strained by the fact that one is ruled by Pope and the other by Prophet. Recently, fundamentalist Protestantism, signaled by Moral Majority it seems, has decided to do "what comes naturally" by extending the pipe of peace to its ancient theological competition (né "papist") on the abortion issue. Pipe smoking is an appropriately masculine symbol for this tripartite cartel for the preservation of male cultural imperialism. All three place "abortion and women's rights" near the top of their "hit" parade.

Before the United States Supreme Court in 1973 legalized abortion in the first trimester, at least one million illegal operations were performed. One in five pregnancies was purposely terminated, 96 percent of them illegally. From two and a half to five times the number of maternal deaths occurred in areas where abortion was prohibited compared with areas that allowed it. So-called "criminal" abortions accounted for half of the maternal mortality statistics in New York and Pennsylvania, 40 percent in Michigan. A new "Against the Law" stamp on a slightly swollen abdomen will not still its owner's dread of the consequences of parturition. One Omaha abortion clinic reported that 35 percent of its patients were Catholic, a clinic in New York, 50 percent, in Milwaukee, 55 percent, according to *Newsweek*. The fear of punishment for sin instilled from early childhood by the enormous admonitory resources of the church apparently does not frighten away Catholic women from terminating a pregnancy when they believe that inescapable considerations of health and well being may require it; these same considerations will be decisive for women of other faiths or none.

Public opinion polls have shown that the majority of North America's adult females believe in the right to abortion. The grim record of social experience proves that for many the necessity of premature (aborted) fetal delivery is urgent enough to override jeopardy to life. Supreme Court Justice Thurgood Marshall warned that a ban on abortion (or on federal or state aid to women who need it) will revive the era of "the back-alley butcher." In lieu of safe, legal, affordable medical care, women will resort to potentially dangerous practices. Clothes-hangers for the indigent are neither imaginary—the pre-1973 years saw them in action—nor obsolete; the rich, as always, have other devices, *viz.*, expensive "surgery," a vacation in Scandinavia, a call to someone they "know." If pre-1973 history is a legitimate guide, some of the poor (*many* would be a demonstrably fair estimate) will die from lack of adequate care.

Pro-Life (*pro* meaning "on behalf of") demands the right it would take from those at whom it hurls the hysterical cry "murderers" to *choose*, and it shouts from the housetops that it chooses life in obedience to Yahweh's command in Deuteronomy: "Choose ye life. . . ." But whose life? Surely the life of a poverty-burdened woman who seeks medical aid for an abortion in instances other than endangerment or impregnation by rape or incest! Does *she* not deserve to live? Instead, she may become an obscure casualty in "Armageddon."

Pro-Life chooses not an actual person in the *present*, but a *potential* person of the *future*, a child deformed in that it lacks the most basic appurtenance of childhood—to be *wanted*. Such a child, in all likelihood, will be subjected to parental abuse and neglect, inexorably plagued by social problems and often crippled by mental or physical handicaps already foreseen in older siblings— a child whose horizon may be so severely narrowed by a hopelessly impoverished and unemployed household that its only outlet will be the reproduction of another generation, in similar circumstances, of welfare dependents.

Pro-Life! Quantity or quality? A geometric rise in the number of kids' lives or a rise in their chances for decent, dignified living? In some feminist circles, in their heyday of exuberance, it may have been "near heresy" to view abortion as more traumatic than an abscessed tooth. It is a melancholy thought, this receptivity to the proposition that a woman approaches without qualms the need to cancel out an extension of her own flesh and blood. I am not hospitable to a dimout of caring and empathy. No normal woman with child endures casually the thought of fetal extinction, whatever her previous count of carrying them to term or the material deprivation she may have suffered. The choice of pregnancy termination is not easy. Poor women are generally driven to it by necessity. It would be good to provide clinical counseling before and after abortion to prevent possible emotional and spiritual hardship. But the choice whether or not to go through with it must be granted to women as a right.

Contrary to popular opinion, nine out of ten abortions are performed for married women around thirty years of age who already have borne three or four children; the rest are chiefly teenagers. During recent times the thousands of normally unwed young girls who annually become pregnant have yielded a considerable proportion who abort the fetus; an increasing number, however, prefer to go the full term and keep the offspring, for whose care and support they are woefully ill-prepared, either in psyche or funds (eventually adding to welfare rolls); both parents frequently become school dropouts, destined for a dead-end: unemployed or unemployable. And an increasing number of their offspring are blighted by illegitimacy. Doesn't birth control to stop the stream of anti-social effects at the source, with abortion as a backup, provide a more life-preserving response to the sexual freedom of a permissive North America than an anti-abortion juggernaut that shrieks "murder"?

In a Nazi concentration camp a Rumanian woman doctor secretly aborted three thousand Jewish women. If they had been recorded as "pregnant" on the medical report all would have died in the ovens. If the fetus is a person, she saved three thousand lives by killing a like number; otherwise all six thousand would have been incinerated. Would Pro-Life convict that physician of mass murder?

On April 2, 1978 the St. Louis Cathedral *Bulletin* announced a date for picketing what it named "The Abortion Chamber." Its final summons to take to the streets sounded these words: "Everyone, regardless of any other interest, should be a part of the Pro-Life movement. . . . *No Christian* (italics mine) will excuse himself lightly from this duty." Unless the cathedral's hierarchy disbars mainline Protestant denominations from Christendom, its *Bulletin* has claimed jurisdiction beyond its proper turf. A legion of clergymen representing the Christian faith of congregations and themselves would denounce as effrontery the claim that their "duty" lies with Pro-Life. A few years ago five Protestant ministers appearing before a New Jersey judge asserted that the right of a woman to follow her conscience to terminate a pregnancy had been violated by a state law stopping Medicaid funds for elective therapeutic abortions. One of them testified that it was the *Christian duty* of a woman to abort a fetus if bearing the child would create undue hardship for the family or if the mother felt she could not support the child properly or provide suitable upbringing. (New Jersey at one time provided as much as $100,000 for abortions to poor women; the most recent allotment was $240!). . . . The United Methodist Church holds that a woman has a Christian duty to consider abortion when faced by an unwanted pregnancy. . . . The noted Baptist cleric Doctor Harvey Cox favors legalized abortion to prevent further killing by illegal means. . . . Reverend Howard Moody, United Church of Christ leader, said that if two people are not prepared emotionally, psychologically and economically to enter parenthood they should have the right to terminate a pregnancy. A chorus of normative Protestant pulpits would resonate these judgments. Reverend Donovan Roberts, co-director of the Center for Religion and Life at the University of Nevada, Reno, reminded a judicial hearing of the Nevada State Legislature that the aggressive "respect for life" demonstrators had not rallied for a "constitutional convention" on behalf of the poor, the sick, the confused, the aged, the minorities, the outcasts or victims of war. "I am not impressed," he said, "with the so-called 'Christian spirit' of a selective and personally painless opposition to abortion which ignores the plight of all persons who suffer. A comprehensive 'respect for life' throughout our society would be truly Christian, rather than the constant reiteration of the 'evil' of abortion!"

A Religious Coalition for Abortion Rights composed of twenty-seven Protestant and a smattering of Jewish and Roman Catholic groups distributed a six-page tract which stated: "A 'human life' amendment which protects the fetus from the moment of conception would no doubt prohibit use of the two most effective contraceptives. Both the IUD and those birth control pills considered safest for the woman (presumably low-estrogen morning-after mini-pills) prevent implantation of an already fertilized egg into the wall of the uterus." (Right-to-Life spokesmen therefore term these devices abortifacient since they and the amendment look upon a fertilized ovum as a person.)

When criminal abortion laws were first introduced in the mid-nineteenth century they did not incorporate the St. Louis

Cathedral's sense of "Christian duty." Their incentives, it seems, sprang from concerns far removed from the church, such as existing health dangers; the desire of the medical profession (invariably male) to eliminate lay healers (generally female) who performed abortions and other health services; women's rejection of their primary role as breeders and home-makers; "pure-Yankee" xenophobic fear that the growing popularity of abortion among upper-crust American blue-bloods would dilute their genetic heritage and ultimately surrender numerical and political power to recent, therefore "inferior," immigrant stock.

But it was not until the United States Supreme Court legalized abortion in 1973 that Armageddon-fever began: first, by proclaiming that personhood begins the instant of a microscopic sperm's triumphant wriggle to and immediate merger with an expectant ovum—in the womb; second, by hurling the word "murderer!" at anyone who would choose or approve the termination of that reproductive romance before its term. Sometimes the word was spat out in a rage, historically fueled by religious frenzy.

For centuries, we Jews were at the receiving end of that cry. "Murderers of our God!" *Christus-Killer—Trauma Meines Lebens* (Christ-Killer—Trauma of My Life) was the title given to the German edition of my book *Storm the Gates of Jericho.* However cruel, primitive and dangerous to life and limb the not yet totally extinct epithet has been for Jews, the "murderers" chant for abortionists is no less the putrid residue of irrationality. "Baby killer"—the current pseudo-Christian word—reached the height of dangerous incitement in bombs tossed at, and clubs and fists swung in, abortion clinics from Anchorage, Alaska to Fairfax, Virginia; the assault troops were acquitted by the court because they believed they had to invade the clinic to save lives. Fanaticism "purged" of evil by its own madness. Incitement reached the depths of obscenity when a glass jar containing a "pickled" fetus was thrust into blanched faces of weeping women to terrify them into bearing kids who, they knew, would carry life-debasing handicaps of poverty and malnutrition, with possibly an alcoholic or absent father.

A crescendo of comicality was set in motion by the demand of a Pro-Life proconsul that the 1973 Supreme Court be summoned in a United States town, fortuitously named Nuremberg, to answer a charge of murdering six million children counted as killed by abortion since the court had given the green light.

Finally, the "murderers!" cry reached the *nec plus ultra* of blatant insensitivity; the head of the San Francisco Medical Society and the communications officer of New York's Archdiocese matched the shrewd, media-courting, off-the-cuff guess of six million embryos— brought to a silent, solitary, reluctant end in the bellies of troubled, compassionate women—with the six million Jews who perished in the horror of Nazism's organized genocide. Forty-two members of my father's family in Lithuania were machine gunned after being bludgeoned into digging their mass grave. Using their unimaginable suffering as a gimmick for such stupid, infantile propaganda is callous insult—indeed, blasphemy. . . . But that was not all! In reply to Protestant and Jewish clergy who declared "acts of intolerance and insensibility" on the part of anti-choice forces to be a "direct outcome of the language of intolerance and the spirit of extremism spoken and exhibited by the Roman Catholic hierarchy," a priest dangled the crowning jewel of single-issue grossness before them. "The people who were silent during the Holocaust," he said, "may have been silent because they were afraid to use inflammatory rhetoric."

If this string of Pro-Life pearls of wisdom seems like a gaudy collection of cheap costume jewelry, what is one to think of a bill introduced in the Indiana Legislature whereby the state would offer money to a woman who consented to carry to term her unwanted pregnancy; then the person who had agreed to adopt the child would reimburse the state, unless the mother decided to keep it, in which case she would have to pay back the money that had been advanced to her.

Exemplified by these cavortings the entire Pro-Life phantasmagoria unfolds from the one basic premise: that a living person comes into being at conception. Was it always a dogma? History says no! In the thirteenth century Pope Innocent III held that abortion was not a sin if the fetus was "ensouled" with an immortal spirit. Thomas Aquinas, to whom successive legions of Catholic scholars have paid homage, favored the Aristotelian principle that "ensoulment" happens eighty days after conception for a female fetus due to the "undeveloped" nature of woman's matter and forty days after conception for the earlier-quickening male. It was Tertullian, touched by suspicion of heretical tendencies and reputedly the most demanding and coercive of all the Church Fathers, who in keeping with an astringent temper synchronized ensoulment with conception.

Then in 1588 Pope Sixtus V forbade all abortions. Three years later Gregory XIV allowed them for all fetuses until "ensoulment" had taken place forty days after conception. In 1869 Pope Pius IX condemned all abortions performed after conception and a year later, at his own insistence, it is said, he was endowed with infallibility on matters of faith and morals, a power held by all those who succeeded him.

The nineteenth century reversed the common law in which abortion was acceptable, by making it a crime against the state. Some students of legal history claim the reversal came because abortion was losing citizens for work or as cannon fodder. Later it also became a crime against the fetus and, ultimately, against God.

Does the entity called "soul" enter the vagina, the womb, then the ovum at the moment of fertilization? Is the schedule of time and place sufficiently indubitable to warrant a decree of stubborn error or heresy against anyone who ignores it? Are observable facts available as evidence? Shall we adopt the premise that mortal beings on receiving "holy orders" from the church also receive supernatural power to know, beyond doubt, what happens inside a woman's body at the junction of sperm and egg? To none of these questions can answers be found—except through *faith* that does not require confirmation by fact or logic. "Soul" itself, the nub of the argument, cannot be detected by a litmus test. It is a mystery wholly indefinable, insubstantial, as fleeting as the vapor of one's breath on a frosty morning. Indeed, primitive man actually deemed his breath to be soul!

The papacy, it has been stated, actually has never determined the time when soul animates the fetus; rather, it bids men think and act *as if* the sublime event occurred at conception. Whether actual or as if, non-Catholics surely must remain immune to papal ukase.

There is no counterpart in Judaism for Catholic theological problems such as baptism and ensoulment. Soul has been "breathed" into all of us by God. The most popular rabbi-analyst of the Law, tenth-century Rashi, held that a child is not called a living being until its head can be seen. (No Jewish funeral service is required for a deceased who has lived less than one month.) Save for mystics, meditators and academic specialists, the time of the beginning of a person's life has no more controversial significance for abortion than the Creation vs. Evolution feud now being revived to pinpoint the beginning of the cosmos.

The sensible way to decide between contradictory positions, when neither can be proven false beyond question, is to ask, "Which provides the greatest good for the greatest number of people?" The *fetus* is born at conception; the *person* is *potential*, to be actualized by delivery. The traits that express personhood— outside viability, self-awareness, perhaps memory and volition— are they present at the sperm-ovum connection? Granted, God moves in wondrous ways His miracles to perform. Sperm-egg fusion in a microscopic space within a female's abdomen *may* generate a soul, just as complete fusion or fission of infinitesimal neutrons and electrons within the atom can generate cosmic power. The difference is that the latter phenomenon is a subject of science, whereas the former is pure supposition. Since proof eludes us, the human mind must resort to a leap in the dark, relying on its own intuition, conscience and logical trend—unless it wishes to abdicate the right to choose in favor of a scientific or, in this instance, ecclesiastical authority. Twenty-five centuries ago Socrates said, "All that I know is that I know nothing." In the domain of spirit, God, immortality, *soul*, the Greek philosopher *did* know as much as *we* know. These are matters of *theology*. Has mankind discovered any *factual knowledge* about them since the time of Socrates? Not an iota—although large segments of people in quest of certitude (or power) uphold the absolute-veracity claims of Holy Writ and of a constellation of revered scholars who wrestle and wrangle over its meaning. We have faith *that* God is; but do we know *What* or *Who* He is? There are myriads of galaxies in the sky and, yes, we are beginning to understand *how* they move in their orbits. But do we understand *why*?

A famed Scottish preacher once described himself as a man who went about thinking that he didn't know much after all, therefore he had to be kind. Similarly, a great Jewish philosopher cautioned us, "If we knew the precise attributes of God, we would be gods ourselves!" Both glimpsed the truth: We can't be God, but we can be kind.

We *can* be kind! But we *can't* be and *must not* play God! Fracas and feud about ensoulment are no less futile than argument about the soul's immortality. Such confrontations only divert men and women from vital issues such as nuclear war on which rest the very existence of the human species, and on which *all* must work *together*. Pro-Life, whose sincerity I do not doubt, is plunging America into a religious war. (Is our country to duplicate the tragedy of Northern Ireland?) I do not quarrel with their creed; that is *their* choice. I only ask the same right of choice for women who do not agree with them.

James Luther Adams, one of America's most distinguished clergymen, deemed it appropriate for the Roman Catholic Church to persuade its own constituency but inappropriate to impose a rigid anti-abortion standard by law on other citizens. The fealty of Catholic women who prefer to risk physical death rather than sin and moral death they believe to be attendant on abortion deserves utmost commendation from every clerical advocate of religious responsibility. I stand, nevertheless, with the women who choose to take a chance on the damnation threatened by a church that claims to have God's imprimatur. In one year, 1.2 million women made such a choice and polls revealed that 73 percent of Americans favor legalized abortions during the first three months. But the 1977 law deposited in the congressional hopper by a Mr. Hyde of Illinois sentenced three million women on Medicaid to potential and possibly unwanted childbirth, at whatever cost to family and society. In 1978 Medicaid-funded abortions dropped 99 percent—from 250,000 to 24,000—a year after the Hyde Amendment *forced* pregnancy on poor women by denying them Medicaid for pregnancy termination except in cases of promptly reported rape, incest or danger to the mother's life—a cruel and unusual punishment for being poor. No wonder that the American bishops refuse to regard as an "acceptable social compromise" the cut in current federal funds to poor women for abortions, spelling out excommunication for any Catholic woman who undergoes or takes part in "the evil practice." By declaring as unconstitutional a state's prohibition of pregnancy-termination during the first trimester, the United States Supreme Court reaffirmed the historic position of the West.

Constitutional amendments reverberate down the corridors of time. At this writing the phraseology of a constitutional amendment proposed by Senator Helms of North Carolina reads as follows: "The paramount right to life is vested in each human being from the moment of fertilization without regard to age, health or a condition of dependency." (A National Right to Life version does not differ in essence.)

Another zealous politico, Representative James Oberstar of Minnesota, phrased his amendment as follows: "With respect to the right to life, the word 'person' as used in this article and 5th and 6th Articles of Amendment to the Constitution . . . applies to all human beings . . . and their unborn offspring at every stage of their biological development."

The arch-conservative sweep into the United States Congress, coupled with the tactics of Right-to-Lifers and allied with ultra-Right phalanxes of fundamentalist Protestants and the Catholic National Committee for a Human Life Amendment (funded by $300,000 in annual contributions from American dioceses), conjures up the macabre nightmare of a two-thirds congressional majority for submitting it to two-thirds of the states for ratification—and total criminalization of abortion for *any* reason. Can a nation's psychopathology show more grievous symptoms? Indisputably, *theological* opinion restricting personal choice is being inserted into a political Constitution that specifically guarantees freedom of religion to every American! It is a monstrous reversion to thought control, desecration of the aim of the Founding Fathers to sever religious dogma from the credo of a democratic state and a leap backward to autocratic rule by inquisitorial speculation on the unknowables.

Reverend Martin E. Marty, Lutheran minister and University of Chicago Professor of Church History, would not join me in this polemic. He points out an apparent inconsistency. The Catholic Church, he reminds us, received grateful accolades for support of civil rights in the sixties and for assistance to conscientious objectors at the time of Vietnam. Now that the bishops are supporting a cause many people don't like, they are being criticized for mixing politics and religion. "Nothing is wrong with having the Catholics—or anyone else—try to legislate morality. It happens all the time."

All true—but slightly irrelevant and immaterial. A ready analogy cannot fill the gap between individual priests counseling lads with religious scruples against combat war service in a situation lasting at most a few years or speaking at a civil rights rally—and recasting the seminal principle on which a nation was fashioned. The entire personnel of the church—from Pope to parish secretary—has been converted into a massive weapon of propaganda plus political pressure, plus panegyrics to piety, plus the peril of Hell—to achieve what? An amending paragraph in the basic American Constitution that will strip from more than a hundred million American women a civil, moral, political and religious right guaranteed by that same Constitution—namely freedom to decide their course in a private, moral crisis. Its pushers would misuse the Bill of Rights, which also and not incidentally separates church and state, to enthrone as basic law an unverifiable theological concept that rests solely on the opinion of a vociferous section of the American people.

A second glance at Marty's statement against my hassle with Catholic Church dignitaries leads me to this counter-perception: in both the civil rights and the Vietnam instances of priestly benediction for liberal causes, the churchmen were extending support to movements that sought release from and relaxation of surveillance by the *state*, the secular arm of government. Coerced anti-abortion, on the other hand, is a superbly orchestrated effort to suppress freedom from and relaxation of discipline exercised by the *church*. Can any two objectives be more clearly polarized?

"We're tired of having pickled fetuses shoved under our noses before every vote," sighed one weary legislator. But the campaign, as it has been relayed to me, already had brought fourteen states into line for a petition to Congress requesting a constitutional convention. After the no-abortion amendment has passed, will a prosecutor indict its violators for murder? Since consistency is the virtue of small minds, the Right to Life committee chairman who plumped for a murder trial of the 1973 Supreme Court can be expected to rouse his foot-soldiers for the same charge against aborters. Doesn't the amendment make abortion tantamount to murder? The horrendous possibilities are already previewed in talk at Pro-Life meetings—as well as in congressional cloak rooms.

The scenario adumbrated by a staff lawyer with the Center for Constitutional Rights, unfolds:

1. The charge? Murder of a fetus, whose remains may be presented in evidence. Prosecutor's statement at opening of case demands verdict of first degree murder, at least manslaughter.

2. Defendant—a woman who aborted herself or obtained an illegal abortion. (Some supporters of the amendment would ask the death penalty for self-abortion.)

3. Since abortion could not be the result of a rational or moral choice, the amendment's backers acknowledge acquittal only on grounds of insanity.

4. Although saving the mother's life lends abortion some legitimacy, it has been said that such "self-defense" applies only when the victim's conduct was wrongful, not in the case of an innocent fetus.

5. If exceptions such as endangerment of the prospective mother are recognized, due process of law probably requires that the doctor seek a court order permitting the abortion. The fetus, being a "person," would be represented by a lawyer, who might ask the court for a deferment until the supposedly endangered woman is on the brink of death, thus verifying the emergent nature of her condition. Thereby early, safe abortions are eliminated.

6. Anyone who assists in an abortion or fails to report it may be prosecuted.

On April 22, 1981 a U.S. Senate judiciary sub-committee met to define the time when human life begins. That agenda shows how far government has gone astray to decide theological enigmas under pressure from special interest "religious" groups. What were the senator-theologians discussing? Scientific evidence in support of a bill establishing that life begins at the moment of conception. Both proponents and opponents of the bill agreed that giving constitutional rights to a fetus, as the bill implies, would make abortion a homicide subject to punishment. In fact, Rhonda Copelon, lawyer for the Center for Constitutional Rights, pointed out that a miscarriage could be treated as negligent homicide, that the majority if not all the scheduled witnesses at the "sham" hearing were anti-abortionists, and that in the current state of man's knowledge the Senate judiciary is not qualified to decide the question of when life begins. The American College of Obstetricians and Gynecologists protested because its president-elect George M. Ryan was not permitted to testify unless he confined his remarks, as an individual only (not as representative of the College), to strict definitions that "ignore the many medical, legal and ethical concerns held by the College." In short, the senators wanted to limit the hearings to what they imagined is their special field of expertise, *viz., theology!*

Catholic, Mormon and Moral Majority leaders have shifted Abortion Armageddon from the conscience of the common people, where the negative absolutism they jointly espouse can be and often is ignored, to the complexities of uncommon law, where their mandate can be imposed on everyone, and where the volatile (violent) pronouncements of clerics will give way to a judge's cold casuistry, which is not apt to produce dramatic heroism. The bedrooms of pregnant women wrestling with prenatal abortion, however, abound with heroes—poor Catholics,

Mormons, Moral Majority-ettes whose loyalty to church makes them carry to term children whose care and support will further blight already over-deprived lives in the here-and-now, and the women whose loyalty to individual ideals makes them risk Divine anger in the world beyond.

Another true hero is U.S. Judge John F. Dooling, Jr., who after thirteen months of study declared the Hyde Amendment unconstitutional. In an unprecedented ruling at the behest of intellect and conscience, he forced Congress and twenty-eight states to resume payment for medically necessary abortions, just as they fund other surgical procedures. (Medicaid to poor women for abortions had been the only funding denied them by the Hyde statute.)

First, Judge Dooling stated that a pregnant woman's poverty is a significant factor in deciding whether her abortion is "medically necessary" since lack of financial means prevents her from dealing optimally with her condition. It increases her risk of health damage—even death—from diseases and complications. Unwanted pregnancies furthermore have a grave impact on the mental health of patients.

Second, by creating the Medicaid program in 1965 Congress established a statutory right for poor people to "medically necessary" health care; a "life-endangerment only" criterion for abortions precludes many needed treatments for health. If Congress intended to deny coverage for them, it had to offer rational reasons and a lawful purpose. This it did not do.

Third, severance of abortion funds interferes with a woman's right to freely exercise her religion. Her option for abortion is a conscientious one that entitles her to the same protection provided by the First Amendment. Many mainstream religions do not forbid abortions; Congress must be tolerant of all beliefs. . . .

Judge Dooling issued a nation-wide injunction which stymied the Hyde Amendment until the Supreme Court overturned it and told him to reconsider. Since then the Court and Congress have hedged the abortion right within further narrowing bounds.

Judge Dooling assembled nineteen lawyers, thirty witnesses, eight exhibits and 329 pages to validate his stand. Whatever the practical results, he has confirmed nay-sayers to Pro-Life in the hope that the outlook is not monotony unrelieved by change but rather a challenge for brave men and women to plant and nurture new ideas and directions. The judge is a septuagenarian and a

Catholic. The elderly can still hew new paths; Catholics are not a monolith.

Comments on Dooling's dissent bring me to Judaism, wherein centralization of religious authority began its ride to extinction in the fifth century of the Christian Era. The Sanhedrin—actually the semblance not the substance of authoritarianism—was scattered to the four winds. (A conclave of rabbis to elect a Pope-style world chief would end up with one vote for each rabbi, I would predict.) On questions of theology the Talmud favored open-ended debate instead of definition. God? He is one and incorporeal; His other attributes are subject to interminable discussion. Immortality? Yes, but without maps of Heaven or instructions on how to get there.

Rabbinic legalism explicitly recognizes the fetus as a non-viable entity while it is in the mother's womb because its life cannot be sustained outside that shelter. Basic sources on abortion in Bible and Talmud are sparse enough to intimate that it was not an issue of absorbing importance. The variety of nuances relegates Judaism to the outer periphery of Armageddon, though it has little traffic with absolute prohibition of early abortion. Incest and rape received little attention from ancient Judaism; less chauvinistic awareness of women as independent personalities later underscored the trauma of rape victims.

That mother's drug addiction or intake of medicine harmful to offspring justifies termination of pregnancy was the talmudic dictum. The question whether a woman has final rights to her own body was answered negatively: no human being was created himself; such rights belong to God alone. Rabbinic sages interpreted a passage in Exodus, chapter 21, to signify the priority of mother over embryo. The verse deals with injury to a pregnant woman during a fight between two men. Destruction of the fetus is redressed by financial indemnity to the father; if the mother is killed during the quarrel, the assailant must die. Another talmudic verse embodies the principle that the embryo is a limb of the mother.

Should permission to abort be granted for life jeopardy alone, or is injury to a woman's health enough? That was a contentious question. Ben-Zion Uziel, a former Chief Rabbi of Israel, condoned abortion even for "a very thin reason," such as the mother's avoidance of severe child-bearing pain, her anguish at the probability of a defective child, or the disgrace and threat of suicide by a woman raped or impregnated in adultery.

A well-worn quip has it that wherever you encounter two Jews you will find at least three clashing opinions. Three postures on abortion are visible in Judaism. First, conservative Rabbi Robert Gordis, although disavowing any inclination to call abortion "murder," calls abortion "on demand" a cheapening of life in an already violence-ridden society; the embryo as a potentially living entity must not be discarded lightly or flippantly. Family planning, though often desirable, should be balanced by unequivocal obligation to add to the human family and to one's own. I unreservedly endorse the overriding moral essentials in the Gordis stance. Reverence for life as the highest value was the central motif of Jewish ethical teaching centuries before Albert Schweitzer verbalized and exemplified it in his hospital at Lambaréné in Africa.

The second posture was taken in the Israeli Parliament by four rabbis representing an ultra-Orthodox religious party whose votes in the Knesset held the balance of power for the coalition government party. When a new abortion bill was introduced for enactment into law, the quartet threatened to resign and bring down the government unless a previous clause was repealed in the bill permitting abortion for reasons of severe social and economic hardship. The ruling party, under duress, eliminated that progressive measure from the bill. As finally approved, it does allow abortions for an under-eighteen or over-forty mother, an extra-marital or incestuous pregnancy, a physically or mentally damaged fetus, physical or mental harm to the mother—with the concurrence of a commission composed of two physicians (one a gynecologist) and one social worker. In 1978 nearly half the abortions under such legal supervision were granted for socioeconomic reasons. A nation-wide poll several months before the blackmail vote showed that almost half of Israel's adult population favored the right to pregnancy termination without any legalistic hindrance whatsoever. In Jerusalem as in Washington secular powers flout the wish and need of the populace at the point of an ecclesiastical gun.

In June 1980 the Central Conference of American Reform Rabbis reaffirmed a resolution adopted thirteen years earlier strongly urging the broad liberalization of abortion laws in various states and calling upon its members to work toward this end, with the following comments:

(a) Jewish legal literature permits therapeutic abortions.
(b) The decision concerning any abortion must be made by the woman and not by the state or any other external agency.
(c) We oppose all constitutional amendments and legislation which would abridge or circumscribe this right.
(d) We call upon our rabbis and upon the Union of American Hebrew Congregations to strengthen their support of the Religious Coalition for Abortion Rights on national, state and local levels.

This statement claims no occult, unique insight or knowledge, nor does it seek to enhance Judaism's own authority under the guise of the old morality; it seeks to open the gates of freedom, not to seal them tight forever; it cares about the right of a woman as a mature, responsible human being to choose the use to be made of her body and the fruit thereof, the right of a *poor* woman to implement her choice, and the right of a child to be wanted.

Although it was an American Rabbis' conference that sponsored these unequivocal sentences, they were also the declared position of Canadian Reform rabbis, all of whom belong to that clerical body. And they may soon be tested. A Canadian Christian Right movement, inspired evidently by the success of such uprising in the United States and impressed by its strategy, has shown signs of birth and development. In the Ontario election of 1980 various groups formed a coalition of the "Christian Right" under the banner of the Pro-Family political action committee, which campaigned vigorously for Pro-Life policies considered instrumental to restore "a higher morality and religious sense in Canada." In further imitation of its U.S. model, it maintains "report cards" on the votes of federal and provincial politicians on issues of critical importance to the Christian right—such as homosexuality, public school religion and *abortion*.

Perhaps it is relevant at this juncture to remind all Pro-Lifers of the debacle of that so-called "noble experiment," the Eighteenth (Prohibition) Amendment. A constitutional lunge toward legally enforced morals, spurred by the churches, became the cradle of organized crime: rackets, gang warfare, police corruption, killer substitutes for liquor, all because Americans felt they *had to drink*! Isn't sex desire more obsessive, more compulsive and more universal than the appetite for alcoholic beverages? Would the amendment abolishing abortions under penalty for murder add a new department to the conglomerate of operations under *cosa nostra* Mafia "families," a business venture devoted, let us say, to the spread, sale and regional distribution of "protected" abortions? During a time of Armageddon that isn't a paranoid fantasy.

But perhaps there is hope that the average American and Canadian citizen is not quite as easily dragooned by the hierarchical establishment after all. During the 1980 U.S. election campaign the Archbishop of Boston issued a letter that was read aloud in all Catholic churches of his area advising their parishioners that it would be "a deadly sin" to vote for anyone who supported abortion. The Archbishop obviously was referring to two congressional candidates who favored federal funding for poor women seeking to terminate pregnancies. Yet the targets of his letter were both elected by huge margins, one of them in a district heavily populated by Catholics.

I cannot end this chapter without envisioning the goal for which we should strive—not against, but with each other. It is a simple, maybe simplistic dream: not so much to make abortions impermissible as to make them less necessary; to set our sights on a time when poor women will not *need* to abort offspring for relief from additional burdens emanating from poverty because no one will be subsisting below the poverty level; a time when teenagers will not be hastened or hassled into sex through ignorance, lack of hope for their future, and alienation from society—a time when sex will be fully accepted by the church as a gift of God for the continuance and enjoyment of life.

12

So You Want To Be a Sex Counselor

Was the King of the Universe indulging a wry sense of humor when He endowed the supreme artifact of His creations with sex, this Divine gift which can raise man and woman to the gates of paradise but also can lower them into the pit? Or did He have second thoughts after investing us with obsolescent tonsils, an appendix and a tail? The genitals would *never* lose their unlimited power to delight or distress.

Sex can be a life-long source of frustration and trouble. A relationship concerned with and riveted to the body alone ceases to be sexual in the fully human sense of that word. Even sex designed to be casual (as with a prostitute) inevitably bores deeper into personhood than we originally intended. Coitus is certainly fun—playful, jubilant—at its best; but to make it simply fun is to make it starkly simple, because without over- and undertones of feeling it becomes enviscerated, enfeebled and eventually emptied of the fun with which it began.

An activity tangled in the unpredictable, vagrant depths of human personality ("subconscious" if one has to be Freudian) cannot be programmed like a computer. Indeed, it is beyond the reckoning of science or any of the disciplines we orderly humans have forged in a futile attempt to systematize life. Who can pigeonhole sex and keep it in a designated place forever? How many adults can boast of a consistently upbeat experience of sexuality? Surveys show that after a few years the majority of couples are less pleased with their sex than when they first went to bed. Even well-suited mates are bedevilled by maladjustments and most suffer from incompatibility.

Why do we have so much difficulty with this all-important component of happiness—or misery? Erudite advisers are not lacking. Mailboxes glow with arty brochures announcing insti-

tutes, workshops, treatment centers and experimental farms purporting to relieve the North American male and female of erotic
dysfunctions. Can sex be reduced to scientific and logical
premises? Is reaching toward a supremely satisfying sexual union
with another human being, like reaching for spiritual communion
with the Supreme Being, a do-it-alone and do-it-yourself job?

All a counselor can do is listen with empathy, light a few
candles and gently lead seekers through the mazes of their minds.
However modestly described, that can be the crucial, all-important
junction-point. And who can make it more acceptable and effective in a one-to-one encounter than a clergyman alerted by our
permissive world to a need for tolerance, by the contradictions in
his own human nature to a need for humility, and by the endless
riddles of sex to a need for earnest and honest recourse to the fact
and fancy his assiduous scholarship has gathered from many
springs? Since the relevance and scope of the world's oldest
profession (sex for hire) are being diminished by amateurs (sex for
fun), North America's newest humanistic profession (sex for
study) glows like sunrise for millions aching to wrap their loneliness around a panacea, a poultice or a placebo to assuage the
emptiness of their sexuality.

Enter the sexologist, who is eager to equip all and sundry
with researched, "authoritative" knowledge (and clashing theories).
Whereas in 1970 Masters and Johnson's *Human Sexual Inadequacy* ushered in the era of therapy for such hitherto closeted
problems as impotence, frigidity, premature ejaculation and
masturbatory compulsiveness, Dr. Lee Birk of Harvard Medical
School said the most striking change their clinic in St. Louis
inaugurated was the degree of acceptance by the practitioners of
medicine. How else would someone like Dr. Helen Singer Kaplan
of New York Hospital-Cornell Medical Center be able to say that
before M. & J. the body was like a Barbie doll, without genitals?

It has been estimated that in the United States about twelve
hundred "certified" professionals and four thousand claimants to
the new techniques are profitably engaged in guiding the sex-
troubled out of the tunnel. Virginia Johnson inveighed against
piano teachers, lawyers and engineers hanging out shingles after
only a weekend lecture attendance. Few states have begun to
regulate the practice of sexology. William H. Masters himself
does not overrate ten years as sufficient time for a "field to evolve
its own ethic." He and his collaborator-wife have already found it

preferable to abandon employing "surrogate" partners to handle the problems of single men. (A surrogate who does not inspire trust can hardly benefit a patient who must first gain confidence in his or her own sexual competence.) Masters and Johnson claim that in sixteen years only 20 percent of 790 patients, chiefly couples, failed to respond to their treatment. Other researchers, unable to duplicate that tally, although using the same techniques, are skeptical about the reliability of the M. & J. deductions. In a 1980 issue of *Psychology Today* Bernie Zilbergeld and Michael Evans stated that they were unable to tell from the gurus' own account precisely what they did and how they did it. They wanted to know who decided whether or not the treatment succeeded. Because of these questions Virginia Johnson had to concede that she and her husband might have published their findings without "painstaking computerization." Other critics even have injected the sly stab that many M. & J. patients showed signs of having been pre-screened and positively motivated, hence inclined toward favorable expectations.

Masters and Johnson prefer to treat couples. A "school" of their disciples enlarges the nuclear unit to process group therapy on the thesis that the shared relationship in a collective would banish a woman's sense of being "alone" with a problem. Evidently females fare better in a group setting. "Those who never had an orgasm," one practitioner explained, "did not benefit from couples therapy!" Apparently, they ended up waiting around with two therapists and one husband for "the poor woman" to have one. The "advanced" therapeutic aim seems to be to make women feel good about being sexual. Prominent in the teaching program is pleasurable masturbation; following these warm-ups they go on to achieve pleasure with their partners through further "homework"—massage and discussion of what they like and don't like in erotic frolic.

What is a tyro preacher with a sex counselor self-image to do as he conscientiously tiptoes through the welter of avant-garde sexology? I have vented my misgivings about the vaunted and occasionally flaunted revelations by "authorities" newly descended from their separate Mount Sinais. A cleric seeking dogmatic certainty about sex has been conditioned by the doctrinal rigidity of the pulpit. The rules for healthful and happy handling of human sexuality have not been chiseled on the Tablets of the Law. A wise pastor-counselor will push on without queasiness through the jungle of human sexual behavior where sexologist-scholars only yesterday hacked a path, learning what they think they have discovered. Then he will filter his findings through the prism of his own sensitivity, insight and experience. The breadth and variety in his own trial-and-error struggle with Eros might well be the decisive "fine print" on his list of qualifications.

The freshly minted sexologist is not the only Messianic trouble-shooter in the North American pantheon of sex oracles. He/she must share the shrine with two others: the physician and the psychiatrist. Each governs in his own constituency. Annointed "Mr. Deity," the physician normally has been conditioned by his traditional Jewish or Christian parentage; he belongs to the socioeconomic middle class and is affluent; because he is probably an archetypal conservative he will be tight-lipped or judgmental about sex. Only the youngest in the profession have become familiar with sex as it is through their more recent medical school training.

While Margaret Sanger made birth control an unavoidable issue in the 1920s, the medical profession forced society to deal with successive generations of unwanted children rather than condone or promote self-limiting reproduction. The profession also set a fifty-year precedent of callous unconcern for over-impregnated mothers, often giving priority to religious beliefs over a rational and socially urgent medical policy. A profession for whom inherited doctrinal beliefs wield compulsive power can liberate itself only by a supreme effort for empathetic attention to a patient's sexual crisis. In a time like ours which prizes individual choice of erotic style, effective counseling is impossible if this moralistic syndrome is allowed to inhibit mutual trust and interchange. The psychiatrist-counselor is hardly one to be hampered by church-bred sexual negativism. Not self-repression, but expression—a principle inviting libertinism in the patient and irresponsibility in the healer—supports his couch. The psychiatrist seems all too generous with behavioral prescriptions, and I cannot evade the opinion that psychiatry's chief handicap in counseling is its success as a calling. The "in" lingo—"libido," "subconscious," "inferiority complex," "oedipal obsession," etc.—rolls lightly off the tongue in singles' bars, king-size beds and during college bull sessions. Even Dear Abby with all her insight steers her troubled correspondents toward "professional help" when a ready solution eludes her. In celebration of the

Freud-begotten axiom that the libido towers over all other determinants of personality, the institutes, workshops, treatment centers and experimental farm brochures all shore up their panacea for erotic dysfunction by sporting a stable of big-name psychiatrists.

In my early pastoral counseling I made two mistakes. The first was to conduct separate interviews with quarrelsome couples, who then would exchange jibes en route to the divorce court, each using my cautious comments as evidence; then both would shoot verbal arrows at me on grounds of partiality. Actually I suspect they felt I knew too much about them. My second mistake was to advise some counselees to see a psychiatrist. For that I received blasts such as "Do you think I'm crazy?" Like many other clergymen of that day, a brush with Freud edged me, I thought, into the ranks of an "amateur" psychiatrist. Yet I soon realized that my irresponsible conceit would lead me into waters beyond my depth, and to the kind of superficial counsel that might endanger a trusting client's psychic future. Subsequently I made it a rule to recommend psychiatric treatment for those cases complicated by processes so far down in the subconscious that only a professional analyst of the mind could do the probing.

That kind of precaution is no less pragmatically a means of protecting the minister. Malpractice, the old hobgoblin of physicians, has become a new occupational hazard threatening North America's clergymen. Enough lawsuits have been filed naming minister and church to induce insurance companies to write malpractice clauses into their policies. In March 1980 a Catholic couple whose son attended the largest Protestant church in Los Angeles before committing suicide sued the church and its pastor, charging "clergy malpractice," wrongful death, negligence and outrageous conduct. "Spiritual counseling malpractice," a Superior Court judge ruled, "was not precluded by the First Amendment," as the defence had maintained. The plaintiffs' attorney argued that in the special relationship between the boy and the clergy, they had had a "special duty" to heal the guilt and anxiety that had afflicted him. Instead, their counseling had exacerbated his malaise.

Most ministerial suits, it is stated, come under the heading "scapegoating," finding someone to blame. They are usually dropped or thrown out by the judge. (Jurists still opt for religion.) But a jury awarded $2.1 million to the twenty-two-year-old plaintiff who said that the Church of Scientology had defrauded her by failing to fulfill promises to improve her life. This award of damages may have been buttressed by the fact that the Church of Scientology exacts a fee for its advice, I am told; in the sight of most law makers, free counseling seems less blameworthy.

About twenty insurance firms offer malpractice coverage to clergy. The Episcopal Church will insure them through an affiliate of its pension fund. Whatever the outcome of a suit may be, its mere appearance in court can cost a church money or its good name. It would not astonish us if a cleric who recommends to an unhappy wife temporary separation from the husband may be charged with alienation of affection. Preferred Risk Mutual of Des Moines, Iowa, will not cover a minister or pay for his defense if he is accused of sexual misconduct with the wife. No more than a doctor shuns malpractice insurance should a pastor reject it in fear of repudiating his pedestal if he can become an inviting target for blackmail.

Weekly sessions with a psychiatrist no longer raise the specter "Am I crazy?" Although marriage American-style may be started by the boy-meets-girl recipe, it often proceeds to husband-and-wife-meet-psychiatrist, and may end there. On a visit to Moscow in 1961 I chatted through an interpreter with a group of work-gnarled housewives gazing at a shop-window display of American-style household appliances. Only half in jest, and with subsequent regret for my crudity, I told them that an American matron who "wanted to belong" had to have not only an electric hair dryer and a refrigerator, but a family psychiatrist ("mind doctor") as well.

Does the vogue of the "shrink" mark the abnormal eroticism of a "sexaturated" society? Unless we are driven to write off as futile any attempts to achieve a mutually enriching, durable, man-woman relationship, we must applaud research psychiatry's unceasing efforts to explore the subconscious. However, it would be counter-productive to abandon one proviso: that the findings it stumbles on are tentative, rudimentary, and subject to exploitation, abuse and shallowness.

High fees for psychiatric ministrations have compelled most prospective patients to substitute impersonal, somewhat formalized group sessions for one-to-one individual encounters and thus reduce the "shrink's" domain of maximal helpfulness to an elite circle of the affluent. That baker's dozen practitioners not only prescribed conjugal adventure for sex-starved women, wed and unwed, but also presented themselves as pharmacists able to fill the prescription, spells out the temptation with which counseling confronts anyone engaged in it—an opportunity no less visible to the clergyman. The minuscule few who succumb need have no significance beyond providing a hot scandal for the media.

Protracted practice of a skill programmed to heal human hurt is liable to bring about the onset of absent-minded habit which erodes sincere concern. The person undergoing treatment can be forgiven for interpreting bored languor as a shallow dimension of caring. In San Francisco, to which I fled to recover a taste for zestful living after my wife's death, depression led me almost furtively to the bolted, nameless doors of three psychiatrists; each left me more hapless than his predecessor. The scenario was like a series of meticulously timed forty-five-minute quiet inquisitions by triplets, each in turn—a bare room save for two chairs, a tape recorder, a small desk and a Buddha-like figure whose movements were wholly manual—turning on the electronic record and labial, addressing toneless queries with a sleepwalker's gaze. And I sat there with innards gutted, having laid the vicissitudes of a lifetime at a heedless idol's feet. What balm accrued to me from those three separate plunges into the memory-haunted caverns of my soul? One of the overseers of my torment enunciated a single declarative sentence after the last of several carefully scheduled seances—"Depression and grief are not the same"— and all three prescribed their respective favorite tranquilizers. I took the pills without demure or deviation, although they darkened my days and stretched into seeming infinity my dream-tossed nights. The final assortment from the drug store had me climbing the wall that flanked a door leading to the balcony of my tenth-storey apartment. Only a sudden awakening from the nightmare and the thrust of my face into a cold shower safely brought me back to bed. Since then I have sought neither pills nor psychiatrists.

Do I recommend a cleric for sex counseling? In the mellowing middle years of my rabbinate, the hub of my operational circle had moved from the cosmic, rhetorical challenges of an intense preacher to a pastor's personal concern for the troubled individuals who pour out their problems across his desk. Did my parishioners prefer the amateur psychiatry of a clergyman to the professional ministrations of a psychiatrist only to escape the stigma and avoid paying the fee? Perhaps the layman in search of a firm footing still assumes that his best bet is to consult a man steeped in God. Should he be warned of the novice with good intentions?

As I grew more comfortable with my own sexuality, the responsibility of sex counseling no longer frightened me, nor did the personal risk I was taking. Several summers of paid counselorship in private outdoor camps in the Pocono Mountains had been a baptismal and toughening preview. The proliferation of youth group rural retreats, with outdoor twilight prayer, careless attire and the slogans of frankness and freedom has widened the scope of Satan's wiles. Clerical innocence, whatever its credentials at the portals of heaven, then becomes a handicap.

Ordinarily a young counselor (often female) has difficulty with the negative edicts of conventional morality, often the source of her client's neurosis. A clerical counselor must shift from public tirades against "sin" to private "sharing" with a potential "sinner." *Pastoral Psychology*, an informative periodical, and popular seminary courses on that subject will not empower the minister to recommend an outlet other than sublimation or a cold shower. Nor do they suggest an alternative for the sexual hunger of a married woman.

The caricatured psychiatrist who carries a couch on his back has no valid replica in clerical counseling. The pulpit must be left behind; to moralize is fatal. A preacher who specializes in regular denunciation of sexual hijinks automatically disqualifies himself for a pastorate in sex counseling, unless he fulminates in a militantly fundamentalist setting that inhibits pew-occupiers from airing their erotic hangups. "Free" clerical sex counseling escapes the intrusion of finance, but it must also interdict the stifling aura of sanctity. Although candor and confidentiality— already jeopardized by the ready tongue of a pulpiteer—are the basic requirement for any worthwhile session, they cannot coexist with missionary righteousness. A pastor on the threshold of the counseling-hour must recognize, however reluctantly, that the goal is not to make his bewildered subject morally right but to make him/her emotionally happy. In the chair facing him sits a "naked" loner stripped of everything but a soul in confusion, not a prospective convert to be seen and heard in relation to the *Summa Theologica* of Aquinas or the carved-in-stone code of

Moses. If his habits to preach prevent him from displaying impeccable honesty, then let him stay in the pulpit.

There are risks, of course. I was once accused of being soft on alleged adultery because I implored an outraged wife to show "benign neglect" toward her husband's single indiscretion, a momentary epidermal itch on a business trip. Before she entered my study she had sworn to punish "the swine"—and splinter a loving family—"before a judge." Afterwards she added a supplement: "I'll tell the world you are an abettor of immorality by a faithful woman's husband!"

Before treating people a counselor accepts the role of a penitent admitting his own shortcomings. That a belief in his own perfection will erect a wall he cannot clear between himself and the seeker for sexual truth seems to me a patent fact. Pomposity and self-importance will dash his hope for counselorship. The inaccessible "prelate," the rabbi lofty enough to be rated with the almost extinct German-style "Ober-Rabbiner," the public figure who is primarily sought for graduation and ribbon-cutting ceremonies, the crusader out to rescue capital "H" Humanity from war, pestilence, famine and its own political foolishness, or the ever-busy administrator should erase sex counseling from his appointment log. Also, the silver hair that crowns advancing years may turn off some young wanderers in the mapless underbrush of their sexuality. Does the veneration offered to a patriarch evoke trembling "gut" speech from people caught up in the vagaries and dangers into which sex has pushed them? I think not. Luckily, temperament has steered me away from playing the "fatherly" role story books have allocated to the "sensible" octogenarian; zest for life rather narrows the generation gap. At the same time decades of experimentation and an active memory have fortified my intuitive alertness to the "problem child" (adult or adolescent) seated across my desk. The accent and attitude of unflappable affinity, rapport, feeling-with, *inside the hide* of that human being facing me—not condescending forbearance toward his/her erotic "troubles"—*there* lies the secret of sex counseling. It is revealed to the cleric-counselor most fully in the recollection of the "troubles" *he* has endured.

Clergymen are under a special mandate to provide honest counseling. Many of the "lost souls" seeking relief are casualties of the revolution against entrenched ecclesiastical control of the bedroom. A spokesman of church or synagogue drawn to sex counseling is really an agent of poetic justice. Father Andrew Greeley, a Roman Catholic priest and syndicated writer on matters of religious import, belied the centuries-old Augustinian view that woman's sexual voracity imperils her salvation: "A man perceives his own worth as a sexual creature when he perceives his mate's hunger for his body and the need to satisfy it; only thus can he become a successful lover." This cogent insight is a remarkably self-directed step toward release from the bondage of church tradition—and toward the kind of honesty essential for effective counsel.

At a seminar in Reno for a group of clergymen, I heard Reverend Jack Elliott make a plea for the intellectual and moral integrity that might fracture Protestant sexual hand-cuffs. Beginning with a claim that the church's canon law and doctrine do not square with reality, he pointed to the evasion of the locked-in concept of one mate for eternity by solemnizing re-marriages and allowing divorce. Yet there is no real confrontation of hypocrisy. "If we have some of Jesus's love and humanity of spirit," I understood him to say, "we can't avoid counseling and deciding contrary to Christian convention. If a pastor is rigid, he's hiding behind church doctrine. He must extract from the Gospel whatever is useful to people; otherwise we come out with sociological statements that circumvent Scripture and conventional custom without getting to the heart of official doctrine. We must take risks by moving from a checklist of allowables to a little creativity, from fear to courage, from law to maturity, from absolutes to relatives, from isolation to reconciliation, away from passive invulnerability to creative passion consonant with the passion of Christ. . . . We may speak of women, men, life, community, yet we link sex with death! . . . Relax defenses, get beyond conventional restrictions of the day, just as Jesus did when he had contact with women. Set the pace. We may not be able to trust ourselves very far, but we can trust the church even less." Why did Jack Elliott release that verbal thunderbolt at the seminar? My feeble eyesight caught a "wrap-up" epigram in my notes that was linked to a quote of Anthony Burgess: "We must trust the State even less." The coupling's exact origin eludes my memory—but its relevance elates my mind. Verily, *neither* church nor state deserve trust more than our own integrity—if we cleave to the line marked by Jack

Elliott and enter the sex counseling chamber as people who embark on the fulfillment of a sacred trust.

What other human endeavor activates the electric waves, the nerve-endings and the infinitely filigreed network of brain tissue more than sex? Almost from the cradle to the grave, people think, fantasize, dream about it, no matter what they like others to think they think. Has not everyone's life-cycle started at the split second of penile ejaculation endlessly repeated in a billion-year cycle of evolution? I'll play the fool who steps "where angels fear to tread," venturing to guess that no adult in this land is permanently immune to sexual anxiety, conflict or bewilderment. The primary rule, therefore, is that no erotic misadventure, however bizarre, should excite astonishment or produce aversion in the counselor. A sharp counselee will sense bias or revulsion, and modify or truncate any disclosures to avoid shocking the questioner. And without full "confession," sex counseling becomes a sham.

What are some of the erogenous war zones a normal seeker is apt to sketch, often with calculated promptings, during a genuine counsel hour? What responses would nestle in my mind, bred by the practical perceptions of psychologist friends, learned through decades of listening, tempered by frequent chastisements for my own faulty, immature choices—and always geared to the perception and readiness of the person who honors me with his/her trust?

Problem: Non-Marital Living Together

Response: If you are engaged to the man who wants to move in with you, cohabitation should positively reinforce the chances for sexual success in your marriage. Believe it or not even Harvey Cox, one of the most influential Protestant clergymen in the United States, said that on a panel discussion sponsored by *Playboy*. For generations, the peasants and proletariat of Eastern Europe dated intercourse from the day of betrothal; they were not ashamed to have their baby as a guest at their wedding. And the New England Puritans condemned premarital hanky-panky in precept, but not in practice. The number of kids born out of wedlock in Concord, Massachusetts, ran close to the number on the church records. Nor do the good burghers of Holland and Sweden scrutinize birth certificates' dates.

According to ancient talmudic law cohabitation under certain rules was one way to institute formal marriage. If a man who bedded a marriageable woman declared, with her consent, that he had meant the act to be an act of marriage, it was so regarded. Later codes of laws considered them husband and wife if their cohabitation had endured for some time and she had lived only with him. You know, I assume, that concubines were a settled part of ménages if their male heads could afford them. The concubine status was undocumented by the wedding rite; she did not belong in the family and her offspring could not inherit. Today she would be called a "common law" wife. Old Jewish tradition technically permits this half-marriage; the Old Testament allotted concubines to patriarchs and kings—a royal privilege still extant in modern Europe.

Today some Protestant churchmen have relaxed their holus-bolus opposition to living together. In Canada an Anglican Church report stated it was time to stop being "prissy" about it. Dr. Allen J. Moore, a highly placed Methodist, Dean of Students at Claremont School of Theology, has stated that intercourse between responsible singles who are committed to each other can be a more meaningful expression of sex than within a marriage, where it can be a weapon to manipulate one's partner. Reverend Howard Moody, a leader in the United Church of Christ, accused Christianity of always talking as though young men and women had never lived together out of wedlock. It should help them make decisions, not look the other way. A minister in Massachusetts performs a marriage ceremony he calls "In God's Eye" for couples who would find legal wedlock a hardship; for example, the case of a widow who would lose her pension.

Granted, these permissive clergymen were thinking about premarital togetherness when "free consent and sexual consummation" occurred in the context of a life commitment. I'm not sure that avoidance of intercourse before matrimony is an infallible preparation for it. Some divorces caused by sexual incompatibility might have been averted had the couple slept together first and found out that they were not suited for each other. Neither the Christian nor the Jewish religion offers a single woman realistic guidance. "Don't do it," they say, "until a minister declares you married!" But you live in a society that often makes marriage impractical or impossible for economic or educational reasons until you're in your late twenties, whereas your sex drive will have reached its peak in your teens. A sensitive girl of sterling character can be driven into a premature, bad marriage. . . . And perhaps marriage is not your goal. Today some young women with good jobs prefer to stay single.

How serious is sex to you? I hope you don't consider it just "a roll in the hay," as Noel Coward once named it, or the reverse—an act which will determine your fate in this world, in the next, or in both. Evidently you don't have an ineradicable disgust for sex but are calmly contemplating it an excellent, mature idea. Some couples prefer unmarried sex. I know some who got divorced after making it legal only to be reunited later without a license.

Let me pass on some notes of caution. The breakup of a non-married union can be more devastating than the separation of legal spouses. A woman once told me she was glad to be rid of two husbands by divorce, but got hysterical when her boyfriend left her. Of course, the pain of the loss will parallel the depth of the relationship. Unless your partner has advanced beyond the macho pattern of the past masculine generation, you will be cooking dinners and washing dishes when you get home from work, and shopping at the supermarket and cleaning house on weekends. Live-in men often are prone to cop out of inside work.

A report in the *Journal of American College Health* showed that the stress of intimate sex relations can load a college student with anxiety and depression, produce headaches, stomach distress and poor sleep. Health professionals on campus may spend a third to half their time dealing with symptoms caused by sexual ties one or both partners are not equipped to handle. We oldsters get a vicarious thrill out of fantasies about the sexual resources and libertinism of the young. Sometimes I visualize a student sitting in his room worrying about how he can ever live up to the shenanigans our society pins on him. Recently a sensational news story headlined an advertisement in the University of Arizona student paper: "Living in sin with your boyfriend without your parents' knowledge? Use the Alibi Service." The service is a student named Lisa who will, for a monthly fee, serve as a surrogate roommate, take unexpected telephone calls from mom or dad, receive mail, deliver messages, and be on hand to replace the boyfriend in case of a parental surprise visit. The customer can even hire Lisa's spare bedroom to make it look as if both of them shared it. That juicy morsel of campus erotica surely must tickle middle-aged palates!

Despite the widespread tolerance of living together, there are elements in our country who treat it with severity. A public school teacher in Missouri lost her job after years of competent service because she had lived with her husband for two months prior to their wedding. Although a judge ruled that her conduct did not make her unfit to teach, the school board considered only her breach of conventional morality.

Once you have slept with each other, are you committed? Do you feel that way? You may be driven by your sense of responsibility or conscience into a premature, fixed relationship that could be destructive. You may not really wish to be bound to each other by intercourse. Nevertheless, by completing instead of suppressing the sexual act you may be spared a miserably wrong marriage. I have officiated at the nuptials of many "nice Jewish girls" (as they are tagged) who had hurried to the marital canopy out of sheer physical need. They could no longer stand virginity. Now a grievous proportion of them are separated or divorced. I venture to say, had they embarked on a kind of trial marriage they might have delayed taking the final vows long enough to change their minds.

Sex without love is better than none at all, you say, but when it continues indefinitely I question whether you can retain the capacity for a deep and lasting relationship. Physical intimacy in itself does not portend depth and ongoing spiritual union. One can be misled by binding them together. I'm sure you recognize that joy in bed, even as play, should express the total personality. It's more than a dance at the senior prom.

Finally, I urge you to regard living together as no less important than a relationship that has been solemnized in your church. Maggie Scarf, in her book *Unfinished Business: Pressure Points in the Lives of Women*, searched for the answer to an arresting statistic: two to six times as many women as men suffer from depression. She maintains that women are vulnerable to depression because emotional attachments are more important to them than to men. When bonds with husbands, lovers, children or close friends break, females sometimes suffer terribly. That psychological trait, she wrote, lies in the female genes; it is a product of evolution from the primitive primate infant who developed the bond of dependency to keep its mother close by. Mind you, I'm not an anthropologist and cannot evaluate Maggie Scarf's reasoning. Of course, men also get depressed, as I have reason to acknowledge. But with males the trigger is likely to be pulled by loss of self-esteem due to failure in some endeavor other than the collapse of a personal relationship.

Now in what way does this apply to you? If I may say so, it is something quite simple: if you are merely interested in a temporary, superficial liaison, someone to share a bed with you and pay half of the housekeeping expenses, that should not be too difficult—and you have every right to join in such a two-some without feeling an iota of guilt. But if you are looking for true intimacy, caring, growing together, getting close to another and to yourself, that's a leap you ought to make only after much, much thought.

(*Note*: These responses were not actually made in continuous form like a speech, but in separate segments, replying to comments and questions.)

Problem: Sex Over Sixty—Over?

Response: I'm glad you asked me about the advisability of seeking sex at seventy. I'm over eighty and sex is not dead for me. Why must it be extinct for you? Some years ago I delivered a series of lectures for seniors at the University of Nevada in Reno. The subject was "Sex Over Sixty—Over?"

There were thirty-three women in the class—and one man. The human male is not as gregarious as the human female and is apt to keep silent when it comes to his love life. Besides, most men refuse to believe they need to learn anything more about sex than they already know—especially from a rabbi. Perhaps men feel uncomfortable about sex and shun a discussion about it like the plague. Deep down, I believe, it's their fear of impotence, real or imagined. Therefore, they might confine sex talk to barnyard jokes or quips about gays. . . . Maybe we can deal with that delicate subject in our next session, if you want. But evidently that is not your immediate concern. You're a widower, as I am, and no longer young. Should you give up sex is your question. Certainly not!

Old-time religions have convinced many people that the body is unclean. Well, old age weakens the body, right? So it sets a man free from his body's power and its pollution. And he can achieve release from the tyranny of his sexual desires. They say old age becomes more conducive to serenity and peace of mind. While grandma bakes cookies for the kiddies and is supposed to be content with that as her only pleasure, grandpa collapses onto a couch, snoozes and maybe smokes a pipe. That's the image drawn for us oldsters. I don't accept it. Nor do you, my friend. Do you know what's the most exciting and instant method of communicating with the human race? The sense of touch, the physical feel of somebody else. Years ago sexual intercourse was known to the boys on the street as a "piece of skin." Remember? A baby explores the world around him by touch—with his mouth and fingers. You and I have elderly acquaintances, widows especially, who have not felt the skin of another person in years; they even hold back from shaking hands out of sheer timidity. Some are afraid to look at their own genitals! Nonsense!

Sex passion does not enslave us; what Freud called libido liberates! Remember the Scottish poet Robert Burns? In his poem "John Anderson My Jo" he describes the ideal aging couple, when carnal heat has died away and they don't feel its tingling any more.

> John Anderson my jo, John,
> When we were first acquent
> Your locks were like the raven,
> Your bonnie brow was breut;
> But now your brow is bald, John,
> Your locks are like the snow;
> But blessings on your frosty pow,
> John Anderson my jo.
>
> John Anderson my jo, John.
> We clamb the hill thegither,
> And many a canty day, John
> We've had wi' ane anither:
> Now we maun tother down, John,
> And hand in hand we'll go,
> And sleep thegither at the foot,
> John Anderson my jo.

People are shocked when they hear of an old man and an old woman wrestling in bed. Vaudeville, opera and movies poke fun at an aging lover and make him out to be a doddering fool. And when a man appears in a restaurant with a woman young enough to be his daughter—or granddaughter—people stare, click their teeth and whisper, "A disgrace! How can that old buzzard make that beautiful girl happy?"

Reject that "second childhood" wrinkled baby image! Replace it with "second manhood." Many of the world's great creative leaders have set inspiring examples. Victor Hugo felt no sense of sexual inferiority in old age; Tolstoy, toward the end of his life, preached total abstinence, yet at seventy he returned from a long ride one day, made strenuous love to his wife and the next day moved around the house as if walking on air. And look at Picasso, Charlie Chaplin, Supreme Court Justice Douglas, Pablo Casals and Doctor Spock! My friend, I don't believe the Lord has prolonged your life on earth and then doomed you to stay lonely, sexless and dehumanized. As I view Him, He would rather see you derive joy from these extra years He's allotted to you and from the genital equipment He's fitted to your body.

You feel inadequate, you say? Can't measure up to an opportunity in bed? There are many techniques for giving a woman sexual satisfaction. The Creative Force, the Almighty who designed this miracle of bone, sinew and nerve called "our body," is delighted when we invent new postures and functions to squeeze from it every moment of joy. Once I came across a question-and-answer column in a newspaper. Someone had asked, "How can I make love? I have severe arthritis." The reply was brief. "You can always cuddle," the columnist said. There are women who go wild when you kiss their ears. A psychiatrist told me once that the erogenous zone, as he termed it, can even encompass the toes.

Catholicism bans every kind of intercourse as unholy except the basic penis-vagina operation; overstepping the line is to be included in confession, I'm told. If you are of that faith, I'll not suggest that you ignore its moral admonitions. Judaism does not set down such limits.

A few months ago I read that Cary Grant, at seventy-seven, married a woman in her thirties. I'm sure he has mastered enough experience over the years to compensate for the chronological gap. The fact is, an elderly man does learn from his own life in far more cases than the critics realize. The chances are he has discovered how to please women in ways that street-corner cowboys and loud-mouthed macho boasters have never heard of.

Mary S. Calderone, executive director and co-founder of the Sex Information and Education Council, contends that society desexualizes the elderly. Well, we oldsters are getting tired and bored with the sneers, leers and snide remarks made by smart-alecks, smug middle-agers and teenage punks at the slightest indication of over-sixty sexuality. Calderone says, in fact, that men don't lose their sexual capacity until *they themselves* believe it, and women are capable and often active all their lives. Keep that in mind, my buddy. I think you and I should sing a quiet requiem over the day when people laughed at an old guy inching up to a lady.

You probably compare your present or suspected lack of sex ability with your achievements when you were young. Of course that's a downer. We all tend to do that. Here's a fundamental rule: don't try to compete with the way you were a half-century ago; you don't need to measure up to anyone else or to the stud you were, or imagine you were, fifty years ago. By doing so you're manufacturing a rival who doesn't exist. Try to meet a woman who wants opposite-sex company as you do, then let things take their course. Forgive my bluntness; I'm leveling with you.

You don't know such women? Do you really keep your eyes open? There isn't a community in North America of any size that doesn't harbor fine women aching to meet a lonely, eligible man: widows left alone by the shorter lifespan of their husbands, divorcées hoping to retrieve a male consort, business executives who sacrificed male companionship to get ahead in a career and now feel the pinch of loneliness. A look-in at my university class about sex over sixty would have amazed you. How eager and excited those middle-class, church-going ladies were! Financially independent too! My lectures and the open discussion following them were unrestricted in language and ideas. I didn't mince words or sanitize my opinions.

Their main concern showed itself when I announced that I would talk to each of them at the end of the series on how to establish contact with a male. "Why put it off until next week? We want to hear it now!" they exclaimed. One of them rose in class with fire in her eyes. "The men I meet would rather go fishing!" My quick answer was practical. "Why not buy a fishing rod and go along and ask him to show you how to put a worm on the hook? He would be thrilled and flattered to act as your teacher!" A week later, as I passed her in the university corridor, she broadly winked at me, held up her fingers in the "V" sign and whispered, "OK."

Maybe you don't hanker to marry again. That's understandable. Matrimony at our age can complicate things. Or you have moral scruples about just living together. More and more, thoroughly decent and understanding couples are doing it. Eighteen thousand was the statistical estimate of the known elderly cohabitants some years ago. That figure didn't count the arrangements in secret. I recently saw a movie on television about a pair gloriously content without a marriage certificate—until their children came for a visit. Then one of them would move out for the few days. I hope you are not afraid of your kids. They know that they weren't brought by the stork.

Of course you need to have a real relationship, not merely a meeting of bodies. But first bring skin to skin together and let the rest develop. A widow or a widower deprived of sex for some years fears that he or she will never again be able to reach the depths of intimacy and the heights of joy. I was married for forty years to a woman of dazzling beauty on every level—body and soul. Yet I have found a richness of sexual expression beyond anything I could have dreamed possible with a lovely, truly alive woman in her early forties. And according to schedule—always subject to change by the Lord without notice—I'm pushing eighty-two.

Do you mind if I offer a few practical tips? First, get around to the senior centers. So many attractive, personable women frequent them for all kinds of educational and social activities. Let these women be aware of your presence. If you're too shy I'll be glad to introduce you and act as a sort of amateur dating and mating bureau. Maybe some day senior centers will set up such projects instead of travel slides and bingo.

Second, keep telling yourself that any part of the body ingenuity can adapt for the act of love should be used. Train your fingers to stroke and massage. If done with skill and care, that will gradually send a woman into rapture.

Three, play down the importance of orgasm. Don't tear yourself apart to reach it, and don't be depressed and frustrated when you don't. In fact, an elderly man's semen count may be low; that may retard the climax. Rather than force coming, leave it for the next time when the semen you save now will help you ejaculate. The real aim is to give sexual happiness to your lady.

Fourth, don't permit yourself to be hung up on the question of morality unless you have strong scruples deeply ingrained by your religion. I would never counsel conduct which violates the law of God as sincerely interpreted by any faith. Such misguidance would be a crime against my own religious heritage and cause a terrible sense of guilt for both of us. It's a profoundly private decision each person must confront in his or her conscience. A man or a woman may earnestly conclude that he or she has paid in full the dues for membership in the human race created in the Divine image and now deserves a bit of happiness in the gathering shadows of twilight. I feel sure God won't begrudge it to you, my friend.

Problem: Impotence

Response: You're not the only one. Impotence can occur in nearly all adult males, at any age, even on a man's wedding night. It can ruin the honeymoon and often will haunt the marriage like a grisly ghost. Intense sexual excitement can freeze the genitals, especially if the groom has had little or no sexual experience.

For centuries men have searched frantically for a magical formula to keep lust alive. Popular folklore has recommended aphrodisiacs such as the mandrake root. People said it was God's gift to men who are duds in bed. The ancient Egyptians called it "phallus of the field," and the Romans spiked wine with mandrake to heat up their orgies. Among African tribesmen the elephant is being doomed to extinction by the notion that its tusks ground into powder can prolong the period of penile penetration. Then there is jimson weed, the thorn apple and belladonna. When I was a kid I used to sell ginseng in a grocery store where I worked; not until years later did I find out why the old men who bought it trembled with anticipated delights while I wrapped up the stuff. And what about monkey glands? Only the rich could afford the surgical implant, but what a storm of hope they aroused!

Today aphrodisiacs promise eternal youth for you and me— but that's all. Making the promises good? That's something else again. The zinc in oysters is supposed to stimulate sex potency. Wonder drugs have a huge market. Listen to some blurbs: "Postiche-flavored Nymphomaniac Drops for the Frigid Female"; "Sta-Power Spray gives complete control to the over-eager male"—it contains benzocaine, an anesthetic; "Get what every man needs with fantastic placebo sex-aids." Here's an admitted placebo, no more effective than sugar and water prescribed for a hypochondriac, yet men in the grip of impotence will buy it. One product, called THP 400, is distributed by mail-order houses; it is touted to cure sterility and frigidity. The ad was canceled when the postal service revealed that the bottle only contained vitamins and minerals. Super-E was removed from circulation; it contained Vitamin E, niacin and cola nut-powder. Are you taking Vitamin E regularly, my friend? I did to postpone the day when I would suffer as you do today—until the Food and Drug Administration said it enhanced no sex interest whatsoever.

In 1978 a widely recognized clinic in Pittsburgh studied one hundred well-educated, happily married couples. Sixty-three women had trouble getting "turned on" or reaching an orgasm; forty men had trouble reaching a climax. Statistics like these are repeated endlessly all over this land. Probably next to the common cold, the complaint general physicians hear most seems to be male impotence. According to estimates, 10 percent of us are impotent all the time and 50 percent have difficulties part of the time.

Why have I gone into so much detail about the universality of the condition you are consulting me about? To reemphasize the basic fact: you are not alone. When the average span of life was, let us say, the early forties, men didn't terminate their sex urges or capacity until they died. Now, with an increased lifespan impotence may well precede our demise. Women do have an advantage. They can enjoy the bedtime story for life because they don't have to work up the energy or the erection. But our bedmates can contribute enormously. A sensitive woman who loves her man and is resolved to protect him from sexual embarrassment and frustration can subtly and surely guide him by physical and psychological manipulation when they are together. His confidence and self-esteem are literally in her hands.

What is the main reason why I lay stress on *everyone's* susceptibility to impotence? To keep you from feeling sorry for yourself. A low-key spirit aggravates and hastens the fading of sex desire. Depression can lead to decrease in passion, eventually to partial or total impotence, and that leads to more depression. A vicious cycle!

Impotence in itself is not easy to deal with. It requires patience, understanding and careful investigation. Medical research has shown that half the cases are rooted in other physical complaints such as diabetes, heart weakness, inadequate blood supply to the brain, hepatitis and rheumatic fever. In fact, almost any debilitating disease can interfere with sex functions. Medications for high blood-pressure, certain anti-depressants, marijuana, believe it or not, according to some recent studies, will reduce potency. Of course some people cover up their sexual hangups because it's less disturbing to the ego to have a stomach ulcer. A common error is the association of impotence with a prostate operation. Apparently that isn't so. May I suggest that you have some thorough medical tests?

Alcohol can wreak havoc. The last time I saw *Macbeth* I took special note of a phrase in the porter's speech to Macduff about the effect of alcohol on sex. Listen to what Shakespeare had him say: "It provokes desire but takes away performance, it sets him on and takes him off." The Bard of Avon would have been intrigued by the findings of a Harvard University project at the Center for Alcohol and Drug Research. Alcoholic beverages reduce the ability of the testicles to manufacture testosterone, that essential hormone which regulates a man's sex drive throughout his life. Other research shows that three-fourths of the people who drink heavily over a prolonged period are incapable of having normal sex.

What can you yourself do about impotence? It isn't so much the why's you need to know, but the how's. Doctors may help you solve the problems of your body but you're here to face the psychological trouble that has attacked your mind. Let's face it, you are anxious to reap the harvest of sex that awaits you. It's really fear that creates the situation you and most men are afraid of. I've preached many a sermon on the contrast between fear and faith. Faith can help bring us victory; fear dooms us to defeat. How can you handle what you fear? Often, the source of impotence is fear that it's arriving, what is called a self-fulfilling prophecy. Although fear makes adrenalin flow, it clogs the way for testosterone, the sexual hormone. Fear resides in your mind and for that reason a psychologist or two will point to the cranium, not the crotch, as the place where a man's genitals operate. Banish fear at the moment of truth. Tell yourself you can—and believe it. Do you remember a bestseller titled *The Power of Positive Thinking*? Think positive. If the woman at your side cares for you at all and is smart in the ways of bedmanship, she will arouse you and gently help you to become a wonderful lover.

Now here's something to make you chuckle. The great movie producer Alexander Korda seduced women by pretending to be impotent; then when they rose to the challenge he bubbled over with gratitude. How's that for a clever trick!

Problem: Oral-Genital Sex

Response: Your husband's request for oral sex obviously has not yet been answered, otherwise you would not seek counsel. You say the fate of your marriage may rest on your reply to him. I appreciate your confidence in me. I realize this presents an emotional wrench to you. Likely you never dreamed of such a suggestion. I'll help you all I can.

What the woman does is called fellatio; the man performs cunnilingus. These are very ancient Latin words. Men and women have likely engaged in these practices from the day Adam first drew near to Eve. All over the world, wherever civilizations older than ours have thrived, there are sculptures, drawings and murals depicting oral sex in action. Isolated primitive tribes practice it more habitually than what we regard as *the* proper way, which they only perform for child bearing. Throughout the ages men and women perceived in oral-genital contact as a natural outlet for their sexual urges; the laws written by church and state couldn't stop it. Countless races have looked upon it as a part of lovemaking, subject only to the desires of the two people involved.

For a long time oral copulation was linked to what is termed perversion and therefore was officially declared taboo in our part of the world. Most sex manuals treated it, if at all, as a preliminary to the main event. Kinsey's block-buster report on the sex behavior of Americans projected a 60 percent proportion of oral sex positives, as I recall. Inasmuch as sin, in the view of some people, attaches only to full consummation at the meeting of penis and vagina, oral sex would be technically if not morally acceptable to them.

But there's been a change in attitude during the last fifteen years or so, especially among groups with above-average incomes. A comprehensive survey by *Redbook* magazine found that 80 percent of the women it questioned found oral sex quite acceptable. A considerable number even preferred it. Yet forty-three states at this time still have laws making oral sex a felony. Five other states in the last decade quietly shifted to the concept that what consenting adults do in privacy is their own business. Great Britain and Canada came to the same conclusion some years ago. California repealed its ban on oral sex—and the severe penalty—some time back. How can government enforce it? With a policeman in every bedroom? St. Paul warned centuries ago against passing moral laws beyond the ability or willingness of people to obey them. So did the Jewish Talmud.

I'm not inciting you to disobey a law, but I firmly believe that the bedroom must remain the final "castle" in a man's and woman's home. Domestic privacy in the rest of the house is frequently invaded by telephone salesmen, Jehovah's Witness missionaries, bill collectors and the delivery of junk mail. Somehow nothing is done to stop that evil. Whatever is done in bed by adults sufficiently mature to give intelligent consent, however, must be out of bounds to policemen and preachers. A legal ban on oral sex is no more enforceable than the Catholic rule against birth control. I can't think of any boudoir episode open to inspection except incest, rape or bestiality. How you and your mate express your love for each other should be, I think, the most jealously guarded secret in your life together.

A preacher in Houston, Texas, while on a crusade for moral orthodoxy, forced the removal of a minister from a Southern Baptist Conference program because he had said that he favored oral sex in marriage; the preacher condemned it as a perversion even between husband and wife. To me, sex is debauched when it exalts only the flesh and is separated from feeling. Must we assume that the carnal union of man and woman designed by God through nature can be carried out in only one way? The Creator devised a swarm of different forms and patterns to evolve into mankind. The imitation of God is the ideal aim of human conduct in both Christianity and Judaism.

Let me conclude by saying that when some power within us urges unity with the soul and body of another, the exact anatomical posture is not a priority.

Problem: Sex—Interest Fading

Response: A psychiatrist once told me he was amazed at the openness of his patients' revelations about their sex experiences and lifestyles. Yet I find that couples rarely talk to *each other*. Your waning interest in lovemaking, my friends, may be diagnosed as just that. The condition is not unique. You show remarkable wisdom in wanting to do something about it. The fact that you are consulting me together is another step in the right direction.

An ongoing sex relationship is not a simple matter. Physical difficulties may require treatment, but sometimes heavy stress may be the cause. And I suppose there are cases when a person simply gets tired of sex. After a few years, couples are usually less and less thrilled with the merger of their bodies and probably this winding-down process is the root of many breakups.

In the conjugal act you must tell the other exactly what it is that might intensify your joy of sex. You aim to give each other maximum satisfaction. That means being absolutely candid about your inclination at the moment of encounter. In other words, communicate your desires and your needs to each other. Surely you discuss a multitude of domestic issues: children, work, housekeeping trivia. Why not confer about sex? The fact that the cumulative crises we all have to meet day after day *out* of bed can affect our mood and mode *in* bed was hinted at in the results of a test conducted during the First World War. Combat soldiers in France were asked to name what they most desired. One would have anticipated their replies to be sex. Well, sex was Number 20 on their lists—after furlough, rest, clean sheets, a hot bath, etc. The constant, exhausting danger, filth and mental stress had pushed sex deprivation to the back burner. The connection works in the opposite direction too; unabashed sex can *relieve* the domestic tensions of marriage.

Sex signs can be transmitted non-verbally. If the invitation by words is too difficult to utter, a nuzzle, a pinch, a glance can spell eagerness for the connubial merger. I wouldn't say that sex by itself is intimacy. Every time you give the green light to your inmost sexual needs, however, you take a step toward the ideal intermingling that makes a marriage worthwhile. Maybe you can call it love.

Problem: Open Marriage

Response: Sex and marriage have special attraction as a testing ground for rebellious temperaments. I recall the story about a groom who refused to apply for a marriage license because he resented the state "butting in" to his personal affairs. In another instance a couple living together decided to make it legal; a month later they divorced, went back to cohabitation and lived happily ever after. This fillip one gets by flouting conventional controls and parents doesn't really connote heroism these days. The institution of marriage is so weak it can't fight back.

I would not have you believe that all the exponents of open marriage are frivolous. You, for example—the mere fact of this session demonstrates to me the maturity and seriousness of your approach. I am trying to help you identify the implicit meaning of open marriage before you decide to espouse it. I pass no judgment on adultery itself. Some of the most influential clergymen in North America are moderating their stand against it. During a recent panel discussion prominent members of church and synagogue aired their personal views on the subject. After defining marriage as a covenant rooted in affection, one conceded that because the covenant cannot be coerced it may have to be ended; and under special circumstances, the term "extraneous sexual intercourse" should be a shock-absorber for "adultery."

Harvey Cox, one of the panelists, said that Jesus believed the church had no business condoning or condemning adultery. And he envisioned instances when an affair could be the lesser of two evils; as an example he referred to Robert Woodruff Anderson's play *Tea and Sympathy* in which the wife of the master of a boys' school sleeps with a student to build confidence in his manhood; the boy was afraid of becoming homosexual. The top-ranking Roman Catholic on the panel was not prepared to say that mutually agreeable infidelity was wrong or immoral, but added that he could not conceive of a happy couple wanting to engage in it. A fourth spokesman of the church cited situations in which human values could actually be preserved by violating neatly formulated regulations. In other words, the church must come up with new guidelines for sex outside marriage that sometimes can be *saved* by an affair. All the clergy on the panel faulted our society because it makes it very difficult for a couple to share their whole life together—illicit sex being a symptom rather than the cause of maladjustment. However, a Lutheran member of the discussion team rejected all compromise. In his eyes marriage is based on the concept of a vow or pledge more than a mere legalism couched in the terms of a civil contract.

That the twenty-first century will see the accepted marriage span *reduced* to about five years and not an entire life is being predicted. You see how ambivalence has invaded the moral bastion of religion!

Does the open marriage contract—that's what it is—sweep under the rug your ingrained objection to adultery? Is it worth scrambling your inherited values? Open marriage offers diversity in your bedmates—more fun. Are you ready to choose a parade of immediate pleasures that can cloy the appetite and become a worse bore than the marital bed?

The pulpit rhetoric we preachers emit occasionally blares out atonement, merging with God, with humanity, with a man or a woman we care about. Lacking that sense of atonement, sex may sink to mere calisthenics—a physical exercise whose emptiness in terms of interpersonal union is not at all diminished by an assortment of gymnastic partners.

There are other dangers. Let me tell you about a group of couples I met at a summer resort I used to frequent. They played the open marriage game. One after the other they would reveal to me, in confidence, the problem they all had in common: subconsciously they were comparing one bedmate with another to the detriment of the husband or wife they were accustomed to live with. Such a development is likely and should be considered.

A further complication arises: should the married couple reveal with whom he or she is sleeping out? In a highly sophisticated marital set-up a clear-cut adulterous adventure can be treated in the Continental European fashion that looks upon extramarital jaunts as strictly private—not to be revealed to one's spouse, who must be shielded from hurt. Telling may end that marriage. In Europe, among the upper classes, marriage is certainly more than love; it's apt to be a business arrangement as well as the proven way to raise children. The average North American, on the other hand, has a twinge of self-torment. His upbringing has made marriage an adventure of mutual trust in ethics. Therefore, a radical breach presents a case of guilt. Open marriage that gives both spouses *carte blanche* in advance for outside sexual interests supposedly does away with moral dilemma. Now, does it? I'm not sure. Any open marriage partner is susceptible to jealousy, fear and insecurity. Just because both parties can play the field with impunity for physical enjoyment, doubts and misgivings can nevertheless assail them.

I'm leery about pitching the word "promiscuity" into our earnest search for truth. A Toronto psychiatrist has decried the use of that term; he considers it judgmental and says it increases the alienation and isolation of the people against whom it is leveled. Moral recrimination is not my thing. Calm, realistic candor is! When people taste sex at will, wherever and whenever, what else can it be if not promiscuous? Blanket permission by husband and wife purges the possibly wholesale ritual of the onus of cheating, but not of "sleeping around" in what can be indiscriminate, loveless profusion.

Venereal disease has been on the rise due to casual sex indulgence. And there is growing evidence that cervical cancer and genital problems can stem from venereal infections. Far more destructive than the sporadic medical side-effects of promiscuity, as I perceive it, is the insidious and well-nigh certain reversal of the pleasure dividend. Promiscuity is self-defeating. The sensual elation confidently anticipated often declines from orgiastic frenzy to satiety, to ennui, to depression, then to what ancient Greece called anomie, a loss of zest for living. I have seen the tragedy etched on the faceless masks of youths scarcely beyond their teens. Easy, casual sex is bound to become a coin from which all traces of value have eroded.

You came to consult me about open marriage, and I have spoken about adultery and promiscuity. The fact is, they are all linked together.

The aforementioned counseling sessions encapsulate some of the major issues for which a cleric's guidance may be sought. Does a clerical sex counselor ever need to sit in the counselee's chair? Early portions of this book leave no doubt that the answer is emphatically in the affirmative. Dilemmas of judgment are legitimate and always imminent in a region covered with so much concealing undergrowth and a thick stratum of historical folly.

Ending on a Personal Note

The history of this book may be of interest. It was born during the night of December 1, 1929. The midwife was *Release*, the title I had chosen for a soliloquy, torn out of my guts all that furious night. It was not a tranquil stream of reveries, but a tumbling torrent of self-addressed, total, often flagellating sexual confessions. RELEASE—slowly, carefully block-scripted, as if to let me take in a deep breath before hunching down over the 114 pages—was typed the next day by a public stenographer sworn to secrecy. I scanned the sheets without revision and placed them into a discarded cigar humidor, never to be seen again until I ferreted them out in 1977 to share the contents with Dr. Jack Clarke, my closest Reno friend, a psychologist and head of the counseling department at the University of Nevada.

In *Release* I also had jotted down the following "pragmatic sex program:"

"Full economic, political and sexual equality of men and women. A single standard of morality. Maximal reduction of female disadvantages arising from monopoly of pregnancy. Divorce by mutual consent after agreement on the care of children—not, like bootleg liquor, the special privilege of the rich and of Rota. Conception by choice, not by ignorance. Elimination of time-worn ecclesiastical codes for the bedroom and of religion's role as policeman-voyeur. A vast nation-wide system of public school sex education and replacement of guilt with guidance by church and school. Homosexuality an alternative lifestyle, not a crime. Unabridged rights for illegitimate children. More rational study of masturbation. Sexual behavior a private matter, of social or religious concern only when it infringes on others' rights."

When we had finished reading the 114 yellowed, fragile but still legible pages Jack cried out, "In 1929! You were the advance agent by decades of the sexual revolution—and you a clergyman to boot!" Although a proudly devout man, he urged me to make

315

Release the seed of a book. "Why not call it *Sex and the Pulpit?*" leaped from my lips.

For the remainder of that afternoon, the university counselor became my confessor. Clenching hands on my knees, I leaned forward and led him into my psyche. Words formed themselves beyond my conscious will and hurried forth.

"The lurid history of sexual vices that has befouled the church for centuries still smells to high heaven. From Augustine to Pope Alexander VI, to Martin Luther, to Henry Ward Beecher, to some rabbis I have known, to legions of intervening prelates (men and women), they all strip any individual miscreant of claim to distinction. I am not unique. That so many shared my violation of the code does not grant me acquittal. There is one significant difference, however. Whereas Catholic yea-sayers to sex indulgence can achieve self-purgation in the aloneness of a confessional under the kindly eyes of a colleague, I may resort only to a pulpit proclamation for the *world* to hear. Two months after entrusting the manuscript of *Release* to that humidor, Jack, the one-word title became flesh. I resigned from Temple Israel of the City of New York. . . . Thirst for a martyr's crown could have produced a sensational *mea culpa*. But I wasn't thirsty."

The chats with Jack Clarke had revived and firmed up a resolve which had been hibernating in my mind for over fifty years: to record and analyze the self- and other-inflicted sexual harassments of the clergy, a breed sharing the perplexities and passions of universal humanity though sentenced to solitary exile by enforced "superhuman" vassalage; a need to identify the historical and ideological strands that had been twisted into a rope by ecclesiastical authorities to strangle divergence from the sex code they had invented; a need to set out the challenges directed at organized religion by a society grappling with radical change.

The exhumation of *Release* from the humidor had sparked my intent to write this book. In the words of Hillel, a revered talmudic sage, "If not now, when?"

Bibliography

Abata, Russell. *Sex Sanity in the Modern World*. Liquori, Md.: Liquori Publications, 1975.

Aquinas, Thomas. *Summa Theologica*.

Barthes, Roland. *A Lover's Discourse: Fragments*. New York: Hill and Wang, 1976.

Bullough, Vern L. *Sexual Variance in Society and History*. New York: John W. Wiley & Sons, 1976.

Butler, Robert N. and Lewis, Myrna I. *Sex After Sixty*. New York: Harper & Row, 1976.

Chesler, Phyllis. *About Men*. New York: Simon & Schuster, 1978.

Comfort, Alex. *Joy of Sex*. New York: Crown, 1972.

Decter, Midge. *The New Chastity and Other Arguments Against Women's Liberation*. Coward, McCann & Geoghegan, 1973.

DeLynn, Jane. *Some Do*. New York: Macmillan, 1978.

Douglas, William. *Ministers' Wives*. New York: Harper & Row, 1965.

Feinberg, Abraham L. *Storm the Gates of Jericho*. Toronto: McClelland & Stewart, 1964; New York: Marzani & Munsell, 1964, 1965.

French, Marilyn. *The Woman's Room*. New York: Summit Books, 1977.

Freud, Sigmund. *Leonardo Da Vinci: A Study in Psychosexuality*. New York: Random House, 1966.

Friday, Nancy. *My Mother, My Self*. New York: Delacorte, 1977.

Friedan, Betty. *The Feminine Mystique*. New York: Norton, 1963.

Gittelson, Natalie. *Dominus: A Woman Looks at Men's Lives*. New York: Farrar, Strauss & Giroux, 1978.

Goldberg, B.Z. *The Sacred Fire*. New York: University Books, 1958.

Goodich, Michael. *The Unmentionable Vice: Homosexuality in the Later Medieval Period*. Santa Barbara, California: American Bibliographical Center, Clio Press, 1979.

Gordis, Robert. *Love & Sex: A Jewish Perspective*. New York: McGraw-Hill, 1978.

Gordon, Sol and Libby, Roger W. *Sexuality Today and Tomorrow*. Belmont, California: Duxbury Press (Wadsworth), 1976.

Greer, Germaine. *The Female Eunuch*. New York: McGraw-Hill, 1971.

Hite, Shere. *The Hite Report.* New York: Macmillan, 1976.

Horsburgh, Russell D. *From Pulpit to Prison.* Toronto: Methuen, 1969.

Jong, Erica. *Fanny.* New York: New American Library, 1980.

Kinsey, Alfred C., Pomeroy, Wardell B. and Martin, Clyde E. *Sexual Behavior in the Human Male.* Philadelphia: Saunders, 1948.

McNeill, John J. *The Church and the Homosexual.* Kansas City, Kansas: Sheed, Andrews & McMeel, 1976.

Marmor, Judd. "Homosexuality in Males," in *Psychiatric Annals*, December 1971.

Masters, William H. and Johnson, Virginia E. *Homosexuality in Perspective.* Boston: Little, Brown, 1979.

_____. *Human Sexual Response.* New York: Bantam Books, 1966.

Pagels, Elaine. *The Gnostic Gospels.* New York: Random House, 1979.

Shea, John. *What A Modern Catholic Believes About Sin.* Chicago: Thomas More Press, 1971.

Singer, Isaac Bashevis. *Shosha.* New York: Farrar, Strauss & Giroux, 1978.

Taylor, G. Rattray. *Sex in History.* London: Panther, 1965.

Tillich, Hannah. *From Time to Time.* Briarcliff Manor, New York: Stein & Day, 1973.

Tripp, C.A. *The Homosexual Matrix.* New York: New American Library, 1976.

Walker, Daniel D. *The Human Problems of the Minister.* New York: Harper & Bros., 1960.